£3,99

(12)

D0343676

OH JOHNNY!

Oh Johnny!

by

MARY DUFFUS

The Memoir Club

© Mary Duffus 2003

First published in 2003 by
The Memoir Club
Whitworth Hall
Spennymoor
County Durham

All rights reserved.
Unauthorised duplication
contravenes existing laws.

British Library Cataloguing in
Publication Data.
A catalogue record for this book
is available from the
British Library.

ISBN: 1 84104 070 3

Typeset by George Wishart & Associates, Whitley Bay.
Printed by CPI Bath

Dedicated to all our family –
past, present, and I hope future.

With grateful appreciation to our family, particularly Guy, Christie, April, Graham and Colleen who all helped me at one time or another. Jo Robertson became my number one typist, so reliable and always showing a genuine spirit of interest which was encouraging. Thank you, Jo.

Dr David Briggs, my grateful thanks to you for your medical support, Irish sense of humour and old fashioned caring.

Susan Wootten Jackson for your enthusiasm.

With special thanks to Ian Mak who has been such a help to me.

Also Bobby and Mary-Jean Otway-Ruthven.

Our Susan gets full marks for sorting out her Mother's brain from time to time . . . thank you dear.

Contents

Illustrations

'Oh Johnny!'

IT SEEMS everything has a beginning, so my story is no different. Back in 1916, when my mother produced me in a wooden-framed overgrown house called 'The West End Hospital' on Thurlow Street in Vancouver, BC, my father said I resembled a Northern Spy apple. That was to be my first insult.

While waiting for their house to be built, my parents and brother, Billy, stayed in an apartment called Kensington Place on Beach Avenue near English Bay. In order to amuse himself, Billy would ride the elevator with a man who knew very few sentences without strong curses. So, during my mother's recuperation from the 'apple', quite a vocabulary was attaching itself to a two-year, nine-month old little boy.

The story goes that my father was deep into his newspaper at the breakfast table and Billy was not happy with the lack of attention, so he said, 'Daddy, for Quith's sake, talk to me!' Mother was told she had better hurry and return home with sister Mary. Speaking of her, much had been said about his playmate-to-be, sister Mary, so when the pink blanket was tossed aside and my mother said, 'Here she is, Billy' – he took one look, probed me with his forefinger and said, 'Is that sister Maywee? Sister M can go to hell!'

When I was ten months old, our grandparents in Peterborough, Ontario sent a young nursemaid to look after us while mother had a kidney removed. It so happened she was in love with a soldier overseas by the name of Johnny and the soon to be very popular

The Northern Spy apple.

Brother Bill and 'the apple'.

song, 'Oh Johnny, Oh Johnny – How You Can Love', came out. With me cradled on her hip doing her work, she would sing and dance to this tune. It was only natural that my first words were 'Oh Johnny'. This was soon to be the only name I would answer to, although I did later feminise the spelling to 'Johnnie'.

There were very few girls I would play with, as I preferred boys. There were times, I recall, that there was a price to pay if you had to keep up; never cry when hurt and learn to fight. One Hallowe'en I was handed a package of firecrackers which, if I was to go around with them at night, I had to hold onto while they put a match to them. Needless to say, I have had a horror of being burned ever since.

Our back garden was a general meeting place and at one time a boxing ring was constructed and the boys whammed away at each other quite regularly. It was agreed that I could fight Michael, who

Brother Bill and sister.

unfortunately was wearing white flannel shorts, white shirt, knee socks and runners. I broke his nose and he was a sorry sight. That evening his father telephoned, returning my father's call. Before my dad could say a word, he was told how happy he was that Michael had been fighting as he did not think his son was cut out for rough sports, 'Who was Michael boxing, Mr Ferguson?' My father had to prick his balloon by saying, 'Johnnie.'

School bells called and off to Crofton House School I went, to become a regular girl with lifelong friendships to be formed. I longed to go away to boarding school where my brother Bill had been for several years and at thirteen was packed and off to Strathcona Lodge School on Vancouver Island. It was situated on Shawnigan Lake, only a few miles from where Bill was. Unfortunately, he only spent one of my years there as his best friend, my pretend second brother Bruce Allan, was at Brentwood College on the other side of the island. Our parents finally gave in to his pleas and he left for Brentwood.

The years, almost three in all, were very happy ones. Minna Gildea, our headmistress, was English. After graduating from Cheltenham Ladies College, she accepted a teaching position at St Margaret's School in Victoria, BC. This was a stepping-stone to opening her own school.

Strathcona had only been functioning for a year when I went and our year saw one hundred and two boarders and three day girls. It was a very happy school. Miss Gildea was in every respect a remarkable person. She was a devout Christian with an incredible ability to inspire. She had a great sense of humour which she often used with her method of discipline. For example, about four seniors crept out to the gym, each carrying a pillow and eiderdown, went upstairs on the balcony and spent the night on the floor. We never did hear how it was discovered. At prayers next morning, Miss Gildea said that a certain group of girls were being given special permission to sleep in the balcony for a week as they obviously preferred the hard floor to their own beds. There was not a straight face at prayers that morning.

With world depression at its worst my boarding years came to an end and it was a very sad day when I had to say goodbye. It was a truly wonderful time in my life and I am so grateful to my parents and Miss Gildea, who left her mark on all her students. Friendships made have lasted all my life and my memories of those inspirational days and years are as clear in my mind as if they had just taken place.

In summer terms we enjoyed our lake, shared by small cottages, the Forest Inn Hotel and the boys' school, called Shawnigan Lake. We had speedboats, canoes and a ship's lifeboat that was filled with singing girls and towed by a speedboat to go on our picnics on one of the islands. There we had a huge bonfire where the coffee and tea water was boiled and marshmallows were roasted. With torches to light our way we would return to school.

The only sports we were not taught were lacrosse and golf. All games were highly competitive; we even had jacks tournaments. Good sportsmanship was never actually taught but prevailed throughout the school.

Miss Gildea's health was plagued by asthma and eventually forced her to retire. Nonie Guthrie became the next Head and, from all I have heard, was held in high esteem.

As times changed, Strathcona was invited to join forces with the boys' school, Shawnigan Lake. Obviously I was born too soon! As letters used to flow between the two schools on a regular basis, I cannot help but think that the local post office must have suffered from the union.

One very special memory I have is the six weeks that I looked after about eighteen Strathcona students whose parents were stranded in Asia during the war. Miss Gildea rented a house in

Maple Bay, on the island, as a change from school and as I had time to put in, I volunteered to do a big sister act. With a large station wagon available, we picknicked and generally had a great time, only spoiled by a matron who gave us all the willies. Mrs Lyons, our wonderful cook, more than made up for the matron. She was a peach!

To back up to leaving SLS, I returned to Crofton as a day girl, which was a huge change but made pleasant by many friends that accepted me back. I am not sure how our parents managed so many parties, dances and good times. Looking back, we never seemed to lack for anything.

Unfortunately, I developed a congested lung and rheumatic fever and was sent up to Kelowna in the Okanagan to get away from the sea. Through family friends I was able to stay, as a paying guest, with a truly lovely young mother of a four year old daughter, whose husband had been killed in an auto accident. Before long, her younger brother returned from army camp and we were besotted and 'floated' on cloud nine. Their family was so good to me and the weeks flew, only to end in sad farewells.

Mother, in her infinite wisdom, threw us together over the following year and I finally graduated to older interests.

As I had missed so much school, and tutoring still left me floundering, I opted to join my good friend Ernle Morgan at a designing and dress-making school called 'The Academy of Useful Arts'. In many ways, I am indebted to that year; time and time again I have utilized what I learned in the academy. My friend Ernle went to London with her knowledge and was able to support herself.

One day, we arranged to meet a friend for tea at what we now call the 'Old Hotel Vancouver', as it was abused dreadfully by soldiers that were billeted there during the war and was torn down. CPR built a new one that, in my estimation, lacks the elegance of the 'Old'.

While waiting for our friend we kept our eyes on the revolving door so we could greet her. A tall, very tall, young man cruised in and I said, 'Ernle, where do you suppose he comes from? Nothing like that ever grew in Vancouver. All I know is he is just the kind of man that I would like to marry!'

Re-reading my diary of those sub-deb/deb days, we were really spoiled. House parties were very special, fraternity dances, rowing club and yacht club dances. Sailing and cruise holidays aboard the *Willeena F*, belonging to the parents of my great friend Nora Farrell. The Farrells had two sisters, cousins of the Farrell girls, who arrived from England to spend the summer. They were older than Nora, more the age of her sister, Dorothy Jane. In order to introduce the cousins, a dance was planned for them and Nora was permitted to invite a few of her friends. Don Millerd and I were included.

I made my evening dress with thirteen and a half yards of material and who knows how many yards of red satin ribbon. The material was white with tiny dashes of red clay all through it. Never will I forget the frustration of sewing it, as the machine would have to face up to every piece of red clay with a bounce of the needle, which obviously resented the whole exercise.

There were eight in our 'young group' and we pretty well stuck together. We were ushered downstairs to the playroom and it was filled with a great variety of games. It was all great fun and an ideal way to relax the English cousins. Around eleven o'clock, we were invited to go upstairs for a light supper which was followed by dancing. As I started up the stairs, I turned to see if my friend Don was following me. Out of the corner of my eye, I spotted the person I had seen enter the Hotel Vancouver some two years or so before. As soon as I could, I asked Nora who he was. 'Oh, that is

1936, taken at the exhibition when we were engaged.

Mort Duffus, he is a friend of Dorothy Jane's.' (Nora's sister, also called 'Didge'.) 'Sometimes when he calls for her and she is not quite ready, he helps me with my math.' Their beautiful garden, which overlooked the Fraser River, was surrounded by trees that had fairy lights throughout. The lawn had a floor of tight canvas stretched across it, sprinkled with a dusting of boracic powder. The orchestra was cozied up on the sun porch. It was a beautiful summer evening with a happy moon.

Don was an exceptionally good dance partner and we were enjoying ourselves when he had a tap on his shoulder and he was cut in on. To my complete amazement it was none other than Mort Duffus! He towered over me and said, 'I know you are Johnnie Ferguson, I am Mort Duffus. I have tried to be introduced to you but they say you are with the younger group, so I have had to introduce myself – let's dance.' Finally, after several more cut-ins, Don said, 'If that long john comes around once more I am going to get on a chair and sock him.'

My mother was always awake when I came home and I would regale her with the fun stories of my evening; this was no exception. I said, 'Mum, have you ever heard of Mort Duffus?' Her reply was, 'Good heavens Johnnie, don't tell me you have reached his age!' Yes, she knew of Mort, knew his parents and played bridge with his grandmother. His father had been the Assistant Commissioner of the RCMP but he had died.

Nora's grandmother entertained the nieces by having a dance at the RVYC and Don and I were invited as Nora's guests. Along came Mort once more, finally saying he would phone me as he would like to ask me out. He had had quite a few drinks that night, which did not impress me that much.

My family were entertaining at a cocktail party a few days later, honouring Adele Herrman, the beautiful bride-to-be daughter of my mother's best friend. The guests were all her friends but I was there because I loved her as if she were my older sister. I happened to be in the dining room with mother and a group of Adele's friends when Charlie, our cook, came to me and said, 'You are wanted on the phone, Miss Johnnie.'

When I returned, Mother said, 'Who was it?'

I replied, 'Mort Duffus.'

'What did he want?'

'He wanted me to go out with him.'

'Did you say you would?'

'I said no.'

'Why?' asked Mother.

'Because he is too old and he drinks too much.'

Little did I know, but one of Mort's great friends, Phil Wootten, happened to overhear our conversation. When he left our house, he bustled up to Mort's family home and with great enjoyment at being able to tease, he regaled Mort with my conversation – unknown to me at the time.

Later that summer, Nora and I were invited to spend a few days at our old camp up the BC coast. As a young girl, I went every summer for eight years and loved it. Nora went only once and drowned me with homesick tears. I was to learn later that Trevor Arkell suggested Mort get a date and they would join forces to go to the Commodore, our favourite place to dance. Mort said, 'I will try and get Johnnie Ferguson.'

'Don't bother, she's up at Kewpie Kamp with Nora,' said Trevor.

That did it! 'Well, I guess I will have to let her grow up,' he said.

In the fall, I happened to be at the Commodore and saw Mort on the dance floor with Joanne Disher so asked my date, who was a very good friend, if he would try and end up on the floor close to Mort. This he did. To my horror, he left Joanne and came to ask me, if he phoned me would I go out with him – to which I said, 'I will tell you when you phone.' A few days later he asked me to go to see Clark Gable in *China Seas*, and that was the beginning of many enjoyable times together.

Mort was an avid skier in 1935 and it didn't take very much persuasion on his part to persuade me to join him. Vancouver is so conveniently situated in proximity to the mountains. Each weekend we would drive up to the foot of the trail leading to Grouse Mountain and our Thunderbird Ski Club. Mort would carry his skies, my skis and both our packs. As I recall, Grouse is about 4,000 feet and we would have several thousand feet under snow. There were two stops, Orange Peel Corner and Lizard's Rest. I am sure I took many more as Mort was always up skiing by the time I arrived.

There were no ski lifts in those days so we really slugged it out, as, for every thrill we got from coming down those runs, we had to snow-plough our way up in order to do so.

Our club membership extended from November until the end of the snow in very early spring. Mike, our cook, was a warm-hearted lovable character who devoted his time and talent to filling us with wonderful hot meals. He did all the catering and would go down for supplies and load them back up on his back. I am sure his pay was minimal as we only paid $30.00 a season – all meals included! I do not think one can buy a day's ski pass for that today. The depression years painted a very different picture to the way of life we have now.

Tradition still existed and December was chosen for Mary MacNeil and me to 'come out'. This took place at the RVYC with many dinner parties beforehand. Mort was my date for the evening and as all the young men were probably told to be sure and dance with us, Mary and I had a fabulous evening.

The next day, Mort had a cocktail party for me and asked me to marry him. It came as quite a shock and I said no. About half an hour later, I asked him if it was true that it is a woman's privilege to change her mind. Obviously, the answer was – yes. I had such mixed feelings, I was so young and having such fun and enjoying life so completely, but I felt Mort might never ask again and I did not want to lose him. We decided to keep our engagement quiet and announce it at the annual Christmas Eve Dance at the Jericho Golf and Country Club, to which Mort belonged. He did, however, do his duty by phoning my parents. They were delighted.

26 September was set for our wedding, which gave us a

Mort and Johnnie, 26 September 1936.

wonderful carefree summer and Mort a chance to save after his extravagant bachelor days. It was decided to have a morning ceremony so we could get a good start in Mort's new car to drive south – first to San Francisco then to LA. In those days we really licked the cream with our dance bands. We both could have danced all night, the music was so wonderful. Griff Williams was at the Mark Hopkins in San Francisco and Henry King, our favourite, was playing at the Ambassador Hotel in LA, where we were staying. The first night we were there, after we were seated at our table, Mort tried to order a drink for us. The waiter refused to bring mine as he said he was not permitted to serve alcohol to minors. Mort finally told the powers that be that we were married and then he signed a statement to that effect. My exotic drink was called 'Clover Club', consisting of a maraschino cherry in the hollow stem liqueur glass of crème de menthe! The Trocadero Restaurant was another superb evening with great music, dancing and dinner. It was a favourite nightspot with the movie stars, and it was a truly entertaining evening. We saw Cary Grant, Jack La Rue, Charles Boyer, Alice Faye, Pat Paterson, Mary Livingstone, Arline Judge, Simon Simone, Evelyn Venables and Frank Morgan. Jack Benny and his wife were there (I bumped square into him), Ruby Keeler and George and Gracie Burns. Ginger Rogers and Ruby K were even more attractive in person.

Our days flew by and we wended our way home, some twelve hundred miles. It was unbearably hot and we made frequent stops on the way – this was to quench our thirst. For twenty-five cents one could buy a huge cardboard tumbler full of freshly squeezed orange juice. I can still savour the thought of them.

It had been a superb two weeks, to be topped off by returning to our first home. It was on Point Grey Road, across the street from the ocean and with a view of the mountains. It consisted of a living room with a fireplace and a small veranda, dining room, kitchen and breakfast room, back veranda and a small garden with a huge cherry tree. There were stairs that led down off the kitchen to a full basement where we were to play some raucous and highly competitive ping-pong games! Upstairs, the master bedroom had a matching veranda. There were two smaller bedrooms, with one bathroom. All of this was our half of a duplex for fifty-five dollars a month, which we felt was an extravagant amount. The car had to stay on the street as we couldn't afford to rent a garage.

Poor Mort had to come down to earth with a thud, as cooking was not one of his bride's attributes. His parents had Jane, a huge woman who cooked mouth-watering meals, and we had our Charlie, who even exceeded my mother's cooking ability. My brother Bill saved me several times by eating one of my horrors before Mort came home for dinner.

The best of plans can go awry and ours certainly was not to have a family our first year, but on 29 June 1937, we were to expect our baby. I remember thinking that if all women felt as I did for all those months, it was strange that there were so many people in the world. In my eighth month, I developed toxic poisoning and our son, weighing just over three pounds, died before birth and I nearly did also. It was about a week before I was able to have labour induced.

Life went on, as it does in bad times in our lives, and the next experience we were to have was for Mort to come home for lunch in January of 1938 and casually hand me a business letter from the head office of The Canadian Canners in Hamilton, Ontario, asking Mort if he and his young bride would consider moving to Britain to represent the company. Would we!! There was no doubt about our reaction. Mort would have to go to Hamilton for two months then I would join him for a week – train to New York and sail to England. We would live in Glasgow for six months for Mort to present the company's large and varied tinned food at the British Empire Exhibition at Ibrox Park. At the end of our time in Glasgow, we would move south to London where Mort would have his office.

Letters from Britain

April '38

c/o 52 St Enoch Square, Glasgow

Dear Mrs Duffus,

I was so delighted to hear from you today. I simply cannot understand Mother, it will be two weeks tomorrow I will have been in London and still no word from her. I've quite given up hope of ever hearing from her.

Mort gave me your letter at Euston Station from where he left this evening – not to return to London again, unhappy thought! In about ten days time I expect to follow him.

I am now on the train and brought this letter along to add a little more to it in my spare time. Today, Esme, Cynthia Bull and I decided to visit the Cathedral in Canterbury – so we took a train from Victoria at 10:30 and arrived two hours later. We had a perfectly lovely day and fortunately had time to go completely through the Cathedral first and then attend a special visitation service by the Archdeacon of Canterbury. We were terribly thrilled with it all. The service was attended by about fifty men of the clergy, all very colourful and impressive, to say nothing of the dear little choir boys in their long robes and ruffles around their necks. The organ was also lovely – no doubt you have been there yourself and were equally impressed. I really think it was far nicer than Westminster Abbey. On the way back I had been invited to stop off at Bromley, Kent, to dine with a cousin of Peter Kayes (Barbara's husband). She met me at the station; such a nice girl too and we went on to her house – her sister later joined us for dinner and I was very delighted as she reminded me slightly of our Dot – so nice finding a kindred spirit.

They wined and dined me very nicely and now I am on my homeward journey at 10:30 p.m. and will take a bus up to the club upon my arrival at Victoria.

Well, here I am all safe and sound in my bed – clean sheets and all. It is quite an event in this club to get them, by the way. I am only sorry the day is over as I really did enjoy it tremendously. Nice things go so quickly and how the horrid things drag.

You will be glad to know that I received my very first letter from Mother today, which I can plainly see is going to take hours to answer as there is so much to tell and so many questions to ask and answer.

Last night Margie Braden and I went to the Mungalls' cocktail party (the third couple on our long weekend). I do wish Mort had been there as I am quite sure I would have enjoyed it more. The people seemed very stiff and formal – the men more affable than the women, the latter didn't say any more than 'How do you do' to us. Seems funny, I think we Canadians are much more pleasant to strangers than English people. We are taking Flora to the Buttery tomorrow for lunch; she's such a pet – I really am terribly fond of her already.

Mort and I have found the most fascinating restaurant called the Queen's Brasserie – it's a German Beer Garden and, of course, had a wonderful Austrian orchestra and all the famous beer songs thrown in. We were there Sunday night for dinner and hated to leave. We guzzled tremendous steins of beer and everyone joined in the singing – perfect place for depressed spirits – it would be impossible to keep from smiling with joy.

Your new hat with the veil sounds perfectly sweet. I know exactly how you feel about veils and I felt the same way. For once I have a hat Mort likes – practically the first.

You and Dot are not the only ones who miss the bridge games and our very frequent dinners with you. We occasionally let ourselves go and have a grand time reminiscing about such sweet things but we find we get so depressed that we try to put it out of our minds until we can bear it a little better. Believe it or not, we are both very homesick for you all.

Well, my loves, it is after twelve and I think I will close an eye or two. It has been such a long day, so until tomorrow when I will finish this off – goodnight! S'funny, you have just called down to Jane to tell her you are awake – nine hours difference as there is also summer time here, and Mum would be calling in an hour. I miss all those things.

Well, today I am going out after lunch to see the flower show near Victoria. I had two tickets given to me, so I thought Margie and I would see it. Next week before I leave – Esme, Cynthia and I want to go down to Brighton for the day. I am quite excited about smelling sea air again. London is so dirty.

Another of my introductions just called me; I am having tea with her at the Piccadilly Hotel on Monday. She sounds very nice.

Well, I cannot think of any more news, so I will close. My very best love to you both and have Dot give Peter a big hug for me when next she sees him.

Johnnie

May 2nd, '38

Dearest Nora,

No doubt you have long ago given up hope of me ever writing you a decent letter, however, please forgive me as this being my first visit to London, naturally I have been very much on the go ever since I arrived and have only written to Mother and Mrs Duffus.

We had quite a nice crossing, not particularly exciting though and I felt very miserable with my cold all the way over and spent three days in bed, so I must admit I was a little relieved to get off. Ten days with no excitement is too long.

We had a grand weekend over Easter, went to Stratford-on-Avon and stayed at the Welcome Hotel – perfectly delightful place. There were six of us in total and we had stacks of fun. Isn't the country beautiful?

This weekend I went to Surrey to Bob Beldham's; I had a very enjoyable time. They have a perfectly lovely place with acres and acres of gardens.

Esme, Cynthia (who by the way looks awfully well), and I went down to Canterbury last week to see the Cathedral. Have you ever been? We were very impressed; we even took in a small service by the Archdeacon. On my way home I stopped off at Bromley to have dinner with Muriel Kaye, a cousin of Peter's. She is very nice and so is her sister. I shall write them soon, but in the meantime you might tell her, will you?

This afternoon I am going to meet Barbara Kaye's bridesmaid. We are having tea together, so will leave this open for further reports for Barbara. This letter is going to be a continued story and very disjointed.

I had tea with Marnie earlier and liked her tremendously; really – she is a darling. I hope to see quite a bit of her when I return to London again.

Esme and Cynthia had me over for a sherry last night. Alistair Smiley was there. Do you remember him? He lived in Vancouver during the badminton club days. Anyway, the four of us giggled and laughed and had loads of fun talking about Vancouver and of all the good times. They have had such a lovely trip over here. After finishing the sherry we all walked over to Oxford Street to the Good Housekeeping restaurant and had soup and waffles and coffee. You really appreciate American meals over here, they are so few and far between.

I am having tea with Joyce Frazee today – I ran into her in the underground station last week. She looked awfully well and very brown. She certainly loves it over here.

Ernle had changed quite a bit – she used to be quite reserved and shy, but now she is on the go all the time and thoroughly enjoys life; she works very hard at her new job as well.

I listened to the King's speech this morning over the radio from Glasgow. The Exhibition opened today – I wish I could have seen it, but had to satisfy myself listening to the crowds yelling and shouting and singing 'God Save The King'.

I had a letter from Mort yesterday from Glasgow, saying that he has located a house – fifteen miles out in the country. We will either take that or else will have a cottage by the Clyde, which I would adore, especially for the summer months.

I find now that Mort is going to be away four days out of every week – this little adventure is not going to be all easy going. He has to visit Manchester, Liverpool and all the other industrial cities each week, poor darling. And I no doubt will be dreadfully lonely.

Of course I have been doing the usual amount of sightseeing – not as much as I would like, but of course I have ample time in the years to come to do all these things.

What I really enjoy is wandering through the shops, they really are wonderful, aren't they, Nora? Harrods so far is my favourite – but what tempting places they are. If I had bought all I wanted to buy, I would be spending $100 a day! It might be fun too. I was very much amazed that their clothes are so frightfully smart. English magazines have the dowdiest pictures and yet the dresses are beautiful, a very pleasant surprise.

I saw Jeanie's wedding picture at the Bulls' last night. It was quite good; didn't Jeanie look happy? They certainly have my blessing. How is Daph? Do give her my love – I do not know when I will write to all the girls I want to – someday soon, I hope. I wish you were coming over this year, and Daph, we could have heaps of fun – London is such a wonderful place.

Remember me to Hugh – I hope he is well and that business has picked up again and that you two will be able to get married when you planned. Be sure to tell me all your plans when you write!

I have only received two letters since I arrived – one from Mum and one from Mrs D and I am good and cross!

My very best love to your mother. I hope you did tell her I phoned on the 19th, remember, and she was at the hospital with your father?

I suppose your garden is looking very lovely by now – and you are having your meals outside again, or is it a little early? I used to love going out to your place so much. Oh, how I am going to miss you – our bicycle trips to the airport, tea at Jericho etc. – maybe someday we will go back. I hope so and yet I really love England. It is all very different from Canada, everything in fact – the people, their ways and so on – it all takes time adjusting.

Well, goose, I must close now and write some more letters. Please write soon and give Mum the odd ring. Heaps of love to you and the family.

Johnnie

May 9th, '38
40 Cranworth Street, Hillhead
Glasgow W2

Mum darling,

At last we are settled in what we can call our 'home'. It has been a long, long time living in an unsettled lifestyle. We have taken an apartment. Mort decided against the house in the country as his hours at the Exhibition are so long – sometimes twelve hours, which would have meant he would not have arrived home until midnight, which is more than anyone could stand. He also figured I would be too lonely so far away from town.

We are one floor up, in what looks like a dingy place, but they all look like that from outside. We have a really large living room, real fireplace and three large high windows with green velvet drapes and valances and a very pretty inlaid table. On the table we have placed a glass vase with branches of a tree in it, a green plate in a stand and also a very old silver incense burner. The living room is furnished with two easy chairs and a love seat covered with green silk cushions. It is a nice room – extremely bright and easy to keep looking pleasant. There is also a big rack of old china that is hung over the mantle which I am not so delighted with, but apart from that it is not too tough to look at. The woodwork is all dark brown and the walls beige and the ceiling cream. The dining room also is large – about the size of Harwood Street – nice big tables and six chairs, fireplace and bronze velvet drapes. These two rooms are next to each other and face out on Cranworth – such a lovely view. Outside these rooms is the hall, with doors from the other rooms opening onto it. The bedroom is nothing to write home about – large, fairly comfortable double bed, fireplace, two large windows, a green dressing table, an easy chair and not a bad rug. The bathroom is very colourful – turquoise bath and basin with brown walls up half-way, then cream. The kitchen, believe it or not, is not too bad. There is a very clean coal stove set right into the wall, which I do not really use – I'd hate to bake a cake in it, needless to say. The sink is a little battered and has wooden drains with a nice big window in front of it. My coal bin is concealed in a big cupboard with my pans next to it, making a table-like affair. Now you know all about it from top to bottom. I quite like our new 'home' considering it's Glasgow and nothing looks new. It is very clean and only six to eight minutes from the centre of the city by bus.

A woman will come to me twice a week for six shillings – half days only, which is quite good. The stores are only a block away and little boys come to your door every morning with baskets of wood to sell, and they will carry down your ashes and garbage for a penny a bucket.

We have your picture, Col. Duffus', and our wedding picture in the living room. We had a little bad luck – my picture (and frame you gave us) was completely squashed. That was really tough luck – $15 shot to the devil.

I went out to have dinner with Mort at the Exhibition last night. What a sight it is! Futuristic fountains, all lit up – avenues of them! One restaurant juts out of a hill and exactly resembles an ocean liner; it's called the Atlantic – wonderful looking place. There is a colossal club with two thousand members, which is unfortunately filled with a waiting list, so we could not join. Honestly, Mum, you could not describe it, it is beyond all description. It was a truly wonderful sight, especially at night.

Mort's exhibit is exceptionally good – a tremendous drawing card in Canada House. There are two Mounties outside the building who knew Mort's father.

It was terribly exciting to see them. Brings home a little closer. Gosh, it is funny seeing every other man in a kilt and nearly all the little boys – they all look so sweet. I stand around and listen to their Scottish brogue, and they are so funny to listen to, I find it impossible to keep from laughing.

Today I phoned Lyndsay Mavor, an introduction. She sounds very nice. We are lunching together in town tomorrow. Hope she's as nice as she sounds. Mort and I walked through the Botanical Gardens this afternoon; quite pretty. Poor Duff has a bad case of sore feet. He is on them all day and for the last week, twelve hours a day, so we did not do very much walking.

Well, Mum, I can think of nothing more to say – so for now, all my love to all of you and for Pete's sake, write. I have had two letters from Mrs Duffus and only one from you since I arrived! It is getting a little too much to bear. Always send them via New York as I do – they will come much faster. Look out for the big boats in the paper and mail the letter c/o them.

As ever – Johnnie

May 16th, '38

Mum Darling,

You have no idea how delighted I was to receive two letters this week. That makes three letters in all since I arrived in Britain. Try and write as often as you can, even if only a note. We long for letters.

No, I never received the dressing gown – did you not put a return address on the parcel or else check up on the Bellingham post office? It's too bad, but surely there is some method to check up on it. Yes, darling, I received your wire and letter at Boston – I beg pardon, but in one letter I did say I had received Mrs Nickerson's wire at North Bend, not Boston. I previously sent her a card; evidently she did not receive it so I have posted a letter to her which she should get before this arrives.

Dorothy Austin is unsettled as to how long she will stay. Her money is going very quickly and if she does not get a job she will more than likely return around June. I'm not sure though. She is very happy over here. Mort hates Glasgow and so do I. It really is not a very clean city.

Poor Daph and her mother. They are continually moving, they must be fed up to the teeth with it. Congrats on the twin foxes, darling. I'll bet you look like a million! It would be lovely to take a jaunt down to San Francisco – wish I could join you.

Sorry to hear about Gladys. I hope she is feeling better now. Hope you didn't get it. Norman is married and separated from his wife. Hence Margie; please don't do any talking about this as I would not want anything to get back to him for the world; it would never do. I hope I will see Muriel Burritt – I liked her tremendously. Bob Rankin knows darned well he hasn't got a chance with Birkie. She has told me she will never marry him 'cause she isn't in love with him. Maybe she's changed her mind.

Now to answer a few questions from the other letter – glad to see you enjoyed the crazy little jigsaw puzzle – thought you would get a kick out of it. Yes, Phil's a perfect darling when he isn't drinking, isn't he? I think Joan has always been quite keen on Phil. What did Eleanor Bossons have – a boy or a girl? And what about Barbara – what did she have?

Yes, Teddy and I had a big row up the mountain one night. It's silly to look back on because we turned out to be good pals right after it. She's a nice girl. I got quite a laugh out of you saying I'd have lots to do and see – my gosh, if you arrived here tomorrow, the only thing I could show you would be the Exhibition. Believe me when I say, there's not one single thing worth looking at!

I only received one club letter, one Philpot Lane, and one St Enoch Square. Maybe one is on the way. I bet little Point Grey Road looks intriguing these days. How I adored that place – wasn't it sweet? It was so clean and fresh looking and our things looked so nice there. We wish we were there too, Mother darling, far too much. But this is our lot and we must make the best of it, and perhaps one day we will be happy here. It is so hard to readjust when your heart is six thousand miles away.

Thank you for the newspaper clipping. If you want to do me a big favour, you can have the *Sun* sent here – either the Sunday or all week. I would love to see what is going on and who is giving parties.

Yesterday I went out to the Exhibition for two hours and spent my time roaming through the British Pavilion; quite the best of them all. It was really wonderful and naturally impossible to describe. I met Mort at seven in the Canadian Pavilion and we hopped on a bus to the Grosvenor Restaurant – supposed to be among the best. Excellent dinner but a very dowdy place and people. Arrived home at ten and I skinned Mort badly at 'Down The River'. We get a bang out of games like that. A lot of good laughs.

Today, Mr & Mrs Caldwell are taking us for a drive. At three we are being called for and oh, I'm so excited I can hardly wait. I suppose I shouldn't speak that way; they are so kind but we simply don't speak the same language.

Am still seeing Lyndsay continuously. She is a grand girl. We had her, her mother and little brother in for tea the other day. Her mother is also very sweet. They have a lovely home. I had lunch with them on Friday; a cousin was also there. They seem to be very fine people. Her uncle is James Brady, the playwright. Lyndsay said she would take me out to meet him some day.

We are hoping to get a ride in this week. Am dying to do some riding again. I am going to cook Mort's birthday dinner on Tuesday and have all his specials, as his mother used to do. Oh, to be able to make his special strawberry ice cream, but with no ice box, I wouldn't dare try. I am giving him a Kodak camera. I bought it yesterday. It takes moving figures and everything and it would be so nice to send some snaps home. With the ten shilling note Emily sent me, I am buying eight rolls of film, and also I will give him my picture in the mirror frame. I had a new frame made down town and they say it should be finished on Tuesday. I hope he likes all the presents as I was most extravagant.

Well, darling, can't think of writing anything else of interest. Thank you for your nice long letters and write often!

Heaps of love to you all, Johnnie

June 9th, '38

Mum Darling

Received a letter from you yesterday from the office. You funny girl, why send it there? You had already sent one addressed to here. I have just written a letter to Walt Somerville at his office in London. I am hoping and praying he will send me a cheque to go up and stay with her. It costs so darned much for a return trip, I couldn't begin to afford it right now. Oh Mum, I could not agree with you more that it wouldn't have hurt her one wee bit to have given you a trip over. I'm afraid she's a bit selfish. She must've known how much you would've appreciated it, as you say. Oh well, but I do say, it burns me up. Well, sweetie, I do hope and pray you may win a sweep – and if I win, you'll come over.

We went out to the Caldwells', and fortunately it rained, so we didn't play outdoor badminton, instead we played a silly game of bridge. They absolutely have no system and never bid more than one or two of anything – a trifle boring, but still they are very kind to us, so we cannot kick.

Mum, I write pages and pages telling you things – won't you make some comment on them? For instance, I wrote pages on my weekend with the Beldams and all about my impression of Bobby, and you never said a single word about it. I always keep your letter open beside me and try and answer or make some comment on what you say. Do you understand what I mean? It seems to me a wee bit boring to write at such length and then never know what you thought of what we did.

This morning we received an invitation to spend the weekend after this one with Cora. It will be lovely and of course we are going. She lives on the east coast, so we are hoping the weather will be nice up there. I am dying to meet her – Mort speaks so highly of her.

You asked me if the 24th was a holiday here. It is in Scotland, but not in England; that was the day Mort left for London, so it did not do either of us one bit of good. Yes, your letters are becoming more regular now. The boats throw the darned things all cock-eyed, so it's pretty hard to know when we're going to receive them. Mort always receives one every Monday or Tuesday morning. I have not bumped into Betty yet, no doubt I will some time. What is her married name?

Mrs Bush is an old devil. Mort and I absolutely gasped when we read your letter. In what way, may I ask, did you ruin her apartment? The old crow! Our Mortie is very well indeed – exceedingly homesick though, but who isn't? Yes, darling, he misses you and many times said he wished the old 'tomato' was here. Me too. I often feel you are so close. We must be thinking of each other at the same time. Every morning when I dust your picture, I talk to you and tell you your face is dirty – it is almost impossible to keep it clean over here – you look so sweet with a dirty face. Wish Bill would send one of himself.

Take care of yourself, darling, and get your blood in better condition.

All my love, my Mummy – Johnnie

June 13th, '38

Mum my darling,

Aren't you a monkey when you get on your own – a new car and silver foxes? That's lovely, Mum, you will certainly be niftied up now. Wish I could catch a glimpse of you riding down good old Cranworth Street. I'd go out like a light from sheer happiness.

Our trip to Edinburgh was a roaring success. We left here at

2 o'clock and arrived under the castle at 3:30. I really don't know when I have been so thrilled. It's a truly magnificent city, isn't it? Fortunately it was a lovely day – cloudy but warm, so we hiked up to the castle pronto and got in on the end of a guided tour. We were shown the various points of particular interest, such as: St Giles' Cathedral, the University, Sir Walter Scott's Memorial, the pillars, etc. – we were finally tired of the Scottish jokes made by the guide, so we set out on our own. We peeked into everything we could get our heads into – ending up being completely overawed by the war memorial. You did see it of course, Mum, didn't you? It is in the castle. Everyone and everything that died or did anything worthy of note is represented – even to the mice, rats and dogs. The women and children are seen in the stained glass windows and of course there are wonderfully carved soldiers all around the walls. It's absolutely impossible to describe.

We could not see in the castle. Unfortunately it is not open to the public on Sundays, so we had to content ourselves with the outside. It is really thrilling to imagine the battles they had in trying to keep the castle; it is a perfect fortress if ever there was one.

Finally, on our way down the famous High Street, we were persuaded to take a carriage. It was such fun jogging along through those wonderful old streets. We saw the residence of John Knox, and of course the driver showed us all the markings on the pavements such as the spot where the famous old country gaol stood. It's marked by a large heart wrought in the pavement – and so on.

He then trotted us down to Holyrood Palace – it's also very lovely, isn't it, Mum? Mort took a snap of me in the carriage outside the palace – hope it turns out. After all of this, the cabby finally dropped us off by Sir Walter Scott's Memorial. The park was crowded with people listening to a band concert, so we walked along Princes Street and finally found a nice restaurant. I really ate the place empty, for I have never been so hungry! By this time it was about 7:30, so we roamed around looking at the shops till 8:45 and got back to the station for our train. All in all, a very lovely day, and my poor feet ached so much they twitched the whole way home. I now know why you loved Edinburgh so very much, Mum – it's a fascinating place and the roads are so wide. I wish we could spend about a week there and go along the Firth of Forth; it would be a lovely trip. I hope this hasn't bored you stiff, I'm afraid I am not very good at describing things I see – it's awfully hard to do. We will, of course, send any snaps we get that are good.

Apart from Edinburgh, darling, there is absolutely nothing to tell you. Lyndsay is away at Cambridge May week, so have been doing absolutely nothing of interest to you, or even myself. We have Cora's weekend to look forward to this coming Friday, which is very exciting.

All my love darling,
Johnnie

June 14th '38

Dearest Mum,

Many thanks for your grand letter with all the news. No doubt Elizabeth is with you and you are having some great old chats. How lovely you can see her again. I hope the trip out wasn't too tiring for her. I was delighted to hear about Forrie and Gwynn. I always thought that someday they might become engaged. I was so delighted to hear the news. She is a peach of a girl; I always liked her tremendously. Mrs Mavor invited me to lunch today to meet Lyndsay's great aunts. They were old darlings – Mrs Mavor and I took in a movie together afterwards, as the old girls were out to buy evening dresses. On our way back, Mrs Mavor said she and Lyndsay were planning a trip in the car about the middle of July to tour the north of Scotland, and wanted me to come along with them. Well, I would be delighted – but I cannot say whether or not I can swing it. We would be away a week; meals and hotels cost so darned much. However, if it is humanly possible, of course, I will go. It certainly would be an ideal way to see the country. The north is meant to be the choice part of Scotland.

Hope to hear all about you and Elizabeth. Give her a kiss for me, Mum, and thank her again for her kindness to me in Hamilton. It was so nice seeing her again, but the visit was all too short.

Well, darling, until after our weekend at Montrose, I really have no news of any description – so for now my love – a big hug and kiss and my very best to Gordon when Bunny next sees him. Also, ask him what happened, that is, how come he is back in Vancouver again? He said he wouldn't be returning.

My love again to you all – Johnnie

Thought I would open this up to add a few words. It's a beautiful day today; my, what a difference the weather makes one feel. I feel simply too good to be true – only wish I could take advantage of it by lying out in a garden, but where's a garden?

Mort and I had so much fun last night. I was feeling in a glorious mood and pretty soon it was contagious. Mort was feeling the same way, so we had a boxing match – me protecting myself with one of those large plush cushions and trying to box with the other hand; somehow I got the worst of the battle. However, next we had a wrestling bout and I find I still remember the tricks of the trade I used in the old days with Bill. Mort didn't fare so well. Later, we did highland flings and cheap ballroom dancing with our fannies – y'know, just a couple of crazy kids, but it was fun.

Tell Elizabeth that when I heard they were coming over, I wrote to Walt c/o Mutual Life on St James' Square. The letter was returned this morning and it said 'not known here'. Walt would certainly get a kick out of that!

Lyndsay is back so we are lunching together down town and I shall hear all about the May Week at Cambridge. Remember when I was asked to attend it several years ago? It makes me laugh to think of the crush I had on Bob Beldham. It is funny how we change.

By the way, ask Gordon if he found as pleasant a travelling companion as myself on his return trip to Vancouver. Probably a more peaceful one anyway. We did have such a grand time together. He's more darned fun when you get to know him. Heaven only knows what the occupants of that train thought of us – what with snowball fights. It certainly made a pleasant trip out of what might have been dreadful. We tried to reach him at the hotel he was staying at in New York and even left our number to call, but never heard a word. Funny, because they were all supposed to be there.

I'm having dinner with our Mortie at the Exhibition tonight. There will be, no doubt, a fiendish crowd – it being such a glorious day. Didn't think Glasgow was capable of such a one as this. Well, my Marmie dear, all things must come to an end and so must this.

All my love – Johnnie

June 20th, '38

Mum darling,

We had a perfectly lovely weekend with Cora and Neil Pattullo; they have a beautiful place and garden just out of Montrose. We arrived a little after 9:00 on Friday night, sat around and chatted with them until after 11:00, then went up to our room to find all of our things unpacked – put away and hung up. Our bed was even turned down, plus hot-water bottles. I love the way the servants do things over here. We were awakened at 8:30 with orange juice, as we do not like tea so early in the morning. Breakfast at 9:00 with sideboard groaning with eggs, bacon, fish etc. after which the men left for golf and Cora and I sat around and chatted, played with the baby and read. They returned at 12:45 and two ladies came in for lunch – they were quite nice and we had a gorgeous lunch. About 3:00, we all went for a drive and saw some very beautiful country. It is a lovely spot around Montrose. The North Sea makes the air so fresh and stimulating.

The weather, all in all, was quite kind to us; we had only a few short showers, with the sun shining all the while. After our drive, we played bridge and had tea and then we dressed for dinner. We played some more bridge after dinner – the first good game since we got off the boat. Sunday arrived all too soon. The men played golf in the morning and Cora and I sat outside together. After lunch, we nearly went to sleep from overeating, then dressed for tennis, as we were invited to some friends of theirs. The young married couple lived in the farmhouse of his father's estate, which is some place! They must have about fifty or sixty acres and the house resembled a small castle. Bowling green, lovely gravel tennis court and beautiful gardens all surrounded by forty foot stone walls. The rhododendrons around the place stood a good twenty feet high. We then went down to their farmhouse for tea; a very charming place filled with wild flowers and dogs.

We finally got back in time to change and rush through our dinner to be down at the station at 8:07 and arrive in dirty old Glasgow at 11:00 – tired but happy. They have two sweet kiddies – a boy who is eight and a wee little girl of a year. Sweet children and so well brought up. Ozzie of course was there and is coming to spend a few days with us after he travels to Cambridge.

So, you see, we had a lovely time and hated to come home. It's an education to see how some people live over here, as Neil has an income of about £20,000 a year, so Mort says, and will someday be a millionaire. They are both awfully nice.

Well, darling Muddie – I will close now as I must get down to the bank. All my love and hope things are better now. I miss you, darling.

Your Johnnie

June 21st, '38

Dearest Mama-in-law,

That doesn't sound so good, does it? I suppose if I'd been ten years older I would have called you Heloise! We are back in the swing of things again after our most enjoyable weekend, which I believe Mort has already told you about. I must admit, I felt a little let down yesterday. All this seems even worse than ever after the beautiful country we saw, but the time does go quickly. I have been away for over three months now and I cannot say it has dragged.

I have been trying to think of a few interesting things to tell you about – one thing that quite amuses me is the man that goes around at 10:30 with his long pole to light the lamps on the street – of course you have more than likely seen them dozens of times. We have those gaslights on our street. It reminds me of the old fairy stories about the angels flying around and lighting the stars at night.

Another thing is the fact that the educated Scotsman has no accent. It apparently is a give-away over here if you have one. The so-called people of Scotland have beautiful speaking voices, and so nice to hear. Neil Pattullo has lived practically all his life in Scotland and hasn't a trace of it – funny isn't it?

One more thing concerning me is shopping for groceries. You

have to specify about practically everything you ask for. They are great bread eaters though, and butter of course. There are about eight varieties and they use margarine always for cooking. I'm using New Zealand, as it is the most like ours. Mort likes Danish, which is more expensive – around forty-five cents a pound – but it smells! Eggs, of course, and there are several varieties and they are more expensive than ours. I think everything is, except the baker's shops, which are very reasonable. Pork is extremely expensive and it is considered quite a luxury to have sausages. I pay a shilling for four pork sausies for Mort's Sunday breakfast. Dreadful, isn't it? New carrots are a shilling a bunch and they are so small you can hardly see them. Strawberries, 1/6 a box, so we don't have them. I am told they will come down.

Please read this to Mother as she was asking how things compare with home. Food, I think, costs me a good two pounds more a month; when I think of London prices I get the jitters!! The trouble with this country is that practically everything has to be imported.

Poor Mum seems to be very upset about her sister. What a shame they couldn't have a nice visit together. I hope Mum's cold is better now too.

Give Dot my very best love and a kiss for Peter. How I do wish we had him here, but of course he would have been in quarantine all during the Glasgow months and this is when I need him most – the darling.

Heaps of love to yourself,

Johnnie

June 26th, '38

Mother darling

You really are an angel. The loveliest of loveliest sweaters arrived for me yesterday. It fits beautifully and oh! how nice it does look on! I have always wanted an angora one, and this more than meets with my approval. Many, many thanks, darling, I cannot tell you how much I love it.

Mort got away to London yesterday – hated to see him go and yet the change will do him so much good. So far things have been far from dull for me, as you probably have heard. Mort gave me a beautiful set of golf clubs. They really are dandies, the darling. So yesterday, Lyndsay and I went forth with all the necessary equipment to a public course. It was a lovely course and only cost nine pence for eighteen holes. Golf is certainly cheap in this country! We had a great time and are terribly enthusiastic about it and will hate from now on to have a nice day go by without playing.

I only just found out the other day that a man at the Exhibition whom I have made good friends with is none other than Barbara Hogg's brother, Bill! It's a small world, isn't it? You might give Barbara a buzz and tell her I am going out with him this afternoon. We had arranged last Saturday that I would play golf with him, but this morning he tells me he had better make our little date a movie instead of the exercise, as he was out very late last night. Rather a pity as I was all pepped up to play again, and believe it or not, it is a nice day – the third in a row! I like Bill a lot – really a peach! He's been away from home for about eight years and his real home is in London now. Give Barbara my love when you phone her.

Also received a nice long letter from my dear Mummie yesterday. I work myself into a frenzy of excitement when I see your handwriting on the envelope and can hardly open them fast enough.

It was too bad the weather was so hot and the people so awful on the boat. However, it was probably a nicer way to go and a very pleasant change after the trains. I suppose by now you are well into the swing of things at home and feel you have never been away. It would be nice to go down to San Francisco, but I do wish you would save to come over here, Mum. We are very anxiously awaiting young John Bird's arrival. It would be just my luck to have him come while Mort is away. He told me to invite him to stay whether he was here or not. That is the right kind of husband to have, isn't it?

Mort is really looking awfully well and I think he is really happy with his work – hard work and long hours appear to agree with him. He really must have the constitution of a horse.

Mum, will you do something for me? When Betty Farris has her baby, can you send some flowers from Mort and me and let me know how much they are and I will send you a money order? I do not think she expects it till October, but you will be seeing her and chances are you will be able to find out more. You won't forget, will you, darling, as we would hate for such an event to pass by with no congratulations?

I am looking forward to hearing about your return. Mort and I took a bus out to Buchanan Arms on Sunday and had dinner. It was a lovely day and the view from their gardens is something I will never forget.

Bye-bye for now, Mum, and keep up the good work. I love your letters so very much.

Heaps of love to you and Bill,

Johnnie – again, many thanks.

June 27th, '38

Mum Darling,

How is my little Mum these days? I suppose by now Elizabeth is home again and you are recuperating from your jaunts to the hospital. Do hope you have a good trip to Victoria and Seattle. Did she give you the outing or just the tickets?

Your daughter is at present suffering from a cold. How I got the stupid thing I do not know – no-one ever does, so Mort is taking every precaution. It's really not much wonder with a climate like this. Today is a beauty. There is a gale blowing out that is so bad I expect my windows to crash through any minute, and rain that is so heavy that even a ghost would be drenched!

Since last writing, our Mortimer has returned. He got back Friday night so we went all out and he spent 7/6 apiece to see the famous Tattoo at Ibrox Park. Honestly, darling, I don't know when I was so thrilled! It is a display staged by the Royal Navy, Army and Royal Air Force – a demonstration of the skill and efficiency reached after comparatively short service training.

The display opened with the Trooping of Colours. Twenty trumpeters sounded the fanfare, and from that moment on, Mort and I became more and more proud of being British. We then saw one excellent field gun display by the RN – Bill would have loved it – then the massed bands – what a thrill! Five enormous bands all marched on the fields in full dress uniforms with the famous Scotch Pipe Band bringing up the rear. There isn't anything so thrilling as watching the latter; they far outshone the others. I loved to watch their kilts swaying with precision as they marched.

The Air Force boys, the average age being nineteen, put on an excellent show of marching and counter-marching, with only five months in the Force.

Then the final appearance of the Musical Ride – they are losing their horses in exchange for machines. It was grand also. Hope I did not bore you with too intricate details. We saw some good trick riding, a toy soldier display, massed pipes and drums, a thrilling motorcycle display, and as the grand finale – the Sunset Ceremony – lowering the flag (the sunset being 10:45). Then they played and we all sang 'Abide With Me' and then 'God Save The King'. I've never been so thrilled in my life before and am looking forward to seeing it again next year in London.

On Thursday last, the Duke and Duchess of Kent arrived for the Ex., so Lyndsay and I went out very early and got a good position in the crowds and managed to see them perfectly as they drove by and tried to get a snapshot – only hope it comes out. He looks terribly attractive. I was surprised to see his hair is a little lighter than Mort's; I always thought he had dark brown hair. We then rushed over to the Women of the Empire Pavilion where we saw a fashion show. We waited in line for about two hours and finally the Duchess arrived and just walked right straight through.

Just this minute a letter arrived from you, so for heavens sake – so you are in the East now. Well I'm nonplussed to say the least. I think it's nice though, Mum, to have a trip. You should have a good time if Liz keeps to her word. I certainly hope so for your sake, darling. I don't know where to send the letter to – to your own place I guess, for chances are you will have left Waterloo. Imagine Colin phoning you at that hour – the damned little fool. What a boy. How does he expect to hold a job if he gets drunk? Boy, I'll bet you were mad, you always disliked him so much anyway – this will top it all. Don't be too hard on him though, Mum, they were awfully kind to me always.

It is a dreadful day. Lyndsay wants me to go over to her place this afternoon while she gets her things together for a week in Wales. This weekend we are hoping to go to Ireland. How I do hope so. We will not be able to stay too long as it costs too much.

Well, angel, I am at the end of my letter for news, so I will close. Hope you were able to go to San Francisco and you saw your friend. I quite agree, Betty is a fool to see Tommy, and Bill is such a nice boy. All my love, sweet, and write often. I wish your picture could talk.

Johnnie

June 31, '38

Willie My Love,

Terribly thrilled to hear from Mother the most excellent reports on your heart. Congratulations and keep up the good work! I am enclosing something that might interest you; have several other things that I might send some day. Only wish you could see the Exhibition. It is truly a magnificent show. Spend a good part of nearly every day there and still have hundreds of things to see. There were 150,000 people there last Saturday night. The fountains – the size of them make ours in Stanley Park look sick – so you can imagine how perfectly beautiful it is at night.

I do hope Gladys is better and Connie is also well; my love to them both. I miss you all so much, Bill – heavens it is lonely at times, and yet I wouldn't have missed the experience for anything in the world. I only wish you could all experience the thrills I have, London in particular. You'd really love it. It's a kind, friendly city and full of interest for everyone. I simply adore the place and it can give you more shivers up and down your spine than New York or any other big city. New York is a laugh compared to it, in my estimation anyway.

There is a good old Glasgow downpour on right now. Hope it washes away a little of the filth; whew, it's a filthy place. Well, Bill, be good to Mother. You are so lucky to have her, and write to your lonesome sister once in a while. My love to you and Connie.

Johnnie

July 4th, '38

Mum Darling,

You will probably be home to receive this one as you spent the last weekend with the Reads. How very nice to see them again. Before I forget to tell you, Margie Braden's dad works for Westinghouse in Hamilton too.

Mort and I both agree that it is a crime not to have come over. The worst part of your trip being over, every time the phone rings (usually Caldwell for Mort), I jump out of my skin expecting to get a cable saying you are on the way. Glasgow would have immediately become a paradise. We could have scraped up some form of amusement, whereas by myself, I can't. Nevertheless, I expect we still could have more fun when we are in London together. After all, we have nothing to offer you here.

Yesterday, Mr and Mrs Caldwell drove us to Troon. There's a very famous golf course there – it's on the Ayrshire coast. It was really very beautiful, and so nice to smell the sea air again. The only thing against it is the extreme cold and wind. The sea nearly always looks like a storm, whitecaps and all. We were amazed to see people in swimming as we shivered in our heavy coats. We drove down through Renfrew to Ayr, then Troon and Prestwick, and had an enormous high tea in Ayr. We had a quick visit to Robert Burns' cottage; it was a fascinating place – old worn stone floors, somewhat like Anne Hathaway's, only far more rugged, because as you know, he did not become famous till after he died. All in all, a very enjoyable day. I saw my first American car yesterday. It was so nice to see the left-hand drive; of course there are loads of US cars here, but they are all made with the right-hand drive.

I am anxiously awaiting the arrival of my new dress and I will write Elizabeth as soon as it comes. It was very good of her to send it. You did not mention the kids or Walt; maybe you will tell me about them in your next letter. Am dying to hear about Anne and Mary, etc. I saw in the paper that my dear old friend Chappy Boehm from Waterloo is marrying a Vancouver girl – I didn't know her. Will you ever forget my crush on him?

Do write me at great length when you are settled and tell me all the news, Mum, and all your impressions – I'd love to hear it all.

I am busy these days making smocks. I promised one to Mrs Beldam for a charity party and am also making one for little Wendy Farris for her birthday – you will probably see it. They are looking very sweet so far, but have not done much.

I am going down town this morning to the Jaeger sale, which is really something! We saw some grand things in their window. Mort wants socks – lovely ones for only 2/6, so I will buy six pairs. I hope to buy a cashmere sweater, which is going for about sixteen shillings.

Well, angel, I must put Johnnie in the tub. Will write again soon. All my love, Mum – to you and Bill.

As ever – Johnnie

July 6th, '38

Mum Darling,

What a difference the sun makes to the way one feels. It is doing its dandiest to be a good day and I certainly hope it succeeds. I will then go over to our corner to the Lilybank Garden with the private sign and put my face in the sun; it's pining for it. I received such a nice long letter from you yesterday. Glad you had some fun with Elizabeth's friends, if not with her. It would be nice seeing Gladys Livingston again; what about Florence Hodgins?

Today I received two letters – one from Ozzie Wootten. He is coming to spend a few days with us, so we will see the Exhibition. He arrives on Friday at 11:55 p.m. so Mort will meet him. Heaven only knows what we will do to entertain him if the weather is lousy, as it usually is. Also had one from Cora. She, Neil and her son Peter also arrive on Friday for the day, so I am meeting them at Mort's stand and we will all have lunch together and roam around the Ex. Something like a postman's holiday for me, but it will be so nice to have someone to talk to. Can you imagine day after day, having nobody to talk to except your husband? – loads of fun! Sometimes I get so depressed I think I will go insane – the women on the prairies have nothing on me.

I have practically finished the smock for Mrs Beldam. It is looking terribly dainty and sweet – only wish it was for my own child. I almost get bitter when I think of mine. How lovely it would have been to have had it here. It would make the difference between happiness and the other; what's the use of thinking about it.

Lyndsay returns in a few more days. It will be grand having her again, if only for a few minutes every day. By the way, tell Bill I really think he would be far wiser to buy that sword at home. By the time he got through duty and all, it would be pretty high.

The dress has not arrived yet – chances are it will come on the Friday delivery, as your letters were airmail and naturally would be quicker. Will write again on Sunday as usual, and I will inform you of our doings with our house guest. All my love, Mum, and try to save your money to come over via Panama next spring.

Your Johnnie

July 11th, '38

Mum Darling

The dress arrived and I simply adore it. It positively fits like a glove except for a small alteration around the waist. My, but it's a sweet thing on, and when altered, I believe it will look as nice as anything I own.

Ozzie did not arrive till Saturday at 5:00 – much to our surprise. Apparently his card telling us went astray. Friday we were invited to be the guests of the Donaldson Line (they do all the Canners' business). We were called for à la chauffeur and two representatives at 5 o'clock. We were driven to the Glasgow Docks and then boarded the *Athenia*. It's a little smaller than the *Carinthia* and not as nice. They took us down for dinner almost immediately, after several martinis. We had a grand feast – much to my usual delight. After dinner we went on deck to watch us sail down the Clyde. It was most interesting as all the docks are there and we also had a good glimpse of the *Queen Elizabeth*, now well under construction. We are, by the way, going to witness the launching of her next month. She certainly is colossal. The trip down took about two and a half hours. We were introduced to several people – very nice; one girl in particular who was sailing for Canada to spend four months, and gosh how I envied her.

We arrived finally at about 8:30 and the tender from Greenock came out for us. I'd have given my right hand to have not got off that ship. It was really sad to watch her steam away. I could have cried. We took a train back, first class – they gave us our tickets – which left about 9:10 and arrived back in Glasgow at about 10:10

Saturday night we took Ozzie to see *Under the Flag*, and Sunday, the three of us took the 11:30 train down to Troon and they played golf while I read in the golf club and had tea. We then went immediately to the hotel for dinner and then later walked along the boardwalk by the good old sea. It felt like nectar after the filthy air we breathe in here. We caught the 8:30 train back and played three-handed bridge all evening. Much to their disgust, I beat them both very badly. I will be sure to write Mrs D all about it as I am sure it will amuse her.

Well, darling, I must amuse my guest – it is hardly polite to keep on writing. Hope you are feeling better after your trip. Many thanks for the papers and tell them only to send the Sunday edition – that's plenty. All my love, Mum dear.

Johnnie

July 13th, '38

Dearest Elizabeth,

You will be delighted to know that the evening dress fits me perfectly and I am mad about it. Really don't know when I have had one I liked better. Apparently we both wear the same size clothes, so if you ever have anything else you have no use for, I would appreciate it no end, and thank you ever so much. Mother, from all accounts, seems to have enjoyed her visit tremendously and seemed very sad at the thought of saying goodbye. How nice you could see her again after all these years. How do you think she was looking? I only wish she could have come right on over here – I can hardly wait to see her again. I am so homesick for her.

We are not very happy over here. The climate in Glasgow is so miserable – we have had two days of sunshine since the 6th of June. I am so sick of rain and dirty clouds I could scream. We are both counting the days till we return to London and have our own furniture and home again. Living in other people's places is not that much fun. Hope you are feeling better now. Mother was saying you were looking much better, so I do hope you can continue the good work. Do drop me a line sometime soon – I would love to hear from you. My regards to Uncle Walt and the children and many thanks again for the perfectly charming little dress.

With love,
Johnnie

July 14th, '38

Mum Darling,

Received two such sweet letters from you on Tuesday. One written from Waterloo and one from Port Nelson. I was delighted to hear you were enjoying your visit with Kathryn Read. They really are the nicest friends you have ever had. Their place sounds so attractive – it must have been such a treat for you after Elizabeth's lovely but unhappy set-up.

I am anxiously awaiting the summer dress, although when it's to be worn, I know not! I am sticking firmly to my woolly shirt and Mort has only gone twice to work without his overcoat since his arrival. Laugh that off – we can't! There have only been three days of sunshine since the 6th of June. I am so sick and tired of the rain and smoky clouds. I would not live here if they made me Queen of Scotland with Holyrood Palace thrown in! Thank you ever so much for the dress and I will write and tell you all about it when it arrives. I wrote Elizabeth to thank her for the dress and hinted that if she had any more she wanted to get rid of, I would be very delighted to relieve her cupboard. Do hope she catches the hint.

Mort is off to Newcastle early this morning and will be back late tonight. Poor boy, he works too hard – I sometimes wonder if he will have a breakdown. How he keeps working day after day, 10-12 hours, I do not know. Two days of it and I would be done for.

This will probably amuse you, darling. You remember me writing about a Mrs Brown, 5 Cranworth Street? Well, you reported she was young, so I took the bull by the horns and phoned her. She was very surprised and sounded quite nice, so we had a long chat, and during the course of our conversation she informed me she had been married for twenty years! I nearly laughed in her face! What can Mr Campbell's idea of an older woman be? Is this his idea of a young one? Anyway, she invited me over yesterday. Her place is almost as bad as mine with the usual amount of junk. She is a weird little person; lame, slightly pop-eyed, and frizzy greyed hair. At first I thought I was going to be bored to extinction, but after a wee while we went down town and had tea – the latter seems to pep everyone up – so before we knew it, we were chatting away like lifelong friends. So now, I think she is very nice, although naturally I do not care to see much of her. She left today with her husband on a two-week holiday, so we will have her over for tea when she returns.

We went to the theatre the other evening and saw an excellent play. *Payment Deferred*, it was called. We were very taken with it and the acting was excellent. I had a long letter from Ernle this morning – she will never go back to Vancouver. London has a fatal grip on her now and, of course, she has an excellent job and lots of friends, so really, why should she?

Had a grand long letter from Betty Farris; they appear to be missing us quite as much as we are missing them. I have been doing extremely well with letters lately. They both cheer me up and depress me at the same time. I have never even had a postcard from my father and I have written two letters and a postcard.

A man out at the Exhibition snapped a candid camera shot of Ozzie, Mort and me as we walked along last Monday, and they turned out very well. Well, my sweet one, I will close now. All my love and many thanks again for the dress. I am sure it will be lovely. My love to Bill, Bun, and I will write them soon.

Your Johnnnie

July 16th, '38

Mum Dear,

Here is Sunday again. How I wish the next two years of Sundays would pass by all in one day and bring me a bit closer to the day I return to Vancouver. Oh, Mum, you can honestly have no conception of how homesick I am. Me, that never knew what it was like those three years at school. I'm so sick and fed up with everything and everyone and I think I will go off my poor noodle. I'd beg, borrow or steal money to go home if I could, but this is my lot, so I will just have to stick it out. I tell myself that every day and where is the consolation? – rain. Where in the devil does all the moisture come from? It may be a beautiful country, but I would take a squatter's shack on Dead Man's Island in preference any day. I know this sounds hateful and nasty, and I am sorry to have to write such letters, but you are the only person I can say such things to as I don't want other people to know what a wretch I really am.

Mum darling, the little dress arrived and is extremely nice, but most unfortunately is too small. The shoulders are a good two inches too narrow for me. It's such a pity and I was most disappointed. I will try to sell it to Lyndsay; she is a wee bit smaller than I, and will ask a pound for it. Hope she can buy it because I could do with the money. No, it came right through without being opened by customs, luckily, as it didn't look like a worn dress. The little sun-hat is sweet, Mum, and if the Mavors ask me out to Kilcreggan in August, I hope I will be able to use it there.

You were asking me what to do if you wanted to send me money. You can get a money order made out in Sterling, either at the post office or the bank – that is what Mrs Duffus did with Mort's birthday cheque. By the way, Mum, I really think it's advisable whenever you get the urge to buy something for me, to just send the money as you can buy very nice things here – quite as nice as home, in a few ways, nicer. Clothes have to be suitable for the damp climate. I have only worn a silk afternoon frock twice since the 6th of May – once to a wedding and once to the Caldwells'. Sweaters and skirts seem to be the most satisfactory clothing, and wool, as you know, is so reasonable over here. I bought a beautiful fawn Jaeger sweater with sleeves for only 30 shillings ($7.50), whereas in Canada it would be $18. There is a colossal difference.

From Saturday, July 15th, till Tuesday, is what is called the

Glasgow Fair. There is no fair, it simply means every man, woman and child vacates the city in one fell swoop. The wealthy ones to the Continent or swish hotels, the middle-class either to mediocre hotels or travel by car, and the great masses of poor gather their few shekels and live in tents anywhere they can pitch one – some even sleeping on the beaches with their bike strapped to their big toe! July is the month for all holidays here. It is really funny to see the blinds drawn down in nearly every tenement. Mort works all day Saturday, the evening, and all Monday too. Hardly what one would call pleasant for us. The Exhibition of course has been getting phenomenal crowds. I really believe every living creature in Glasgow feels it is up to him or her to make the thing a success; hence many aching limbs at the end of each day, including me. As the only alternative for me when Mort is out, I will naturally go out where I can see and hear people, if not to speak to them.

I had hoped to go on a motor trip with Mrs Mavor and L. this week, but it now looks impossible as they are getting a new servant and feel they cannot leave her. Mort saw Mr and Mrs Sandy Douglas at the Exhibition yesterday – they have been over six weeks touring England and Scotland and are leaving the end of the month, lucky devils.

Wish young John Bird would hurry it up and arrive so I would have someone to play around with; it is so lonely. Well, my sweet one, I will not trouble you any longer. Sorry this letter sounds so depressed but believe me, I am, and cannot help it. Again, many thanks for the dress – too bad it did not fit.

All my love – Johnnie

July 19th, '38

Mum darling,

I could really cry about your letter I just received, telling me of how very nearly you came over. Oh Mum, you can have no idea of how many times Mort has said he had wanted you to come over. We simply could not figure out why you didn't, when you were half-way here. You silly, silly darling, in thinking we wouldn't want you. We have been praying you would just come and drive up in a taxi as you said. In fact, these last few days I have been popping up to the window every time I heard an unfamiliar car door shut – thinking it might be you. No such luck though, and now I know you won't be here, it's even worse. Ages ago we thought of cabling you and decided it would be silly because you definitely couldn't afford it; now I wish I had done so – it seems all you really needed was some encouragement.

You seem to have had a lovely time, Mum; I am so glad. How nice to have seen Jim and all the others you mentioned and your old house. It had changed considerably I imagine. No, we never have had any of those photos developed – on the boat or leaving Vancouver. You see, our projector will have to be changed – the current or something is different over here. We will get them done one of these days, soon no doubt.

I finished the little smock for Mrs Beldam; it does look so sweet and dainty. It has a small rosebud pattern in the material and it looks so sweet with the smocking too. Hope she likes it as there are lots of wee babies at home that would like to have it. Will get busy on Wendy Farris' now. Mort took me to the theatre last night. It was awfully funny and called *Yes and No*. Thank goodness there is one diversion from ordinary life here. Had a letter and parcel from Margie Braden this morning. She sails from Liverpool on the 22nd and is in Greenock on the 23rd, so I will go down and see her off at the latter. It is only an hour from here. She sent me a beautiful purse as a farewell present – pigskin I think it must be. She will be going back to Hamilton for a few days and then out to Calgary and maybe out to Vancouver. If she does, I will have her look you up. She's a nice little thing, small, about a year my senior.

All my love, darling. Am really sorry you are not here now.
Johnnie

July 22nd, '38

Dearest Nora,

I feel very badly not having sent your birthday gift off before this. The only reason being that I have not been down town for centuries. I never go because the shops are so dowdy and awful – it is no wonder the women in Scotland look so messy. I have hardly seen any really smartly dressed people. However, my love, this afternoon I am going with the express purpose of finding something you will like and I hope not to pay duty on. I have been making inquiries though, and find they nearly always allow a parcel through when it is marked 'birthday gift'.

Mort leaves for London this coming Monday, lucky devil. He will be away about eight days. It is so terribly lonely for me when he is not here – the evenings are so dreadfully long.

I suppose you have been away on the boat several times already. Are you taking a cruise this year, and if so, who are you taking with you? We had such fun last year. Remember the mouse that came aboard at Hardy Island? I would give my all to be doing that again. Whenever I think of summer at home, my mind auto-matically turns to the good times I have had with you and your family on the good old *Willeena F.*

Only about three more months and we'll be moving. Lovely thought. It can't come too soon for me. The idea of having our own furniture again is positively thrilling. I saw in the paper where Mary and Billie had done awfully well at Crofton; are either of them going away to school this year? Your mother and father must have been awfully pleased with them.

Did I tell you before that we had Ozzie stay with us for a few days? We took him down to Troon for golf and, of course, the Exhibition – there is really very little one can do here with a visitor. We are hoping John Bird will be here – it would be my luck for him to arrive while Mort is in London. Will write again soon. My very best to Hugh, your mother, and father.

Heaps of love,

Johnnie

July 23rd, '38

Mum Darling,

Don't die of heart failure about the Canada postmark. Just thought it would be a good idea to post it on the *Duchess of Richmond* when it sails with Margie this morning. How I wish it was bringing me home to you, darling. When do you suppose I wll ever go back? I'd certainly like to think I could go next spring via the Panama, but I won't be able to, so must forget about it. Had a postcard from you yesterday – Uncle George, yes, he was always my sort of dream uncle. I don't remember him, but I do recall his picture. It used to be on your dresser in our first house.

Mort is buying me a set of golf clubs today so I am starting religiously on Monday. We came to the conclusion I simply must do something or I will go batty. Must close, dear, my train leaves at 11:45. All my love. Wish I was meeting your boat.

Johnnie

July 29th, '38

Mother Darling,

Your daughter is an addict! Only golf though. Gosh, I love it. Everything seems much easier now; only wish I had my clubs ages ago. Lyndsay and I have played three times this week and believe it or not, I'm making darned good progress – considering no lessons. We went out early this afternoon and got in eight holes while it showered and the skies let loose and then it came down in buckets. We both got thoroughly drenched and whizzed home and now I'm all bathed and feeling like a million. Can hardly wait to go out with M.S. and have him correct my mistakes. The duck arrives home at eight tonight so I am going to blow myself to dinner in town and meet the train. Won't be able to put on my very best as I usually do when I meet him, as it's one devil of a day. Had a lovely long letter from Dad; very interesting. Said you were looking awfully nice when you left Vancouver – I bet you did too – wish you had continued your trip over here though. I miss my Mummie so much and can hardly wait to see you again. There isn't a bit of news except golf and I just had to tell you how much I love it, so this will be short and sweet.

Bill Hogg phoned again yesterday and wanted me to play golf today. Said he had been feeling terrible and was sorry for Tuesday's game, but was raring to go again. He is quite nice, but nobody is 1,2,3 to my Mort. I really love him more and more every day. We are certainly getting to be the old married couple – almost two years now. It doesn't seem that long. Time goes so quickly, doesn't it?

Well, my sweet, I will close now and go down and get some butter and bacon for our breakfast. One must eat, unfortunately. All my love – please write as often as you can.

Your loving Johnnie

P.S. How is Bill? I'm looking forward to hearing from him sometime soon.

Aug 2nd, '38

Dear Mum,

Have only a few jiffies in which to dash off a line or two. Mrs Duffus tells Mort you are home again, so am expecting to hear shortly. Chances are you have been pretty busy settling again. I am going down to Kilcreggan with Lyndsay this coming Monday and will stay till Friday afternoon. It will be a nice change for me and they have such a lovely summer place there.

Today in fact, just as I finish writing this, I will be having lunch with Mary Riddell, who is an ex-Vancouver gal. She has a child that is nine, and is divorced from her husband who is an Englishman. She is coming back here to live. She came via the Panama and her boat stays here a week. I am to have lunch on board. I did not know her, but Mort did. I do hope I like her as it will be nice to have her in London.

Have been doing nothing but playing golf lately. Yesterday I did nine holes in 54, which isn't bad for a week's playing. Mort played with me on Sunday. We had heaps of fun and he helped me considerably. Will write again later in the week.

All my love darling,

Johnnie

P.S. Forgot to tell you something funny. We took our golf clubs on the bus to our nine-hole course and when we arrived we had to wait quite a while as there were so many players. I was very nervous as there were many people standing around the first hole. When our turn came up, Mort took my bag and the four remaining clubs along with his massive bag full of clubs, and sent me to the tee with, 'Keep your head down and you will be just fine.' To my complete and utter delight, the ball sailed away and landed just over 200 yards away! Mort was most impressed and took my place on the tee, took a mighty swing, and topped the ball, which bounced and hobbled thirty-odd feet down the fairway! Poor Mort! People laughed because of his professional bag and the clubs, and from then on, he played his usual super game and I did not play another really good shot. With his golfing record behind him, it must have been an awful shock to his pride as I don't suppose he has flubbed a shot since he was a young boy in Calgary.

Aug 6th, '38

Mum Darling,

Many thanks for your letter – it was the first since you arrived home. Yes, it is a pity that you didn't just come on over. We would have adored having you with us, but will look forward to the time it does actually happen.

You wanted our telephone number – it's Western 3683. It would certainly be nice to hear your voice although it will probably upset us both. Don't forget the nine hours difference, will you? We wouldn't mind a scrap being wakened though. It would be a shame to call during the day and perhaps only get my cleaning woman. Mort is always home till 8:45 a.m. and gets in about 6:45 p.m., so you can figure it out yourself. The phone service over here is simply appalling. Mort and I get cut off on long-distance calls and everything, so choose an hour when everyone else will not be on the phone at the same time. If your friend Murray doesn't kick through with the free call, you mustn't do it yourself as it would be a dreadful waste of money with the poor connections over here.

No, Billy Livingstone has not arrived yet. Chances are he won't either; kids don't like looking up strangers. I leave on Monday for Kilcreggan and come home Friday. Hope I have a good time. If the weather will only stay decent, it will be grand.

What heat you are having and all those awful fires. I wouldn't mind a bit of it myself, although we had three good days this week.

Mort and I go down to Troon tomorrow and will have a game of golf and dinner. Mary C. Riddell and her son and I went down to Edinburgh for the day on Thursday. We had a lot of fun and nearly walked our legs off. I met Bill Hogg and Mort at the Exhibition for dinner. I like Mary very much and we will no doubt have some rare times together in London later. I am awfully well, Mum. I guess the reason I never mention my health is because I never felt better in all my life. Mort says he has never seen me look better than I do now – apparently this life agrees with me. It certainly ought to – I am in bed by twelve every night of my life. Mort looks better than at home too, and all the exercise, such as the Exhibition and all the walking instead of using a car, has reduced his waistline about six inches.

His work keeps him busy. He puts in about four or five hours a day at the stand (waiting on customers and generally supervising the girl demonstrators), and is also about five hours at the office on St Enoch's Square. He certainly works for every penny he gets. Everybody seems to like him a lot.

Well, Mother, my darling, I can think of nothing more to say, so will write from Lyndsay's next week. All my love to you all.

Your loving Johnnie

Aug 15th, '38

Darling Mum,

Had such a lovely holiday and I am looking 100% better for it. My face has taken a new lease on life and glows with health and sunburn. We spent almost every minute sunning ourselves in the garden and went swimming only once – the water was grand too.

Yesterday, Sunday, Bill Hogg, Mort and I took the train down to Troon and played golf. They nearly walked the legs off me. It was, in length, 6700 yards and I felt every last hundred lugging our clubs, etc. Mort figured I walked about seven miles in all, chasing balls etc. However, I enjoyed myself thoroughly and did not really feel tired until today – which leads up to another little tale.

This afternoon I was pooped out, so I lay down for a while. Next thing I knew, of course, I was well into the land of nod. I dreamt I had just returned from buying two lamb chops and some corn for our dinner and was puttering around in the kitchen when the doorbell rang and in you walked! After we got through giving you the royal welcome, it seemed apparent you were not staying with us, so I said very formally, 'You will of course stay for dinner?' You said you would and with that you walked to your suitcase and brought out one lamb chop and some corn! After that I awakened. Next dream was that I heard you so realistically say, 'Johnnie, it is such a lovely day, you shouldn't be inside sleeping. Why don't you go for a walk?' Your voice was so clear, and it was as if you were really here, that I jumped up off the bed and dashed into the hall before I realised it was only a dream! I felt queer all day about it.

You will be glad to know, Mum, that I am really feeling better about this whole situation and have not got that burning feeling inside me that I must go home. It is really a relief, Mum; I was unbearably homesick for so long. I miss you all so terribly but in a different way from before. I must close, sweetie, as Marge Hamilton is meeting me at 10:40 for a special preview.

All my love darling,
Your Johnnie

Aug 20th, '38

Mum darling,

Was so glad to receive your letter this morning. I miss them so much when you miss a week; however, was pleased to hear Helen had been up. It is so nice to have company. Am getting all excited about the big surprise you say you have in store for my birthday. Can't imagine what it will be, but knowing you, I can be assured of liking it. It will be a funny kind of a birthday – my very first away from my very dear Mummie and I will no doubt feel very blue instead of bursting with happiness as I usually have before. But never mind, old sweet, there are lots more birthdays and chances are, we'll be together for them. Let us hope so at any rate. Twenty-two; it's amazing how the years roll around. I wish for a birthday gift I could have a baby – nothing in all the world would make me happier.

Mort leaves me again for London a week from Monday and hopes to be back the day of or before my birthday. He is trying to persuade me to use the money I have been saving for my fur, to go up to London, but nothing could make me spend that until I have enough to buy that fox – not even a weekend in London, and that is giving up a lot.

We are going to a big football match this afternoon – it is a lovely day too – really too hot for the players, poor devils. It will be our first English football game. Hope we enjoy it. Am meeting Mr Caldwell and Mort for lunch at 1:15 in town and then on to the game.

And by the way, Eva, did you find those pictures of Flora and me at Stratford? I would like them back and know they aren't really very interesting to you, and to me they represent my first week in London. As Margie Braden has the negatives, I cannot get any more.

Had such a nice letter from Mrs Duffus today too. She has had such a time with her teeth, poor dear. So glad Bill enjoyed himself so much; the change of air would do him a lot of good too. Tell him to write and tell me all about it. Hope Bunny receives his birthday gift all right – I thought it was such a good-looking hanky. Will write again soon, but wanted to thank you for your letter and the newspaper you sent. Do you ever see Gordon S at all? How are Daphne and her mother? Yes, Bill H is very nice and not like his brother.

All My Love Mum, As Ever

Johnnie

Sept 11th, '38

London (For My Birthday)

Dearest Nora,

Have had a perfectly glorious week with Mum and Mort here for three of the days. We have done just about everything imaginable, including three excellent theatre shows which were *French Without Tears*, *Golden Boy* and *The Fleet's Lit Up*. Had dinner at Quaglino's and on to the Florida Night Club, lunch at Mungall's, saw Ascot, Windsor Castle, Hampton Court Palace and drove all over Surrey. All in all, we have done an awful lot in such a short time, including today, which we spent at the Beldams' beautiful house.

I hate to think of settling down in Glasgow again, but it is only a matter of about six more weeks and the time will probably pass quickly with Mother there. She expects to sail about the middle of October and plans on spending some time in the east and will, I think, be back in Vancouver about the middle of November. By then I hope we will be settled here.

Enough for now, Nora my love, and my very best love to you and your mother and Hugh.

As Ever

Johnnie

Oct 14th, '38

Mum darling,

I hate to think the time has come to write this letter; it really is dreadful. We will hold the thought, Mum dear, that we will be able to see each other again soon. I will never forget what it has meant to me to have you here. How would I have got through the last six weeks I honestly do not know. You were a brick, darling, and there will be other times to look forward to, I know! Take good care of yourself on the ship! Write full details of all the passengers. I will be so anxious to know about it all and post it immediately to Cranworth, and your next letter to London. I will write often, darling, if only a postcard. Give Bill, Bunny, Mrs D and Dot a big hug for me. Bless their hearts. We will miss you so much. The weeks and days ahead are not pleasant to look forward to for either of us, but with spring comes a new hope that you might get over again. Do everything in your power, sweet, to save and get ahead, because with travelling one does meet such attractive people, and I won't be happy until I know how you are settled with your future plans. Hope our flowers are nice and help to cheer those first few minutes of lost feelings as she steams down the Clyde. If only we were making the trip together, what fun we would have; maybe we will some day. I will keep my fingers crossed during the Irish Sweep days and expect to see your sweet face back again if you should win!! I hope Emily will be there to meet you, so give her my very best love – Roy and Judie also. All my love to Kath, and Royal, Margie and Elizabeth, and to you my darling, all my love always. I hope some day I will be able to repay you for your kindness in coming and all the sweet things you have done for me. I always think of you so often. Who knows, we may not always be here, Mum. Bye-bye sweet, and we will both try and be so brave tomorrow.

Your Mary Ann

Oct 14th, '38

Dearest Nora,

Mort had a letter from Phil yesterday, telling us of your wedding date. How thrilled and excited the two of you must be and how I do wish I was going to be there to give you a party. It doesn't seem fair to be away for it. Am dying to know who your bridesmaids are etc. It gives me the shivers down my back just thinking of it. Damn, I wish we were going to be there!

Mother sails tomorrow. I have a very empty feeling in my tummy and God only knows what it will be like tomorrow. As I think I said before, we push out of here on about the 3rd or 4th. certainly won't shed any tears over that. We are going to be in a service flat till we find our house. We shouldn't have any difficulty. There seem to be hundreds in the papers and they all sound so attractive.

Please write in between fittings and tell me all your news – where you are going for your honeymoon and is your house ready etc.? If only I could talk to you both. My very best love, Nora dear, to you both, and your mother.

Johnnie

Oct 17th, '38

Mum Darling,

How lonely it seems here this morning. It's dull and gloomy and no idiotic Eva to laugh with. I almost have to pinch myself to believe that you are not going to come around that kitchen door yelling – coal, coal – or something silly. It was not so dreadful over the weekend as we were busy all the time and Mort kept up a stream of crazy conversation, but now it's so quiet and awful.

After you steamed away down the Clyde, we immediately caught the train back to Glasgow and got off for the Exhibition.

Shortly after we arrived, Norman Brann turned up and the two of us went off to look for toys for his nephew. Norman is an awfully nice boy and we had such a lovely evening with him. Before going to dinner, we came home and brushed up. My black gloves and tears had done a good job on my face. We dined at the Grosvenor as arranged – had a lovely dinner and then went to the theatre. It was not *Tovarich* as we thought, but quite a good show called *Saloon Bar*. We came straight home afterwards, played a few card games and so to bed.

Sunday, the weather looked very unsettled and in the afternoon it turned for the better, so the three of us went to Troon on the 1:30 train. They played golf and I walked, at least I struggled around after them. There was a fifty-mile gale blowing. You poor darling, I am afraid you were in for a very rough trip. It was an amusing game – they never knew where the ball was going to land. The wind would catch it in mid-air and twirl and toss it around to finally arrive on the fairway in every place but where it was supposed to be. By the end of the 18th, we were all blue with cold, so we headed directly for the South Beach Hotel and your little bar. I had two Manhattans and they a couple of double whiskies, then their famous steaks to top it all. Norman had to catch the train at 8:00, so we had to hurry back, as he was returning to Ireland.

Last night I taught Mort our builders game and played a ha'penny a card and made a little money off him. Today Lizzie arrives and I think I shall spend the day helping her. I will pack the trunk in the kitchen as a starter and tidy my drawers, which are, as usual, in a dreadful state.

I do hope, darling, your trip wasn't too ghastly. The people we saw looked very pleasant and knowing your winsome manner, we felt assured that it would not be too long before you had made friends. Your stateroom looked very comfy and I imagine you had letters and things to keep your mind occupied for a little while anyway.

I must get busy now, darling, and put myself in 'Greenland's Icy Waters'. It is going to be awful here. Everything reminds me so of you, but in two more weeks we will be almost out of here and then new places and faces to help forget the dearest mother in the world. Not forget you – in true sense – just that you were here and to hold the thought that you will be back again.

All my love, darling, and take good care of yourself.

Your Johnnie

Oct 24th, '38

Mum darling,

All going well, you should be in Toronto today. I have thought of you so often this week, and wondered how you were getting along on your trip etc. and kept my fingers crossed for a smooth crossing. The weather here has been ghastly; rain or cloudy and dull – I hope the Atlantic was not as unkind to you as Glasgow has been to us. This week Mort has had three evenings at the Exhibition, poor boy, so we have not had a very exciting time of it.

Lyndsay has been in a couple of times, once for tea. She is so busy these days she cannot spare much time consoling a lonely gal like me. However, when Mort was not going to the Exhibition, he took me to the movies. Saw *Jezebel* and enjoyed it thoroughly. Also saw *Divorce of Lady X*. It was, as well, darned good entertainment.

Mrs Mavor took me down shopping and we had afternoon tea. (Remember St Andrews?) All these little things and a bit of packing has helped pass the week away, and right at this very moment we are listening to a Canadian program, headquarters being in Toronto and then it's to take us all the way out to dear old Vancouver. You might this very moment be listening to this from

Mother.

the Woodcocks. If only we could be transported as quickly as we are by radio and could spend Sunday in Vancouver.

We are definitely leaving on Friday the 4th, and find to our dismay our furniture does not arrive over here till the 29th, so we will have about three weeks to look around and really find what we want. We are going to take a room in the place Mary Riddell spoke of – it sounds quite comfortable and certainly central. We can always move if we don't like it.

Mr Cummings (the person who has the wonderful collection of silver), has invited us to his place tomorrow evening. It should be most interesting. Tuesday, Mort leaves for Newcastle and returns late Wednesday evening and misses out on a dinner party given by Bill Hogg at the Grant Arms, to consume some partridge he had sent him from Canada. Another couple are going and I will trot along, minus one husband.

Thursday night about ten of us (Lyndsay's friends) are all going to the Piccadilly Club for dinner and dancing. It will be the first time in Glasgow, so it will be fun to see what their night spots are like. What evening gown I should wear I know not, but chances are the blue with the silver jacket. It is nice to know that people have not seen my evening gowns, as no doubt they shall see several more seasons.

Next week Mr Caldwell is taking all the demonstrators including his wife and us, to Coopers for dinner and then a movie. All in all my days are not empty and they will all be gone before I know it. Lizzie starts her cleaning bug tomorrow – altogether she will be here five days. Am looking forward so much to your first letter. I miss you so much, Mum. I try hard to not even think of you. One cannot and must not live on memories. They do not afford happiness, so instead we must look forward to our next meeting and may it be as happy as our last!

There is no more news now, my darling, so will busy myself with our dinner. So for now, bye-bye Eva and be good to yourself.

Your loving Mary Ann

Park Chambers
35 Queens Gardens
London W2
Nov 5th, '38

Mum Darling,

Here we are back again. It does not seem possible really, after all the work and confusion of those last few days in Glasgow. Thank goodness it is all over now and we can relax for a few days.

This place is really not too bad at all. We have lots of room – twin beds (at least day couches), two tremendous wardrobes and dresser, and our own concealed wash-b. The other business is just down the hall – telephone, modern furnishings and a large green rug. You probably won't believe it, but we had a little snow and lots of sleet before we left, and down here it is glorious. Mort is off today without an overcoat on and sun is streaming in our window. It sounds fantastic, but it is true nevertheless.

We both have colds – as usual. I have a break of three weeks between each one. Maybe down here we will stop it. The weather in Glasgow was enough to drive anyone into their grave. Lyndsay and three others and ourselves all went out last Tuesday and Mrs Mavor very kindly had Mort and me for dinner first. They really have been so kind; we had quite a bit of fun and weren't late. On Wednesday night, Mort and I packed vigorously and finished things up pretty well. Thursday he stepped out to the big dinner and I went to a movie very early. I did the final touches on the house. Yesterday morning, Lizzie came in for the brushing up and I left to meet Mort at the station at 1:00. Mr Caldwell had tears in his eyes when he said goodbye to Mort – they will miss each other so much. Big thrills in store for the Duffus family. We are going down to Reigate this afternoon to be shown around our prospects. By the time you receive this, I hope we have definitely made up our minds. If only we can find a cheap but nice place, all our financial troubles will end. As you know, it costs dearly to live over here.

I simply cannot get over the sun. I had given up hope of ever seeing it again. It has been ghastly since you left. I was so sure there would be a letter for me c/o Philpot Lane, but Mort says no. Do not write to this address that is on my letter; keep on with the Philpot till I tell you not to. Will keep you posted to tell you how we are all making out.

London seems a little queer without you, darling. All my love to you, Bill and Bun.

Johnnie

35-39 Queens Gardens W2

Nov 15th, '38

Mum darling

Intended to write yesterday but have been so dreadfully busy! We have definitely decided on 'Tall Trees' in Reigate. We really love the place and are only waiting to hear the OK from the house agent to cinch the thing. It's so exciting, Mum, and I will one day very soon, when I have a breather, describe the house fully to you, so when you next write, send your letter to me at this address –

Tall Trees

Wray Park Road

Reigate, Surrey

It is a lovely feeling to have our own address again and no more c/o's! All going well we hope to be in by December 1st, but it all depends.

We had a lovely evening at Flora and Finlays – dinner and 'vanti' afterwards. They both asked very kindly for you. We sailed home at 3:00 a.m. and Sunday we spent the day in Epping Forest with the Browns. They have the loveliest dog and are going to try and get one of the puppies for us. We mooched all around, saw Boudicca's famous wall where she made her last stand against the Romans; also an 11th century abbey and some 16th century beer taverns. It's really a beautiful county, but we like our Reigate.

Yesterday I bought our Xmas cards. They are quite attractive and will try and get them all addressed as the last week in Nov. will be such a rush for us without Xmas things to worry us too. Today Mary Riddell and I are going to do the rounds of the second-hand shops so as to get a rough idea of what we can get for

Tall Trees, Reigate.

our money. It is going to be an awful struggle, I think, but struggling is rather fun.

Had a long letter from Dad yesterday, also one from Jeanie Alexander. They expect their babe in January, lucky kids! Also got one from Miss Wylie, thanking me for leaving such a clean flat. She said if anything, it was far cleaner than when I got it, which was very sweet of her. I will enclose her letter.

Well, darling – enough about us. Are you OK? I am longing to hear after you got home. Did Royal Read forward you my first letter? Wasn't it simply dreadful about Margaret and wee Stewart? My God, some dreadful things happen. That poor wee baby and how my heart aches for Jock; he loved the child so much. I will write to him soon.

Well, dear, I must close – I am meeting Mary at 10:45 and it is getting late now. Have you had any luck, if you know what I mean?

Heaps of love darling,

Your Johnnie

Nov 12th, '38

(From the Landlady)

Dear Mrs Duffus,

Just a line to tell you how much I appreciate your goodness in cleaning the flat – so beautifully clean, I think it was cleaner now than when you got it; how you managed I do not know – what with all your heavy luggage and stuff to get away at the last moment. It was wonderful. Also the food, and your flowers are still lovely. I do hope you find a nice house and are very happy in it. You deserve to be, I think.

This letter should have been written last week, but you will excuse me when I tell you my lifelong friend died on Wednesday. Kindest regards to you both.

From yours very sincerely,

Mary Wylie

Looking back on all the letters I wrote home to Vancouver, I am more than a little ashamed to have been so homesick. No wonder my mother packed herself off to Glasgow. She certainly put a smile back on my face as the three of us celebrated my 22nd in London. Fortunately, Mort got along famously with her, so it was no hardship to have his mother-in-law with us for three weeks. I do not remember why his nickname for her was 'The Old Tomato', but she loved it. Coming from a Scottish mother and an Irish father, she had a great sense of humour and a wonderful disposition. She was very generous and compassionate, never discussing her many good deeds to those less fortunate. My father adored her. All of the latter is to prepare anyone reading Oh Johnny! *to understand why letters to her were so filled with devotion.*

Some sixty years later, I stayed in Glasgow and was very impressed with the transformation that had taken place. Where it had been a grey and dirty city, it is now bright, clean and attractive, with beautiful buildings which you will read about in my diary. Lyndsay Mavor Sandeman, who was so wonderfully kind to me when we lived there, had died a few years prior to my last time in Scotland. However, I had four glorious days with her and her husband Cargill, at their home, before she became ill with cancer. They drove me to have tea with Lyndsay's mother, who was close to ninety. It was wonderful to see her again, I was so fond of her and they were unbelievably kind to us when we lived in Glasgow.

Tall Trees
Wray Park Road, Surrey
Nov '38

Dearest Nora,

You have never been out of my mind all this week. If all things come true that I have been wishing for you and Hughie, you should both be a very happy couple! I even wished for a beautiful day for the 30th and I hope I was not betrayed.

Your twenty-page letter arrived yesterday. I was so thrilled with it, Nora, and your gown sounded too lovely and your bridesmaids should do you credit. How I ached to be there, it simply does not seem right that I wasn't. Mother was very thrilled that you invited her and said she would be writing me full details. It is maddening to wait so long to hear about it all.

We cannot get into our house till the 5th or 6th and are both simply furious, as we expected to be in yesterday. It's the d—— customs, and then our furniture was in the bottom of the hold. Here is hoping we are settled by Christmas! Your little present I sent you is very small, Nora my love, but things have been terribly hard – living in a hotel for a month and all our moving expenses – it has been very bad, but it is just to wish you both a very Merry first Christmas together, and may all your New Years be as happy as the first should be. While I remember, do send me Eileen's address (what is her last name?), as I would love to see her and the baby.

We have been having the most glorious weather, every day, bright and sunny and so far no fog. Of course it is mighty cold, but as long as it is sunny, I don't care. Today Mort and I are going out to the Regent's Park Zoo – he has not been for ten years and they have a lot of baby penguins, which I am dying to see! London is such fun, there is always something to do. If you ever get the chance, see a French film, *Katia*. It is the grandest film I have seen in many years. My love and every good wish to your Mum, and meantime – Merry Xmas.

Lovingly,
Johnnie

Nov. 19th '38

Mum darling,

Your sixteen-page letter arrived from Regina yesterday. Thanks, darling, it was lovely and so newsy. What a grand visit you have had with the Irvines; it is such years since last we saw them. This letter is not going to have any paragraphs as I have this one sheet until I can get out and buy some, so won't waste any space. My letters of late haven't been very newsy or long – we have had a terribly busy time and it's not over by any means. I was down in Reigate yesterday trying to locate a maid – they are expensive in England unless you get a schoolgirl minus all knowledge. Do not know what I will do. If it wasn't for all the fireplaces, I would almost rather do it all myself. Last night we played bridge with Dr Thomas and had a lovely time. They are so nice and their kiddies are sweet. Before, we went to a cocktail party given by Phyllis Burley-Smith (old Woodward's granddaughter – she came into a fortune) who has a lovely flat in Mayfair. It was an almost all Canadian party. Young Roderick Bell-Irving was there (Henry's son) and a finer lad I haven't met. Mrs Campbell, Margie and Doug (Mrs Covernton's sister). Remember during camp days at Roberts Creek I had such a crush on Dougie? Also an American chap with his girl and a most amusing Hungarian author who was most attentive and intriguing, and one Englishman who was a little overpowered by so many Canadians and their loud voices. It is simply teeming today and we are hoping to go to Covent Garden to hear the symphony. We have been so lucky with the weather, every day being perfect. Bob Caldwell told Mort the weather in Glasgow has been terrrrrrrrible! Can't you just hear him? Yes, I knew about Margaret and the baby, my heart aches for Jock. I will write him as soon as I get our paper. I will really write a good descriptive letter about Tall Trees when we get in next month, but at present it is hard to describe, apart from it being a lovely place with a large garden. We have all the downstairs and basement, with our own separate entrance. The upstairs is not finished as yet. Our bedroom is very large with a fireplace and wash basin. Three eight foot windows facing south and over the garden. The living room is all beamed with a very large fireplace. Have not had the boat pictures developed as yet because I haven't finished the roll, but will send them along as soon as possible. My love to Bill and Dad. I must get caught up on my letter writing. The days seem to fly. All my love to you, Mum dear.

Your John

Still London
but –
Tall Trees
Wray Park Road
Reigate, Surrey
Dec 1st, '38

Darling Mum,

This is in the way of being a Christmas letter so that I can wish you and Bill a very merry one and a happy and prosperous New Year! Let us hope it will be the last one we will all be separated from each other.

We have both decided to write to our respective Ma-ma's and tell them not to cable at Xmas. It is very silly to waste the money expressing what we know the other is thinking and wishing. Please promise not to cable, Mum, as we are not and it would only make us feel badly if we didn't and you did. All the moving has made Xmas a bit hard, so we feel we cannot add more. I know you will understand.

We are trying to get Flora and Finlay to come down for the 25th and have dinner with us but don't know as yet if they are able to or not. This failing, we may ask Betty and Joe Thomas and their children.

We are still undecided as to whether tomorrow will be the big day or Saturday – the Customs are being a little tiresome and can't make up their stupid minds when they will release our furniture. In the meantime I have been busily attending to gas stove and hall heater, electricity and what not. I am quickly becoming a very business-like woman. Mort, of course, cannot leave the office, so have had to do it all and must admit I have thoroughly enjoyed myself.

I do so hope you won't open your Xmas parcel that will arrive for you and Bill – please don't, and we hope you will both be pleased. I would give my all to see Willie's face when he opens his. I may be wrong, but I think he will be quite thrilled. Tell him not to shake it!!! We would have liked to do more but not this year, I'm afraid.

Well, dear Mum, I will close now and will be writing as soon as I get a breather in Reigate and will tell you all the details which I know you are so anxious to hear about.

All my love to you and Bill. My heart is full of good wishes for you both and may this coming year bring you both every happiness you both so rightly deserve.

Your Mary Ann

December 17th, '38

Dearest Mum,

Am feeling so full of myself today, I had to write and tell you all about it. The drapes are up!! They look so nice, especially the living room. You remember the red that was blended in them, well, they had to be dropped nine inches just to bring them to the window sill as the ceilings are so high. So, they have matched them exactly and run the addition up both the outer sides, if you understand? When they are drawn they form a 'U'. The windows are set into an alcove so when they are drawn back during the daytime, they completely cover the windows on the sides and as they are casement windows, they really look very nice.

The same had to be done to the bedroom, so they have a gold border added to match the gold stripe and they are not too bad. The spare room, unfurnished as it is at the moment, has our dining room drapes, also with a piece added. They are quite presentable for the time being, and after all, they were all made of lovely material. The maid's room is very nice. It makes all the difference in the world to the look of the house and certainly makes it feel warmer. The furniture I bought at the auction looks very nice and is comfortable. It was a pity we couldn't bring everything over, but we are pleased with what we have achieved so far. We feel pretty well settled now except for our maid and with any luck she should arrive about January 1st.

Last night we had the Caldwells for dinner. They arrived from Glasgow a few days ago so it gave us a golden opportunity to repay their hospitality. They are on their way to the South of France, which is nice. Hope we will be able to do the same one day. I cooked a scrumptious leg of lamb, mint sauce, scalloped potatoes and mixed vegetables, which all turned out very well. Mince pies that also turned out very well. They seemed to enjoy themselves.

Yesterday was Dad's birthday. Please tell him I will be dashing off belated greetings soon. I have been busy. This is a large place to run without any help.

Mary Riddell and Flora and the Caldwells all received your Xmas cards and said to thank you. They were certainly well ahead of time but I never know how long to allow either.

We have secured a cook who is coming for four days, from Friday-Monday to do us over Xmas, so we will have nothing to worry about. Have ordered our turkey and all the trimmings. She should be good; her references are perfect. A really typical English servant – yes madam, no madam. My daily can't come any more as her husband had an accident and she has to look after him. Hence my days have been full. With no central heating Mort is always bringing coal and wood for me. We have an electric heater in our bedroom which he very kindly lights before we go to bed and first thing in the morning, and on Tuesday, an electric towel rack goes in, as the towels are always damp. We got a gas radiator for the hall.

The pinky-beige rug is going to fit very nicely into Mort's dressing room, also the wicker chair and his chiffonier. We picked up a colossal wardrobe at an auction in London. It really is a pip as well as a very good bargain. We are both able to hang all our clothes, hats and linen in the one wardrobe, which is darned convenient.

Our guest room is empty except for the large cedar chest and our dining room drapes – maybe someday it will be furnished. Furniture is quite reasonable over here but we do find food is outrageously high. I paid 1/2 for a tin of Aylmer peaches the other day and soup, 5d. a tin! We are going to buy them in London. I'd be broke if I had to buy them in Reigate.

There are a lot of shops to choose from here and very good service. Even my butcher calls for my order every morning and one lad, from a vegetable and flower shop, is a lamb; he runs all kinds of errands for me and always has a bright answer to everything I say. Yesterday he arrived in a drenching rain with a bright 'Good morning, Mrs Duffus', which really is a silly salutation!! I really look forward to him coming every morning. I will keep on having them come for my order until I get a bicycle. I love the walk into the town but find it a bit much carrying all the parcels.

We have a home for the blind and crippled children next door to us and I have been invited to attend their Xmas party on the 21st. I intend to go as I will meet other people, I hope. The head matron is awfully nice, but her tongue wags at both ends.

Sunday – Mort and I have had the nicest day. It was brilliantly sunny and as cold as the dickens. There were icicles hanging off our outside windows and all the puddles are frozen. We put on all our warmies and had the grandest walk all up in the hills and had lunch in the log cabin lunch and tea house. It's quite attractive but its real charm will be in the summer as they have tables made of slabs of logs on the verandahs which overlook a clear sweep of Surrey, in all its beauty. On our way home we came upon about thirty hikers all singing marching songs. They looked so nice in their bright sweaters and caps, trudging along so gaily. England is a very fascinating place and I really think it will completely captivate me before long.

We are now sherried and dined and are feeling comfortably tired in front of our fire. It is so cozy and so very cold outside. I seem to be doing a lot of writing about us, no doubt because we are so happy to finally have a place of our own. From the time we closed Point Grey Road and Mort went east, it has run into eight months, so you will understand how very pleased we are to be settled at long last.

I must close now as I have Xmas letters to write and it is getting late. Oh yes, one more thing I forgot to tell you. Granny Smith sent us some money which we used to buy a card table. It was such a shame Crone's Moving Co. somehow or other managed to lose our nice white one.

All my love to you and my big brother Bill. One of these days I will find time to write to him. Meantime, you will have to share these lengthy epistles.

Your loving Mary Ann

December 27th, '38

Dearest Mum and Bill,

This letter ought to be written as a book and it would have the title *Tragedy Versus Joy*. It might make a better film as there are some very comical sides to all I have to tell you, all of which will come later. First and foremost let me thank you for our perfectly wonderful Christmas present from you both. You can have no idea how thrilled we are. As you obviously remembered, the only missing pieces from Uncle Walt and Elizabeth's wedding gift to us were the fish knives and forks, and now, thanks to both of you, we are looking forward to our next fish dinner. They are really beautiful. We feel sure our Dover sole will taste twice as good. A million thanks, although we thought you were very naughty, but we loved you for it.

And now for our long tale of woe . . . woe . . . woe (and joy).

First and foremost, on Friday our cook, Mrs Burt, was supposed to arrive; did so and left again because I had changed our Xmas dinner from the 25th to the 26th because Flora and Finlay couldn't come due to her illness. This of course was a dreadful disappointment. However, they invited us to go to them instead, in order to save Flora from going out in the cold. Mort arrived home to find me in tears as I had had an upsetting conversation with Mrs Burt on the phone. She was cross because being a widow, she wouldn't spend Xmas in her own home. She was very rude, but before she hung up she said a Mrs Jordan would come on the 26th instead.

On the strength of knowing we had help on the 26th, we invited Kythe MacKenzie and Bob Hyndman to come down to us from London and we would have our postponed Xmas turkey.

Christmas day arrived and we had our breakfast, lit the living room fire and then opened our presents. One big thrill was a beautiful belt from Etoline Watt. It's a Jaeger one and had always fascinated me when I saw them on others. It was terribly sweet of her. Mort gave me a beautiful red scarf to wear with the suit Mrs Duffus gave me (which by the way, is a knock-out), also 100 Gold Flake and Cadbury's chocolates. We had both made a bargain not to spend more than a pound on each other. Lyndsay sent me powder puffs. Emily, four pairs of silk stockings, which I would gladly walk ten miles to kiss her for. Dot also sent me stockings and Margie Braden, an evening hanky. Dad sent us a huge box of delicious apples. Cables from Betty and Ralph, Betty Birks, Alan, yourselves, and Mrs D and Dot. You were all so very good to us and we were thrilled to get them and only wished we could have done the same for you. They are very proudly sitting on our mantelpiece. Of course I got masses of hankies and Mort got some lovely things also. I gave him a very good-looking scarf from Austin Reed's and some tongs for the coal!

We then had a grand clean up and made reservations to spend the night in London as the snowstorm had muddled all the train schedules in Surrey. We went into London about 3:00 and bathed and dressed for dinner at Mungall's at 7:00. We had a most delectable dinner and we played silly card games wherein we lost a pound. Two others dropped in during the evening and we had lots of fun and laughs. They gave us a game of Autobridge, which hopefully will help boost my game. Sallied home about 2:00 o'clock, feeling full of Xmas dinner, champagne and laughter.

We caught the 12:00 o'clock train back and expected to find Mrs Jordan waiting for us, but no, she never showed up. Likely took umbrage about her friend Mrs Burt. We'll never know as she was conspicuous by her absence.

With our expected guests for dinner, Mort buried himself into fireplaces and the Electrolux, while I stuffed the turkey, peeled the potatoes, etc., etc. – including a fair quantity of silver polishing. Finally, half dead and finished our work, we settled ourselves to have a sandwich and a quick drink before changing to meet Kythe and Bob at the station. We had just finished saying the worst is over and congratulating ourselves on the amount we had achieved in such a short time, when we heard a strange swishing sound we thought came from the kitchen, as if I had left a large pan of grease in the oven. I ran out to see and there was nothing wrong there. The noise got louder and louder, and to our horror, if a torrent of water wasn't surging from the hall ceiling onto our hall runners. Mort rushed upstairs, which isn't occupied as yet, and called out to tell me to telephone our landlord Mr Hume. He said he would be right over and for Mort to try and find the water main and to turn it off. It was pitch black upstairs and Mort grabbed any tap he could find and felt considerably relieved to find the pressure easing somewhat, and then two pipes burst, one over the bedroom and the other over the front hall!!

Meanwhile, while all of this was being a problem for Mort, I put in a call to Kythe and fortunately caught them as they were about to put their coats on. She was terribly upset for us and equally for them, as they had been looking forward to coming out to us and having a square meal as they were both terribly hard up.

Meanwhile water swished and gushed in every conceivable spot. By this time I was almost hysterical at the front steps, calling wildly for Mr Hume to hurry up or we would be flooded out. He finally arrived after what seemed like a lifetime, bearing everything he could lay his hands on to mop up the water, followed by his plumber in tow. From then on everything happened and was done in such a frenzy of haste, all by candlelight, that really it's pretty hard to describe. Practically everything in sight was used to wipe up – blankets, bedspreads, towels, bath mats – and from Hume's house, even coats! When the water came through on our bedspreads, it put the finishing touches on me and I buried my head in a wet towel and made it even wetter.

I do so wish we could have had the odd picture taken of the whole scene. One of me that you would have loved, Mum, would have been of me wringing out, to the best of my ability, everything that they threw in the bathroom door. I thought my hands would never be warm again.

We really had a contrast of emotions on Boxing Day. At one point we decided there and then to move out bag and baggage; everything had gone wrong from beginning to end and we felt we could not bear one more day. Lease or no lease, we would quit on the spot.

It took three hours to get things under control. Mr Hume, the plumber, and the two of us had a couple of good drinks, after which they went on their way. It wasn't long before there was a healthy knock on our door and it was Mr Hume, laden with blankets for us and an invitation to join their fancy dress party and forget the whole wretched business until morning! We thought it was a great idea; tucked the turkey into the pantry with all its trimmings, and proceeded to enjoy a bacon and egg dinner. We then put on fresh dry clothes and up to Belmont we went on snow-covered Wray Park Road. Their house is named Belmont! He really is a perfect brick and saw to it that we met everyone and our glasses were filled all evening. We parted the best of friends at 12:00 o'clock and slid all the way back to Niagara Falls, weary and good humoured due to Belmont specials.

The awakening was grim, both having felt we had enjoyed ourselves far too much. No water in the taps and our beautifully clean flat looking like nothing on this earth. To say we worked is a very, very mild way of putting it. We pulled up all the rugs and had all the fires and heaters going like mad. In fact, it was all heat and steam everywhere.

By night-time we had accomplished wonders. Dried and put down all the rugs and underfelts, cooked our turkey dinner and sat down to a candlelight feast for two – topped off with a movie and a clear conscience. It probably sounds unbelievable to you, but it is all too true, unfortunately. What I would have done without Mort I do not know. He joked all the time and worked like a fiend. He was simply marvellous! I will never forget our first Christmas in freezing cold England which, in spite of everything, I loved.

The only bad bits still are the wet ceilings and one hall runner isn't down yet, but really, things don't look too badly, considering.

We keep saying we thank God we came back from London when we did. If we had been five hours later there is no telling what we would have found, to say nothing of the horrendous expense Hume would have been faced with.

We can laugh about it now, but by gum, it was no laughing matter. I felt at the time, I wanted to cry until I finally died from exhaustion, but there wasn't time for such experiments and instead only had one flood! We thought of our respective mothers, saying how you were both probably thinking of us having our first cozy Christmas in our new home. So ends the saga.

I am amazed to hear about Adele's divorce. How come? Her baby? Everyone thinks I know all about these things. Ducky Miller wrote telling me Adele had a baby. Is it a boy or girl and are they still living together? Do please tell me. I love her, she was always like a sister to me. The difference in our ages never seemed to bother her.

We had a screamingly funny card from Betty Meyers. I feel so badly – I forgot to send her one. My mind was in such a state before we moved that there really is little wonder I guess, but to forget Bruce and Betty!

This letter is brimming with exclamation marks, but they are warranted.

We are looking forward to our girl arriving from Germany. All that is holding it up is the permit from the Ministry of Labour. Once we have that we are told it will then only be a week before she arrives. It is an ordeal, but after our experience with Mrs Burt and now Mrs Jordan, I think we made a wise decision to have someone young, and her references are excellent. We may have a language problem, but we will work things out.

We are going to the Aldershot Fancy Dress Ball at New Year with the Beldams, and staying with them, which is very kind of them. I am going to wear the Chinese costume I modelled in

Chinatown for their jubilee, remember? Thank goodness I brought it over, slippers as well. Mort intends to rent one in London. He only knows Bob, so I am hoping he will like his parents as much as I do.

Thank heaven it has started to thaw at long last. Over a week of ice and snow. The overflow from the tank above the toilet has a wee pipe that drains to the outside. This has been freezing which means we had to climb up on the windowsill and pour boiling water over the pipe so the flush could take place. Great fun. I was beginning to get very irritable due to the cold and discomfort. The flat is lovely and warm now, so hopefully the worst is over and everything will go smoothly from here on – let us hope so. The damage done to the houses in Reigate reaches thousands of pounds. There are seventy-eight houses with burst pipes, so you can imagine for yourselves how cold it must have been, especially when houses are built of stone and have foot thick walls. We hope it is our one experience with such things.

Business in London has been at a standstill all week. Mort is only making spasmodic appearances at his office, which is lovely for me. There is no business at all, so he only goes in to see if there are any cables.

Mort joins me in thanking you both again for your lovely gift. We are delighted beyond words.

My love to Mrs Duffus. I will be writing shortly, but would like you to share this letter with her as I couldn't bring myself to write it all again.

All my love to you, Mum, and to Bill.

As ever,

John

I intended to give this to Mort to post and forgot, so will add a few more lines.

Your birthday is almost here and we will be drinking a toast to your good health, Mother. Wouldn't it be nice if we could all be together for your special day?

I meant to tell you that I actually won a prize! My new laundry had a draw and the prize was a Seven Dwarfs baby fire screen. It is really very sweet and if not used for its original purpose, it will make a darling ornament in a nursery (if we ever have one). We had a good laugh when I went to pick it up as he reminded me that I had remarked that I never win anything.

Guess who I am having to tea on Friday? Heather Maitland and Betty Beddall. The latter is living only about ten miles from here. It will be grand seeing Heather again; I always liked her. She and her husband are over here for three weeks.

Love again,
John

163 Queen Victoria St.,
London EC2
January 7th, '39

Dear Eve and Bill,

You can't imagine the thrill John and I got when we received your Christmas present this year. Really, you two, it was much too kind of you and for it, many many thanks.

We certainly are going to eat our fish in grand style from now on. You do, however, need a sound scolding for being so very extravagant.

John, of course, has told you all about our Christmas and New Year celebration, so there is very little for me to add on that subject. We did miss Vancouver very much and would have given a lot to have 'lifted' a few with you – instead we drank your health with great gusto. Had a very nice dinner at Flora and Finlay's, but as nice as it was, there is no place like home.

Have been leading a very quiet life lately but are going into town for tea and supper tomorrow (Sunday). Tuesday night we are going to have dinner in town and take in the ballet as guests of some friends. The following weekend the Beldams have invited us to spend with them. So you see we are not exactly stagnating. After that I am leaving to tour the UK. Fortunately, however, these trips will only be necessary every two months. Most of my work is in London which is something to be thankful for.

What do you think about Old Baldy doing the marriage act? We shall be awaiting your report with the greatest of interest. We got off a cable to him which we hope found him. Guess old Al will feel very much the bachelor, or is he still going about with Dorothy?

I must be off, so will close with many, many thanks for your lovely gift. Love and every good wish for 1939.

As ever,

Mort

P.S. Eva – Forgot to mention your daughter's health – the kid is looking extremely well and regained all her lost weight. Even the lack of central heating doesn't seem to faze her.

M.

> Tall Trees,
> Wray Park Road,
> Reigate, Surrey
> Tel. Reigate 3767
> January 31st, '39

Mum darling,

Such a lovely long letter from you. They really are worth waiting for and so full of news. Also received a chatty one from dear Bun. Please thank him for me.

First of all, we have never received any socks or silk stockings. Where they can be heaven only knows. Birkie said in her cable that she was sending me a photograph; that hasn't arrived either – there is something queer somewhere. It is such a pity because I need stockings very badly as I have shot through all my Xmas ones so quickly. I'm furious about the loss of them.

Mum, will you please phone Dawson or whoever sold your things and have them check their lists to see if they by any misfortune got hold of our card table and glass top to our table? Crone's swear they have no record of them and that they may have been dropped off somewhere. Please write by return post as Mort has to get onto them again.

Yes, isn't it too wonderful about Emily and Mrs Duffus coming over. She told us it was a big secret, but guess she hasn't been doing very well. We are terribly excited and can hardly contain ourselves. How I do wish you were coming with them! We are very busy looking for furniture now as we hope they will spend weekends with us. Mort had a letter from Emily this morning and she is almost out of her mind with excitement.

It's still bitterly cold here – if only the wind would drop – but it blows all day long and nearly chills you to the bone.

We had a heap of fun last night. Flora and Finlay came down for dinner and I put on a royal spread for them. We played Pick-Up-Sticks and rummy games and both men consumed quantities. The dinner was a roaring success. Chicken, tomatoes stuffed with sweetcorn and buttered crumbs, roast 'tatoes, soup and your famous rice with whipped cream, topped off with hot maple syrup for dessert. I bought a bottle about six inches high and paid 2/6 for it. The cost of living is a real killer. Everything we like is so expensive.

Am attending my first Red Cross meeting this afternoon at 5:15. I hope I enjoy it. I must do something and this is the kind of work I would rather do than anything else. In case of war, it will be better to be busy and they say I can choose my own hours –

either morning or afternoons. Mort is going to see about his volunteer work also. England is definitely preparing itself for the worst – let us hope and pray that nothing occurs to put it all into work. The papers over here don't say anything about it, but all the same it's quite worrying. I wonder what Hitler will say in his speech this week.

Well, darling, I must go and prepare our dinner as I will not be home until after 6:30. We go to our big dinner party at the Park Lane tomorrow and will remember you to Polly if we see him. Didn't we have fun there? Will write and tell you all about it later this week.

Heaps and heaps of love, Mum dear, and do keep the letters flowing.

Your John.

P.S. Nickie sends his love.

Monday, March '39

Mum darling,

No doubt you are very busy as no mail has rolled my way since the week before last and none in today's mail. However, I know from my own experience what moving and unpacking etc. is like so will forgive you this time.

I heard today I passed my Red Cross examination. Although I'm not one little bit keen on this nursing angle, I feel it is nice to have the knowledge of it, especially with everyone saying we are in for a war any day now.

There is really very little to tell you. I had the Boultbee Thomas tribe over for dinner yesterday – Gardner, Mrs Boultbee, Betty and Joe. They arrived about 5:00 o'clock and we chatted, then two London pals dropped in for a drink and left at 7:00. We had dinner at 7:15, consisting of tomato soup, fricassee of chicken on puff pastry (which I made) and baby peas. Then we had a lovely chocolate sweet with whipped cream and coffee. The table looked very pretty with yellow freesias. Mrs Boultbee brought me two dozen manor tulips which are looking very gorgeous.

We listened in to the news broadcasts and talked about the prospects of war nearly all evening. Mrs B has bought a car which G will buy from her when she leaves. They are all off to Paris for Easter and will be gone two weeks. It must be nice to have money, that's all I can say. She also bought Betty a grey squirrel fur coat and a silver fox and herself a Persian lamb coat – nice work if you can get it!! Mrs B is looking much older. It was three years ago since old W.W. died so Betty was thrilled to have us to come to. They seemed to enjoy themselves and left about 10:15 as it takes an hour to drive into London.

We can't help wondering if Mrs Duffus and Emily will be over with all this damned Hitler business. Isn't it dreadful?

We have thought of you many a time lately. It reminds us so of Glasgow with you, although of course it hasn't really got started yet. Poor old Chamberlain, what a 70th birthday gift Hitler gave him. Well, no matter what happens, here I stay. I must admit it's much nicer and 100% safer in Reigate than in London. I will not envy Mort going in by train every day, however I must not be so pessimistic. Let us hope nothing does happen.

We had a lovely time Saturday night. Gay and Edward Lacy-Hulbert had us over to their place for dinner. Gay called for us and brought us home. There was another young couple there and we hope to see more of them. Of course, Gay pops in and out all the time, but it's the first time we had met Edward. They have an adorable two year old boy who wears four year old clothes.

Did you know that, all going well, Birkie will be over to spend the summer with us, arriving on about the 1st of June? I'm terribly thrilled about it. Birks and I get along beautifully, as she does with Mort. If she does come, Mort is going to raise my allowance two pounds and Mum, do you think you could possibly spare about $5 or $10 to help me while she is with me? I don't make both ends meet as it is and with another to feed I get a little worried about it and I do want her to come so badly. I hate to ask you but I'm so darned bust always, it's dreadful. Damn England and all its expenses. The maddening part of it is that we are forced to do so much entertaining and it does run into money.

Barbara and Peter arrive about the 27th. That means another do for them. I love doing it so, but oh dear me.

March is definitely a bad month in England. It's windy and very cold and bleak every day. I'm trying very hard to get my vegetable garden done but my hands get so cold I can't move the implements. It's really mean after our summer-like February. I had to put my big coat on today and it made me mad – I've been without one for so long now. I hope to put some of my seeds in tomorrow. I may be very thankful I have my own vegetables before I'm through. I have a large and angry blister on my hand today, which is sure proof of my hard work!!

Have you heard any more about Uncle Walt coming over and if so when should we expect him?

Well darling, do write a long letter and tell me all about your house and furnishings etc. Where would I sleep if I ever come home for a vist?

Heaps of love to you, Dad and Bill.

Your John

March 2nd, '39

Mum darling,

No letter from you this week, I guess you are busy. I do wish though that I could rely on one letter a week like Mort does with his mother.

How do you like my paper? I think it is quite nice. You have to get your own plate. Writing paper is really very reasonable over here, I think.

How quickly the time does fly – it is grand; it evidently pays to keep busy. It certainly agrees with me anyway.

We have had a nice week. Tuesday we went to the English's and had a lovely time – met Bunny's friend Mr McAdam and his wife. I liked him tremendously and she was quite nice. It was a grand dinner. Wednesday, had Gay and Betty in for tea and then got the 5:23 in to London to be wined and dined by Norman Brann – remember Mort's Irish boy? We went to the Morocco for dinner and stuffed ourselves gloriously on Chicken Paprika (wonderful!). Then he took us to see Leslie Henson in *Running Riot* – it was awfully good, and darned funny. Last night I had Norman down for dinner and Kythe MacKenzie came down at 3:00 o'clock and we had tea and fixed up the tables. It was grand fun and we thoroughly enjoyed ourselves. Norman is a nice boy – brought me two dozen beautiful tulips which are looking too lovely in my large white vase. We played dominoes all evening and they left at 11:05. Everyone seems to like the house and certainly the living room.

We had more snow – all Wednesday and part of Thursday. Miserable wet stuff. It thawed a bit and now it's all cold and freezy again. It's apparently England's worst winter.

I may join the Red Cross; in any event I think I will attend their lectures. I don't like the thought of exams again tho' – however, I'll see, and if it's very interesting, do it thoroughly. M. doesn't approve as he says I'm not strong enough to nurse during the war – but I'd surely do a part-time shift. I've always been interested in nursing, so now is my chance.

Darling, sometime when you are in Bellingham, would you pick me up a large drip coffee pot as I only have my two-cup one and it's not large enough when we have guests? You can't buy them over here!

We are having Flora and Finlay down on Sunday for supper. I'm terribly worried about it as they always have such lovely meals. Still, it must be done and I can't put them off any longer. Thought I'd have a chicken, consommé and a dessert of some description! Wish you were here to help me, darling.

Must go and do some shopping, my love, so will post this letter. Heaps and heaps of love and *do* write often.

Your John

Lucky Jeanie with her baby girl.

March 6th, '39

Mum my darling,

'Spected a letter this morning from you but no luck. Had a darling one from Jeanie Alex F. She is so thrilled about her baby – also tells me Mrs A had a breast removed.

This has been a fairly busy week for me. Monday, Gay and her German maid came to tea. Wednesday, a girl called for me and took me out to golf, back to her place for a bite of lunch and here for tea. The girl is not bad, a little shy, very dumb, Scotch and anti-English. However, it was fun playing golf again and the weather was perfect. Mort played squash that night and was very ill after it – apparently played too soon after eating and looked like death all the next day. That same day, Peggy Jennings, our dogs and self went for a long walk on the Downs and had lunch at what is known as the Bridge House, a charming place which serves rotten food at exorbitant prices. Peg came back for dinner as her husband had to work late. Friday, the latter had a three-table bridge party. We nearly died of suffocation due to her smoky fireplace and no open window. Managed also to lose about 3/6. The party broke up with the chimes of twelve, so got an early night.

Forgot to tell you Lyndsay M spent the night on her way back from skiing in Switzerland. She was thoroughly disgusted with it as the weather was dreadful all the time she was away. She left Saturday morning with Mort and says she wants to come back for a week during the summer. Mort and Fred Jennings played golf all day, so Peggy drove me down to her mother's for lunch. She lives in Hove, a city adjoining Brighton. I adored Hove, but loathed B. Mrs L – Peggy's mother – has a nine-room flat which is separated from the sea by the boardwalk. You couldn't imagine how thrilled I was to see the old ocean again and smell the sea air. I'm sure they must have thought I was batty, I raved so about it. All I needed to complete it was the mountains. There was quite a wind blowing and the breakers were crashing in. What a thrill after so long away from it. Troon was my last sea spot.

We went for a long drive after lunch, all along the waterfront. They even have a baby train that takes passengers along the seaside from B to the cliffs – it's really adorable. We had tea at a new modern hotel called the Ocean View. It was a dreadful abortion, and upon entering we promptly lost our appetites due to an aroma of disinfectant which wafted its way around the corridors from the swimming pool. The tea was actually fair.

It was so warm down there we could easily have sun-bathed. In fact, sitting on the verandah after lunch, we were so hot we both fell asleep.

We drove home at 5:30 and arrived at the golf club at 6:30 for a drink with the men, then we came back here and had soup, sandwiches, coffee and cake and several rubbers of bridge wherein we won about 6/-. The poor Jennings, we trounce them every time – 8/- last week, 6/- this. At that they were lucky as I played badly.

Today Margaret and I have started our spring cleaning. We are going to do one room a day – woodwork and windows. My room is done and looks grand, except for the ruined walls from the flood, which will surely be fixed this month.

My vegetable garden has the soil turned now and am hoping to get my seeds in this month. I seem to be so busy these days. I don't get a minute to myself and the days go by so quickly it's really dreadful. Tonight I have the Red Cross – next week is the exam – woe is me!! I'm afraid I'll flunk it badly. I hate the whole idea of it.

Everybody here seems frightfully optimistic about the war situation these days; hope they are right.

Well darling, must trot along and do my shopping and will post this then. Do write often.

Your loving John

March 12th, '39

Mum darling,

Many thanks for your long and sweet letter. We get such a kick out of them and are always disappointed when there isn't a local scoop. Yes, we are sorry too, darling, that you can't just pick up stakes and come over any old time you feel like it, or as you say, send me a ticket to go home. I often do wonder what my impression of Vancouver would be now. I'd probably adore it for about three months and then long for England, it's pretty hard to say. In only a year, one drifts so far away from old friends. I haven't even heard from Birkie since Xmas and at first I used to get so many letters from all of them. Of course I also haven't the yen for writing that I had.

Margaret is as happy as a child. She bought a bicycle on the hire purchase, as they so aptly call it over here. 10/- down and 18/- a month. It's a beauty and only cost £4.10s. Bikes are dirt cheap in England. Remember granddad paying about $60.00 or more for Bill's?

I seem to have been dreadfully busy this week doing a lot of nothing – gardening, cooking, spring-cleaning, walking, etc., etc. I'm on the go from 8:00-12:00 every day and look and feel better than ever before. We have breakfast together every morning at 8:15 then dress. How times have changed says Ma-Ma!! I can't stay in bed any more; I guess it's a good sign.

I'm listening to an American program called 'A Drive Around New York'. It's a good reception. I must say it's nice to hear an American accent!

Mort arrives back at 10:00 tonight from a day trip to Bristol. Poor darling is having a busy time while Mr Pearce is here. He should phone any minute then Nickie and I will walk down and meet him. It looks as if my whole life will be a continuous meeting of trains and seeing them off. Ah well, my time may come. Who knows?

Tomorrow (Sat) we are having a Miss Dennoff and a Mr Anstey over. Both live at Park Chambers and Mort and I used to play a lot of bridge with them. Anyway, they are coming for tea and dinner. They are awfully nice – he an Englishman, she an Austrian – and very, very anti-Nazi! She is an artist and has exhibitions in all the famous galleries. I like her tremendously and so does Mort. He is quite a darling – rather the Bob Rankin type, with flirty eyes and a devilish mouth. Both play very good bridge. I used to get a bang out of sitting back and listening to the three accents – Canadian, Austrian and English.

It seems ages since I was last in London. Mort says it's really fascinating these days. The parks are filled with crocuses and the leaves are beginning to burst out so quickly you would think you could hear them. England is a truly beautiful country and as each day goes by I think it creeps further and further into my heart.

I do hope we will be able to move out of this house next year. I really hate it now – it's simply impossible to keep clean. We work all day – sweep, Electrolux, dust, etc., etc., and still the dirt is there an hour later. With a coal stove to heat the water in the kitchen, it's simply impossible to keep it clean. Then the dirt is tracked all over the house. Poor Margaret doesn't get a minute's peace from it. Apart from it being such a hard place to keep clean, I love it, but there it is – work all the time. Where we would go I don't know, but I'm really going to speak to Mort about it. Surely we can find a decent house within our means. I would rather hate to leave Reigate, especially now I know so many people. It's such a pretty place too – damn, damn, I wish I could have known how dreadful it would be.

Well, darling, I really think I'd better close. My mind is wandering all over the place and I'm sure it cannot be very interesting to read. Before I close, I want you to know how thrilled I am about the stockings; also many thanks for attending to the newspaper.

Heaps of love to you and Bill.

John

March 13th

Just got a letter yesterday morning, so kept this over to add a few more pages. Was very surprised to hear all your news and I must say delighted. You and Dad can start all over again and make a go of things once more. Your house sounds lovely, Mum, and you will be busy and neither of you alone any more. Mort is really thrilled about it and we both want to wish you and Dad every success in your new home. The only thing we are cross about is that you three have three cars and we two have none!! Ain't it hell!

We simply adored old Elsie's letter; she really is priceless. If she went in for writing and somebody could publish a book of letters and drawings with her and the cats, they would probably make a fortune. You will break her heart taking Bobbie away from her, I'm afraid.

Your letter was posted on March 2nd and I got it on the 11th. That's pretty good time and, of course, means I won't receive one this week on account of two last week. No doubt you will be pretty busy these days anyway with moving and settling – do take some snaps of the house someday soon; am most excited about it.

You ask about your grandchild – we seriously hope to be bouncing a wee fellow on our laps by a year from this month. It's the only sensible time to have a child in England. The houses are so cold and damp before March.

Had a nice morning Saturday and Sunday. We walked for miles. We walked so far we got lost and the last mile home I felt like crawling, my legs were so tired – Nickie was exhausted. The country is so beautiful – daffs are out, pussy willows, primroses, the leaves out two inches, birds are singing – it's simply glorious. How I would miss England.

Well Mum, I must close now. I have a million and one things to do. Had a sweet letter from Betty F. Said she was going to phone you as soon as she was moved and settled.

Heaps of love to the three of you.

John

March 16th, '39

Mother my love,

It's really just like Christmas! Two letters waiting for me from you and one from Dad! All brimful of interesting news. I will go into great detail about the latter in a minute, but first let me tell you about what is uppermost in my mind at present! My little Nickie has only just been taken away to the 'Nursing Home For Dogs' with distemper. I've shed buckets over him. It came on while we were in London, so he is in his third day now. He was absolutely pathetic and my heart aches for him. I never dreamt I could love any animal as I do my Nick, and now, well I guess it's anybody's guess whether I will see him again. I'll just die if he does.

We are sending him to the hospital for three weeks to get him over the worst and are paying $7.50 a week for it. Nice work if you can get it. Mort is really mad about the whole business because he had told me to have him inoculated several times and I never got around to it and now look what my punishment is. I blame the man I got him from because he told me not to do it, that they are finding it most unsatisfactory. Well, I won't depress you further altho' I can't bring myself to think of anything else.

Mum, the things you are sending over sound too exciting for words and as for your fur coat, my gosh Mum, you shouldn't have done that – you need it yourself. Naturally I'm thrilled to pieces but I do feel I'm depriving you badly. It's such a beautiful one and I will take wonderful care of it. However, if you do by any chance change your mind please don't hesitate to tell me and I will send it back with Betty. The other things sound equally lovely and I will write and thank you all properly once they arrive and I have seen and tried them on. In the meantime, a million thanks to all of you. I am indeed a lucky girl.

It wasn't until yours and Mrs Birk's letters arrived that we really felt Betts was coming. No doubt there are letters in the mail for us and should be in Monday or next Thursday. We should have a lot of fun. I like Bett so much.

You wondered why we have put off having a baby for so long. Well Mum, I don't want it born any earlier than March because it's so damp and cold it would be murder to have one sooner, so if it's started in June it should be about right – giving a month or so for 'no go'. Another thing, I would not need a nurse. I could manage on the train and there are nurses which you get automatically on the boat. However, we'll wait and see how things pan out.

Monday, April '39

Mum darling,

Received a letter from you today. What a big job you must have had with all the moving etc. Evidently Mrs Fagg was conspicuous by her absence. Hope you are all settled nicely now. Wish I could have been there to help you.

Well, I've been quite busy this last week with one thing and another. Thursday, Peggy Jennings and I went into London to see the arrival of President and Mrs Le Brun. We stood on Victoria Street and had the most perfect view of everything. It was a sight I shall never forget. We saw the King and Queen, the Le Bruns, the Duke and Duchess of Gloucester and the Kents, all of whom were in their carriages which passed by within ten feet of me. They looked simply lovely – their colouring is perfect. What amazed me was the King – he looked so young and with his hat off it showed a fair lock of hair which I never knew he had. Everybody remarked how much like Edward he is. I had shivers running up and down my spine for half an hour after it was over; I was so thrilled with the whole business.

After it was over we went to Selfridges and I bought some 'Scots Tissue'. I'm absolutely fed up with the English brands. They want 7d. per roll, but it's worth it. Then we went and had tea at Fullers and mozied around the Regent and Oxford Street shops and arrived home at 7:15 p.m. It was a wonderful day.

Saturday, Peggy and her husband and Mort and I went to a Point-to-Point. If you don't know what they are, it's a horse race which takes place in all the fields they can lay their hands on, usually consisting of a three-mile course. They put up flags and jumps and the horses belong to the gentry of the country and are sometimes raced by their owners. It's quite a spectacle. Tents and funny stalls are pitched up overnight and anyone can go to it. The wealthy people take their cars right onto the fields and are parked alongside the finishing lines – this costs them two quid – otherwise there is no entrance fee. I've never heard anything so funny in all my life as the bookies and tipsters. One was an Oxford grad who wore his grad cloak and cut apples in half with a sword to find the name of the winning horse inside. All very stupid and silly but screamingly funny. Mort won about 5/- and I lost about 10/-. There are five races and you pay 2/- a bet, only for first place.

After it was all over, during which I forgot to mention came the damnedest weather – snow one minute, sunshine, sleet, rainbows and more snow – crazy day and very cold; anyway as I was going to say, we came back here for tea. Peggy brought a cake and then we had a two rubber bridge session which we won 5/-. After dinner we went over to their house (across the street) and played vante and won!

Sunday, yesterday, was loads of fun also. Flora and Finlay invited us in for the afternoon and dinner. We started early, intending to have lunch together and stupid Johnnie, bright little thing that she is, left her purse in the train when we changed at East Croydon. I missed it immediately but nevertheless too late, and so when we arrived at Victoria Station I went on to London Bridge to make inquiries – but no luck, it hadn't been turned in. I met Mort at the Mungalls at 3:00; he couldn't come with me as he was hugging a squash racket and suitcase. Anyway, he had lunch and I didn't and then not to find my bag, (money, compact, lipstick, etc.) – I was fit to be tied! We went directly to Regent's Park Zoo to see the baby giant panda. It is the sweetest darned thing I've ever seen. No doubt you have seen pictures of it. The man in charge picks it up like a child and it puts its funny fat paws on his face and licks him all over. He's so cute I couldn't describe him. Then we were taken by a guard to see the tiger cub. It was three months old and just like an overgrown tom-cat; playful as the dickens. It licked us all over and chewed my glove. It would be strange to go back about a year or two from now and see it grown up when we had all patted and played with it. There had been four of them but the mother killed the others and ate them, so they rescued this one and had a collie dog (should say bitch) feed it. It was the cutest little devil. The keeper said it might always be tame with the people it knew but so few of the keepers like to take the chance of finding out once they are older. He said it (Maurice by name) only weighed a pound when born and it was as big as a rat.

We had a very sumptuous tea at Gunters (it used to be a favourite haunt of the Duchess of Kent till everyone found out about it). Lovely place. Mort and Finlay played squash and then when they arrived home we had a couple of cocktails and then dinner, which was, as usual, up to the Mungall standard.

Glen Blackstone came in. You remember him – he was at Quaglino's with us and at The Florida? The five of us played a crazy new game they have and Mort and I walked away with 10/-. We need it – we've been having dreadful luck due to my bad playing at bridge. We caught the 11:20 home and spent the night in our own guest room as the painters were to arrive at 8:00 o'clock this morning to do our bedroom. Of course they arrived at 9:15, but fortunately he tells me they will be all finished tomorrow. I think Barbara K arrives this week and Mrs Duffus a week this Thursday.

Mort has left for Scotland today and will return this Thursday night, so Margaret and I are spring cleaning thoroughly before Mrs Duffus arrives. Tell Bill to thank Connie for her very nice letters. Had a nice one from Dot Rowell also. Heaps of love to you, Dad and Bill.

John.

April 3rd, '39

Mum darling,

Here we are into another month, how the days do fly. In only three more days Mrs D and Emily will be here. We are dreadfully excited and keep saying this time in three days – so and so.

Mort is away again but will be home tomorrow night. I am at present in bed trying to shake a bad throat. Evidently I got a chill last Saturday at the Point-to-Point as I haven't felt human since. Cold, cough, and throat. An awful lot of it is going around – very mild flu! Nevertheless, am staying put in order to be quite fit when they arrive.

On Friday I had some pals in for tea for Mrs Hill upstairs. She is a darling, and her husband a silly child. I felt like hell but went through with it as it would be my last chance of doing anything for six weeks. That night, Mr Pearce (the Director) had invited us to a theatre party so couldn't break that very well. It was a variety show – 'Goodness How Sad'; of course screamingly funny. It amazes me how they get away with all their smutty stories.

Saturday we stayed in all afternoon and then dressed to go into a party that Jack Norris gave. Six of us in all – we went to Mary C's flat and had drinks. The latter was away and her room-mate was with us. After, we went downstairs to the Dolphin Square dinner dance. It was very good really and we thoroughly enjoyed ourselves. It was one of those times when you didn't think you would, and did. Got home at 2:00 o'clock.

Sunday we lolled around till after lunch, took Nickie for a walk and then Peggy and Freddie came over and we played bridge. Had them down 32 points at 2*d*. a 100 at one time and they said they'd stay till they at least halved it. Ended up eventually by having them for tea and dinner and taking two shillings only from them. All in all a very amusing day, except for my throat.

This brings us to today. Mort left at 6:00 o'clock this morning with strict instructions to stay in bed, so heah ah is!

No letter from you last week and none so far today. No doubt you are dreadfully busy. How I would love to see your house. Do take some snaps soon.

Had a very long and newsy letter from Nora. Saturday, she sent me a lot of pictures of her house. It's certainly adorable. She sounds very happy. Yes, D.J. is having a baby, also many others apparently, including Nancy N (supposed to be a secret).

It's a wonderful feeling seeing the spring arriving. All the trees are bursting into bud, our rose climber is in bud, violets and prim-roses everywhere and the birds – they never stop singing all day.

Well, Mum, it's hard writing this way but will write after they arrive Thursday. Happy Easter to you all.

With heaps of love,

John

April '39

Mamie dear,

Received such a pleasant letter from you today from Harrison. So glad you were able to pick up stakes and have a rest. It sounded very restful and lovely and I imagine the scenery alone would pep you up to scramble bigger and better meals and swing the old broom with even greater zest.

I hardly seem to be able to rest for a minute in any one spot these days with the family here. It's in and out of London continuously. I came home yesterday after lunching and shopping with Mrs D. Emily was elsewhere. We had spent Wednesday with them – did White City and a theatre. The former and I started off brilliantly by winning 10/6 for a two-bob ticket. It rather went to my head a bit and, of course, ended up by being down about 10/-. All in the day's fun I guess. Mrs D bought me two beautiful slips and as she had given me two pounds for Easter, I bought myself three sweaters and a spring hat and am feeling like Mrs Rich Bitch herself. Haven't had so many new things for years, it seems. Also assisted at the buying of a gift for you which you will adore!

Now for a few questions to be answered. Betty is figuring on a three-month visit, at my invitation, I might add, never dreaming of going home at this time. Another thing that is agin my going is the fact I would be preggy, as we are most anxious to try to have one started in June and every precaution is going to be taken this time. I would die if anything happened again. I still think it much wiser to wait and save more money so I could come with the baby next year. I don't think Mort would be too terribly keen on me travelling so far with it but I would go nevertheless.

Now about Mort joining up – no darling, his business is needed so badly during war time he can't do anything but work and will spend his free hours offering his services for ARP work. I will no doubt be up to my ears with my two evacuee children. If war was to break out I wouldn't try to have a baby I don't think. Mort seems very doubtful if there will be one now and said only this morning if Russia is really to be an ally, Hitler's chances of starting war are very unlikely. The old devil is busy at this point celebrating his birthday. Nobody seems very worried about things these days and all say we'll worry about it when it comes and to hell with the whole bloody business.

I'm going in now to London to a party (farewell given by Mort's director). It will no doubt be one ghastly bore but one must do these things and he is so terribly fond of Mort and will no doubt go back to Canada boosting his stock to the skies.

I will write again before the Tuesday mail, as I must get away to my train. They are coming tomorrow for the weekend. The weather is grand – hot as summer. My carrots and lettuce are well up. Have planted sweet peas, parsley and radishes and love doing it.

Heaps of love to all,
Johnnie

Grosvenor Court Hotel,
Davies Street,
London, W1
April 14th, '39

Mum darling,

Here we are in residence, thanks to Mrs Duffus. We came in yesterday, early, and had lunch with a relation of theirs at the St Regis. All very swish and elegant. Then Emily and I covered London by underground and finally ended up for tea with Emily's cousin. Came home for dinner upstairs and Mrs Duffus took us to see *Dear Octopus*, with Marie Tempest. It was absolutely super. Don't know when I have enjoyed myself so much. The latter was wonderful. No doubt you have seen her yourself.

Today, Nancy Heard is coming to lunch and then we are going to mooch around Harrods and size up all their wonderful counters. Tonight we are going to see Deanna Durbin in her new film *Three Smart Girls Grow Up!* I hear it's quite good. Tomorrow I'm being given a present of a permanent by Mort and then having lunch here and going home. They are coming down on Sunday for the day.

We have all spoken of you so many times. Mrs D tells me you are up to your ears in gardening and housework and looking exceptionally well in spite of it all. Keep it up, Evie my love, but don't overdo it.

On Tuesday, Flora and Finlay are having us up for cocktails and then we are all off to the White City for dinner and the dogs. It should be lots of fun. Only hope I have a little better luck this time. The old brain isn't functioning very well today for some reason.

For the past five days we had a lovely April heat-wave, all of 75° and for three days I did nothing but lie in the garden and have the most glorious tan as a result of it and am feeling better than ever before in all my life. Mrs D thinks I've never looked better, so you need have no qualms about me.

I suppose you know Birkie is definitely coming, at least she will if there isn't a war and there can't very well be till the crops are finished.

Well, my mother dear, bye bye for the present.

Heaps and heaps of love to you and the family.

John

Tall Trees,
Wray Park Road,
Reigate, Surrey
Tel. Reigate 3767
April 15th, '39

Mum darling,

Here we are home again after a very enjoyable two nights with Mrs Duffus.

I had my hair done this morning. It really will be lovely, I think, and Mort and the others like it very much. It's very curly in the back and slanting from my ears right down almost to a point in the centre of my neck. I tried to draw the front but couldn't – anyway, it's like the Seattle man did it before I left – swooped up both sides with a swoop up the centre. I'm terribly thrilled about it.

Mrs Duffus gave me two pounds as an Easter gift, so am going to buy two hats or else a twin sweater set and one hat. Haven't quite made up my mind yet.

We came back directly after lunch and did the weekend shopping in the village. Saturday is always a big day in these little places. I get such a bang out of it.

Received such a sweet letter from you upon my arrival. How I do love to hear from you. You always mention the Glasgow things that I remember too – and the time we did two shows in one afternoon and rushed you around Troon golf course, still dizzy from the ship; and remember our Edinburgh jaunts? It was all such fun. Never mind, Evie darlin', we will have more good times – we're bound to.

You wondered why I never mention the European situation. I will gladly tell you how the opinion is here, but by the time you read it, you've read it in your local papers. Roosevelt made his demands to Hitler in a letter today and, of course, we are very anxiously awaiting his reply. He will be put on a spot all right, for if he won't reply we'll pretty well know he has his mind set on war. The general opinion seems to be there will be a war all right, but it's doubtful if it would be before the crops are in. Also, you wondered what I would do. Well, Mum, I guess I'd stay here, after all, Mort has to have a home and it would be dreadful for him all alone here. There is one thing, Reigate is pretty safe. I wouldn't be worried here at all and I'd have my refugee kids to look after. No, of course they aren't with me now, silly, it's only if war breaks out or it gets pretty hot and then of course I'll be stuck. Here's hoping I get two decent ones. We get exactly 10/- a week – in other words, $10 a month – for their keep. What a laugh. If we are to live at all I guess it will be on porridge and bread. I must start getting in supplies of sugar – just in case. Somehow tea without sugar sounds revolting!

Sunday afternoon – Mrs Duffus and Emily are here now. They look awfully well. Do tell Dot that Mrs D is extremely well and is thoroughly enjoying herself. It's so darned much fun having them both. I like Emily tremendously – we seem to hit it off better than I dreamed it could be possible.

Thanks for all the lowdown on the kids having babies. There are certainly enough people having them. Joanie Lamprey was the one that really thrilled me. Everyone figured she couldn't have one, she's taken so many years to make up her mind about the situation.

Nickie is simply delighted with his bone. It was sweet of you to think of him. He's a darling, only he adores the garbage the same way Peter used to. If anything happens to him I will *never* have another cocker – they are such gluttons. On Wednesday I left my 1lb. box of chocolates under a rug in the garden and came in to bring my lunch tray out and found Nicks looking fat and bloated five minutes later, having completely tucked the whole pound into his little belly. I was so damned mad I hit him so hard I could have cried with pain myself. I'll bet he would have liked to rub his behind.

Mort is writing to you in the morning so no doubt you will receive his with this. In fact, you should receive three letters from me as this makes my third this week – I'm feeling really noble.

Apparently, from all newspaper reports, we are in for a dandy summer – statistics show if there is a heatwave in April it means a darned good summer. Let's hope so, I'm in the mood for heat – the more the merrier. And, of course, if Birkie comes, it's the easiest way to entertain her imaginable.

Well darlin', I must write to Dot and give her a report on Mrs D. Many thanks for your grand letter and write often.

Heaps n' heaps of love,

Your John

May 3rd, '39

Mum darling,

No letter from you this week, you are naughty! Mort's been away all week and returns tonight. Had Mary R down and went back up to London with her in her car for lunch and had dinner at Betty's. I got home about 11:15; felt very devilish all by myself.

Believe it or not, my maid arrives on Monday. I simply *can't* believe it. In some ways I'll be sorry because I've really enjoyed keeping the place myself and it's very easy once you get a system! It will cost much more and I'm always broke without one, so heaven knows what will happen now.

We have been having glorious weather – keeping all the doors and windows open all day. Nickie and I have such grand games in the garden; he retrieves beautifully.

There honestly isn't a single thing to say to you, darling. Haven't heard anything exciting for an age now.

Will write again during the next few days but wanted to get this into the mail for tomorrow's boat.

Heaps of love to you and Bill – how is he liking his new club?

John

P.S. I must try and do something about Bill's sword but I'm so seldom in London unless it's to go in for dinner. When the maid's here, I can go in for the day and leave the dog so will try and let you know.

Sunday, May '39

Mum darling,

When I wrote last night I neglected to mention your proposition about a trip home! Well, darling, it's all terribly thrilling and I'll tell you what I think about the whole business – between you and me and the gatepost (not Ted O'D!!). The Director that's here now says Mort is almost sure to go back to Hamilton next summer for a month, and as you know I hope to start a baby in June. Well, all going nicely (and being no war), I think it would be very much more sensible if we both wait until next summer and then maybe Mort and I and a three-month old baby could all go over together and then the kidlet and I would go on to you for two months visit. Don't you agree that it would be better, and you would so adore having a baby in the house, wouldn't you? I couldn't go this summer, darling, and as you know, Birkie arrives June 1st and I want to get going on a baby at that time. After all, a year isn't such an awfully long time and by then we would both have more money. This year has been a hard one financially for us both and I will feel better able to leave Mort next year than this. His business is very worrying, especially with the European situation in such a precarious position, and he needs any home comforts that are available to make life a little more pleasant to live in. Maybe by squeezing things I could get home and back on $500, I don't know. But of course we can thrash all that out next year. No, Mort doesn't get all wrought up any more. He is still getting enough work for three months to do and gets unbearably tired, so much so that he is now in bed with tonsillitis. We got the doctor in tonight as his temperature rose to 102° and he was vomiting and we were frightened of pneumonia. However, the doctor reassured us that he would be feeling himself in three days and gave him some pneumonia precaution pills – some miraculous new things on the market that cure the hopeless cases. Poor boy, he was pretty sick today. Emily and I were really quite worried. We kept it from Mrs Duffus and she, of course, hasn't been near him at all.

Well Evie dearest, I must close now. Hope I have answered all your questions this time and that you will agree with me that this is best.

All my love darling,

John

Monday, May 10th, '39

Mum my love,

The family are gone after another weekend. It's simply dreadful how quickly the days go by. They will be sailing before we know it – on Mort's birthday too – a very sad day it will be, but I must not be thinking of such things now. Bad enough to cope with when the time comes!

We had a lovely Saturday and Sunday. They came at 3:30 and Mort got back from Southampton at 5:30. Unfortunately there were April showers both days so were confined to the house. Played dominoes, bridge, etc., read and talked and so the days flew by. They are coming again next weekend and we are going in to them Wednesday for the night and to see Bernard Shaw's *Geneva* on Thursday. Mort and I are taking them to Genaro's Italian restaurant in Soho and coming home after a rubber of bridge. In again on Friday to dine as Emily's guests and see Jack Hulbert and Cicely Courtneidge – none of us like them but the show itself is supposed to be wonderful. It's all very lovely, as you can imagine. We seem to do so much and such lovely things. We are a badly spoiled couple.

Had a very long and newsy letter from Ginnie Lefergy saying how very much she enjoyed your dinner party and gave me all the latest news of the pregnant younger generation. Vancouver seems to breed like cats!

The dear darling director has gone at last. He took us to the casino Friday night. It's supposed to be quite a smart place but we thought it stank! So did the people.

Tomorrow I am entertaining Mrs Beldam at lunch and tea here. She arrives at 10:00 o'clock. Here's hoping everything goes off with a bang. It's really dreadful that I have never had her in the house. I owe so many people it's positively disgusting but am going to forget them till after the family go.

Dot would be delighted at the way Mrs Duffus looks. Tell her

her voice never cracks and she never gets that tired look about her face.

Nickie is a scream about his bone. It literally reeks of chocolate and he licks it all day long. His poor little tongue must be worn to threads. He is a darling.

The country is really beautiful – it's day by day acquiring its luscious greens and the leaves are all out. The daffs are all over the fields and the tulips are selling for 6*d*. a dozen and roses a shilling a dozen. How I do love England. Have not seen our pet squirrel recently. Do hope Nick has not frightened it away.

Our dearest friend Hitler speaks soon – wonder what he will say to Roosevelt – probably ignore the whole business. Russia is practically signed up and when they do our pal Adolf will not be quite so happy. Fighting on two lines would not be very pleasant for him, to say the least.

Will keep you posted, darling, and you write often.

Heaps and heaps of love to you and the family,

John

Mrs Duffus says it will take hours to tell you how well I look. We had a lovely visit with Mrs D and Emily on Wednesday, Thursday and home late Friday. We saw two very good shows – one of Bernard Shaw's called *The Doctor's Dilemma* and the other, a perfectly adorable thing called *Her Little Ladyship*. Friday night we topped off the whole delightful three days by hearing Paul Robeson at the Queens Hall. He was simply delightful and has the most charming personality I have ever come across. He sang 'My Old Kentucky Home', 'Old Man River', 'No John', 'Shortnin' Bread'; etc., etc. I clapped until my hands ached. We then rushed back to the hotel, changed into our suits and got the last train home. On Thursday, Mrs Duffus presented me with five pounds to buy myself a dress as a parting gift. You know what she is like and nothing I could do or say would alter her mind about it, so I got a two-piece affair at a sale – a black light wool dress and a coat. The dress is very plain with short sleeves and the coat just meets in the centre, is belted and slightly flared at the back with smallish sticky-out sleeves. I will, I believe, get a considerable amount of pleasure out of it and it certainly is a most suitable outfit for going in and out of London in the trains. They are so hard on one's clothes – even my black skirt is beginning to look a little shabby from so much sitting in it. Nevertheless, it's still lovely. I never tire of it.

We are going into town on Thursday and will remain with them till their train draws out on Friday – oh sad, sad day. We are all feeling a little sad-eyed even now, so what we will be like by Friday I rather hate to think. Mrs Duffus gave Mort a parting gift of a new set of tails. They are not made yet but I believe on order. I've never known anyone quite like her – if you say no you hurt her feelings and to continually say yes is equally dreadful. She must sit up nights thinking of things to do for all of us.

Mum, I can't tell you how thrilled I am you and Dad are getting about so much. Bridge, poker and one thing or another. You seem to be quite lucky at them, which helps. Your house and garden sound lovely. Do you like it better than the old Harwood house, or is it only the garden that is so much nicer? I really know so very little about it.

I am sending a little gift back to you with Mrs Duffus. Hope you will find them useful.

Will write soon darling – my many, many thanks again to all of you, also for your letter.

While I think of it, *please cancel* all the *Sun* papers. Gordon Southam has presented us with a two-year subscription to the *Province*!

Heaps and heaps of love,
John

Monday, May '39

Mum darling,

They are gone now and probably are feeling the awful let-down we are experiencing. Yesterday, Mort and I sat and looked vacantly at each other all day. It didn't seem right not calling them for breakfast, etc. Darn it all, why do all good things have to come to an end? They left, as you probably know, on Friday morning for Liverpool. We didn't go there to see them off as it's almost a four-hour train journey, but saw them off at the Euston Station. I don't know which is worse, seeing a person off on a ship or on a train. In my estimation, a poisonous pastime.

The Saturday after they left we went to Gatwick to the races. I managed to win two races and broke about 2/- up in the end; Mort not so well, being down two pounds!

Yesterday as I said, we just sat, altho' I did do two hours weeding in my vegetable garden and have a beastly blister on my hand as proof of my effort with the trowel.

We grow a wicked thistle in England, or is it just in my garden they flourish so well? My sweet peas are up three inches, my lettuce about an inch and a half – I'm getting terribly excited.

Am enclosing a snapshot which Margaret took of us on about February 15th, and only just had developed. The wisteria climbing up the house is so beautiful now – a mass of blooms. My sweet peas are well along the right, under the bathroom window. It's fun watching things grow. It certainly doesn't take long for them to get started.

Betty arrives on the 29th. Only two more weeks to amuse myself. We should have good fun.

Mort is off to Bristol for today and tomorrow and leaves on a long trip next week. Am afraid he is going to miss the Derby. Betty Balfour is back and four months gone and wants us to go there for dinner, the Derby and go to the fair in the evening. The whole thing takes place on the Epsom Downs. It would be such fun. It's on the 24th (early this year), only I'm afraid Mort will be away and I will have to follow with my original plans with Peggy Jennings. It leaves me a little flat after Betty's invitation – hope I can wangle out of it.

Saw in the *Province* where Rookie died. He went crazy, didn't he? What really happened – just too much alchy?

Rita Hill and I are off this afternoon to spend a very wet afternoon in the cinema listening to Jeanette MacDonald and Nelson Eddy in *Springtime*. Hope it's good.

Heaps of love to you all and a big packet to yourself.

John

Nickie is progressing slowly at the hospital and should be home, if no more fits, in two weeks. In the meantime, Margaret has found a hedgehog which is in a box outside the kitchen door, much to my disgust. She picks it up and everything – nutty about all animals.

May 21st, '39

Dearest Mum,

This makes exactly the 17th day with no letter from you. I'm afraid I cannot understand it and nothing will convince me anybody could be so busy not to even be able to write a postcard.

What happened about the phone call? We set our alarm for 1:45 and waited till 2:15 – finally the Canadian Exchange informed us the call had been cancelled. I had been so excited about it, having known the call was coming since 1:30 p.m., a good twelve hours of looking forward to it! Do write and tell us all about it. I must say tho', if you were going to pay for the call I am thankful it was cancelled. It would be dreadfully foolish to waste so much money.

Betty arrives on Saturday. Jeanie MacMillan is in London and is coming out to have lunch with me on Thursday.

We saw Barbara and Peter last Wednesday. I went in and took her out for lunch and Peter, Barb and I had tea, then we, including Mort, went to Genarro's for dinner and they went on to see *Under Your Hat* which we had already seen so didn't accept their kind invitation to join them. Barbara has lost pounds since I saw her last and was looking so pretty. What a lovely complexion she has.

Surely a letter will come this week and when it does I will answer it immediately. In the meantime, I can't think of a damned thing to say.

Best love to you all,

Johnnie

May 22nd, '39

Mum darling,

A letter just arrived from you so I thought I would quickly drop off another note to say it had at last arrived. Very newsy. Everyone seems cross with me for not writing; I don't notice any letters streaming in for me.

So Betty Myers may be over next summer. My gracious – where I'll put her I don't know, 'cause I will have to use my guest room as the baby's room. There's nothing else for it (if I have one) and where she'd sleep heaven only knows! I'll believe it when I see it nevertheless.

Isn't Peggy Lang's baby adorable?

Your garden sounds too lovely for words, Mum. Don't tell me you do all the work yourself – you'll kill yourself. Surely Bill or Dad do the lawn-cutting!

Have not heard from Dot yet. How lovely for her taking the trip south. She must have made up her mind on the spur of the moment.

Betty Balfour said if I'd wait two years from now we could both go home together with our two kids – she's four months. Might be better to wait, then the child would be past the wetting stage with any luck. It's all so far away, anything might happen. We can only wait and hope for the best.

Will try and get another letter off this week. Have to get the dinner as Margaret is washing all the windows.

Heaps of love,

John

May 27th, '39

Mum darling,

My, what delightful weather we are having. It's just like our hottest summer days in Vancouver. I am in my romper bathing suit in the garden. Nickie is romping around with his tongue hanging out a foot and Mort is sitting here with his hairy chest exposed to the sun in a very un-gentlemanly manner! It's Whitsun weekend and millions of people will be going to the country.

Betty doesn't arrive till Monday, damn it all, and Mort leaves for a ten-day trip on Tuesday.

Wednesday, Betty and I are lunching at the Savoy with Jeanie MacMillan who, by the way, came out on Thursday for tea and dinner and we asked her to stay on for the night. She didn't need any persuading; she was thrilled to death with our place and the simple country life we have – and who isn't? I would be loathe to leave here; it's so pretty and green and so different from anything in Canada. If only all of you could come and live in England it would be really perfect.

On Monday we will inquire and see what train Betty will arrive on and if it's a reasonable hour we will both meet her, otherwise Mort will go alone. Rather expensive, trotting in and out – three shillings a crack. Mrs Duffus was always so thoughtful and sweet and used to give me my fare.

Mum, the *Sunday Sun* is still rolling in by the dozens and as we now have the *Province*, something really ought to be done about it. Please will you give them a ring? Saw an adorable picture of Jeanie's baby in one of them. It really is a darling child. She must be terribly thrilled. Rather reminded me of Jeanie's baby brother Jackie – did you see it?

Tomorrow, Sunday, Peggy Jennings and Freddie are driving us down to Brighton to spend the day with Peggy's mother and dad. I have been before but Mort never has. The men will probably go swimming if it remains fine, but can't say I'd like to dip myself in the briny as yet.

Brighton over Whitsun is like a three-ring circus – thousands of people, vaudeville shows on the beach, coconut shies, etc., and lots of nice girls being led astray by not such nice boys – or so they say. It should be a good day's entertainment. We shan't be able to come home till about 11:30 as the holiday crowds are like our Bellingham ones on the 24th of May – if not worse.

I knew I had something terrific to tell all of you, but couldn't think for the life of me what it was. On Wednesday, we – Mort, Peggy and I – went to the Derby. I will never forget it as long as I live; it's quite the most unusual affair. We took a picnic lunch with us and drank pop, ate ice cream by the bushel and had a thoroughly happy day. There were half a million people there – over the population of Vancouver – so you may well imagine the 'fair' was crowded to a degree. Cars were lined up for miles and of course it was a beautifully hot day, so hot I wore a silk blouse and skirt and nearly died with heat.

Jeanie Mac told me she had seen you while pouring tea at The Riding Club and you were looking very attractive and smartly dressed. Good old Marmie, you always did know how to dress. You used to make me proud to be seen with you, and Glasgow will never be the same after the splash you made there in your fur coat and wine suit. Remember the pinkie sweater we bought you in Edinburgh? Wasn't it fun!! And as for pushing you up to Cranworth Street, I have to laugh every time I think about it.

Nickie is a little upset this evening (have been writing off and on all day): diarrhoea and vomiting. Only hope it's not a relapse. Poor darling, if he gets any worse the doctor is coming in to look at him. Seems very lifeless and droopy, poor baby. How we do adore him.

Will write after Birkie arrives and tell you all.

My very bestest love and hugs to you, Mum my sweet, and to my Pa-Pa and brother Bill. (Saw a very good picture of Bruce. It's wonderful to see him looking so well. Give him my love when you see him.)

Johnathon

P.S. Airmail letters from you reach me now in as little as seven days. If it wasn't so darned much more money here, I'd always use it. A letter written by you on a Monday reached me the following Monday. Remarkable, isn't it?

June 5th, '39

Mum darling,

I can't tell you how much I adore my little cape and how absolutely sweet it does look on. I've worn it already over my lovely green dress and was complimented no end! What a thrill it is to know you look nice!! Thank you a million, million times, my love, and for the two pairs of stockings. I do feel so happy about everything and the joy I will get out of being warm next winter in your black seal. I hate to take it from you tho'. If you change your mind, do promise to tell me and Bett can take it back. The scarf, hanky and belt are so attractive and fit beautifully. You are a whiz at picking things the right size and style!

Betty and I are having loads of fun. Tommy Meyer (remember

he used to bring B and me champagne and beer all the time when Mort was away?) came out for dinner and Kenneth Keith dropped in after and we all drove over to a delightful hotel five miles from here. We drank Pimms and looked at their beautiful pool and came home. Full moon n'everything. I wore my green and leopard!

Saturday he came down for lunch and drove us from Surrey to Berkshire to Windsor Castle (remember?) and Eton in Buckinghamshire, then to a crazy little pub in Aylesbury called the Bull's Inn. We played darts, saw gypsies, went punting on the Thames, two fairs and oh such beautiful scenery. Bett was thrilled. Tom has a beautiful two-seater sports drop-head Bentley and we felt very impressed. We arrived home at 12:30 and Tom spent the night in the guest room and Bett was with me in Mort's bed. Margaret was horrified.

Next day we lazed around till 1:00, then drove to Oxted for lunch at a pub called Ye Old Whyte Hart Inne! Roast Beef and Yorkshire Pud! And gooseberry tart – so typical of pub food. We then drove to Sevenoaks, a beautiful spot, and Kent and home for dinner. All so beautiful. We completely exhausted our vocabularies with fitting adjectives. We then played silly games and Tom left early for London. He is a dear boy.

Tonight, Kenneth is coming to take us out driving also; he is so nice. Bett is going out with Tom on Wednesday to a theatre in London, so she is having a good time I think.

The weather is unbelievably lovely day after day – streaming sunshine and so hot we can't even stay out for very long.

I am enclosing some snaps Mort and I took the weekend before Bett arrived. Hope you like them.

Mort seems to be thoroughly enjoying his trip, having had a delightful weekend in Ireland at a little country hotel twenty-three miles from Belfast. He is longing to get home tho'.

Tomorrow, Freddie and Peggy and we two are driving to

Oxford and I am going to try and look up the Coolings in Reading.

Have so many letters to write, Mum, I must close and get busy.

A million thanks. Tell Dad and Bill I will write when it gets cooler – it's so sticky writing letters these days.

Tons of love and again many thanks for the lovely things.

John

P.S. I have written on t'other side of pictures. Please pass them on to Mrs Duffus.

June 20th, '39

Dearest Mum and Dad,

Received a lovely long letter from you yesterday. It was very newsy and oh so secretive about this new engagement. Well darlin', my guess is Molly Winkler? Let me know if I'm right.

Glad to know Mort's shirt can go back. I will post it off to you and maybe you'd get a size 15 instead of 16 – he liked it so much he would like to have it so it really fits properly instead of gaping at the neck. He never did get whatever you sent him for Xmas. He will be writing this week as regards the shirt – he has been dreadfully busy since his return from his eleven-day trip.

We have been on a steady 'go' it seems ever since Betty arrived. Last Thursday, Kenneth Keith, Mort, B and I all drove to Aldershot Tattoo. Left here at 6:45, stopped off at a pub on the way for a warmer and then on our way – it's an hour and a half drive. The Tattoo started at 9:30 and was opened by the Duke of Kent accompanied by the Duchess. Everybody stood on their little wooden camp chairs to see them. I craned my neck an inch too far and the next thing I knew I was floundering two rows down, seeing stars, umbrellas and raincoats from a most uncomfortable position and feeling very battered and bruised on my poor sit-down and having seen nothing of their Royal H's! I will never forget the Tattoo as long as I live. My gosh, it's an amazing sight – I couldn't begin to describe it; massed bands, the Highlanders – hundreds of them. Sets of five hundred men at a time doing massed drills; all so colourful and too perfect for words. It rained off and on lightly until the end and on our way home, poured. We took a picnic supper with us which we had to eat in the car at 12:00 o'clock. Everybody always does that so we did and it was fun. Betty and I drank two thermoses of tea and the boys drank beer by the quart. We got home at 2:30 which wasn't bad. Betty was so thrilled she was speechless.

Betty and I are very full of our proposed bicycle trip. We are thinking of taking a train and bikes down to Devon. From there we go on our own steam for a week's tour all over Devonshire and Cornwall, probably averaging 25 to 30 miles a day, staying the night at cheap places and eating at quaint cottages etc. on our way. It should be perfect fun and only hope we will get some fairly decent weather. We will, I think, plan on it for the first week in July – hope it comes off.

We have just finished reading all the Vancouver papers about the King's visit. They certainly received a wonderful reception.

Keep us posted about Dave Manley, will you? – what a dreadful thing. He's such a darned nice chap. I guess his love of gambling got the better of him. Mort used to play golf against him every weekend and loved gambling on anything at all.

Betty Balfour had the three of us over to her place for dinner last night. Her house is so lovely. She is expecting her child the first week in October. Tonight (Sunday), the Hills upstairs have invited us to go up for supper of sausages and beer. We are all bleary-eyed and stupid as it's a rainy stupid sort of day and are not feeling like A1 company with anybody, however as it's Margaret's day out we won't have to bother making any supper.

The weather has been pretty foul lately – cloudy and rainy. Apparently June is always a bad month in England.

By the way, I wore my new blue and striped dress yesterday and thought I was quite a smarty. Mort loves it. The dressmaker made a nifty job of it; I had the skirt taken off the bodice and put on a band so I could wear it with jumpers as they are not thick enough to not show the blue bodice, if you follow me.

Am terribly sorry not to have remembered about your wedding anniversary. Many happy returns to the two of you! 27 years is a long time and here I am ambling along only to my third.

Do send along those snapshots. Do you know I haven't one picture of you, Dad, and only about a 1928 number of Bill. Couldn't you take an hour off and do a little snapping?

Well, my dear Mama and Papa, I must away and dress for the beer and sausage do, so will close with a large prayer that you will all write often. It's bad enough being 6,000 miles away from home, but it's worse still to be 6,000 and no letters – even a postcard will keep me quiet.

Heaps of love to you all,

As Ever,

John

163 Queen Victoria Street,
London, England
July 1st, '39

Dear Eva,

Just a note to thank you so very much for sending me the very smart sport shirt with a tie to match. Unfortunately it is the wrong size but Johnnie tells me that it can easily be exchanged for the right size. I am therefore sending it back by Betty and will look forward to sporting the new one in the autumn.

Your daughter is looking very well and seems to be enjoying life to the full. I feel quite sure there are going to be rivers of tears if and when we have to leave England. The child simply adores it.

Reigate is looking extremely beautiful and Johnnie's vegetable garden is flourishing – and she did it all herself.

I am sending her off for a week's holiday to Devon. She and Betty are going, along with some friends, so they should have a good time. I should love to do it myself but I'm afraid I have neither the time or the money to do so.

The war scares are on again but I don't really think anything will come of them, although there will be some very anxious moments.

Betty seems to be enjoying herself and judging from the attention she is receiving, I am quite sure she could make her home in England if she desired. However, she has not met anyone who has really made her heart flutter dangerously.

Well, Eva, I must be on my way as there is lots of work at hand. My best regards to the family and my love to you.

Affectionately,

Mort

Tall Trees,
Wray Park Road,
Reigate, Surrey
Tel. Reigate 3767
July '39

Mum darling,

Another week gone by. My golly how the time does fly and with such awful weather. I imagine we are both having identical summers. When it's not raining it's warming up to it – black clouds, thunder etc. Oh well, the devil with the weather; maybe we'll have a really good August instead and September is always nice here.

My sweet peas are really quite nice. I pressed my first one out and have it in between our London directories and when it's finished I'll send it along to you. My stalks are now a good 15-18 inches long. Next year though, I will have much better ones still.

We have met some very nice people called Evans. We met them a week ago Saturday night at a bridge party and they asked us out for dinner the following Friday. They have three children; one little girl – Sally – a beauty if ever there was one. The little boys are devils and stop at nothing. They have pots of money I guess. He's a member of the Stock Exchange, has a chauffeur, cook, children's nurse and a butler – some fun. The house was left to him so it's full of old bits and pieces. We had a lovely dinner. I seem to think I've already told you this.

Saturday they popped in and brought me some beautiful flowers from their garden. Sunday, he dropped in and asked Mort out to play golf with him, which he did, and we went there for supper. Fried eggs and bacon and Spanish spaghetti. It was their 9th anniversary so we helped celebrate and drank a magnum of champagne. I still loathe it – but this was very good. Played bridge afterwards.

He was born in Cuba and educated in England – Oxford etc. – and is the image of David Niven in the movies; aged 31, married at 21. She is rather large, quite untidy about her person but very nice. We really like them both enormously! And he is far more a contemporary of Mort's than anyone he has met here yet. It's strange how out of nearly all our Reigate friends, the men are so young. He plays a wonderful game of golf – shot a 75 with Mort on Sunday – with a 6 and a 5 in two of the holes. His handicap is 4!

Had a letter from you written on that funny paper you found in Dad's room. It's quite something. Eva!

I still haven't posted the shirt back to you. I must remember to do that!

Am still waiting for the pictures – hope they come in this week. They sound so lovely. I don't know when Bett leaves. She expects to leave somewhere around the end of August. Wish she did not have to pay duty on the china, Mum. She had trouble getting Canadian pottery she brought us in here. Can you find out?

About the fur coat. I haven't got around to that either as yet. I don't know where to take it, unless I lug her into London one day. As soon as I do I'll send you an SOS for some money as I'm flatter than fifty pancakes. So's Mort. We've been doing quite a bit; new refrigerator etc., and my trip to Devon. I wonder how much it will cost. As you say, the lining is pretty awful for a young girl, but I might have it dyed black? It's so much too big. I will probably get quite a bit back. It's most exciting. You'd better count the alteration as a birthday gift. By the way, if Mrs Duffus says anything to you about whether or not to send money or a present, do please tell her money because I need shoes and gloves and nobody else can buy those sort of things for one. Will you, darling? There seems to be so many things I need.

Am having the Evans couple in for dinner tomorrow night so think I will do them a baked ham, beginner's style. I love them so. Hope they will fit into our self-waiting meals. It will be a good test of the type of people they are. Finlay and Flora fit in so well and seem to enjoy themselves tremendously, so we shall see if it's too much of a comedown for them – minus butler etc! I will try and remember to tell you in my next letter about it.

Had an invitation today from Joanne Disher to her wedding. Betty tells me she is marrying an exceptionally fine boy. Whereabouts is she to live? I heard Hamilton – I hope so. Chances are it will be our home eventually. Who knows?

Hear Ted O'Donnell broke his leg. Poor devil – it must be

dreadfully painful. He does write Mort the funniest letters; he ought to go in for it.

Well, all you crazy kids, I seem to have come to the end of my letter. Heaps of love Mamie dear, and to dear Bill.

Lovingly,

John

July 10th, '39

Hallo Mrs 'Firgy'. Your daughter and I are having <u>more</u> fun – they are both being so nice to me. Hope you are well.

Lots of love,

Betty.

Mum darling,

Received a nice long letter from you this week. Thanks, my little Marmie. You seem to be experiencing such awful weather. Well, cheer up leetle fish, we are having and have had now for weeks, dreadful stuff – rain, rain and more rain. My sweet peas are crying for sun. If I had a sun lamp I'd be tempted to use it on them – and after all my hard work too!

How the days do fly by. We had a lovely day yesterday. Tommy Meyer came down at 10:00 a.m. and took us out for the day. We went to a summer home of theirs and had a lovely lunch; good old roast beef and new potatoes etc.

After lunch we walked all over their grounds, which are vast and beautiful with all sorts of fruit trees and every possible vegetable in their kitchen garden. They have everything from raspberries to corn on the cob, chickpeas, hens, baby chicks, etc. Really lovely, all of it. We then collapsed on rugs, chairs and chesterfields and slept till tea-time. After tea and a dozen chocolate biscuits, we drove to Bournemouth, and what a place it is! Hundreds of tired and cross parents pulling and snapping at their even more cross and tired children. Music, breakers, ice cream cones, flappers, penny slot machines and so on! We walked out on the pier for 3*d*. each and saw nothing; walked back again and decided to go out in a speedboat. It was an enormous one and gave us a big thrill as it was just rough enough to make a spray. The poor devils behind us got soaked. Don't imagine we were doing much more than 25 knots, but it did seem pretty fast. We left there about 8:00 o'clock and went back to Tommy's in time for supper at 9:00. Cold chicken and hot vegetables from the garden, then fresh raspberries and cream – all very super!

The house was lovely; a good 100 years old. Fairly large sort of place I'd adore – of course it's a good 60 miles from London. Tommy is so kind. He gave me a huge hamper of eggs, carrots and potatoes and a kind of pea that you eat in the shell. You cook the whole works and they are quite a delicacy. Also about three dozen of the most exquisite delphiniums I have ever seen. They must stand easily 3 feet high and are literally covered with flowers. You would adore them, darling. Also a huge bouquet of sweet peas. My drawing room smells like a very exclusive florists's – it also has honeysuckle from the garden on the mantelpiece. Can't you almost smell it, darling?

Saturday night some people we met at Nora Pierce's invited us to dinner – dress n'everything. We really had a lovely time. They had only us for dinner, then four others came in and we had two tables of bridge. Had some amazing hands and altho' we were playing a 20th cut-in, I only lost 1/6, which was very clever of me, don't you think? We had a lift home by an elderly couple and it was a little difficult driving as there was a 'black-out'. It was a weird feeling. Policemen everywhere, motor cycles rushing about and not a light anywhere. We were driving along quite gaily with our headlights and a Bobby rushed up and had us put on our dimmers only – it was about a 1,000 square mile black-out; quite successful, I think. Betty was not with us that night. She went to Selsdon Park with Bo Berrick and to the dance at his hotel and got a big thrill out of driving home in the black-out.

On Friday coming, Bo is taking Betty and me to Lords to see the Eton and Harrow match. Heaven only knows what I will wear – my black taffeta I guess, and on my head – *I don't know*!; a sort of turbany thing maybe. But shan't worry about it for a few days yet. It's such a dressy affair. Fortunately the other girls going won't be wearing long dresses – that would finish me completely!

Had such a sweet letter from Betty Farris. She is a grand girl. Wish they could live over here for a year or two and play around with us. She says her babies are so sweet now. I'll bet they are. I still miss Bett terribly and I guess always will. We did have some good times with them, remember?

Oh dearie me – I do owe so many letters. When will I ever get them all answered? I feel so ashamed!

Posting off a little dress to Jocelyn Crompton today – that little flowered taffeta you bought me after I came home from the hospital. It looks a little young on me now, darling, and I'm sure she would like it very much. Give it a little rub-off with the cleaner and it should be as good as new. Tell her I will try and send some more, but really I seem to wear all the things I have now.

Betty and I are going on our holiday on July 29th, till the 5th, to a place in South Devon called Beer – a little fishing village – for £2 10s. a week inclusive. Pretty cheap holiday and we'll probably have a grand time. Will try and get lots of pictures to send – if the weather will *only* be nice!

Bye for now, Mum dear. Write often; I love your letters so. Very best love to Bill and Dad. No, I've never heard from Elizabeth since Xmas.

Heaps of love,
John

July '39

Mum darling,

Once more I cannot thank you for a letter. None last week and today. Canadian mail came in and none from my dearest Mamie. What am I going to do with you?

Mrs Birks sent me two beautiful pairs of silk stockings in some newspapers. She is being too generous and kind. I will write her tomorrow. Her Betts seems to be enjoying herself tremendously, quite as much as we are loving having her. She's always ready for a laugh and doesn't seem to mind everyone (including ourselves) teasing her about her accent – it sounds so American after listening only to the English accent for so long. Tonight Bett and Mort and I are all having cocktails with a very great friend from Montreal, now of London – a Mr Whyteside. It should be fun. Then we meet Tom Meyer after at the Café de Gourmet (gluttons). Supposed to be very good. Then on to a theatre to see *The Little Revue*, and then, of course, a mad dash to get our last train. It should be a lovely evening and will remind me of the many equally glorious busts we went on with Mrs Duffus.

The weather hasn't been any whiz lately, but it never seems to depress me. I just get happier and happier every day. It's such a nice feeling. I love England so. I really think I shall die when I leave here. It seems part of me now. I almost feel ashamed at how quickly I have changed from Canada to England. All I need is all of you and I'd never care if I went back again. Am I so dreadful to think that way? Or perhaps I' m lucky. It would be misery if I loathed it as much as I love it.

Yesterday we had a thoroughly lazy day; lit a fire, it was so chilly. Played games, read and ate chocolates by the pound. Had a make-your-own dinner and went to a movie. Seems funny doing a show on Sunday. We so seldom do.

Four of us went to a beautiful place near Steines called Great

Fosters – somebody's gorgeous estate turned into a hotel. Flood-lit gardens, acres and acres of them with the most beautiful hedges all trimmed to resemble ducks and animals, and pools and ponds with swans and ducks swimming around – and such flowers!! The house itself is 450 years old and quite the most fascinating place I ever hope to see. However, there had to be some drawback, and it came in the food and the orchestra. They were not so good.

Well, Mum, *if if* I hear from you during this week, I will write again. I must rush and get dressed now.

Heaps of love to you all – John

Kenwood
The Meadows
Beer, South Devon
July '39

Mum darling

Here we are happy as clams in a little room on a funny street overlooking the English Channel. We arrived last night about 6:00, had dinner and a walk and into bed at 9:30! It was a dreadful introduction to our little village as the weather was terrible – cold and bleak, with a heavy mist all over the hills and water. However, we managed to realise the place had possibilities.

We had breakfast at 9:00 which consisted of cold ham, a boiled egg, bread, butter and marmalade and tea. We were so hungry we ate it but can't say we enjoyed it very much. We then went on a tour of inspection. The sun was able to make temporary appearances from behind clouds. We walked way up onto the cliffs and really, Mum, you could never even imagine the view – miles and miles of blue blue sea and the cliffs of red and white brick behind, all jutting out from all angles with the green fields at the back of them. Cows mooing, horses, wild flowers; all so lovely it almost left us breathless.

We returned through the little village of Beer – it's terribly quaint. Funny old fishermen standing around. They nearly all look like Popeye – weather-beaten faces and gnarled hands. They are a study in themselves.

After lunch we had a sleep and then walked from Beer over the cliffs to the next village; a place called Seaton. All in all I think we covered six miles. It's so beautiful you hate to stop in case you miss something.

We are having a grand flirtation across the way – his window faces ours and he keeps himself busy going in and out of the house or up to his bedroom so he can have a look over here. Imagine, he's about 23 or 4. It's rather fun and hope it remains at this coy stage – it's far more fun.

Here we are in our 2*d*. deckchairs on the beach. We have found two perfectly sweet fishermen; an old one and a young one. Uncle and nephew. The old one was in the Navy for twenty years and now he's finishing up his life here fishing for a living. The young one was sent to Redhill a couple of years ago to train as an electrician and said he couldn't stand it and ran away back to the sea, so his family gave up and now he's here living the life he likes. We are going out fishing for mackerel one afternoon with him and early one morning at 6:00 we are going with him to bring in the crabs and lobsters. It will be about a four-hour trip and should cover about twelve miles in all.

Excuse the mess on the paper but we have about ten minutes sitting outside then it rains and we rush for cover to a bathing house. During the rush I seemed to get this sheet covered with pencil marks.

There is the cutest little 'Peke' here – two years old and called Chang. It amuses itself chasing after the seagulls. It reminds me of Mother's Peke, or Mrs McRae as it sits up just the same way and takes such an interest in everything. Betty hates them and I nearly drive her mad calling her attention to its crazy antics.

There are really an awful lot of people here for such a small place. Can't imagine where they all sleep.

Our room looks onto a church steeple, other houses and over to the right, the sea. You can't imagine, Mum, how much I adore the sea. I guess it's born in me – the smell of it and the rollers crashing in, seagulls screeching, seaweed smells, etc. Oh, I could rave on for hours. If we ever have the money I would adore a little cottage by the sea somewhere. I'd just sit and sniff all day and be perfectly happy.

There must be at least thirty fishing boats drawn up on the beach now and every few minutes one is rolled down to the water and out they go to sea for their morning's fishing. They look as if they hadn't a worry in the world – just fish, sleep, eat and smoke their pipes. We were talking to an old fellow last night and he was telling us what he did all day and he said, 'I gits up in the marnin' and I puts me kittle on...' and so on. The way they talk is fascinating.

Well, the Cornwall trip is on. Tommy is coming here on Thursday by car and will spend the night in a pub along with another man of about 35. Then, on Friday morning, we all drive to Mullion in Cornwall to Tommy's parents' summer place. The four of us spend Friday night alone. I'm acting as chaperone!! We are then joined on Saturday by Mr and Mrs Meyer, Tom's brother John and girlfriend Delores. All of the young ones have their own cottage and we only go up to the big house for one meal a day – family breakfast at 11:00 o'clock. From all we can gather, Mrs Meyer is somewhat of a b. As Tom has said, 'Don't let Mother get you down because she gripes at everybody.' Don't judge Tom by this because he's really a darling. However, we feel we can put up with Mrs for five days to live on the cream of the land – servants rushing about, fishing trips, rage on, Mrs M, see if we give a rap! The family are having friends down also so there will be about ten of us in all. It's a shame Mort couldn't get away too. He needs the holiday far more than I do, but maybe it will be a holiday for him without me there. No doubt Margaret will take even better care of him than I do. She's petrified and yet adores him and the whole house moves around what he likes and doesn't like.

The Evans are figuring on taking charge of him. They seem to be absolutely mad about him and wanted him to stay there but, of course, Mort refused.

We helped celebrate Owen's birthday the night before we left. Peggy called for me *à la* chauffeur and Buick and we went up to London to have a couple of cocktails at Mort's club first, then we four went to Luigi's for dinner – champagne etc. Mort and I gave Owen a couple of silly Woolworth presents and I made up a silly poem for them which highly amused him. After dinner he took us to a marvellous show, or review I guess it was, called *The Band Wagon*. It was screamingly funny and quite risqué in spots. We went back to our place and had beer and about five games of tiddleywinks. We seem to get more childish as the days go by!

Will be dropping the odd card from here to show you what it's like. Heaps of love, Mummie dear, to you, Dad and Bill.

Your John

Mullion Cove
Cornwall
August 7th, 1939

Dearest Mum,

This letter is going to be taken back to London by a Canadian who is staying with the Meyers, by the name of Colonel John Donally, a dear man who is a great friend of Major Swan of Vancouver – Bill's father. If Bunny should see him do tell him about this. By the way, Mrs Meyer knows you, and was entertained at a luncheon you gave for her in 1926. Imagine her remembering. She stayed with the Herrmanns and knows you as Gineva. Do you remember her? She has been perfectly sweet to me, thanks to you, I feel sure.

Oh Mum, this is the most delightful place you could ever imagine. Six of us are living in the cottage, and the elders are in their house, fortunately far enough away so as to not be bothered by our noise. Tommy, his brother John and his girl, Delores, another man, who is a little older but very nice, and Betty and myself. We have our meals here which are brought down to us from the family's. The boys call their place 'The Retreat'! Music blaring most of the time, so think the family planned things well for their boys. Have been fishing and caught two mackerel and tried to eat them for breakfast and couldn't bear them. Every night we go to a pub in Helston called the Blue Anchor and play skittles. Ask Dad about it. The pub has the original skittle house. You play with huge wooden balls that Betts and I can hardly lift to roll down at the pins. They in turn are rolled back to the players on a thing like a kiddies' slide. Quite an amazing place really, and they brew their own beer on the property for tuppence a glass and it is considered to be the best in the country. From family down to family they have been in business for 400 years.

I can hardly understand the fishermen; their accents are indescribable and only use nouns and say more in one sentence than we do in ten.

We are going home on Wednesday. It's a ten-hour drive in their open car which is a beauty. It should be a beautiful trip; Betts certainly will never enjoy anything as much as this holiday with the Meyers. The coast here is terribly rugged – green hills, jagged rocks and emerald green water. What a country this is – if only all of you could see it, how happy I would be. Cornwall is very different from South Devon, which is soft and glorious, and depending on the weather, Cornwall can look bleak. We have not had good weather – foul in fact – but when the sun has come through it is truly beautiful. I hate to leave here as I'll probably never see it again, which is sad. I watch the big liners going by on their way over to Canada, no doubt, so many of them too. I suppose one day in a few years I will be crying my eyes out as I leave here for good, bag and baggage.

I am now weighing 128 pounds and have gained a terrific amount of weight since leaving home, so much so, I can't button my shorts. The cream here is my downfall; it is so delicious I can't resist it on anything, particularly with the berries and desserts they send down to us.

The days are flying by so quickly and yet I will be happy to be going home. I miss Mort terribly and keep wishing he was here to enjoy everything with me. I telephoned him this morning and he sounded very lonely for me.

I will write when I am home again, Mum, and tell you more than I have here as it's hard to write when so many people are rushing about. Colonel John will take this into London and post it for me. Betty says to phone her mother and tell her what we are all doing as she doesn't want her to worry about her and that she will write when she is back in Reigate, not from Mullion Cove! The noise is really something with all the fun we are having. If only Mort was with me. He would love it.

Lots of love to all the family,

John

Tall Trees
Wray Park Road
Reigate, Surrey
August 14th, 1939

Mum dear,

Such a perfect letter from you on Saturday, posted from Vancouver on Monday! It made me feel so close to all of you again. The mail leaves here on Saturdays so will 'do' you a Clipper letter soon. A million thanks, Mum, for your cheque for the alterations. Will tell you all about it when it is finished. We got a terrific kick out of the pictures of Betty; they are sweet.

Your letters are never dull, Mum. To think you are taking over the big house, I really am overcome. Granddaddy would love to think you were going into one of his Harwood Street houses. It will seem strange to be living on Harwood again. It seems like a huge undertaking with the large garden etc., but I guess you know what you are doing. Must say I have always loved that house and wish you great times. Only wish we could be there for the housewarming.

Well, we have been leading a very gay life since we returned 11:30 Wednesday night from Mullion, having left at 10:30 a.m. It was a glorious drive thru' the most beautiful country I have ever seen. My, we did have fun down there, Mum. It simply couldn't have been nicer – crazy fun, when everyone did or said as they felt inclined. Tom and John are quite a pair of brothers and obviously get along famously. What one didn't think of the other one did. They can say the worst things and get away with it. Even their parents have to laugh at them – especially John.

While we were there, Gunner Knutzen telephoned from Norway and said he would be over on Thursday, so immediately a party was arranged for him. Betty and I went into London early Friday afternoon and went straight to Delores' flat. Mort stayed at his club. We dressed and met everyone at No. 1 Wimpole Street (the Meyers'), had a couple of Martinis and in two taxis toddled off to the Dorchester and went into the dance. We drank Courdin Rouge '28 all evening and I thought it the best Champagne I have ever tasted. Everbody merry, but not too much so. I was very impressed with the Dorchester. Everyone was beautifully dressed, the food and service absolute perfection. Gunner was in fine form and we laughed so hard recalling the evening we all had dinner at the Wincklers'. Do you remember him? Mort liked him tremendously. He dances very well and is such a nice person. We sallied forth at 2:00 a.m. to a nightclub that reminded me of the Commodore a bit as it had a similar large floor with super indirect lighting. We had bacon and eggs, toast and fried potatoes and more Champagne before leaving there at 5:00 a.m. Drove to Delores' where we made tea and talked for half an hour, then went to bed to the tune of milk wagons clopping up and down the streets.

Mort played 36 holes of golf that day, with John, and said he nearly sold out after the 26th. I hate to even think of it. Tommy called for us three girls and took us to a cinema after lunch. I felt perfect all day, much to the disgust of the others. We all fell asleep in the film. The boys didn't get back from golf until 9:30 that night, so Tom took us out for dinner. We caught the 11:15 home. Sunday Mort played golf in the afternoon and brought Owen and Peggy back for tea after which the four of us played French cricket in the garden. In the evening Peggy and Freddie Jennings came over for bridge and once more we beat them badly for 13 shillings, poor dears. We play tuppence a 100, and have suggested we play for a penny, but they say oh no their luck will change, so there is nothing we can do about it.

So sorry to hear about your back. My, it must hurt. Betty said she had the same thing happen to her and had to carry a cushion around with her everywhere she went. Did Dr Schinbein say anything else to you? Are you really quite well apart from the broken bone? Please tell me in your next letter, Mum.

I am feeling terribly well. The five pounds I gained when I was away makes me feel and look better. If I had stayed there much longer I would have lost my figure for sure. Poor Betts is having to have her clothes let out.

Mort went away yesterday for a two-week trip, poor darling, and only just as the weather has taken a turn for the better. It was very bad when we were away, but we have had two good days now so maybe it's here to stay for a while.

My, it was nice getting your letter so quickly because I could visualise so much better when you had done things, knowing it was only a week before instead of ten or eleven days. So glad you like the earrings. Please tell me quite honestly, Mum, were they broken by any chance? I thought afterwards that they should have been in a larger box. I do hope not because they were lovely.

We were invited to Peg and Owen's for dinner last night and they ran off a lot of their movies for us of their two trips to Spain. My, what a gorgeous country it must have been, but practically everything we saw they said was now in ruins. Wars, endless wars, and what do they really prove?

Mort seems to think if the world gets by the next four weeks with no war we will probably go thru' until next spring. We have been having quite a few blackouts lately and the balloon barrage is up in London all the time, at least it has been every time I've been in lately. They are the weirdest looking things. It doesn't mean a thing, but feel we should be prepared for the worst.

When next I write, Mort asked me to send his love. He is in a fabulous mood these days and getting better looking every day, it seems.

Arrived home to a spotlessly clean house. Margaret must have worked like a fiend. She did all the floors with steel wool and then polished them. Washed all the windows in and out, all the washable curtains, all woodwork, tidied all my drawers and Mort's and my wardobe; in fact everything was so clean I hated to touch anything. She is a fabulous little worker and quite a good cook. Even my dresses are pressed for me, to say nothing of exercising Nickie every day. She absolutely dotes on him. She is very keen to go to one of the hospitals to train this autumn; only hope we won't lose her.

I must get busy and try and get some of the people I know off my list. It's really dreadful and how I hate ruining a good afternoon by trying to be sociable over a cup of tea.

Well, Mum darling, I've come to the end of my news. Again, many thanks for your cheque.

Heaps and heaps of love to you all,

John

August 27th, 1939

Dearest Mum,

Well, I feel lower than a snake's belly at this point – Betty sailed from Southampton last night at 10:00 on the *Empress of Australia.* We honestly didn't know what to tell her to do. How can anyone tell what can happen in the next few days or what it will bring forth? If we had persuaded her to stay over and something happened to her we would never forgive ourselves and have to live with it for the rest of our lives. As her family didn't approve of her remaining over to nurse and she didn't have a job, there really was no alternative for her. We, or I should say Mort, was terribly lucky to get her a passage at all this week. As it was she got the very last bunk available and even then she is in a stateroom with two other girls! At least she will have company. I felt dreadful and we both made shocking exhibitions of ourselves; gosh, I hated to see her go, and she just adores it over here.

Tommy drove us down in the large family Rolls with Bett's trunk and bags in the back. We probably looked as if we were delivering a corpse with our faces set like death masks. We had dinner with farewell Champagne toasts and then took her aboard the ship. Poor Betts; don't tell her mother as she might be hurt that she so hated leaving here.

Mary Riddell called me to say goodbye as she is working overtime to obtain passage on the *Queen Mary* on Wednesday but isn't holding out too much hope that she will succeed. She also hates to leave but wants to get her son out. She feels as much love for this country as your daughter.

Mort is home again looking extremely well but quite tired as he had been doing a rip-roaring business up until Sterling dropped. He was so happy to be home. He couldn't phone me as all the long distance lines are being kept open for official use only. It is bad enough getting through to London from here. The other day it took me half an hour to get through to CPR for Betty.

It's so peaceful here today; the sun is shining as hard as it can go and the wind is brushing through the trees as if it was playing tag. We are sitting out in the garden. Mort and Owen are off to play golf this afternoon, unless I can persuade them that a swim would do them far more good as it is such a perfect day for it.

Mort has definitely made up his mind that if there is a war, to get into the Auxiliary Fire Service with Owen where he will receive the large sum of three pounds a week on which we will have to live – others will be doing the same so we won't be alone having to change our way of living. I am thinking of joining the Fire Service also and I will leave Margaret to take care of the refugee children. I'd want to do something and I could answer the phone and do odd jobs. They need women badly with all the men being called up. I'll wait and see what the next days bring forth.

I will finish this later as I don't seem capable of keeping my mind on it sufficiently to make any sense.

Monday 10:00 a.m. – received a letter from you this morning, Mum – you are certainly having a busy time. I wonder if you are regretting your move. If Bill wants to join up you will be stuck with that great big house with only two of you in it – but you are no doubt obligated by now. You seem to be thinking about us last year as I am, and especially now with all this crisis upset around us again. It does so remind us of being pinned to the news. Never mind, Mum, we will hope for the best and with a little luck we will all be together again next year.

Yesterday, Mort, Owen and I went swimming and after went back to Pegs for tea and played cricket and games with the children in their lovely garden. Their sweet peas alone stand ten feet high, believe it or not. After dinner we played bridge and tiddleywinks, arrived home by 11:00, and this evening we are going to a cinema with them. You would like them both, they are such good fun. It is nice that Mort likes Owen so much as he is the only one of our friends that is a contemporary of his.

My, I miss Betty terribly. It will take a long time to become accustomed to her not being with us. She was always so bright and sweet in the house, never got cross or upset about anything and we laughed 80 per cent of the day.

Your present to me sounds as if it will be a muff. I do hope so as I love them and my hands do get so cold. Mort took your cheque in for me today to cash and I'm having him keep it intact until things decide themselves before I go down to have my coat finished as I honestly don't think I would be wise to spend that much if there is to be a war on our hands, do you?

So Nancy is off to the Sacred Heart. I do hope she will like it and that everyone will be good to that little American girl. Have you seen the new school? If so, what is it like?

Well, Mum dear, will close now and drop off a note to Betty. She should receive it in Montreal.

Heaps and heaps of love to you all and please write as often as you can, if only a card.

John

There seems to be a huge gap in my letters leading up to the declaration of war in September 1939. It was a very busy time for everyone during those days, although I feel sure I did write regularly. I have a feeling my parents shared my letters with Mort's mother as he certainly didn't have time to write. The Ministry of Food was demanding as much food as he could bring over from Canada.

Margaret and I had our hands full with blackout curtains to be made, supplies to be safely stored and me doing my shift at the Auxiliary Fire Service. I had been on duty until midnight and was sound asleep the morning Chamberlain made his speech declaring war. Mort was home that day and had the wireless on and was keeping his ear cocked for any news. When he heard the Prime Minister was going to speak he wakened me in time to hear the ominous news that we were at war with Germany. This was followed instantly by the wailing blast of the air-raid siren which really shook Margaret and me into action with poor Nickie bundled between us as we took shelter under the staircase! No sooner did we settle ourselves than the all-clear sounded. I'm sure Mort thought he had a couple of terrified females on his hands. Every newsreel we had seen up to then showed the German air power flying in formation in the hundreds, to say nothing of the phenomenal strength of their army.

Peg Evans called me to ask if I would please help her as she had to cook some eggs and bacon for Owen and she didn't know how!! Their cook and butler had been called up and Nanny needed to be with the children.

Our refuse tins had our initial 'D' on them as we shared Tall Trees with the Hills who had the flat upstairs. The first day of war our terrified little Margaret painted over the initial so the Germans couldn't see it from the air!

My means of transportation to and from the fire station was on a kindly loan of Margaret's little bicycle. Riding in the dark blacked out streets holding a dimly lit torch for my half-mile ride was always a bit scary. I never knew who was more pleased to see my safe return, Mort or Margaret.

FIRE SERVICE REPORT CENTRE
September 16th, 1939

Mum darling,

It looks as if I have a quiet time so will start a letter to you. There really isn't a lot to say, except that Mort has been recalled to his office. Business is booming, literally, and try as he did, for a week, working all night and going to London every day, he has finally had to go on part-time voluntary service to be on hand if there is an air-raid at night. I do think supplying the country with food is a far greater service than sitting on his rear end night after night in Owen's garage and sleeping all day. He is putting in his last night there this evening. He is looking very tired; the excitement is carrying him but he really couldn't keep it up much longer.

I go on day duty next week. 8:00-4:00 in the afternoon. Mort wants me to give it up and I don't at all. I have worked hard to learn how to be useful down here and I feel capable of handling things during an air-raid. I don't feel like giving up all that to sew or roll bandages all afternoon, unless of course someone needs the money more than I do, then I would. We will have to see how it works out in the next weeks to come. I know it isn't fair to Mort.

There has been no Canadian mail in for ages – guess we will have to make the best of it, Mum, when our letters don't arrive for each other; at least no news is good news, don't forget. What is Connie doing with herself without Bill? She must miss him terribly. It is a wonder they didn't get married like everyone over here – hundreds of them a day I see in the papers. What kind of pay does he receive? Do send me his address as soon as you can as I would like to write him; also what is his rank?

On Sunday, for two weeks only, we are going to look after a little girl of three as a boarder – won't it be fun? One of Mort's men asked him if we would and, of course, we are only too delighted; from all accounts she is a darling child. Will tell you all about her in my next letter. If we have some good weather I will take a picture for you.

Am getting a full day off next week as well as this week, which will be nice. I may go into London on one of them and say goodbye to dear Tommy Meyer. He expects to leave for France almost any day; damn the war.

We all wonder when the first raid will be. It would seem they want to finish off the poor Poles first. I wonder if all the unrest one reads about in the newspapers is true or not? There is so much propaganda these days one doesn't know quite what to believe about Germany. If we are to believe what we read there may really be a chance of a revolution and then this miserable war would end. I wonder how long it will last, as I am sure everyone did in the First World War.

Our anniversary is only ten days away – my, how the time does fly. Three years married. Remember what a beautiful day it was? It seems such a short time ago. I feel as if I am much older than the three years and certainly have had a great many experiences since that day. It has been a full three years, hasn't it?

It's now 5:30 a.m. and 3:00 p.m. with you. It is strange to think of your night just coming and our day just starting.

Well, Mum darling, I am going to close now and try and stay awake to hear my buzzer.

Heaps of love,
Your John

Tall Trees
September 19th, 1939

Mum darling,

We are still waiting for a boat to bring in some mail. It is now two and a half weeks since I last received a letter. There is nothing one can do about it so we just consider ourselves lucky to get any mail during these times.

There is literally nothing to tell you, Mum, but I know you must long for letters also so I will drop off one, even if it is only a postcard saying we are well, which we are, remarkably so.

The three year old baby girl we are taking didn't arrive Sunday as expected but will definitely be here tomorrow, Wednesday, so will write and tell you all about her later. I am so looking forward to having her. Margaret is thrilled beyond words about her coming – only wish I could keep her for the duration of the war.

Peg and Owen are coming to dine with us on our wedding anniversary. We decided against our big night in London. With our future so unpredictable these days we felt it would be foolish to be so extravagant right now. Remember last year we went to the Beresford Hotel and then to *Quiet Wedding* and read newspapers on the train re the looming war?

Well, Mum dear, must get ready for dinner. All my love to all.

John

FIRE SERVICE MESSAGE FORM
September 25th, 1939

Mum darling,

Am on day duty now from 8:00 a.m. until 4:00 p.m. and it's simply great. Lots to do and one feels as if it is worthwhile, war effort wise.

Still no letters. It's three weeks now, but there is no Canadian mail whatsoever. Mort hasn't even had any office mail. Isn't it rotten – I suppose mine aren't reaching you either? No doubt we will both receive a packet all at one time and then wait another month. We can only hope our ships are not being sunk. After what happened to the *Athenia*, one wonders.

There is less than no news. I will be on day duty for ten days now so it does give me time to be with Mort and see my friends. This evening we are going to a party, two tables of bridge. Before I go home to have a little rest I am going down to buy Mort an anniversary present. I think I will try and find a nice Cashmere sweater, if possible. Woollies have gone up 29 per cent. Everything is on the up and up these days. Petrol rations are in force now and food starts any day. We are wondering what they will allow us. Butter and egg prices are fixed now.

Went into London on my day off and bought myself a pair of black shoes as the ones you bought me in Glasgow are threadbare. Mort gave a lovely pair of Daks (trousers) as a present for the 26th. I just love them. Also a lipstick and a smashing white case for my gas mask container. We then went up to Flora's as Finlay has been called up and she seemed to think he will be leaving for France in about three weeks. I can't bear to think about it. We had a few cocktails with her and then the three of us went to Quag's for dinner – downstairs, not where you went with us that night a year ago. We had a gorgeous dinner and received quite a shock when we went out to find London as black as ink. It's impossible to see anyone and everyone bumps one another. The taxis creep about like ghosts. We went back to Flora's as it was late and I spent the night with her and Mort went to his club. We came home together next morning. We did miss Finlay terribly as you can imagine; he is such a special person.

London was so different – sandbags everywhere and men, masses of them in uniform. The barrage balloons up by the hundreds and signs everywhere saying 'this way to the air-raid shelter', and of course everybody is carrying their gas mask.

Must close, Mum dear, my time is up here. It has been very quiet as far as the switchboard has been concerned, so managed to catch up with a bit of news to you. Hope to be able to write soon and tell you we had masses of letters.

Heaps and heaps of love to all,

John

FIRE SERVICE REPORT CENTRE
October 11th, 1939

Mum dear,

Was delighted to receive another letter from you the other day, making five letters all at one time, as I had already had one from you that morning, and answered it – then came home from work to find another sitting on my pillow! Too good to be true. Thank you.

We are hoping to hear you are regaining your lost weight. I can't imagine you being 136 pounds. You were asking how I am. I'm really terribly well, so much so that Mort has had a cold, as well as all the girls I work with over the past six weeks, and so far I am scot-free.

I stop my full-time work here exactly a week today but will continue on my hours of 4:00 until midnight until that time. I come down here in daylight and am driven home at midnight so you need have no further worries about me cycling home in the blackout. I will miss coming down here in a way but will be keeping in touch by doing four daytime hours every so often as they will be needing part-time girls.

So glad you are happy in the big house. Do you have the large bedroom with the bay window and fireplace? Please answer all my questions in your next letter.

As I wrote only a few days ago I have totally run out of news.

Loads of love to you and Dad and to Bill when next you write to him. It must take you back to our boarding school days having to write to both of us again.

Your John

FIRE SERVICE REPORT CENTRE
October 18th, 1939

Mum darling,

As I wrote twice during last week I didn't manage my customary letter off to you on Monday, so hope it's all right with you. My hours are so arranged that I don't seem to be able to settle down to writing letters, but as tonight is my last full-time duty, no doubt I will settle back into a normal routine again and my letters will also.

There has been little or nothing to write about. A Canadian mail came yesterday but nothing from you or friends – only business for Mort and a *Life* magazine

I meant to tell you, I saw a picture in the August *Mayfair* magazine of the wedding of one of the Rogers taken at Highland Hall with the wedding group standing around the swimming pool. What a heavenly time you three girls must have had growing up there. I remember you telling me that Granddaddy built that pool because a great friend of his had lost his daughter by drowning because she had never been taught to swim and he had said no daughter of his will drown for they will be taught in their own pool. So often things you have said over the years come popping into my head. Did they sell Highland Hall after you three were married? Do hope you saw the picture.

From tomorrow on I do part-time and will have from 2:00-4:00 tomorrow, 4:00-8:00 on Monday and each week no doubt it will vary considerably, but never more than four hours at a stretch and chances are only a couple of times a week. It will seem strange to be a lady of leisure again. After a week off I will see what I can do to help where I am needed. I have a goodly amount to catch up on at home. Summer clothes to be put away, perfecting the wretched blackouts that look very tacky as they are. I have had a roller system going with them that was always a temporary deal, but that time has run out. It's very eerie at night and if I want to put on my make-up I have to go into the bathroom as it has good lighting with excellent curtains, and then carry all my paraphernalia back to my dressing table.

Had a lovely letter from Mrs Duffus last week. She is so sweet to write as often as she does, bless her heart. We think of all of you so often. I do envy you your ease of shopping these days. Mort brought me a pound of bacon from London the other day. We haven't been able to buy any in Reigate for a few weeks now so it was like manna from heaven. Shopping is becoming more and more difficult each day and we are told will do so until they get food rationing. I can't complain because only bacon has been impossible to buy and other things can only be purchased in annoying quantities.

Really must close – heaps of love to all of you.
John

October 21st, 1939

Mum dear,

What a dreadful shock I just received when I opened your letter just now! You neglected to put an airmail stamp on it and it came by ordinary post instead. Oh, I do hope you are all right now; if only I was there to help nurse you back to health again. I do hope Bill was able to obtain leave over Thanksgiving as Mrs Duffus said and that he will write and tell me how you are. Do, please take good care of yourself when you do return home. It would be so easy to get another chill when you are as run-down as you must be. I am so worried about you. You never would take care of yourself – so please do this time? Nothing must ever happen to you.

Margaret is going to run to the post office with this now so it will reach you as soon as possible . . . so all my love for now. I am so sorry you have been so ill.

GET BETTER SOON

Your John

October 23rd, 1939

Dearest Mum,

I do hope by the time this letter reaches you that you are home again and feeling more yourself. I have been so worried since your letter arrived the other day, but keep saying to myself that no news is good news, but want to see it in print that you are well on the mend.

Haven't been doing very much lately. Saturday night we walked up to Peg and Owen's and played silly paper games as we call them and laughed until we ached at a dreadful game they taught us. There are never any dull moments when we are with them.

Sunday we had 10:00 o'clock breakfast and did odd jobs around the house, had our lunch and Mort went off to play golf with Douglas Thompson and I did two hours work at the Station, then Hilary and Douglas came for dinner. We had never dined them before so did a baked ham, corn, etc., all of which was delicious. We played games until 12.30 and had a most enjoyable evening. This is all very boring to relate but it was lots of fun at the time.

Will you please ask Mrs Duffus if she received a letter from me thanking her for the money she sent us after the declaration of war? Darn it all, I can't remember for the life of me whether I finished it and if I did, did I post it! I know I started it at the

Brother Bill.

Station; where it has gone I don't know. I will have another thorough search for it. I would feel very badly if she never heard from me. Those days were so upsetting I could easily have done some stupid things with it.

Old man winter is settling in very quickly and Margaret is going through what I experienced last year with a bad attack of chilblains. They are such painful things – I feel terribly sorry for her.

I telephoned the Beldams the other evening and they have between 60-70 people living there. Mr Beldam has his entire office staff in their house, using the drawing room and billiard room. The dining room is a general dining room for all the staff and the Beldams dine in a small room elsewhere. Not satisfied with this as doing her duty, Mrs Beldam is now taking over the job of making 150,000 linen bags for sick soldiers to keep their clothes in while in hospital. She is a remarkable little person, isn't she? Mrs Beldam told Bobby to tell me that if ever I needed a home I was to go to her and she would always find me a bed no matter how crowded she was. She is so kind. However, there is no chance of that happening, but I will write and thank her for her very kind offer. She probably thinks Mort might be called up, but she doesn't realise Mort can never be called up over here. Being Canadian he was told he must return to Canada to join up.

Am off to the Station again so will try and finish this off there if we have a quiet spell. In case I don't, I will say goodbye, with lots and lots of love.

John

Canada House
Trafalgar Square
London, SW1
October 25th, 1939

Hello Mum,

Came into London with Hilary by car on the spur of the moment and as Mort is lunching with me at Simpsons on the Strand at 1:15, I thought I would put in a few minutes here and tell you what I am up to.

It's the most glorious day and all the trees in Hyde Park are turning the most heavenly shade of scarlet. It's as cold as old billy, and my nose, I feel sure, is a most unbecoming red. I just bought a pair of white wool gloves which are really quite attractive considering they are woollies.

I haven't seen a familiar face as yet and there are so many people in here – isn't it strange?

Had a long letter from Betty Birks yesterday, also one from my nurse Kitty Gould. Did you have her by any chance or did she call you for our address? I became so fond of her and she was so good to me during that sad time.

Must close, Mum, as I will have to walk quickly for my date with Mort to do full justice to their delicious roasts at Simpsons, to say nothing of their English Stilton.

Lovingly,

John

Tall Trees

October 30th, 1939

Mum dear,

Have only had the one letter from you written in hospital and am hoping to hear one day this week that you are home. It is so worrying being so far away and never knowing from one day to the next how you are doing.

There isn't much to tell you really. The weekend was a very wet one so Mort didn't get in any golf at all and we played bridge on Saturday night for our usual 2*d*. a 100 (approximately a 20th) with the Jennings. As usual we beat them badly – a pound this time – it is beyond a joke at this point. It is strange that we always beat them. The Pierces always win against us and the Jennings always win against the Pierces. It seems to go in a triangle of money exchange.

Didn't have time to finish this so here goes once more. Such good news from Mrs Duffus in her letter to Mort yesterday, saying that you are home and that Bill is there with you. She said you were doing very well and that Mrs Kinsman is looking after all your meals. Now I know you are in good hands with her superb cooking. Hopefully, with her help, you will regain your lost weight.

About twenty newspapers arrived and I had a good afternoon's reading. Did you see the column called Bric-a-Brac? Pat ought to get her facts straight.

Rain, rain all day. Only the nights are nice and a full moon bursts up about 8:00 every night. We can't resist standing out in the garden to look at it and to feel the peace and quiet around us. It is hard to imagine there is a war.

Am doing a lot of part-time at the Station. They need us badly now as the staff has been cut so drastically.

Saw where Diana Whittal was married over here. Strange that I never have seen her in London. I hope she will be very happy. Is her mother pleased?

Haven't heard a word from Ernle or Dorothy so don't know any news about them. Forgot to tell you that Betty Beddal had a baby boy. I would love to go over to see them but it isn't so easy any more.

Well, Mum dear, I have completely run out of news that is worth repeating so will close.

Heaps and heaps of love to you, Dad and Bill – hope he is able to have a decent visit with you and will write and tell me how you are.

John

November 3rd, 1939

Dear Eva

This letter is a rather belated effort but perhaps it is better late than never. Needless to say I was extremely sorry to hear of your unfortunate illness. You certainly do have miserable luck. However, we both felt much better when your letter arrived to John. You sounded so much better. Graham's letter also arrived and he corroborated the fact. Am pleased to learn that Dr Wallace Wilson is taking a firm hand with you and keeping you in bed. For heaven's sake do take it easy.

Am sure you will be happy to hear that John is and has been extremely well and is happy as a clam. Has lots to do what with supervising the household and putting in about sixteen hours a week at the Fire Hall.

We have been playing a lot of bridge and I become quite disagreeable with her play. Apart from that all is serene in the Duffus ménage.

We have a five-year old evacuee arriving on Sunday. It is a boy, and John who has seen him says he is a 'dandy'. It will be rather fun having a moppet running around and no doubt will be telling you all about him soon.

Have been very busy and during the last eight weeks will have done a tremendous business. I still do fire drill on the odd evenings and, of course, have to report for duty when the air-raid warning goes. Fortunately we have had no calls since the first week of the war.

Well, Eva, I seem to have run out of space. My regards to Graham, Bill and love to you.

As ever,
Mort

November 4th, 1939

Mum dear,

Had two letters this morning, one from you and one from Bunny. It was wonderful to hear so much news of family all in one day. I will write to Bunny as soon as I finish this one. It's a letter-writing day, dull and misty, and I don't have to do any shopping which is always a blessing.

We are taking an evacuee on Sunday; he arrives at 3:00. I saw him yesterday and really, Mum, he is adorable – by the name of Peter, very well built, fair hair, huge blue eyes, clean as a whistle and beautifully dressed. I fell for him on the spot and said I would take him right away but his mother looked a little upset and said she would like to keep him until Sunday. As far as I can see the only trouble we will have is trying not to spoil him; it will be hard not to as he really is a dear little boy. Will give you a full report when I write on Tuesday.

Was so pleased to hear Bill is looking much better. I would imagine the change into the Navy will do him the world of good. I'd give anything to see him. It will soon be two years since we said goodbye.

I told you we were going to buy a Cozy Stove didn't I? It is installed – hardly a thing of beauty but it certainly serves the purpose beautifully which is to heat the house this winter. We are amazed at the heat it throws as it seems to take the chill off the entire house which is quite remarkable considering the size of the little thing. I washed a pair of silk stockings and hung them up above the fire and they were dry in a matter of minutes, so you can imagine the heat it throws.

Apart from work at the Station and the odd cinema and bridge, we really haven't been doing very much. We never seem to get to bed very early these nights and I blame it on the German broadcast. Lord Ha Ha is the announcer and it is so darned funny we just have to stay up to listen to him. You have never heard such dreadful rot. The lies are so terrible that they are humorous, so we stay up to have our laugh. It comes on at 11:20 every night. There are news broadcasts every hour all day long but there is seldom any real news as you know. The general opinion over here is for a short war. I like to kid myself there will be a revolution in Germany before many months have passed, otherwise why doesn't he arm his reserve army?

What did the Americans think of Lindbergh's speech? That man has sunk beneath my contempt. I think his mind must be a little unbalanced since he lost his dear little boy.

So pleased you have seen Betty Birks. She is such a pretty girl, isn't she? It was too bad she had to go home. She would have been married within a year had she remained, then her mother would have been happy. She really upsets Betty. I wish you could tick her off. I certainly would if I was there. How different she is from you.

Saw where you were hoping I was having a baby – no, dear Mum, sorry. I do so love your letters, so write as often as you can, please?

Your John, with lots of love.

November 7th, 1939

Mum dear,

Received a Clipper letter from you yesterday and was so sorry to hear your temperature had gone up again, so more bed rest, obviously. Fortunately Mort also had a letter this morning from Mrs D, saying you were feeling cheery and as it was posted after yours, we can only surmise it was a temporary setback.

Was very surprised to hear Bill wasn't all that thrilled with Navy life thus far. Strange, as I thought he would be delighted with it. Hope he likes his dockyard life better and certainly living aboard the Duke of Sutherland's yacht shouldn't be hard to take. He can feel very thankful that he isn't over here serving in a destroyer patrolling the North Sea and nearly freezing to death with cold, to say nothing of dodging torpedoes from the loathsome U boats. He might indeed be far worse off.

I go for a fitting for my uniform for the AFS on Friday. It is really very smart, so will have Mort take a picture to send you.

About the only thing that is new with me is about our little evacuee, Peter Norris, aged five and really a darling little boy. He was very homesick his first night but is settling down beautifully. He calls me Auntie. I took him down to his little kindergarten yesterday and picked him up at 12:15 to have lunch at home. Mort now takes him there in the morning and I call for him. He plays with his toys and Nickie all afternoon, has his tea at 6:00, bath and bed by 7:00. No wet beds, so really feel we are most fortunate that he has adjusted so quickly. Mort is very taken with him, which is nice for both of them. He is a bit of a tie, but he is a joy.

Mort's business is booming and he is very well. I am exceptionally healthy. So many at the Station have had rotten colds, but I am happy to say I have never caught them.

Peggy Jennings has just telephoned to tell me to hurry up if I am going shopping as it is after 11:00 now, so will trot along and post this on our way.

Heaps of love as always,

John

November 21st, 1939

Dearest Mum,

Had hoped if I waited until today to write maybe the Canadian post would come in, but no such luck. Will write when I hear from you.

Have been frightfully busy this past week. Peter was quite ill with tonsillitis and had a temperature of 102° and felt utterly miserable, poor darling. He was terribly good and took his medicine and the doctor's examination like a man. He is a darling child. Apparently his tonsils are dreadfully bad and after Christmas they are coming out in hospital, to which his parents have consented, so it must be done. If this letter is all disjointed it's because I'm trying to play Motor Transport with Peter. He has guns, lorries, soldiers, etc., etc. and they are all being pushed across the chesterfield, presumably on the way to France. He says when he grows up he is going to shoot Hitler and then the war will be over.

Another little thing that is keeping me busy is pre-Xmas house cleaning. Margaret and I washed all the outside windows yesterday and the inside today. We really have covered a lot and the house is smelling more like a rose every minute. I am as bad as you used to be – I can't stand dirt and won't have dirt. As time goes on I am liking our place less and less because it is so very hard to keep clean. If only the war wasn't on, we would move into a house of our own as we can afford it now. There is no sense contemplating moving in war-time.

The general opinion over here seems to be that the war will be over within a year; how I do hope so. Can't think what makes people feel so optimistic, but sincerely hope they are right.

We went into London last Wednesday and had a good day's shopping. It was such fun. After we were finished we dropped in to see Flora and had a drink with her, then Mort took me to the Café Royal for dinner, which was gorgeous. We had Sole Mornay au Crabbe, Melba Toast, Crepes Suzette, petit fours and black coffee. All in all a delightful dinner. We arrived much too early for our train so went to a news cinema. I always enjoy them so much and can't think why we don't have them in Canada.

That seems to be the end of my news so will close. Hope you are starting to feel like yourself again.

Much, much love,

John

November 28th, 1939

Dearest Mum,

Still no letter from you; I only hope you are all right. I had a letter from Betty this morning and she says you wouldn't be a good patient and remain quiet long enough to regain your strength. Mum, please, it will be worth it in the long run. She also said you were going away somewhere but didn't say where. Please take care, if not for your own sake – mine.

We posted off our Christmas cards yesterday. I only hope everything arrives over there safely and do please promise not to open anything before Xmas, will you? I would be dreadfully disappointed if you did.

We've been having frightful weather – windy, rainy and cold, but when the old sun does make a rare appearance it more than makes up for the rain and wind.

There is very little to tell you. Very happy to say that Peter is well again and doesn't have his tonsils out until after Xmas, so we have a month's grace before that little episode.

On Saturday we entertained the Army – Norman Brann (now a captain aged 25, Mort's Irish friend), also Major Scott (also Irish), who is the man who knows Bunny's brother. He said he left him in Belfast looking very well. They both looked absolutely smashing in their uniforms and intrigued Margaret and Peter no end. They came over from Aldershot at 3:00 o'clock and had tea and dinner, then left during a driving rainstorm at 9:45. They both speak with just a trace of an Irish brogue which I find delightful and fascinating. Norman is always a treat to look at; he is such a handsome young man. Mort and I had him all picked out for Betty but she never had the chance to meet him.

Sunday, we took Peter up to Hilary and Douglas Thompson's for tea, then Peg and Owen came over after dinner and we played our usual mad games. Peg is having a baby in April so we have had to give up tiddleywinks on the floor, but manage to find other ways of amusing ourselves. Owen and Peg won't play bridge together so that lets out that form of entertainment.

We have started a bridge bank and in three days have put $7.00

into it so feel we have a little to go and come on. We really are most frightfully lucky, or is it all Mort's skill?

Well, Mum dear, as I said there is nothing worth writing about so won't prattle along any more.

A big hug and lots of love,

John

December 7th, 1939

Darling Mum,

This letter is to express my very best wishes for a very happy Christmas day and also to say we will be thinking of you on the 30th and will drink a toast to you on your birthday and a Happy New Year too. A very special one comes from me – 'God Bless my Mother'. I hope you will be feeling well enough by then to go out and enjoy yourself over those days. Maybe you will go over to Victoria to see Bill, or better still, that he will have leave to stay with you? It would be so nice for you to have him home over the holiday. If he is there tell him all these good wishes are for him also.

We will have our hands full with Peter all day and the excitement will be something terrific. I have visions of Peter and 'Auntie', as he calls me, sneaking out early to take one present to open in bed.

Peggy and Owen are coming to us for Christmas dinner and the fumes from our turkey are already reaching my nose. How I do love turkey! They now have an Austrian girl to help them so she suggested that they bring their girl to give Margaret a hand, also to be company for her, which seems to be a good idea all around.

We are having a tree this year or my name isn't Johnnie Duffus. I saw some of the trees they are selling when I was out this morning and I really had to laugh when I look back on some of the trees we have had on Harwood. Daddy used to say if they got any larger he would have to take the door off to get them in the house. I wouldn't be the least bit surprised if we have a white Christmas again this year as it has turned very cold and there is a snowy smell in the air. I hope it does. It is so pretty but it would be very hard on the soldiers, and as for the poor anti-aircraft men stationed all over England watching and waiting and the searchlights that are always manned etc., they must be perishing with cold, so on second thoughts I hope we don't have a white Christmas!

Must close, Mum dear, with every good wish for a very Merry Christmas and New Year that will see an end to this blasted war and all of us back together once more, and you right back to good health.

All my love, tons of it, Mum

John

December 19th, 1939

Mum dear,

A large mail came in yesterday, including a letter from Mrs Duffus for me, but none from you as yet. Do hope I hear some kind of a peep from you before Christmas – but it's very doubtful if another ship will come in by then – what a pity because I know you will have written so I will keep my fingers crossed and hope for the best.

The big event of this week, and it really is a big one, was Mr Birks arriving. We were bowled over with excitement. He didn't arrive in England until Saturday night, four days ago, and phoned us on Sunday. Fortunately we were home so we invited him to come down immediately, so he had tea and dinner with us. We talked and talked and he did us a world of good and brought such a cozy, homey feeling into our house when we most needed it so badly. He looks awfully well after his long trip and he thoroughly enjoyed his visit. He tells us now that he shan't be able to return home for New Year as he planned, so we have invited him to dine with us at Christmas and will try and persuade him to spend the night. Peter has gone to be with his parents, who couldn't face the holiday without him. There is a chance that Flora may also be here, so we will have Bett's room free and Arnold will have my bed in with Mort, in the other twin. It should all work out very well and naturally we are only too delighted to have him with us. He is such a grand person. I can't begin to tell you how excited I was to see him. There is nothing like someone from home over Christmas.

Parcel after parcel is arriving from Mrs Duffus. She is much too kind; it will take me a month to write her a thank you letter. Dear Granny Smith sent me some money, which was so kind of her to think of us. A hamper arrived from Chivers from Mrs D, with a Christmas pudding and umpteen other goodies. I really will try and post off a letter to her tomorrow and tell her how thrilled I am with her gifts and for her reports on your health. I can't tell you how happy I am that you are so well again. You have always had such good recuperative ability.

Mr Birks is treating Mort and me to dinner and a theatre tomorrow and I am lunching with Ernle (she can't manage the 25th which is too bad), then I am having tea with Flora. It will be a big day!

Today is Fire Station; it's so cold out I dread it, but it's always warm inside.

Will hope to dash off a letter before Christmas, Mum, meantime all my thoughts are with you and they are plum full of love too.

John

Looking Back

WHEN WE MOVED to Reigate we didn't know a soul. Several months went by before I was called on by Peggy Jennings who also lived on Wray Park Road with her husband, Freddie. She had heard about the lonely Canadian neighbours who lived across the street from an artist by the name of Michael Lewis, who had called on us. He specialised in painting miniatures on ivory. He was quite charming and we had a very interesting and amusing hour or so while he showed me photographs of his work. I couldn't afford to have him do one of me, but as he was departing he saw a photograph of me that Mort had and asked if I would lend it to him as he was giving an exhibit of his work in London and he wanted to do a miniature of it to include in his show. Naturally I was flattered, so agreed to lend it to him. He then called on others, among whom was Peggy Jennings, at which time he suggested I would probably love to have her as a friend. How true it was, as I was alone all day while Mort was in London. Some weeks later I received my miniature as a gift. It is still with me and was greatly appreciated. The frame was damaged which he compensated for by giving me the miniature with his apology. He also did us a favour by speaking to Peggy about me as we became great friends. We played a lot of bridge with them and were introduced to many of their friends. Names I remember were Gay Lacey-Hulbert and her husband, also Hilary and Douglas Thompson.

With the war rearing its ugly self, I joined the Red Cross that summer of '39 and as I entered the church hall where we were to enrol and have our first lecture, I remember standing at the back of all the chairs that were filling up so rapidly, wondering where I would sit. I spotted one empty chair beside two very attractive girls, so I asked if they were saving it for anyone; as they were not, I joined them. It wasn't long before I was asked where I came from as I did not sound English. They were Sonia Reid and Rhoda (Bobbie) Garrick, cousins, who turned out to be our friends forever. Sonia's mother had been an Alan of Alan Shipping Line in Canada. The Reid family adopted us, as you will read about in other parts of these memoirs. I am a firm believer in fate. They filled our lives with warmth and happiness. We, in turn, changed their lives considerably by introducing our attractive friend, Rupert Ross, to Sonia on a blind date and they have now been married for sixty-three years. We adopted our treasure, Susan, and when they found they couldn't have children, they followed suit and adopted their two wonderful children, Fiona and Allistair.

Going back a little – Mort was also spoken to by a total stranger in the train, travelling to London from Reigate. His name was Owen Evans. We used to think he was a dead-ringer for David Niven. When he discovered we were new to Reigate and from Canada, upon returning home he picked a huge bouquet of sweet peas (which were his pride and joy) and dropped them off with a note from his wife, Peggy. This was to invite us to dine with them the following Saturday. We became friends for life. They in turn introduced us to all their friends. They loved our guest Betty Birks, who stayed with us all that summer and of whom I have written elsewhere.

In those days you created your own fun. Television was in its early infancy and I remember standing in front of a wireless shop looking at one they had playing in the window and shaking my head in total disbelief, little dreaming it would take over the world in the years to come.

Our amusement in those days, apart from bridge, was paper games of every description, or sitting on the floor playing tiddly-winks. I'm sure their three children thought their parents and Canadian friends were in their second childhood as we were convulsed with laughter most of the time.

To add to my recollections of Peg (nicknamed Nim, Nimmer or Nimrod) she had a wonderful sense of humour and she wrote and illustrated enchanting poems and stories for their children. Owen, also with a nickname – 'Dood' – taken from the street they lived on, Dood's Way, was a member of the Stock Exchange. He enjoyed life immensely and adored Nim as well as their children. They had a super nanny, an excellent cook and a chauffeur as well as a butler. Owen loved gardening and was an able assistant to their gardener. Between them they had a very beautiful garden with the finest growth of sweet peas I have ever seen. The stalks alone were as thick as my little finger, topped with eight and nine blossoms. He told me they dug a three foot deep bed which was well fertilized every year and they were trained to bamboo poles that must have been seven feet tall.

Sometimes it was hard to know what they were all talking about as they had a language of their own. The only phrase that I recall was when the children were brought in to say goodnight, and Peg would say, 'Bouncing to beebles?' which meant going to bed. In all the hours we spent in their company, I never heard a child crying or a cross word – only laughter. All the children were born at home in Little Batts, the name of their house. Their fourth child, James, became Mort's godson, and many years later became badly smitten with Susan.

In the early months of the war, Owen and Mort joined the Auxiliary Fire Service, AFS for short, and spent many hours together during the 'cold war' days. There were no incendiary fires then, so they played chess and dominoes by the hour. I was on the switchboard at the AFS station. Their stint came to an end at a later date when Owen joined the Army – which took place after I returned to Canada. Mort moved to Little Batts where he stayed until he returned to Canada. He travelled to London every day that the trains ran during the Blitz. Supplying food from Canada was a very demanding job, at which he was extremely knowledgeable. He was not permitted to join up in the UK, so it wasn't until he was able to return to Canada that he was able to join the RCNVR, and was sent on loan to the RN.

Both Peg and Owen have been gone many years now but they were never far from our thoughts when Mort was alive, to keep them in our reminiscences.

Peggy, Owen, Mort and I became great friends with an American couple by the names of Lois and Bob Joyce. They lived in Redhill, the next little town to Reigate. When we visited them we liked to walk home via a shortcut through a cemetery in a churchyard. The nightingales' songs were incredibly clear and beautiful, so we would sit, perched on an ancient tombstone, and listen to them, finally having to tear ourselves away and wend our way home in the blackout.

Lois and Bob were soon to sail on the United States Lines aboard the SS *Washington*. I was to follow them shortly after they departed. Mort had wasted no time calling on Canada House to set up my departure and I was to sail from Liverpool on what was, in all secrecy, called 'the late June B sailing'. By this time I was in my seventh month with our second baby. The following is a copy of the letter Lois and Bob sent us from the SS *Washington*.

UNITED STATES LINES
SS *Washington*
June 20 – 1940

Dearest Johnnie & Mort:

Before we dock tomorrow morning I want to have a note ready to mail to you first thing! How we have talked of and missed you! – you've no idea. Of course it was pick-making not to see Mort before we left – but we did appreciate Johnnie's special trip to the Chantry – and the sweet etching that will always be one of our treasures.

Everything has gone much more smoothly than we expected. Had a short stay in Dublin where the night-lights simply dazzled us. Then on to Galway where the customs officials were absolutely sweet. They passed our trunks so fast that we got on the first tender going out to the *Washington*. You'd have loved the crowd – it looked like immigrants bound for Ellis Island and children – absolutely millions of them! There's so much French and Spanish spoken on board that we keep pinching ourselves to see if we're really on an American boat. Of course there are twice as many passengers as there should be – so they've drained the swimming pool and put beds in – also have them in the gym and Palm Court – just like dormitories. We had a weak moment when we came on board and found our cabin occupied. But miraculously they gave us another one and we're living like kings.

The voyage has been grand and we've met some really good scouts. We've heard the most hair-raising tales about some very interesting and innocent people. And, of course, wild stories about submarines following us, etc.

We absolutely hang on the news broadcasts which came from England until two nights ago – now hear Lowel Thomas. Of course it doesn't sound too good to us. But I hope it may seem brighter to you over there. Will be so anxious to hear the real dope from you. And tell us all about your Saturday or Sunday evenings with the Evans. We hate to be missing out. Hope all is well with you. Much love to you both from,

    Bob and Lois

War Service in Britain and Canada

IT WAS AT THE Evans' suggestion that we would give up our place when I left and Mort would store our furniture and move in with them. Owen was waiting to go into the Army and didn't like the idea of Peg being alone. Our Margaret would take our beloved dog and would work for a family that was very kindly going to accept them both. Even now I can't bear remembering how devastated I was at the thought of leaving Mort and England, that had so totally captivated me. It was truly awful.

On my last Sunday, we took the train to Penshurst, in Kent, so we could go to our favourite pub, the Spotted Dog. We called ourselves a couple of sad sacks, which indeed we were.

'D Day' arrived and sad farewells at Tall Trees; a goodbye present from Sonia, for my breakfast, of fresh-picked wild strawberries, and tears, then we trained for Liverpool, along with hundreds of others. Mort was worried sick that we wouldn't make it safely across the Atlantic. I, on the other hand, felt I might never see him again, as at that time his company wanted him to remain in Britain to supply the much needed food. We had to part in the train station as he was not allowed to accompany me to the ship. I remember so clearly standing out on the deck crying like a child and one of the crew came up to me and put his arm around my shoulder with the most comforting words he could think of. I was so touched, I cried harder.

We had no idea when we were to sail; I believe we slipped away during the night. We were a full ship. She was the *Empress of*

Scotland. There were five hundred and six children and over a thousand adult passengers. As it happened, I discovered Colonel and Mrs J.P. Fell were aboard. They had been neighbours of our family when I was growing up. They were extremely kind to me and I used to walk the deck with them regularly. Apart from one incident when destroyers smoke-screened us near the Irish Sea, we had a good crossing. One thing I do recall was seeing tables of women in the lounge after dinner, spreading the contents of chamois draw-string bags of jewels on the tables. Diamonds, rubies, sapphires, rings, bracelets set with diamonds and necklaces, but mostly single stones, many of breathtaking dimensions. The story circulating the ship was that they had brought them out of Germany.

My beloved sister-in-law, Jane, met me and I stayed with her for a few days before training through to Vancouver from Montreal. My feelings were very mixed as was to be expected. My heart was in England with Mort but I was naturally excited at the thought of seeing all the family and our many friends after an absence of nearly two and a half years.

My mother had prepared an adorable nursery for our expected baby. My brother Bill was to be married to a beautiful blonde in Victoria, by the name of Doreen Cattroll, whom he had met while in the Navy. After life in the UK with blackouts, strict rationing of clothes and food, I found that life in Vancouver really hadn't changed very much. Inconceivable as it may seem, I resented it.

Our baby and the Blitz arrived at much the same time. Mort received the news that he had a son and lived on cloud nine for close to a week as my cable telling him the very sad news was delayed because of the air-raids. Three days was the short-lived life of our baby.

After Roy, Jane's husband, was killed on the beach at Dieppe, Jane had had time to alter her whole lifestyle and with their little daughter Judie, had come out to Vancouver to live with her mother. Although she had her own sorrow to deal with, she was a great source of strength for me. She went out of her way to cheer me up and we became very good friends. Mrs Duffus and her companion, Dorothy Rowell, were wonderfully kind to me. As always, Mother and I fully enjoyed each other's company and time passed.

Mort was finally returned to Canada a few months after Pearl Harbour. He wasted no time in applying to the Naval recruiting office at HMCS *Discovery*. They obviously recognised a good man when they saw one, as they gave him a medical and a commission with orders to report to a training establishment in Montreal, where he would receive his uniform as a Lieutenant in the RCNVR. Although I couldn't bear to see him leave, I knew it wasn't in his make-up to sit at a desk organising the shipment of food to Britain, needed as it was. The 'Yachtsmen's Group', as they were called, all knew each other and Mort was to train east with friends, Freddie Whitehead, Armour Bull and Gordon Stead. I travelled as far as Agassiz with Mort as we couldn't bear to say goodbye in Vancouver. I went on to Harrison Hot Springs Hotel to spend the night with my wet pillow, once more wondering if I would ever see him again.

After two weeks in Montreal, he was appointed to *King Alfred* in Portsmouth, where he was put through his paces in no uncertain way, before being sent to a Hunt Class Destroyer, HMS *Brocklesby*. He wasn't able to tell me very much in his letters, but there was no doubt that he was delighted beyond words with his appointment.

Hoping beyond hope, I once more expected a baby and to our utter dismay, we lost our third son, who also lived for three days. As soon as I could, and Mort agreeing to the idea, I applied for an exit permit to return to the UK as I wanted to join the Wrens, officially known as the Women's Royal Naval Service. The once famous hockey player, Cyclone Taylor, was the man in charge of the immigration office where I applied. For a civilian to obtain an exit permit to cross the Atlantic to join up was unheard of, so I was told. However, he filled out my application form, which I duly signed. With a twinkle in his eye he asked, 'And what will you do for me if I am successful in obtaining this for you?' to which I replied, 'I'll give you a nice kiss.'

When I related all of this to my mother, she didn't think it sounded too hopeful and she knew how desperately I wanted to go. Royal Read, a great friend of our parents, lived in Burlington, Ontario, and they seemed to think he just might be the right person for me to talk to and suggested I telephone him to see if there was any way that he could help me.

After briefing him as to my plight he told me he just might be able to help me as he was leaving for Ottawa the next day and would be seeing his good friend, C.D. Howe, the Defence Minister. He said that he would phone me on his return home. The call came through several days later saying, 'Your exit permit has been approved and you may pick it up in a few days time. C.D. glanced over your file and as your furniture is over there, you are a returning resident.' I was overwhelmed with gratitude. A few days later Cyclone Taylor called me to say, 'You've got your permit and I'm collecting, young lady!'

When my brother Bill was serving in Halifax he and his wife Doreen and their baby daughter Ann had taken a house there and when I was told to report to Halifax for an unknown sailing date, they very kindly invited us to stay with them as Mother was keen to go east with me. When I arrived I was told I was to be on-call with twenty-four hours notice to be at the dockyard. Fortunately we were able to have a great visit with them and time to lose my heart to little Ann, who was to be my goddaughter.

Meanwhile, in Britain, Mort had been to see the Super-intendent WRNS Officer, Western Approaches, to ask if I would be able to join the service when I arrived and was told it would indeed be quite possible and to have me make an appointment for an interview.

After sad farewells I was dropped at the dockyard and finally squeezed into an overcrowded lifeboat with two girls about my age and a huge number of men, who we gleaned were Merchant Seamen. As we drew away from the wharf, the men burst into song, at the end of which I remarked, 'That must mean something. Tell us, please.' We were told they had been torpedoed four times. I said, 'Your worries are over, I will bring you all good luck.' To which they roared, 'Three cheers!' It came as a bit of a shock to come alongside an Egyptian freighter by the name of *El Nil*. We three girls were taken to our cabin which we shared very happily. They were delightful girls, both English, who had been staying with relatives to finish their education and were returning to join up. It was moderately comfortable with a bath, basin and loo, no door, only a chintz curtain which we were told would not jam us in if we were called upon to abandon ship. There was no running water; we had to pop our heads out of our curtain and ask one of the crew to bring us a large jug. There never seemed to be any shortage of men out there. A very formidable group would be talking fiercely, all in full regalia, which consisted of white full-length robes called *galibiyeh*, worn over baggy white trousers. Tucked into their trousers at the waist could be seen a mean handle of a scabbard, as I called it (a curved knife). Although they always looked furious and very frightening to us, they were, at all times, polite and respectful. Our captain was an unmarried Welshman and the dining stewards were Sudanese. Our delightful one was called 'Joe' who always favoured me with an orange and any titbits he could find.

The young men were a great asset, showering us with attention and teasing. My special friend was a young Irishman by the name of Tommy Barer. I hope he survived the war with no further sinkings as he was full of Irish charm and good looks.

Much to the delight of my new friends, I would receive frequent requests to join the captain for tea. He would always present me with the leftover cake or cookies, which I in turn would give to them. To my amazement, before we docked in Liverpool, he asked if I would consider leaving my husband and sailing with him! Oh, what a dreamer he was! Mort was highly amused. Dear Joe, with his Sidney Poitier good looks, asked me to have dinner with him that night in Liverpool. Both offers were graciously refused and I caught the first possible train to London.

It is so very sad that I neglected to ask my mother to keep my letters as they were such interesting times that we all lived in during the war and naturally I recall a lot of things, but certainly most is swallowed up in the years gone by. So, I will rack my brains.

Our time together after my arrival from Canada was only about four days before Mort had to report back to his ship, which was based in Plymouth. When he left me I went to Reigate to stay with Sonia and her wonderful parents, Thelma and Graham Reid. There I stayed until I received orders to report to the WRNS, with an open invitation to spend any time I ever wanted with the Reids at Yewtye. A home away from home is what they gave us and we loved them all and were so grateful to them.

So, off to Plymouth I went and checked in to the Grand Hotel where Mort and I made our HQ. Fortunately his ship was in when I arrived so we had more time together. The morning after my arrival I had my interview, which was made very pleasant by the warmth and friendliness of Superintendent Welby, as she put me at ease immediately. I had no training to offer except with boats and asked if I could possibly be a Boat Wren. No such luck and I quote, 'No, you are not going to be wasted as a Boater, I need you in Regulating.' I had no idea what that meant but it was looking after the Wrens. I was told to report to the Moorfield Training Establishment in two days time when I would undergo two weeks basic training. A very large house had been taken over for this purpose, with accommodation in Moorfield, where I was to be, and several other houses nearby were also for trainees.

Owing to my advanced seniority of twenty-three years and married, I was given the lower berth of a triple decker in a cabin for six. It was a lot more Spartan than boarding school. My cabin mates couldn't have been nicer and made me feel most welcome. We were issued a cotton smock to wear for the ensuing two weeks for our basic training, to consist of lectures and squad drill, early to bed and early to rise. I blotted my copybook in no uncertain way a few days after I arrived. We were all allocated a bath time and while I was watching the water pouring into the bathtub, there was a loud knock on the door and a commanding voice saying, 'Duffus, Duffus, may I come in please?' Entered one Wren officer bearing a vase of flowers that obviously needed water. All of a sudden she caught sight of my bath and she shouted, 'The Plimsoll, the Plimsoll!!' I hadn't a clue what she was talking about. Obviously she had a very stupid trainee on her hands, so she fled to the taps and turned them off, pointed to the dark blue line on the bath and said, 'That is the Plimsoll line. No water is drawn past that line!!' and swept out. The ignorant Canadian fully enjoyed her last well-filled bath!

After we had completed our basic training and had passed our so-called exams, we were all transported to the Devonport Barracks where we were issued our uniforms. If they had been the latest models from Vogue we couldn't have felt more proud or

Mort on leave in Reigate.

happier. Shoes were to be my bug-bear for the rest of my days as I have long narrow feet and the Admiralty didn't think such things existed. If only they had been right.

We were then called, one by one, to see Second Officer Ann Hodge who gave us our appointments. Mine was to remain in Moorfield, on staff to train incoming trainees. Also, I would become a Leading Wren to give me the authority I would need. I was very pleased because Mort was based in Plymouth so this meant we would see each other often and I could request a 'sleeping-out pass' when he was in port.

No sooner had I been told this news than I was called to the telephone. It was Mort telling me to apply for seventeen days leave as of the next day, as that was what he had due to the Dieppe raid. I couldn't believe what I was hearing. He went on to say, 'Johnnie, I am not going to enjoy this leave without you. Please apply for leave!' I went back to my cabin, collapsed on my bunk and told my friends the predicament that I was in. They agreed that if only I had waited to join up for only two more weeks, I would have had no problems. About fifteen minutes later I was told 2/O Hodge wished to see me at once. My remark was, 'What do you suppose I have done wrong now?' After being asked to sit down I was asked why I hadn't requested leave to be with my husband. When I voiced my astonishment that she knew of my quandary, she told me there was a wonderful system called 'The Grape Vine' and that I was excused from duty the next morning and that she had made an appointment for me to see Mrs Welby, or 'Super', as she was nicknamed. I was then told that I was granted seventeen days leave automatically, but that if for any reason my husband was to have any extra days, I had only to send her a signal and the extra time would also be granted. I am sure my mouth dropped in amazement. When I thanked her profusely, she told me that our men come first in the Navy.

When Mort called to hear the good news we arranged to meet, and off to Torquay and the Imperial Hotel we went. What a start for such a squeaky new uniform! On the way there, Mort told me about the severe damage that was done to *Brocklesby*. They had gone aground with shore batteries opening at point blank range. They tried in vain many times to get her off the sand and finally, in spite of the severe damage that she suffered, they were freed.

Mort was filled with admiration for Nigel Pumphrey who was his captain. From all I heard about him, before I was privileged to meet him, he was completely fearless and was awarded the bar to his DSO, which was to be his second such honour. On their return they had saved the lives of a great number of Canadians by hauling them out of the sea and treating them royally on their return to England, which I doubt they thought they would see again.

As I have skipped ahead a bit, I must also mention that Alan Miller, Lieutenant RNVR, who served as First Lieutenant in the *Brocklesby*, was also commended, with their Chief Engineer, Lt. (E) Albert Lee RN, both receiving the DSC.

Now back to the Imperial Hotel. We had a fabulous holiday. There was a good dance band which we enjoyed every evening, as we were never happier than when we were dancing. Our rooms were a far cry from Moorfield. Alan Miller and his lovely wife Kirsteen were staying there also. During the day we took bus trips to nearby towns and villages and walked our legs off. We walked so far one day that I got terrible blisters on my heels, finally finding them so painful I took off my shoes and caught the bus back to Torquay in my socks. I was not in uniform, fortunately, or my blisters would have been far worse.

All good things come to an end, as did our seventeen wonderful days, and back to Plymouth we went, Mort to 'The Brock' and me to Moorfield. Unknown to me, I was in a rapid promotion category, Leading Wren for six weeks and then to Petty Officer. The latter had a few perks. I shared a private dining room with another Petty Officer by the name of Jackman. She was a bit forbidding at first but she taught me a lot and we grew fond of each other. We were well looked after by a young Wren steward and our meals were beautifully served. I graduated to a cabin by myself, which was very pleasant. 2/O Hodge had her cabin down the hall and as my door was open until I went to bed, she would very often stop by and we would sit and talk. Mrs Duffus used to send me Welch's chocolates which we both enjoyed. We became very close friends in the years to come. She eventually married a delightful doctor by the name of Kirk Forsythe.

Mort was able to introduce me to many Wrens in Plymouth,

namely Margaret Jeffries, who was a P/O Boater, and Cynthia Ratcliffe, a smashing redhead who caught every eye in her bellbottoms and sailor cap. She is now living in Washington and is now Helm. Her portrait hangs in the National Gallery. When Doug Brown, from Vancouver, asked me to get him a date, I produced Cynthia and he was delighted. Another very attractive Wren was Barbara Hatton. In Moorfield, my great friend was Margaret Edney.

As I had to teach about forty trainees throughout their two-week period, I had to perfect commanding a squad on the parade ground. Except when a young tomboy when I could yell as loud as the boys, I was obviously not producing enough volume to satisfy Third Officer Spence. I was sent to the farthest point away from my squad and told to put them through their paces. It's amazing how you can throw your voice if it's a case of do or die. As my confidence grew I would take my squad out onto Mannamead Road and send them marching while I remained stationary. In Canada we would say it was a block before I would give them the command to 'about turn'. They were all highly amused and admitted, with much laughter, that they wondered where they would end up as they didn't expect to be able to hear me. In the three months that I trained Wrens I never met one that I didn't like.

By this time, Mort had become First Lieutenant, or No 1, which was quite a feat from his humble beginnings in the Yachtsmen's Group, to being second in command in the Royal Navy Hunt Class Destroyer. I was very proud of him. He sailed off to Rosyth when I was in Greenwich attending my OTC at the Naval College. This was to be a very special experience. There were about twenty-four of us in my class. We attended lectures all day with very demanding squad drills by a Marine. We slept in our beautiful building and walked to the Painted Hall for our meals.

The tables were a treat to look at, with white linen tablecloths, beautifully set with silver place settings. The menu was held in little silver stands. We decided that the Navy looked after the Navy very well, as the meals were absolutely outstanding. The Wren stewards stood behind us in their starched white uniforms, and white gloves, with one hand behind their backs. Our table napkins were kept in a numbered silver ring. Mine was thirty-five. The Wren in charge of the pigeon hole where the napkins were kept had only to be told your name once and from then on when she saw you coming, she drew out your napkin ring and handed it to you. Very impressive!! The hall itself was very spacious. I have no idea how many Naval men and women could dine there. The staff tables were raised as if on a stage. There were silver candelabra on all the tables everywhere. When one became accustomed to the grandeur, you had but to look up to the ceiling, which was a painted masterpiece that Michaelangelo would have approved of.

Squad drill was masterminded by the Royal Marines and we were well taught and drilled to perfection. I loved every single minute of it.

While I was at Greenwich I had one long weekend with Mort. I took the night train and met him in Edinburgh where he had come in from Rosyth prior to leaving for the Med. It was all too short a time for greeting and farewells once more, which was the story of our lives, it seemed. When we caught up with all the news, Mort said that he had tried to book a reservation in the Grill as they advertised a dinner dance. To his bitter disappointment he was told every table was taken. I told him maître d's have a soft spot for the ladies, so took off to try my wiles. To his delight I related my appeal, saying we were Canadians who had had very little time together and were about to be separated again for many months. Was there any possible way that he could squeeze in one more table, to which he had told me, yes, he would put a table on the dance floor. Never let it be said that Mort wasn't impressed.

We dined and danced our legs off. Next day we walked miles and talked a blue streak, knowing there were only to be letters ahead of us. We finally ended up in a very nice shop for tea on Princes Street. To our surprise the waitress placed a pre-war array of tea cakes cozied on a three-tiered stand. When the poor girl arrived back at our table with the bill she literally gasped as she whispered, 'Did you eat all those?' Mort said, 'Obviously we shouldn't have, but you didn't warn us.' With a glowering look she snapped, 'It's the honour system, one each!!' We hurriedly left the poor waitress, saying how sorry we were to be so ignorant. We were also sorry neither of us had Canadian patches.

We then went to Rosyth to see the *Brocklesby* and to wish all those very special men 'farewell'. As we were walking along the jetty we were passing other destroyers and Mort said, 'Prince Philip is serving in her.' I was duly impressed as there were few young females at that time that were not besotted.

And so it was yet another sad farewell.

Back to Greenwich with one more treat in store for me before my appointment – my adopted uncle, Jock MacLean.

He had moved from Peterborough, Ontario to Vancouver after he returned from the first war – about five years after my parents were married. He adored children and Bill and I adopted him as our uncle. He had served with the engineers and became a full major at quite a young age.

While on the subject of Jock, there are so many, many memories that I treasure of him that I must share some of them. When I was quite young I would be playing with our dog and creep by his shoes countless times to undo his laces, and he would always rise to the occasion, saying, 'Isn't it strange, I was sure I had done my laces up this morning.' Or, 'I really will have to buy

Brig. A.T. MacLean: our adopted Uncle Jock.

some new laces, these just will not stay done up.' I would have to
laugh but would pretend it was our dog 'Boots' who had done it.
Skin the rabbit was great fun for Bill and me and I'm sure poor
Jock must have been worn out flipping us through the air time
and again, as children never have enough of what they like.

It was my firm belief that I would grow up one day and that I
would marry my dear uncle. He looked totally devastated when I
told him I had decided I would not marry him because he would
be too old to look after all the babies.

So back to Greenwich, where I received a call from London,
from Brigadier A.T. MacLean, asking me if I would be able to
meet him for dinner at the Dorchester. Would I! With a late pass
until twelve on our one free evening a week, I walked into the

hotel at 7:00 to be greeted with a bear hug. I wondered afterwards if any others dining that night thought it amusing as we were so happy and obviously enjoyed each other. He never let me forget that I had wet the bed when we were at our family cottage in the North Arm and I had insisted on sleeping in his bed. We came down to earth with a terrible bang when Cinderella glanced at her watch! Time had vanished. We literally fled, with Jock telling the maître d' that he would return to settle the bill. A taxi was hailed with a very handsome tip for the driver to try and return the young lady to the College before twelve. Driving at high speed in the blackout could only have been done so masterfully by a London cabbie. We got there. It did amuse me to think of that 'old married gal of twenty-four' playing the role of a Cinderella. I never knew how he did it, but I checked in exactly one minute before my bewitching hour was up.

I was asked if I would take another Canadian under my wing and be of any help to her that she might need. This person was to be the future director of the Canadian Wrens, Adelaide Sinclair, who had been sent over to the UK to learn as much as she could and to have two of the WRNS officers travel to Canada to assist her in forming the WRCNS.

With our exams behind us, we waited to learn our fate. Pass? Fail? If pass, then where to?

The director of WRNS, Vera Laughton Mathews, and three other Wren officers, sat on our board. We were called into the office one after the other, told we were now Third Officers and I was asked what type of place would I be happiest in, which came as a surprise. I told them that as my husband was serving in the Med., I really didn't mind where I went but that I liked people and would enjoy a large establishment. This obviously met with their approval. I was then asked to wait outside and told that they would send for me. My appointment was to be the Quarters

Officer in charge of Wrens in Ugadale Arms Hotel at the Royal Naval Air Station in HMS *Landrail*, Machrihanish, Argyll, Scotland. Four of us from our class were appointed to *Landrail*, to different departments of the station. We said our goodbyes to all our new friends and our instructors who had plied us with so much knowledge that had little or no help for my future, such as navigation. We trained to Glasgow and by coach and boat we arrived. I was met by Mary Gow, whom I was to replace. We were to have a three-day turnover and she really did put herself out to take me to as many places on the main station as we could cover on foot, introducing me to everyone we met. I should explain that my position as Quarters Officer at the Ugadale Arms Hotel was about three miles away from the main station. I had over three hundred Wrens and twenty-two Wren officers living there. I had a staff of twenty-eight, consisting of a Regulating Petty Officer and Leading Wren and Wren in the office, who were a never-ending source of help and support for me in all the days and months to come. There was a very competent team of cooks and stewards who looked after the Wrens and the Ward Room and kept our quarters spotlessly clean. Stokers kept the boilers steaming and were quartered at the far end of the hotel with about five radar lads. I always hoped they stayed there.

The Ugadale officers and ratings that worked at the main station were taken by transport at various times throughout the day. There always seemed to be one at the door when we were to go over to a dance in the gymnasium, which as I recall was twice a week. We had an excellent band made up from the thousands of men that were there on the station. I was quite isolated from the busy part of that world of ours, but I loved it, as apparently we all did. It was so quiet and restful – and a happy place.

We were situated seven miles of palm trees away from Campbeltown, which was a submarine base. The climate was

HMS Landrail, *Machrihanish, Argyll (3rd right, back row).*

wonderful owing to the west coast being favoured by the Gulf
Stream. The Fleet Air Arm Station was built on nine holes of a
once-popular eighteen-hole golf course that Ugadale was built for,
as we looked out over the first tee. I don't believe I ever wore my
great-coat as I never seemed to feel cold. The wind could be really
strong at times, so much so that it would send balls of foam that
had been whipped up from the breakers flying through the air, to
land with a resounding smack against our windows. They were
always streaked with salt.

Having grown up beside the ocean, I loved it. One very windy
day, I picked up a sou'wester, oilskin coat and pants from our gym
instructor, who had told me I could borrow his if I enjoyed
getting out in that kind of weather. I think I swallowed more salt
than I would normally eat in a week, but I had a wonderful time;
my only problem was trying to stay on my feet.

Once a week, or whenever the Commander and Paymaster
Commander got bored with their lives (I thought), they would

Nora Carey & Johnnie, Machrihanish, Argyll.

phone over to say they would love a 'cuppa' after Pay did rounds. The latter was a complete tour of my quarters, poking his cane into every nook and cranny, hoping to unearth something that shouldn't have been there. I don't think he was quite used to my total disregard for his elevated rank, as it wasn't long before I told him he reminded me of Captain Bligh. He slightly resembled Charles Laughton. We became great friends and played golf together and danced very compatibly. He was a frightful tease, making fun of my Canadian accent with emphasis on the rrrrrr's.

One day the Commander phoned to ask me to arrange a luncheon for the captain to honour three Sea Lords who were to be the guests of the station. There would be ten of us altogether. My number one cook, Wren Peacock, and I planned the menu. My wonderful Anne Fitch arranged the table and I took off to the

Winifred Hawkesworth, Machrihanish.

golf course to pick wild flowers. I am sure nobody will ever believe me but there were seventeen different species of every colour. I picked them in batches of one colour, finally returning to dampen them thoroughly, then took off to call on a house that had a stream running through the grounds that I would pass on my way up to the Moors to buy our eggs from the Shepherds. I had no idea who lived in the house but was ushered in by a pretty maid and informed that her mistress would see me. I introduced myself and instantly liked the person I wanted a favour from. I explained that I had noticed she had banks of thick moss gracing her stream and could I please take a piece of it large enough to cover a long platter, which I would fill with wild flowers for our very special guests. This was instantly granted, followed by an invitation to remain for tea. I had to refuse, as the flowers had to be arranged. I have often wished I could have had a picture of the finished centrepiece, as it really was lovely. Each colour was grouped together against the dark green moss, which stood out against the white tablecloth. It was, to my delight and surprise, admired by the 'top brass'. It had been a painstaking effort, separating flowers into bundles of white, pink, purple, yellow, mauve, all the blues, and everything in between.

The next major spree from the norm was to put on a breakfast party to be held on the beach at the home of the Duke and Duchess of Argyll. This was to honour Captain Nelson Lay(e?) RCN (Canadian) who was coming to us on a learning mission prior to taking over the command of HMCS *Nabob*. With a large basket, I was able to acquire the dozens of eggs required and Pay produced the rest of an excellent breakfast for about thirty of us. The reason eggs were in such availability during such strict rationing, was that the great distance the eggs had to travel made it impossible to transport them. I paid five shillings a dozen for them, and had a wonderful walk, with an excellent view of Jura and Islay, the two islands that Machrihanish faced. Also, to my delight, I could see Northern Ireland, the birthplace of my Grandfather Irwin.

A never-to-be-forgotten memory I also have of that day was to step off our transport in the large driveway and to walk at least one hundred yards on newly-mowed, weedless grass, between a forsythia hedge in full bloom that was at least five feet wide on either side of us. I am tall, but standing on tiptoe I could not touch the top of that magnificent hedge. The Gulf Stream does wonders for that part of Scotland.

The friends I made in Machrihanish I have enjoyed for fifty-seven years. When in London, I visit my great friend Margot Redford, who now lives in Oxted. She was in Admin. and worked in the office on the station under First Officer Lorna Strath, but lived in Ugadale. I spent one leave with Margot, or Mag, as I called her. More about that later. We had two visits from her in Vancouver and at our summer cottage. All our family loved her. I

*Lieut. (A) Harry Housser RCNVR, a very good
friend from Vancouver flew in with his Squadron.*

have twice stayed with Paddy (Ailsa) Massey Stewart and her dear
Ian, when he was alive, in Campbeltown. They gave us the
pleasure of entertaining them many years ago. Winifred (Winkie)
Hawkesworth Simpson, I visited in Hillsborough, Northern
Ireland a few years ago, which was a non-stop talk, wonderful
visit. Two other great friends with whom I spent three great days
in Bath were Nora and John Malloy. They met in Machrihanish.
He was a Sub-Lieutenant, and she a Third Officer. John spent
many years as Mayor of Bath.

We have had several reunions with our close-knit group of
Wren officers from Mach., which took place in London. Unfor-
tunately I don't recall the married names but they were Cynthia
Hebron, Elizabeth Briggs, Doreen Pitman, Paddy, Winkie, Margot

A pencil portrait as a gift from a Radar rating
quartered in the far end of my Wren quarters.

and Teddy Taylor. Many of our friends lived too far away to join
us.

The war took a heavy toll on the young flyers and the day we
heard Graham Reid, from New Zealand, had been killed, there
wasn't a dry eye. He had lost his brother and never expected to
survive himself. When Mort and I were in New Zealand, I did my
utmost to locate his parents to tell them how terribly fond we all
were of that charming, delightful, young chap. Reg Holdsworth
was dreadfully, badly burned when his aircraft 'pranged' in a field
near our station. He asked to see me and when the Senior Medical
Officer called to tell me, he warned me I would be very shocked
at the sight I was to have of this handsome young lad. I was
grateful for his warning. His entire head and face were swathed in

bandages, with small slits for his eyes, two little holes for his nose and a hole for his mouth. He told me his Mae West saved him from body burns he would have had inflicted and please would I light a cigarette and hold it to his mouth for him. No tears or complaints – just sheer guts. I hope he was able to come out of all the skin grafts he had ahead of him with his face even partially like it was. They were all such wonderful young men to whom we became devoted.

Whenever a squadron flew in, of which there were many, they would fly over Ugadale to land. There would be a gunning of their motors to announce their arrival. About half an hour later the phone would ring with an invitation to join them in their wardroom to attend a cocktail party. Life was never dull. We worked hard and had lots of fun.

My friend Margot was on leave near Manchester and before she departed she invited me to try and arrange to pick up a flight with one of our aircraft and spend the weekend with her. We could apply to Commander Flying to see if it would be possible to fit in flights with our leaves. This I did, and was told Lieut. Commander Flying was going south as it happened and he would be pleased to drop me off at Ringle Airport. With leave granted I was on the spot at the right time. To my delight it was a two-seater and I settled myself behind a first-class pilot, so I had been told. We were alongside one of the hangars that looked as if it was being propped up by sailors – they seemed to be everywhere, many of them giving us the V for victory sign. I was at a loss to know what it all meant as it certainly had to mean something. With a 'thumbs up' for my benefit, we taxied off to a resounding cheer from our entertaining audience. It was a beautiful day, we were low enough to really clearly see what was below and I relaxed and enjoyed the flight. Ringle was pointed out to me as we circled a few times while waiting for permission to land. Finally, down we went to approach the landing strip and crunch, crunch and up we went. This happened too many times for comfort as it dawned on me that he couldn't get the landing gear to go down. Finally, plop, and we cruised in to land. Profuse apologies followed, saying how terribly sorry he was to have no doubt frightened the life out of me. I finally asked why we had had such an amusing send-off. He said the sailors had been working on her for weeks trying to put her into shape as she was going to be junked – those lads were just wishing us well. As I was safely on the ground, I laughed and thanked him profusely. I had a great weekend and took other means of transportation on my return.

After I had been at Mach. for about fifteen months, a letter arrived from Mort from the Med., saying he had been given two months Foreign Service leave to return to Canada and that he wouldn't go home without me. My feelings were very mixed; excited at the thought of being together again and great sadness at the thought of leaving all my wonderful friends and my fabulous career in the Wrens. I was given an approximate date to meet Mort in London. I applied for leave and a request to see the Director. I had to remain until my relief arrived and after a few days turnover to her, a signal arrived telling me Mort was waiting for me at the Savoy. There were many sad farewells and a promise from my exceptional Wardroom Attendant, Anne Fitch, who had looked after my every need for so long, who said she would seriously consider going to Canada at the end of the war to work for us. I felt very sad when my 'D' day arrived.

I went straight to the Savoy, having signalled my ETA to Mort. The receptionist gave me our room number and promised not to phone that I was on my way up. I can still sense the excitement I felt walking down the hall and knocking on the door; fourteen months was a long separation, always wondering if I really would ever see him again. He looked absolutely fabulous, a lot thinner

The day before my sad departure from Ugadale and all my friends in the Fleet Air Arm. Paddy Massey, Johnnie, Cynthia Hebron and Margot Redford.

with an excellent tan. When we finally settled down he showed me the huge accumulation of ingredients from his parcels that had been held in the GPO (General Post Office) as they couldn't send them out to his ship. Tins of peaches, crab, lobster, butter, bacon, boxes of chocolates, such things as neither of us had even thought of, much less eaten. At our request, the chef on duty came up to see us and his eyes nearly popped out of their sockets. I had brought a dozen eggs from my shepherds' wives and bottles of gin and whisky as gifts for Mort. The chef said he would be delighted to look after breakfasts and lunches, which he did, to our mouth-watering enjoyment. There was an air-raid that night but nothing was dropped close to us, just lots of Ack-Ack noise and a constant play of searchlights in our blacked out room. This was a new experience for me as we never had one warning in Mach., Plymouth, Greenwich or Rosyth when I was there, although Plymouth had been through devastating raids before I arrived.

Next day I reported to the Wrens Headquarters as previously arranged. The rather frightening officer who saw me said that I was badly needed but that they wouldn't detain me if I must go with my husband. As Mort had served for three years without a proper leave I couldn't possibly deprive him of seeing his mother in Vancouver. So my discharge was granted and tears splashed down my face all the way to the Savoy. We were told it would be anything up to twelve days that we would have to wait for a ship but to be prepared to leave when we were notified. We were on call for eleven of our twelve days before we finally received our sailing orders. My third safe crossing it was to be and a restful change for Mort to be at sea without any responsibility.

When we landed in Montreal he said there was one thing he had to do; he had to satisfy the craving he had had for three years, so we ended up on high stools in an ice-cream parlour. The girl that served him couldn't believe her ears when she took his order! Why he wasn't as sick as a dog I will never know.

After a few days with Mort's sister Emily and their little girl, Judie, we boarded the train for Vancouver. There was nothing we enjoyed more than our CPR trains in those days. We were pampered by the porters, and served the most delectable meals by the stewards who always seemed to enjoy you and their work. We played rummy, honeymoon bridge, double solitaire, and as we always played for favours I am sure he never collected half I must have owed him. I used to tell him he had to have been born with a pack of cards in his hands, whereas I was born with my thumb in my mouth, so my mother told me. It was wonderful to see our families again and our friends, who all spoiled us with welcome home parties. A mild form of rationing existed but after the UK it was almost non-existent. The lack of alcohol seemed to cause a few moans and groans but I can't recall any other problems. Many of our close friends were overseas in the forces or lost to the war. We found a dear little apartment in the West End which we were hardly ever in, but at least it was ours.

Time flew as it always does when you least want it to. And hope as I did that he would be based in Newfie or Halifax, it was not to be. When the dreaded signal arrived, he was to return to the UK in command of a Castle Class corvette, HMCS *Bowmanville*. It was quite a feat to have achieved such a promotion and I was, indeed, very proud of him.

One more goodbye was in order as there was absolutely no way that I was going to be allowed to return with him. To put it mildly, I was miserable. I simply could not sit out the war in Vancouver, so I applied to the WRCNS and was accepted, without my seniority, but I could retain my Commission. I was to report to Ottawa to do a Canadian OTC. I thought it somewhat ludicrous, as I was senior in service time to every Wren in the country. Prior to reporting, I was able to stay with my beloved cousin Anne Somerville, in Waterloo, for a few days, which I thoroughly enjoyed. It wasn't long after that she joined the Wrens as a driver in Motor Transport.

I was terribly fortunate with the group of Wrens I was to be with in Ottawa. Roma Dodds, Sheila Mappin and Athol Hughes were just my cup of tea. Right up to the present, I have kept up a great friendship with Roma. I still think of the others with great fondness, as they too were delightful.

Unlike Greenwich, we were in a huge old house on Daly Avenue and other than the intense heat and humidity, there isn't very much I remember. Summer uniforms helped. On the day that we had our 'Passing Out Parade', it was hotter than Hades when we marched on bubbling tar. For a person who never

WRCNS summer uniform (taken by Roma Dodds).

perspired, my sleeves shrank over an inch in my new uniform. Mr and Mrs Jackson Dodds very kindly invited me to spend my last few days in Ottawa before departing for Gault, Ontario, to become a Divisional Officer in HMCS *Connestoga*, Training Establishment. Roma's parents were charming and their house very special indeed. Mr Dodds was to do me a big favour the following year. I was also able to spend a few days with Barbara Kaye and her three children at Kingsmere, where they had rented a house on the lake for the summer. I have since learned that Peter, her husband, was on some kind of hush-hush work for the government. The Prime Minister also had a summer residence on the lake.

Connestoga was interesting. There were about six divisions of about thirty Wrens in each. Each officer had a Leading Wren to

John and Bill.

assist her and mine was a very pretty, intelligent and extremely nice person by the name of Johnson, and we got along famously. What I didn't know, she did. Some things were quite new to me, one of which was raising the White Ensign in the morning and lowering it at sundown. Captain Isabel MacNeil was the officer in charge and I had met her in her early days in the Canadian Navy when she was sent to the UK to see how things were done over there. It so happened she was sent up to Machrihanish and I was not overly impressed with her at the time. I found her a bit formidable at first, but soon found I was wrong. I thought she was mannish in her ways, there again to be proved wrong.

At the end of our six weeks we were given our appointments. Mine was to report to HMCS *Kings*, Halifax, as Unit Officer in charge of the Wrens. I was absolutely thrilled as it was a real plum of an appointment. This was later explained to me when I was told that 'Ma-am' wished to see me in her cabin. To my surprise she was out of uniform and feminine. She asked me to sit down and proceeded to tell me I would be the only Wren Officer and would share the Naval Officers' Ward Room with thirty-five of them in Kings College, which had been turned into a Sub Lieutenants' training establishment. I would live in a separate building with my Regulating Petty Officer and Leading Wren, and about one hundred and twenty Wrens who, apart from the Captain's Wren Writers, would mostly be cooks and stewards. She went on to tell me that, as Mort used to say, a considerable amount of 'hanky panky' was going on down there, so this old lady of twenty-six was told to go down and clean it up.

The officer I replaced had been lax, indubitably, but it wasn't long before I felt I had the respect of my Wrens and Ward Room. My Petty Officer Swift and Leading Wren Lewis were great supports, each with a good sense of humour when a good laugh helped with some situations, one of which I remember most clearly. A Wren, who shall remain nameless, was frequently being brought before me for her behaviour with the sailors. This particular time she was discovered in the stoke-hole, of all places, having sex. After the charge had been read I said, 'Quite honestly, Wren so and so, I don't know what to do about you!' To this, with an angelic look on her face, she responded, 'I'm sorry, Ma'm, the trouble is, I like it.'

Whenever there was a serious charge the Wrens were dealt with by the Commanding Officer who was an unusual man by the name of Ben Sivertz, who fortunately I got along with very well. Two of my Wrens went 'absent without leave'. This caused their dismissal from the service, a situation I was thankful to have been spared in Britain. In front of all their friends, they were court-martialled and their caps removed and the Tilley-band cut off. It was my worst day by far of my three years in the service.

Aboard HMCS Oriole, *Lake Ontario.*

Without any competition I was very spoiled with a convoy to dances, much teasing and loads of fun and friendships that were to last all my life.

It was always a hope that Mort's convoy duties would bring him into Halifax as he was escorting convoys to Canada from Britain. I forget how I learned he would be in St John's, Newfie, for three days and to get leave and meet him there but fortunately there always seemed to be a way of secretly finding out these things. Away I went, pronto, allowing travel time to fit in with his three days. Famous last thought. I got as far as Sydney, NS, by air, when fog socked in to ceiling zero. I checked into a hotel to sit it out. A Naval Officer was also questioning the desk and after meeting there at the same time with the same questions – the weather – we joined forces and had our meals together. He was

With my Wrens at HMCS Kings.

returning to St John, or Newfie John, as it was affectionately called, on leave and his family were expecting him. He was a thoroughly nice person and we shared our frustration. The next day he suggested we should apply for permission to cross the Cabot Strait by boat and take the train to St John, neither of which journeys would ever have been by choice. Many a ship had been sunk in the strait and the train was called 'The Milk Run' and would take forever.

So – away we went. When we were soon to be drawing into Gander station, Reg said we might just be lucky enough to pick up a flight at the Air Force Base. His plan was to leave me with our luggage while he would jump off the train to make inquiries. If we had a chance of a flight he would give me the high-sign to pick up our two bags and get off the train as fast as possible. I finally got the go signal and joined him. With several Air Force types, we were driven in a jeep to the RCAF Officers' Mess and told where we were to wait. It was in an enormous area filled with uniforms from all the services. We could only hope they didn't all want our destination. After what seemed an endless wait, as only time can crawl when you least want it to, an agile young Air Force lad leaped up on a table, called for silence and said, 'The fog is starting to sock in, so there can be only one flight out and that is to St John.' Our luck was in – we were included.

Looking back over the years I do seem to have had some rare flights and this one was no exception. I neglected to say that this all took place a few weeks before Christmas and it was COLD. There were no seats, only a steel-ridged deck to that aircraft and we were huddled together like sardines in a tin. At least they don't feel the cold. I have no idea what altitude we were enduring without any heat, but it was freezing! At long last we touched down, for which we all cheered our gratitude. We climbed into a taxi and I was given no option but to go with Reg to his family and he would track down Mort for me. His mother was charming. I was looked after like a child, and instructed to follow their maid who would take me upstairs and run a hot bath for me. As I started up the stairs, Reg handed me a goodly measure of whisky, with strict instructions to drink it and he hoped to have good news for me when I came down. I have always abhorred scotch whisky but it did warm me through and through. When I had thawed out in that heaven-sent bath, I changed my shirt and dressed back into my uniform and felt like a million. Mort had left a message at the hotel that, if by any chance his wife telephoned or appeared on the horizon, to have her get to such and such an address where he was attending an oyster party. In all my excitement, I hope my good manners, in some way, convinced mother and son how deeply grateful I was for their great kindness to me. I have often thought of those four days and how indebted I was to Reg, as I would never have made it to Newfie without his ingenious organisation.

Since writing about this experience, I have unearthed a signal that was in with some of Mort's memorabilia, saying 'Johnnie will arrive in St John, Saturday P.M.' It was signed W. G. Ross. His name was not Reg, as I thought, and I have no idea what the initials stand for. I have tried to trace him through Jenny Akhurst, who came to Vancouver after she married into our large family, but no luck.

Had I been one day later, Mort would have sailed, as he was to report to his ship at 5:00 a.m. next morning. As a crowning touch to this heartbreaking get-together, I was struck with oyster poisoning. Was I sick! Our farewell was goodbye through the bathroom door. It took me quite a few years to face another oyster. My trip back to Halifax was quite uneventful.

Through our correspondence we agreed that we should adopt a baby as I had had the devil's own luck achieving success in this field. We felt the war was surely to be over fairly soon. I had a very good contact in the Children's Aid Society, with an exceptionally nice social worker. We had a lengthy conversation on the telephone to fill her in on my history and I asked her to keep us in mind. About a month later, Mort steamed into Halifax, which was almost too good to be true. As we were walking down Barrington Street, Mort noticed that we were just below the office of the Children's Aid Society and suggested we drop in and introduce ourselves to the person I had made friends with. This we did. As we entered the large office, on our left behind a huge plate glass window, a social worker was on the telephone and when she saw us waved her hand for us to sit down, which we did. When we were beckoned into her office she said, 'You must be the Duffuses. You aren't going to believe this, I had my hand on the

Decommissioning Ceremony HMCS Kings, *Halifax, 1945.*

phone to call you when my phone rang and that is the call from which I just hung up.' She handed us each a history of the parents of a baby that was to be born three months hence. We both agreed, without a moment's hesitation, that we would indeed be very happy to be registered as the future parents.

My first duty was to apply to the Director of Wrens to release me when our baby arrived. This request was approved. When the time came, it so happened that the Director was in Halifax and had come to have lunch in *Kings*. She was freshening up in my cabin when the phone rang with, 'Mrs Duffus, you and your husband are the parents of a seven pound baby daughter.' The thrill of that moment will live with me forever, and it happened to be 'Mother's Day'.

It was common knowledge in the Ward Room that I hoped to hear news of our baby any day so when the two of us crossed the parade ground to go up to the Ward Room, where we always met

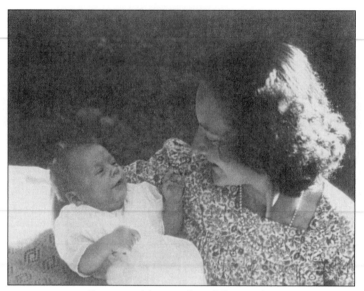

Susan and her mother, 2¹/₂ months.

before our sojourn up the hill to Dalhousie for our meals, we walked in and in a loud voice I said, 'Have a drink on me everyone, I have just had a baby daughter.' How I wished Mort had been there as they all toasted our Susan. All glasses were raised in a heartwarming toast to the oblivious babe. A signal was sent off to Mort, followed very quickly with one back to me, saying they had spliced the main-brace to celebrate the momentous occasion. Telegrams flew back and forth to our parents. Leave was granted to me and I was able to catch a flight to see our baby. A picture was taken of me proudly holding our little Susan. Fortunately she was very well cared for and I had only to apply for my immediate discharge and make my plans.

There is no way I can adequately express the excitement of VE Day, 8 May 1945. We were all delirious with happiness, added to which we were told HMCS *Kings* was to be the first ship to be decommissioned, as we were a training establishment for Sub

Lieutenants and they would no longer be required. By this time we must have resembled Cheshire cats, as we all wore a perpetual grin our faces, from ear to ear.

With unbelievable alacrity our plans were drawn up for our final parade and lowering of the White Ensign and office work finalised. Meanwhile, by this time, Susan was safe and sound in Halifax. Thanks to Marj McRae and other naval wives with whom she shared a huge house, Susan was being very well looked after. When I could be spared from *Kings*, I escaped to be with her, if only for an hour or two. I was so grateful to those mothers, who seemed to think nothing of one more baby to look after. They really were wonderful. As I had been given permission to be discharged in Vancouver, it was looking too good to be true – which it was.

The captain sent for me, so I hurried up to his office. When I entered he asked me to sit down. He then handed me a signal which he had just received, which read, and I quote: 'Sub Lieut. Mary Duffus is re-appointed to HMCS *Peregrin* (temp) as Unit Officer in Charge of Wrens.' To say I was stunned would be a gross understatement as I was one step from being on my way. Before I could speak he said, 'I have never received this signal,' and dropped it in the waste basket, adding, 'Go, and go with all my good wishes to you and your baby, and God bless you both.' I could have hugged him! Over the years we kept in touch with each other and spent several hours together the year before he died. I hope he finished the book he was writing.

That was my last day in uniform. When I had packed and said goodbye to all my Wrens and Ward Room friends who had been so good to me, I took a taxi to pick up Susan and all her equipment, and we checked into the Lord Nelson Hotel. I had only been able to obtain a compartment on the train, which was going to be a nightmare with a small baby. I took a chance and called Jackson Dodds, Roma's father. If anyone could produce a miracle I felt he was the person to talk to. When I explained my predicament he said he should be able to call me back within half an hour. True to his word, back came the operator to say there was a long-distance call from Mr Jackson Dodds. 'Johnnie, they are putting on another car and you have a drawing room all the way to Vancouver.' Instead of looking forward to a ghastly trip home, I was able to enjoy the whole experience, thanks to that wonderful father.

Our night in the hotel for the two of us was without incident and I realised what a little gem I had to travel with. Susan settled down very contentedly after a bottle, in one of the drawers and slept like a top all night. Fortunately she was oblivious to the fact that her mother was a complete novice and had few instructions, other than how to make her formula. Graham Thompson, who was one of the instructors at *Kings*, told me he had telephoned his wife Madelaine to meet me at the train when we arrived in Montreal. It was so thoughtful and kind of him as he knew I was not happy with my ignorance and felt his wife would be a great help, as she was an expert on this mother business. Thankfully, there was no doubt in her assessment of the passengers that were disembarking from that train. She drove us to their house where we were met by a very happy-faced nanny who swept off with our sleeping beauty.

We had a carefree day and got to know each other. She was so easy to talk to and took all my questions in her stride, never once giving me the feeling that she felt a great sympathy for the subject of our discussions. We were driven to the train late that afternoon and were duly handed over to my porter who looked absolutely delighted to have a very small problem in his particular car. Goodbye and many, many thanks to Madelaine and Graham for their thoughtfulness.

It didn't take long before I was to discover some familiar faces in our train, as there were quite a few Sub Lieutenants aboard that had received their discharge from *Kings*. Those I did know introduced me to the ones I didn't, and as many of them were returning to little ones of their own and had probably missed out on the very early stage of Susan, not only were they intrigued but helpful, babysitting when I wanted to go to the dining car or make up her formula. My porter would be given the message that the galley was cleared for action and I would find a large cauldron of boiling water waiting for me and bottles were sterilised while I made up the formula. They were all so kind and helpful. Susan slept and tossed off those bottles like a little pro.

Never can I say enough about my wonderful porter. Those men were a very special breed of the human race. No matter what time of the day or night that I ever rang my bell, he greeted me with a contagious smile flashing his sparkling teeth. In daytime I left my door open to welcome the boys when they passed by hoping for a peek at Susan or to offer to babysit at the next stop so I could stretch my legs.

As we neared Winnipeg I realised I had an hour to dash up to a drug store to obtain very necessary items to ensure continued comfort for Susan. As all my sitters were availing themselves of a good stretch of their limbs, I asked my porter if he would keep an eye on Susan, to which he seemed delighted. Off I ran. This sojourn was to be the worst decision of my life. Although I ran, it turned out to be a lot farther away than I anticipated, so, clutching my parcels, I ran back to the station. To my horror, HORROR looks better, and more appropriate, the train was pulling out!!! Standing against the railing of the observation car with his arms outstretched was my porter and I took off and was pulled aboard by those strong black arms into a bear hug. The whites of his eyes still very much in evidence, he said, 'Thank God, young Missus, I wasn't sure how I was going to look after that little bambino of yours.' What a mother!

Susan flourished and, thinking she needed a boost in her formula, I increased it shortly before arriving in Vancouver to meet her new grandparents who would be waiting for us at the top of the escalator. Gathering all my things together I realised there was an insurmountable amount, including her bassinet, for me to cope with. At that moment of despair I saw John Nichol, one of the King's Sub's, son and grandson of friends of our families. I called out to him to ask if he would take the other end of the bassinet with me. His quick reply was, 'Yes, I will, but if my grandmother is at the top of the escalator, she's all yours!!' Fortunately for me, she wasn't.

Ignorance certainly wasn't bliss: increasing the formula was a huge mistake and that first night with my parents Susan was in pain all night and screamed her poor little lungs out. Into hospital she went as soon as the doctor could admit her and was diagnosed as having colic – all my ignorant fault and I felt so awful. One thing was certain, I had to find a place of my own to do us until Mort got his leave, pending his discharge. Fortunately it wasn't a problem, and four months passed by and Susan thrived and soon learned to captivate her father.

There was one sour note for me. By leaving Britain when I did, I lost my seniority and promotion status. When I joined the Canadian Wrens I was senior to every Wren in the country but as they didn't exist in Canada when I joined overseas, they took away my seniority. The only reason I cared was in the amount of benefits I would have accrued. We needed a house and furniture. Fortunately, Mort's record served us in good stead and we were soon settled into a very comfortable house which we bought from a delightful couple who introduced us to her sister and brother-in-law, Helen and Wendell Craig. They became wonderful neighbours who were always there for us at all times.

Mort's sister, Emily, lost her husband, who was killed during the landing at Dieppe. With their young daughter Judie, they lived for some time with Mrs Duffus and her companion, Dorothy Rowell, rather than in Montreal which was filled with so many memories. As the years passed, Emily met and married Norman Hurd when he was on leave. While waiting for him to obtain his discharge from the Army, Emily and Judie stayed with us for three months. She lost her heart to Susan, as did we for Judie. When Susan was baptised in St Mary's Church, by the Rev Canon Kemp, my brother Bill was godfather and Emily and my friend Nora Martin were asked to be godmothers. Judes, as we called her, attended the Convent of The Sacred Heart and we all got along famously. Sister and brother were tarred with the same brush when it came to playing every conceivable game of cards, both convinced they were the superior. I could hear them voicing their glee if they trounced each other. It was a very sad day when they departed for the east.

As we so hoped, my wonderful Wren, Anne Fitch, came over to work for us and took on a new career as a nanny. Being the super human being that she was, she became everything rolled into one. Much to my distress, she was very homesick at first and my heart ached for her as I could well remember how I felt when we lived in Glasgow in '38. She was a gem with Susan and they got along famously.

Anne saw me through my fourth and last pregnancy which led to the birth of Drue. She was so good to me. I could never begin to thank her. Unfortunately, from our point of view, Anne met and married Roland Stevens and they moved to Kelowna.

When Mort was to attend a meeting up there I went with him and was able to spend some time with Anne which was fun for

Anne Fitch, my very special Wren at Ugadale,
Machrihanish, later to come to us as Nanny.

both of us as we were able to re-live our times in Scotland when
we were in the Wrens.

Our next time together was in Toronto which is mentioned
elsewhere. I made a phone call to Toronto recently to enquire for
Anne and she is in a nursing home. She is working up to her
ninetieth!

Fate is a strange thing. If I hadn't been sent to the same Fleet
Air Arm Quarters as Anne and she hadn't been my Ward Room
Attendant, she never would have met and married Roland or had
the life she had in Canada.

The Family

My mother – Evelyn Maud Ferguson 1888-1974

I HAVE WRITTEN so much about our mother, that anyone reading my memoirs can skip this part!

Eve, she was called by her many friends, Auntie Eve by many young people such as Adele Herrmann, Pat Burns, Jocelyn Crompton etc. She had a fantastic memory for stories and told them well. She had a distinctive flair with her clothes and loved nice things.

Becoming a grandmother was a special time in her life. Doreen and Bill's Ann was to be her first, followed by her sister Gillian, and our Susan and Drue. She lived to see them all married.

Between Bill and me we had every disease there was. Bill had scarlet fever and was in the isolation building of our Vancouver General Hospital. The day he was to be signed out he developed it again, which was unheard of. In later years he had a bad heart and spent several months in bed with Mother caring for him.

When Dr Carder diagnosed me with smallpox he had to call in a second doctor as Mother would not believe one of their children could have such an illness. It was verified and she nursed me through that, painting my spots with iodine every few hours. She wrapped my hands in cotton wool and bound them with linen thread so I couldn't scratch myself. I did manage to work one finger free and took the top off one sore on my head. Thanks to her painstaking care I have no scars from that horrible disease.

My Aunt Annie, Mother, Aunt Elizabeth.

We had never been vaccinated because when Mother had hers, as a child, she had a dreadfully sore arm.

Mumps, measles, German measles, whooping cough, chicken-pox, near mastoid – all nursed by Mother. I hope we repaid her with love. Never, never was she ever too tired or too busy to do something for us.

When beyond our youthful diseases and with Bill away boarding at school, I was still at Crofton House and Mother would come dancing into my room in her nightie singing a made-up tune with these words: 'Oh it's a beautiful day, how would you like to drive to Seattle?' Could I say no? No! She really was naughty as it didn't help my education one little bit, which I was to rue a great many times over my lifetime.

Bill and I could only feel a great sense of relief when our parents got back together when they were much older as they had

Mother, 18 years.

lots of mutual memories and friends in the East as well as the West. They were well looked after, within walking distance from our house, up until our father died of a heart attack and fell off the chair while they were having breakfast. Mother wouldn't stay on there after that happened, so she opted to go to the same nursing home that Mort's mother was in for some years before she died.

I remember taking Ann's daughter Gillian (Doreen and Bill's granddaughter) in to see her one day and Mother couldn't get over being a great-grandmother.

Good, unsung deeds deserve to be recorded. When Mother belonged to the Toc-H it was discovered that a mother had committed her daughter, Claire, to a mentally retarded institution when she was only partially physically disabled. Her mother, the story went, had remarried and they didn't want to burden themselves with a demanding child. Mother removed Claire from the institution and paid a woman to care for her in a private home. I don't remember how old Claire was when she died, but she was grateful to Mother all through the years.

When Mother and I were returning to Vancouver from the East when I was fourteen, parents of my friend Kitty Lake (better known as 'Puddle') were aboard the same train. We had the drawing room in the observation car and as it was getting late we went out into the lounge area to make our room available to the porter. Sir Richard and Lady Lake were in the lounge so we joined them. After a while she left to return to their car. At that point our porter waved to us and, assuming our beds were made up, we said goodnight and walked to the end of the car to find the porter turning down our beds. The wave had meant he would do ours, not that they were ready for us. Mother said we could wait at our door, rather than go back to the lounge, as obviously it couldn't take long.

While we were standing there watching that efficient porter tossing and fluffing pillows, suddenly there was a horrendous crash and we were on about a 45° angle and our porter, with his eyes popping said, 'My Gawd, it's a train accident. Stay where you are and I will come back and tell you what to do.' We had the feeling that if we moved we could topple the train car over a precipice as it was pitch dark, no lights anywhere. Back he came with a torch to guide us back to the lounge – it wasn't easy at that angle. Sir Richard was frantic with worry that his wife could have been hurt and he was told he couldn't leave the car to look for her. The huge lounge chairs were every which way. Word finally came back to us that we were halfway between Medicine Hat and Brandon, that the dining car had split the tracks and that all the cars following were resting against a bank. We would have to wait until another train could rescue us – they had no idea how long that would take.

Much to the relief of Sir Richard, his beloved wife was carefully escorted along the empty tracks and heaved aboard our car. Her hat was well on the back of her head and she laughingly said, 'Richard dear, I've been in bed with another man!' Apparently when the train went over she was thrown from her side of the aisle to the other side, where a man was already in bed. She got a clapping reception from all of us that were sitting on the floor.

As the hours went by it got very cold as there was no heat. An emergency lighting system came on which was a relief. Bottles of whisky were passed around and everybody made the best of a bad situation. We all said, 'Thank God we had a bank to rest against instead of where we might have been!'

Finally, around 3:00 a.m., we were helped to the ground and boarded another train.

My father said he was picking up the paper when the telegraph boy arrived to say we were all right. This he read before opening the paper to see the headlines, 'Westbound CPR Train Wreck.'

Fortunately, no lives were lost and injuries were minimal. Mother had made a large purchase of unusual food items at a speciality shop called 'Micky's' and they had packed it in a long wooden box. It weighed about twelve pounds. The porter had stored it on a rack situated high up against the wall opposite to where we would be sitting during the daytime and she would have been sleeping. If we hadn't gone to sit in the lounge, or if Mother had been in bed, she would have been killed as the box landed where she would have had her head on the pillow, or where she would have been sitting had her bed not been made up. On the other hand our porter happened to be folding the extra blanket at the foot of her bed when the crash occurred, or he would have been struck had he been fixing her pillows. A stroke of fate or an act of God?

My father – William Graham Ferguson 1884-1969

My father was born in Peterborough, Ontario, of Scottish parents with one sister, Kathryn, and one brother, Tom. He grew up loving sports of every description and hunting and fishing were top priority all through his life.

After my parents were married, Dad was soon to be moved to Windsor, Ontario, with the bank and from all I gleaned about that period, neither of them cared for it sufficiently to want to live there, finally grow to like it and then be sent somewhere else, as banks are accustomed to doing. Dad had been to Vancouver once and they decided to leave the East and move to the West. Although my grandfather Irwin had a beautiful house built at Stoney Lake to persuade them at least to spend holidays with their families, it ended up instead with our grandparents spending two summer months in Vancouver.

The Ferguson Higman Ford Motor Company was Dad's first business position and from all I ever heard, there wasn't much about cars that he did not know. Next came Canadian Fairbanks Morse Company. Little did he know that one day his granddaughter Drue would marry his boss's grandson. It was a huge company that sold large machinery and each year they had an office picnic which entailed driving from our cottage in the North Arm to Balcarra Park (I think it was) and we looked forward to this day with our father every year. I remember one year in particular when Bill and I won every race we entered. The prizes were fabulous, such as baseball bats and balls, tennis rackets, dolls, etc. Mother was not able to go with us one year so Dad said, 'Let's play a joke on your mum. We will leave all your prizes in the car, so when she asks how you got along we will look very sad and say, not very well.' We thought this was great fun. Finally, we were asked to fetch something

My father, Graham Ferguson.

from the car that he wanted and we ran out and brought in all the prizes.

Another fun thing we used to do with our father was to fish off our wharf at night using a torch, which would attract large bass. One fat one he pressed with his fingers and some baby fish came out. I couldn't do it now for the life of me but I used to put the sea worms on the hooks. Dad taught us to swim and row our dinghy. We had some wonderful summers up there; the only thing we didn't like was the cold water in the North Arm.

Bill was lucky to be taken on fishing trips and duck hunting while one of my special treats was to sit on my father's knees and steer his car – this I really loved; granted it was only down our back lane.

When I was about four and Bill was two years and nine months older, we were both soundly spanked by our father and, believe

Our Dad.

me, we deserved it. Granny had sent us each new sailor coats and caps for Christmas, which we had put on while waiting for our parents to take us out for dinner. We must have become bored waiting for them, so we went down to our basement. There, we discovered the painter had left several paintbrushes that he had used to paint our verandah. Bill painted a skull and crossbones on my back and a cross on my sailor cap, and I painted his new shoes. We had so much paint on us we ended up being rubbed hard with turpentine and spanked on our bare bottoms. In those days, 'spare the rod, and spoil the child' was accepted. I don't know why it is forbidden today; we grew up knowing right from wrong.

Smelt fishing was fun with our father. I forget when they 'ran' but we would go down to English Bay with him in the early evening. He would have a long pole with a wire cage attached to it and when the schools of smelt rippled the water, Dad would

Our parents.

stretch out the pole and draw in the fish and we would put them in a pail which gave Boots, our cocker spaniel, an hour of total entertainment.

Our idea of a fun evening consisted of two types of entertainment which will sound incomprehensible to young people today. One was to have Dad set long division and multiplication sums for me, which I loved doing, and math problems for Bill that he found challenging. As our father was a whiz at math, he enjoyed those times as much as his pupils.

As I have said before, I was a tomboy and our other fun evenings were spent with the two of us having wrestling matches with Dad refereeing in a highly professional manner, with furniture moved out of the way of flying arms and legs. Our mother was our sole audience and always clapped at the appropriate times.

Every year Bill and I put on a fund-raiser in our back garden to assure that underprivileged children would have two weeks at a camp at Crescent Beach. Our father helped in every way to set up and ready us for the great event. Fortunately, our neighbours were always very supportive, knowing that it was for charity and not for us to squander. They came and played 'knock the teddy off the stand', had their fortunes told, guessed weights, heights and so on – thankfully we always managed to send two children to camp.

I remember one night when we had, as a family, been out for dinner and when we arrived home and went upstairs, our mother walked into her bedroom and called, 'Graham, Graham, come up please – there is a bird in our bedroom!' The next morning the telegraph boy brought our father a telegram from Peterborough to say that his Aunt Isabella had died. I remember my mother saying that she was not a superstitious person but she had once heard that a bird flying into a house meant a death.

When we were older and off to boarding school, we weren't around to notice that all was not well at home with our parents. Perhaps we had been their anchors, but they separated though they stayed friends throughout many years. Several times they tried living together again but it just did not work. They had such totally different interests. Dad loved sports, his fishing trips and hunting, whereas our mother loved to entertain, always had vast numbers of friends and kept herself busy with many interests. Fortunately they went back together when they were much older, and were together up until my father's death from cancer.

Looking back, I think we had a very good childhood with our parents together throughout those years. Fortunately, they remained friends, which in fairness to children, I think is essential – unfortunately today that does not happen too often.

My brother – William Irwin Ferguson 10 December 1913-1993

Of course there is a lot in my writings that include Bill but much has been excluded that I would like to write about here.

Growing up, Bill and Bruce Allan were great friends and I suppose I was their shadow. They had their own telephone system as our houses were back-to-back, only separated by a lane. They rigged wire from their three-pound jam tins from house to house. Don't ask me how it worked but they swore they conversed. They had a hideaway under the Allans' large verandah, set up with apple boxes for chairs, and candles in tins as they couldn't show a light. This place was called the boogie hole – unknown to Bruce's family or ours.

Every Saturday we pooled our allowances and bought a loaf of bread, a box of Puffed Wheat and some cent candy, along with all the cigarette butts we could pick up at home, and matches, of course. We rolled dried chestnut leaves in toilet paper when they were available. How our parents were oblivious to all these antics I don't know.

Meantime, they attended the Vancouver Preparatory School – Bill went off to board as I have previously mentioned, leaving the Sea Scouts that he loved dearly behind.

With the depression there was no chance of him going to University so he went to work with the Mutual Life of Canada, of which our Uncle Walter Somerville was the President and General Manager.

When war was declared, being in the Naval Reserve he was given a commission as lieutenant, and I am sure couldn't have been happier as he was always fascinated with anything to do with the Navy.

Although Bill had been keen on several girls, he completely lost his heart to Doreen Cattroll and they were married in Victoria.

I was with Mother at that time so we attended their lovely wedding.

I will skip ahead to the end of the war which found Bill diagnosed with epilepsy, which was a dreadful shock to all of us. This was more or less controlled by medication. They settled in Vancouver and raised their two lovely girls, Ann and Gillian. Bill went back to the Mutual Life. Unfortunately the time came when he had to retire on a pension as he also became diabetic. Meanwhile the girls did well. Ann went into nursing and Gill into radiology. Doreen became Bill's chauffeur and strong supporter. They sold their house in Vancouver and moved to a waterfront house on Maine Island. They had a boat for as long as he was able to handle it. Sadly, Bill died just before his eightieth birthday.

One thing that has eluded me was my brother's priceless sense of humour. He could twist almost anything that was said into something worthy of a good laugh. I still miss him.

Thank you, Doreen, for caring for Bill over many trying years.

Grandparents

Living in the west and our grandparents three thousand miles away in Peterborough Ontario, we were geographically separated. Mother travelled east with my brother Bill when he was about two, with platinum curls, navy blue eyes and adorable. There are some wonderful pictures of him taken on the farm that was part of his grandparents' beautiful estate. One of these pictures shows little Billy eyeing the baby chicks – then another shows him endeavouring to pluck the feathers off one of them!

When I came into the picture, I was about two when we were both taken east to stay at Highland Hall. Unfortunately, I don't recall anything about that holiday but there are pictures of me – totally opposite in colouring from my brother when he was my age. Dark brown hair with a slight wave and green eyes – very average I would say.

There must have been something that soured the relationship between our paternal grandparents and our parents because I never met my grandmother Ferguson, and my grandfather only once at the last of our visits to Peterborough when I was eleven, and my Aunt Anne died of cancer. It was as if they never existed, which shocks me to think of now as I'm sure they were very nice. I remember being driven by their house which was beautiful, but that is as far as it went. We both adored the Irwins so much I suppose we never thought to ask any questions. Strange.

Highland Hall had been sold by the time I was eleven and our grandparents were living with Uncle Jim Hamilton and Aunt Anne because she was ailing in health. They had, as one of their servants, Mary-Ellen Cushing, who was deaf and dumb. She looked after the laundry and cleaning and had originally been employed as a nursemaid for my mother who, from all accounts, screamed her lungs out and nearly drove the family mad. Mary-Ellen knew the little howler was screaming when her mouth was open. She conveyed her thoughts by sign language to the distraught parents that baby Eva would stop screaming if she was given some scraped raw steak. It worked like a charm and baby Eva never screamed thereafter. My mother grew up with sign language and I always wished I had learned it from her. Children can learn anything – good and bad. I remember when I met Mary-Ellen I was so sorry I couldn't understand her or she, me.

Mother's sister Elizabeth Somerville, from Waterloo, had preceded our visit and had rented a duplex so that we could all stay together. She had her four-year old daughter, Anne, and her governess and the two of us, so we all fitted in very well. Anne was adorable. On Mam'selle's day off our two mothers were urgently called to go up to Aunt Anne as she was failing rapidly. I was left to look after my little cousin. Elizabeth said she would pay me $5.00 if I could teach Anne how to do the Charleston. Another time I was to go up the hill to church with her – I think they must have wanted to have an hour's peace – so off we went. All went well for about fifteen minutes until Anne stood up on the pew and in a loud voice said, 'Let's go home, Johnnie, this is a kee-kee picture show!' I swept her out as fast as her little legs would go.

Before we left Peterborough, Granddaddy called for Mother and me and had the chauffeur drive to the furrier where he bought Mother a beautiful black seal coat and whispered something to the furrier who nodded his head, disappeared, and returned bearing a fur coat for me. I can picture it as if it was yesterday – brown muskrat with a beaver collar and cuffs. I was speechless. From there we were driven to Hoy's ice cream shop and I was given a $10.00 bill to go in and buy myself an ice cream cone. When I climbed back in beside him I handed him all the change. He proceeded to lay out the bills and folded them tightly around the change. He then took my hand and flattened out the palm, placed the roll of money on it, and then carefully curled my fingers around it. He really was a very special person.

Peterborough had a market that my grandmother frequented and she invited me to go with her one day. I learned several things – one of which was that she was well-known by the people selling and those buying. Fowl was not only bought by looking at it, she pressed on the muscle part of the centre bone and if it moved easily she bought it. The farm produce was a sight to behold; fruit was sold in oblong baskets, all with mouth-watering freshness. We left the market well laden, having both enjoyed my first experience in country shopping. I could now picture Granny buying the many things she used to send to us in Vancouver. She would send a tin trunk full of all sorts of things – string bags of onions, brussels sprouts, carrots, chickens or a turkey at

Christmas, always rolled in dish towels inside a Hudson Bay blanket; a box of Laura Secord chocolates; maple sugar – all of which travelled by freight in the CPR trains. Granny must have had lots of good help because she wasn't young then.

Granny and our grandfather used to spend two months of every summer at the Hotel Vancouver as he had a lot of business out west and Mother was pretty much at his beck and call to drive him everywhere. He had a lawsuit in New Westminster that would often start their day and Mum would remark upon arrival home, 'As if we hadn't covered enough miles, Dad asked me to drive him around Stanley Park!' As he gave her a new Buick every other year, she could hardly complain. He was a strange combination – frugal and extravagant. He felt if he paid the CPR Hotel Vancouver for a suite, he shouldn't have to pay ten cents a

Mother in Stanley Park.

WM. J. IRWIN BIG WOODSMAN IS LAID TO REST

Short Private Service is Held in House of Deceased.

"MAN OF THE WOODS."

Late Mr. Irwin Was Born in Ireland and Came To Canada At Early Age.

The respect and esteem with which the late William John Irwin was regarded was reflected in the large gathering of friends and relatives who were present at the graveside in Little Lake Cemetery yesterday and the numerous floral tributes which were received by the bereaved relatives as tokens of sympathy in their great loss.

Prior to the interment a private service was held at the family residence conducted by Rev. William Allan and Rev. Dr. R. C. Blagrave.

Mr. Irwin leaves besides his widow, two daughters, Mrs. Walter Somerville of Waterloo and Mrs. W. Graham Ferguson of Vancouver, who are in the city for the funeral. One other daughter, Mrs. James Hamilton, predeceased her father two years ago; also included among the chief mourners were James Hamilton, son-in-law, and Mrs. Walter Wood of Peterborough, sister-in-law.

The pall-bearers were: Mayor Roland Denne, R. R. Hall, K.C., E. H. D. Hall, E. H. Howson, His Honor Judge Huycke, and Theodore McWilliams.

Born In Ireland.

The late Mr. Irwin was born in Ballymena, County Antrim, Ireland, in July, 1849, and came to Canada at the age of 17 years when he was engaged by the late John Ludgate in the lumbering camps, later becoming foreman and woods manager. He was also employed in a similar capacity with lumbering concerns in Fort Frances and subsequently became contractor for the taking-out of logs both at the last named place and in the waters tributary to the Georgian Bay.

At the time of his retirement fifteen years ago after a well earned rest the deceased gentleman was connected with the Georgian Bay Lumber Company, Lachine, where he was in charge of the woods operations, and right up to the time of his death he continued to take a keen interest in the business in its many branches.

He had a very extensive acquaintance throughout the Dominion and particularly in Ontario and British Columbia. He was regarded by lumbermen as a careful, prudent and successful operator in taking-out merchantable timber and transporting it to its destination, and was affectionately regarded by all men under his control.

Mr. Irwin married Susan Stewart of this city, who it is learned with regret is at the present time in failing health and is confined to her bed.

Since coming to the city over sixty years ago Mr. Irwin has made his permanent home here except during his residence in Fort Frances, and was a regular attendant at St. Paul's Presbyterian Church.

He was a freemason and belonged to the Corinthian Chapter R.A.M. No. 36 and was also a Shriner and was connected with Ramsees Shrine.

R. R. Hall, K.C., who has known the late Mr. Irwin for the past forty years said: "His sudden demise will be deeply mourned by a wide circle of friends and acquaintances throughout Canada, by whom he was regarded with highest respect and admiration."

call to use the telephone – so he would walk down Granville Street to E.E. Rand & Fowler's office (they looked after all the property he owned and collected people's mortgage payments) and use their phone. Then again he would give mother a list of names to set up business appointments for him.

I remember Bill and me showing off our swimming feats while our grandfather sat on a bench at English Bay, and although I could stand on my head under water, I could only swim with my water-wings, which one day I didn't have – so I propelled myself along with one foot on the bottom. I'm sure I never fooled him but I couldn't let Bill show me up! Granny must have been at our house with Mother on those occasions as we seemed to be out on excursions without Mother or Granny, except for long times in the car. I remember hearing them talking one day and Granny said she thought Vancouver would one day have a crime rate like Chicago. When asked why, she replied, 'Because it's a sea port.' When I look back on my childhood and the complete trust I felt in everyone. with our doors unlocked at all times, it was a strange remark for her to make. Today, some seventy-five or so years later, we batten down the hatches as it isn't as it was, I'm sad to say.

I was twelve years old when our grandparents died. Granny had cancer and was very distressed that she would die first and leave her beloved Will, as she called him, because he was so dependent on her. She said she prayed constantly that he would go first, which is exactly what happened. He died two weeks to the day before Granny, which was an answer to her prayers.

Bill and I missed them terribly as we had both loved them dearly.

I only wish they had written their memoirs as I am doing for our grandchildren and the generations that follow.

Grandfather William Irwin 1842-1928

Many mentions have been made about our grandfather and considering I was only twelve when he died in 1928, my love for him has never faded. He was a very special man.

As the eldest of six children he left his parents, twin brother and siblings to work his way to Canada owing to the potato famine in Northern Ireland. With his trunk on his back and a shilling in his pocket he came to Canada and as soon as he could he sent for his twin, David (Uncle Dave), whom he bought a house for in Vancouver.

I'll leave 'Big Bill', as he was known, and tell a few stories about his twin, who was married and lived a few blocks from our house on Harwood Street. He kept chickens, as did our next door neighbour! It seems incredible that it could ever have been possible, particularly as Harwood Street is filling up with monster high-rise apartments.

Uncle Dave would very often call our parents and ask if Billy and Johnnie would be able to bring him a wagonload of sand for his chickens to scratch in. With a firm wag of her forefinger Mother would say, 'If Uncle Dave wants to pay you, you are to say no thank you.' When we returned home on Saturday we were asked as to why we each had ten cents.

'You didn't ask for anything, did you?'

My dear brother piped up, 'I didn't!'

'Johnnie, what did you say?'

'I didn't ask for anything, I said, "That is a lot of sand, it should be worth something!"' All this was followed up by a phone call from Uncle Dave to Mother informing her that she need have no worries about her daughter.

While on the subject of chickens, one of our neighbour's chickens wandered into our garden and Bill and I were practising

Mother on European tour with their chaperone.

shooting his BB gun. Never dreaming he would hit this poor bird, he aimed, fired and killed the unfortunate stray. We were horrified and terrified of the consequences so we had a quick conference and decided on a proper burial. It was some years later that we confessed.

Now back to 'Big Bill Irwin'. I still find it hard to believe that a young lad could, in his lifetime, achieve such recognition in Canada. He met our grandmother, Susan Fraser, in Peterborough where they were married. Their eldest daughter Annie was a twin but her twin died at birth, then there were Elizabeth and our mother, Evelyn. The two eldest went to Havergal in Toronto and Mother to the Lillian Massey School of Household Science, from which we were to benefit as she was a superb cook.

The three young sisters were taken by a youngish teacher, with three of their friends, on an extended tour of England, Ireland,

Scotland, Italy, France and Austria. One story we were told about their experiences was as follows: The 'girls' were taken to the theatre in London to see No, No Nanette and it came to the part in one of the hit songs 'Tea for two and two for tea, a boy for you and a girl for me.' Their chaperone quickly leaned towards them and said, or hissed, 'Come, come, girls, this is no place for us,' and swept them out!

Goodness knows what land cost in those days but apart from Highland Hall, their beautiful home in Peterborough, they had Headlands on Stoney Lake, which I have already written about. Obviously 'Big Bill' was a great believer in real estate which would have been very beneficial, but he died in 1928 and the stock market died also. Mother never really benefited from all the real estate he had acquired in Vancouver. The depression was a devastating experience for so many families; ours escaped many years of it but my grandfather thought CPR stock was like the Bank of England, so he had very heavily invested in it. CPR ceased to pay dividends. A good lesson for all of us not to put too many eggs in one basket.

The announcement of his death is significant proof of what an outstanding man William Irwin was.

Mort 1905-1997

Naturally there is a great deal in these memoirs that Mort shared with me over the years, but these statistics should be recorded.

Mort was born in Calgary in 1905 when his father was serving with the North-West Mounted Police, as it was called in those days. As soon as he was able to ride he had his own pony called Daisy Bell, much to the amusement of our girls, and rode in the first Calgary Stampede. As his father was constantly being moved

Mort back in civvies.

– Coutts, Saskatoon, Winnipeg, Brandon, Toronto, Ottawa – schooling required stability, and he was to board at St Andrews College in Toronto. This he loved dearly. Once he settled into this new routine his marks improved with each year and he completed his final year by topping his class.

When Mort was twenty-one his maternal grandfather left him $10,000.00 which enabled him to travel. He sailed to England, and took in as many shows as possible (favouring Beatrice Lilley), while at the same time squeezing in fittings with his newly-acquired tailor who produced tails and dinner jacket.

Off to Paris he flew, very very slowly and very rough as many of the passengers were air sick. As opera was always the joy of his life, he attended many and was captivated by the Paris Opera House. His only other entertainment while there was to attend the Follies.

Upon returning to Canada he thought he could greatly increase

The Colonel and little Mort.   *Mort.*

his inheritance by playing the very active stock market. All went well for a time but the stock market crash hit the bottom, as did his bank account.

Having six months working in a bank convinced him it was not for him so when a friend said he could promise him a job in Calgary with the Canadian Canners Ltd. for forty cents an hour in the packing house, he moved into 'digs' with his friends and took the job, which was a brief stint before being moved to Vancouver in 1930 at the age of twenty-five.

When we were married in 1936, Mort was manager of the jam department. In early 1938 he was made manager of the United Kingdom sales. The war and his role providing food for Britain has been recorded elsewhere. In 1941 he returned to Canada and joined the Royal Canadian Naval Reserve. He was given the rank of Lieutenant, spent two weeks in Montreal and was sent on loan to the Royal Navy where he trained in Portsmouth, after which he was appointed to a Hunt Class Destroyer, HMS *Brocklesby*, based in Plymouth. This was followed by a Gunnery course at Whale

Lieut. M.S. Duffus, Petty Officer Duffus.

Island, then serving as Gunnery Officer in the *Brocklesby*; subsequently he saw action at Dieppe, Sicily and Salerno, at the latter two as First Lieutenant.

With accumulated leave he returned to Canada and his next appointment was to return to the UK to take command of a Castle Class Corvette, HMCS *Bowmanville*. For the next year he did convoy duty on the Atlantic. When the European war ended, Mort received his discharge with his rank of Lieut. Commander.

After a brief holiday he accepted a position with Kelly Douglas and Co. with Reg Arkell as President until his death, followed by Victor Maclean. Mort met his many challenges and fully enjoyed the wonderful friendships he made there and the challenge of creating one hundred and five supermarkets, for which he was responsible.

On 31 October 1967 Mort retired but remained in an advisory

Mort's mother.

capacity for a year. He was sixty-two and lived to enjoy twenty-nine more years and to celebrate our sixty-one years of marriage.

My mother-in-law: Heloise Denham Rae Duffus 1882-1966

The first time I met Mrs Duffus (as I was to always call her), was in 1935 when Mort first started to take me out. Daphne Arkell was my friend and her brother, Trevor, was Mort's. Their parents were going to Harrison Hot Springs for a weekend and we were invited to join them. We were to leave Saturday after lunch. Mort said to be ready just after noon; he would pick me up and we would have lunch with his mother and her companion, Dorothy Rowell, before driving to Harrison Lake.

I was nineteen and Mort was a young thirty. I thought I had outgrown my shyness but remember when Mrs Duffus walked towards me with her hand held to her ear, holding a tortoiseshell hearing aid, and I had to raise my voice, I felt very shy. I had not realised she was fairly deaf and Mort had neglected to tell me. Dorothy Rowell came into the room to meet me and was a friendly relaxed person, bearing a tray with sherry glasses. The sherry must have helped because I soon got over my shyness. Their housekeeper, Jane, produced a delicious lunch and off we went for what proved to be a very nice weekend.

I had several visits with Mrs Duffus and Dorothy before they departed on an extended trip to South America. Meantime, we were skiing every weekend and my coming out dance with Mary MacNeill took place, followed by our engagement, about which I have already written.

Mort sent off a cable to his mother to which we soon received one in return, saying how delighted they were. We had a great celebration on their return. Mrs Duffus brought me two beautiful nightgowns and Dorothy a hammered silver ashtray. I soon got to know them both very well and grew very fond of them. They were very keen bridge players and tolerated my infantile efforts with great patience.

To jump ahead to the time before we were to be moved to the UK, Mort had to spend a month in Hamilton at the head office, prior to us sailing, so I spent that month with Mrs Duffus. I felt I was quite the most blessed to have such a truly wonderful person as my mother-in-law. I am sure I would have loved the Colonel also had he not died three years before as everyone that knew him spoke so highly of him. Our mothers became great friends, which was a big plus.

When Mrs Duffus and Emily, Mort's sister, came to England to see us we had an unbelievably good time. We would spend three days in London as their guests and they spent weekends with us in Reigate. When we were with them, we saw three plays each week.

They loved our quiet weekends quite as much as we enjoyed our wonderful times in London.

Mrs Duffus was born in Halifax and attended Bryn Mawr College in Pennsylvania. I don't know whether they turned out a special breed of women or not, but I always thought I had the finest and quite the most remarkable mother-in-law in the world. She was kindness in itself, had a delightful sense of humour, was generous to a fault and always most appreciative. If Mort ever left his clothes lying around when Mrs Duffus was staying with us she would say, 'I'm sorry I spoiled "your husband" so badly, but it was easier.' As an expression of affection she would hold out her hand, palm side up and I would place my hand palm side down on her hand. She didn't kiss or hug; you knew how much she cared.

When Dorothy Rowell died of cancer Mrs Duffus went to Ottawa to live with her daughter Emily (Jane, Ginny), her husband Norman Hurd and daughter, Judie. It was very sad for us but we had been fortunate to have her as long as we did. I'm not sure when Norman was moved to Detroit but they all moved together.

After a few summers I received a letter asking if I would try and find good accommodation for Mrs Duffus in a seniors convalescent nursing home. She had been coming to us for two months every summer to get away from the intense heat in the east but she felt the travelling to and fro was becoming too stressful. Fortunately there was a new one being built and we were able to reserve her accommodation before it was completed.

Our girls loved their grandmother. Mrs Duffus they called 'Grandie' and my mother, 'Ga Ga' (Gaw Gaw). Maybe they got that from my brother Bill and Doreen's children. Fortunately we had both mothers alive when the girls were married (Susan's first marriage) and their only very devoted grandfather also.

There weren't many days that I didn't drop by and pick up

Grandie for a drive, lunch, tea or dinner. My parents had each other but Mrs Duffus was alone and all her friends had departed this world. She stayed there for nine years but sadly caught the toe of her shoe on one of our chairs and fell, breaking her hip. When I worked in emergency at VGH, I came to admire the manner and ability of Dr Miller who was the orthopaedic surgeon who fortunately was on duty that day and he x-rayed her immediately. I was with her when he told her he would have to put a pin in her hip and she said, 'I must be one of the few girls that have ever been pinned twice.' He really got a good laugh over that. I don't know whether the boys today still give their best girl their fraternity pin but Dr Miller certainly knew that that was what she meant.

For three days after her operation she seemed to do very well but I think that her system suffered a shock from the fall and she failed very rapidly. Fortunately, Jane arrived out from Detroit in good time to see her beloved mother. I know I for one cried myself to sleep as I loved her with all my heart.

Throughout my life, in the role of mother-in-law, I kept mine as a role model and hope in a small way I will leave pleasant memories of our relationships.

My father-in-law, Lieutenant-Colonel A.W. Duffus 1871-1933

It was always a great disappointment to me that I never knew my father-in-law as Mort so often said we would have got along very well. For our grandchildren I will include clippings and pictures so they will know about their great-grandfather Duffus. He died of a stroke and Mort was thankful he didn't linger as he said he would have hated to be left in a wheelchair or speech impaired.

The colonel's sister, Edith Duffus, is pictured with their three children; the little boy being Ernest T. Troubridge who grew up to

Obituary

THE ANNOUNCEMENT, on September 7th, of the death of Lieutenant-Colonel A. W. Duffus removes a figure whose association with the Mounted Police endured, except for a brief interval of two years, from 1896 to 1931.

Entering the North West Mounted Police in 1896, Arthur William Duffus served as a constable and corporal until 1901. His service carried him from the Regina depot to the Calgary district and then to the Yukon.

On returning to the Force in 1903 with the rank of Inspector, he served at Coutts and Calgary, Alberta; Saskatoon, Brandon and Winnipeg, in order, until 1917.

Promoted Superintendent in 1917, he returned to Depot Division where he remained until his departure for Siberia with the Royal North West Mounted Police Overseas "B" Squadron of Cavalry.

On his return to Canada he was stationed at Brandon and Winnipeg until 1920, when he assumed command of the Western Ontario district, "O" Division, with headquarters at Toronto.

The year 1923 saw another move for Superintendent Duffus, this time back to Regina again, whence, after another few years, he went to Vancouver to command "E" Division. In 1927 his last promotion came, in the form of an assistant-commissionership. With the assumption by the Force of additional duties in 1928, another change came, and Lieutenant-Colonel Duffus was brought to Ottawa as second in command at Headquarters.

All who knew Lieutenant-Colonel Duffus during his long period of service, a service which covered much territory and comprised a great variety of experience including the celebrated Cashel case at Calgary, can testify to his unfailing geniality and courtesy. His death comes as a shock to all his friends, and the sympathy of all ranks of the Force will be extended to his family.

*　　　*　　　*

POLICE OFFICER IS GIVEN PROMOTION

A. W. DUFFUS, R.C.M.P.

COL. A. W. DUFFUS WINS PROMOTION

Royal Canadian Mounted Police Head Here Is Advanced.

DISTINGUISHED RECORD

Lieut.-Colonel A. W. Duffus, officer commanding the Royal Canadian Mounted Police in British Columbia, has been promoted to the post of assistant commissioner, effective November 5 last.

Promotion to this distinguished post came to Colonel Duffus as a reward for long and meritorious service in the famous force, extending from 1897, in the original Northwest Mounted Police, to the present time.

The new assistant commissioner is one of the best-known officers of Western Canada. He has been stationed at Vancouver during the past few years. Six years of service as a constable won him his commission and an appointment as inspector. He then served in Saskatchewan, Alberta, Manitoba, and for a brief time in Ontario. For ten years he was stationed in Calgary, and during that period was active in bringing to justice a number of notorious criminals. He solved the Tucker-Peach murder mystery.

A.D.C. TO GOVERNORS.

In 1914 he was appointed superintendent, and when a cavalry squadron was formed in connection with the Canadian Expeditionary Force he was appointed second in command.

Colonel Duffus has the distinction of having served as A.D.C. to three lieutenant-governors—Sir R. Lake of Saskatchewan, Hon. A. G. Jones of Nova Scotia, and Hon. R. Randolph Bruce of British Columbia.

MAY GO TO OTTAWA.

The new assistant commissioner was born in Nova Scotia of stock that is associated with the salt sea. Sir Samuel Cunard, founder of the great Cunard Line, was his great-uncle.

No word as to what effect the appointment will have on Colonel Duffus' residence here has been received, but it is quite probable he will eventually be stationed permanently at Ottawa.

Edith Duffus Troubridge with the
future 5th Sea Lord.

Cousin Troubridge.

be Admiral RN, Fifth Sea Lord. Mort had the great pleasure of being invited aboard his ship while in the Mediterranean. He said he found him very friendly and charming.

If only I had started my memoirs when Mort was alive, he could have added many interesting anecdotes, particularly about his father. One thing we did do when we moved from our house was to put together many things he had kept of his father's, namely his pith helmet, service medals, riding crop, uniform buttons and other items which the RCMP were delighted to receive as they wrote such a grateful letter of thanks.

The Colonel apparently hoped Mort would follow him into the RCMP but I do think he would have been very proud of his Naval son's accomplishments.

Susan.

Susan: born 12 May 1945

There are many highlights in Susan's life that must be recorded. I will start from her very early days when the two of us moved into a rented furnished house prior to the arrival of Mort, who was waiting for his discharge from the Navy. Finally, at four and a half months she was held in her daddy's arms, which was an emotional moment for him and as she was a remarkably happy baby, she took to him as he took to her.

We did not waste any time looking for a place of our own and we were very fortunate in finding a house that we both loved with adequate bedrooms, a nice garden and, soon to be discovered, exceptionally nice neighbours. All our furniture was in England, still in storage. We moved in with a crib for Susan, dining room furniture left for us because they had no place to put it

Nora Martin, Johnnie Ferguson.

(thankfully), and two very pretty chairs we bought, as well as several tables and our beds, and that was the extent of our possessions. We finally sold our furniture to the Halton family of CBC fame as they were desperately in need in England as I believe all their furniture was in Canada. Shipping furniture after the war ended would have cost a fortune.

It was only a short time after we got settled that Jane, Mort's sister, and her daughter Judie stayed with us for about four months. Fortunately it worked: they competed with a capital C at crib, rap rummy, or any other game at which they could challenge each other. Susan got along famously with her aunt and cousin and time passed all too quickly. They went back to the east to finally settle down to Jane's newly-married life to Norman Hurd, who had been waiting for his discharge from the Army. I have already written about her first husband and father of Judie, who was killed after landing on the beach at Dieppe.

Susan was baptized at St Mary's Anglican Church in Kerrisdale by the Reverend Dudley Kemp. This was our first introduction to this remarkable man but was to be the beginning of a long and wonderful friendship with him and his wife Muriel. Susan wore Mort's christening gown; she looked adorable. Jane and Nora Martin, as she was then, were her godmothers and she grew up to love them both dearly. My brother Bill was her godfather. We never knew what it was to even scold Susan; she was an amazingly good baby and child.

We had an enormous playpen loaned to us by Nora that we started her out in, surrounded by her toys, doll and pram, and I retreated into the house. This was the only time I ever heard her scream and all hell broke loose. Some book on child behaviour that I had read said cold water stopped tantrums, so I flicked some at her. She was so flabbergasted she stopped in her tracks and settled down quite happily. My mother gave her a rocking chair which she adored, singing as she rocked.

Prince Philip was courting Princess Elizabeth and Susan imagined them as her playmates. She would walk around the garden chatting away to the two of them. She referred to Elizabeth as Lizzabizzet, who usually sat on her shoulder.

Susan was two and a half when Drue was born and she was delighted with her living doll and called her 'Baby Do'. Perhaps as time moved on one is inclined only to remember the best, not the worst. I do not remember disagreements or squabbles or mean tricks; they simply got along. My brother and I used to have some royal battles. They were very different – Susan was dedicated to her ballet, was always meticulously clean and organised, and loved pretty things. We could take her anywhere and she rose to every occasion. Drue, on the other hand, was untidy and loved a tomboy lifestyle. My mother used to say, 'I swear if Susan was taken to Buckingham Palace for lunch, she would know which fork to use.'

When Susie went on her 'points' her teacher, Kay Armstrong,

Susan and 'Baby Do'.

with whom she had been training since she was about five, told me I was to take her to a specialist to check her feet as she was disappointed to see Susan was having unexpected problems. It turned out to be true. Dr Donald Starr examined her bone structure and asked her how badly she wanted to become a ballerina. Her answer was, 'Very.' He then told her that if that were to be, she would never be without pain or be able to do what others could do without pain. It was a sad pronouncement after all the years she had taken lessons and, for over a year, private lessons. Kay had told us both prior to Susie's problem that she had the ability in every aspect to achieve her goal as a dancer – the will and drive must come from her. Kay was genuinely sorry when we went for her next lesson but not surprised as she had felt there had to be a faulty bone structure. To cheer us up, Kay said dancing does not stop with ballet and that she had a young man who was training for dancing in musicals and that he would enjoy her as a

Susan, favourite time.

partner. They had such fun and he was a delight to watch. All good things come to an end, and Tommy went off to New York.

Up to this point, Susan had very good health with the exception of the usual childhood diseases, but she became ill and was diagnosed with having encephalitis lethargica. Thankfully, it was a mild case and she recovered very well and quickly. The only after-effect she had was a problem with her eyes. A specialist said she could continue with her schooling but was not to take any notes from the blackboard. Somehow she managed to pass and graduate from Crofton House; she carried out her duties as a prefect and won a cup on Sports Day.

After her trip abroad with all her friends, and her debut, she took a business course and worked for a few years before getting married – which unfortunately did not work out. Her second marriage was to Crozier (Cro) Lucas, who came out here from Montreal when his parents, Berenice and Seymour, moved to

Susan, aged 18.

Drue and I seeing Susan off to Europe.

Vancouver. Nine days before the big day they were up skiing at Whistler Mountain and Susan had a bad fall, ending up with a compound fracture in her leg. Instead of a wedding in a chapel, we had it in our house with our much-loved Reverend George Kelly officiating. He provided a cross for the mantelpiece; Cammy, standing inside the front door, handed each guest a hymn book which seemed to set the tone for the service that followed. Our laundry room had been converted into a bedroom with its own bathroom, so Susie could be on the main floor. Mort wheeled the beautiful invalid down the hall and in to the waiting groom, parents and guests. Crozier's sister, Anne Suche, and her husband Tony, who also had a cast on his leg (mother and father of Cammy), had come from Calgary for the wedding. Although we were sorry it could not be at our church, St Mary's, it was truly lovely. When the time came for the couple to depart, it took quite a while to pack all their trappings into the station wagon. Wheelchair, crutches, suitcases – they left with laughter and cheers for the Bay Shore Hotel.

Two and a half years later, John Seymour Guy was given a royal welcome into the family and was baptised wearing Dad Mort's christening gown, which he would never have approved of much less been told he looked adorable in. Guy and his cousins were to have some great times together.

Although Susie did not travel with us she managed to see quite a bit of this world, but is always happy to be home with roots well dug in. Having spent seventeen years of her summers with us at Cowan's Point on Bowen Island, she became more and more determined to live up there. Crozier, with Susan and Guy, would share a cottage every other two weeks with Drue and Bruce, which fortunately he loved every bit as much as did the others. There will be much more written about their love for the Point, so I will leave Susan and family there for the present.

Mort and Crozier with the invalid bride, Susan.

Crozier Lucas: born 23 May 1942

Little did I know, when I received a letter from my friend Ernle telling me that her friends Berenice and Seymour Lucas were moving to Vancouver from Montreal and would we please take them under our wing, that their son would marry our daughter. I arranged to meet Berenice, shortly after which they joined us for dinner. Berenice and I became fast friends and our husbands didn't do too badly either; they fell on their feet very quickly when they vied with each other as to who played the best game of crib or made the best Martinis. At a later date, when Crozier arrived, he was introduced to lots of girls and finally decided our Susan was the one he wanted to share the rest of his life with.

Susie and Cro's wedding has been covered elsewhere and now, as I write, they have been very happily married for thirty-one years. I will back-track more fully to describe our son-in-law.

The crippled bride with her dad.

Susan and Guy.

Susan and Crozier.

The family lived in Montreal. There was one sister, Anne, who is six years senior to Cro, which meant they really didn't see much of each other as they were growing up. After completing his education he travelled extensively in Europe but had to return home owing to his father being very seriously hurt in an accident, from which it took many months to recover. They sold their summer and Montreal homes and his parents moved west.

After the Lucas-Duffus wedding they moved into a charming house in Vancouver, soon after which Seymour died from a brain tumour which was devastatingly sad. Fortunately, Guy arrived to cheer everyone up.

Crozier has had an amazing capacity to go headlong into varied business careers, showing ingenuity, creativity and temerity. At present he has an office in their Cowan's Point, Bowen Island house (which he helped build) where he runs a thriving business providing holidays in three sports, namely fishing, skiing at

Whistler Mountain, and golf. Groups fly in from the USA, Germany, Japan etc.; they are met and catered for from arrival to departure.

An office in Vancouver finds him involved three times a week in his marketing business. In his spare time (?) he helps Susan to create their beautiful garden or attends their property owners' meetings. As I write, this morning he caught the 5:30 a.m. ferry to take a group to catch a plane to further their pre-arranged holiday. It exhausts me to think about it!

Thank you, Cro, for marrying our daughter Susie.

Guy Lucas: born 23 January 1974

John Seymour Guy, as he was christened wearing his grandfather's beautiful christening gown, was born on 23 January 1974, followed shortly after by his cousin Ryan.

Guy.

Guy.

As little fellows, Guy and Ryan saw a great deal of each other because Susan and Drue were so close. They used to have some great tussles, not always peacefully, much to the amusement of their mothers and anyone else that saw them.

Unfortunately, Guy never spent the summers with his cousins because his parents shared alternate fortnights in the cottage at Cowan's Point. They all grew up loving life there and this feeling has remained with them all to this day. Guy, however, with his parents living there, can go up to the Point pretty well any time he wishes. I would love to think that one day the Cowan's Point grandchildren will all have a summer house up there so their children will grow up together in that wonderful environment.

Guy attended French immersion school up to grade seven and high school years at Vancouver College. Langara College followed, interrupted by an extensive trip to Europe which he loved every minute of – and which whetted his appetite for more.

Graham, Guy, Ryan, Christie.

Whether being an only child explains the ease with which Guy gets along with adults I don't know, but this gift he certainly has.

Unlike his cousins, Guy hasn't had a family business to enter so has yet to make up his mind where he wants his career in this highly competitive world. I have every confidence that he will do well when the time comes, as he has done at anything he has undertaken.

Crozier's mother, Berenice, lives close to Guy so she sees much more of him than I but he is always there for both of us and we are devoted to him.

Drue: born 18 October 1947; died 7 March 1986

When Susan was two years old we contemplated adopting a baby so she would have a brother or sister. I found myself expecting a baby, which was more than a little upsetting. With my dreadful history behind me, the mere thought of nine more months to produce another baby that once more would only live for a few days was more than I could bear to think about.

My doctor, Jack Harrison, said I could expect our baby in October (1947) but that I had two options. The first was that I could carry on with post-war shots of hormones plus vitamins and could possibly have a full-weight baby that would survive. Secondly, because of losing three, I could legally be allowed to have an abortion. He went on to say he couldn't or wouldn't be satisfied to have me accept his one opinion without requesting a second. Would I see Dr Trites, and if he agreed with him, would I go through with it? I offered my hand and we shook on it. With that, he picked up the phone and booked my appointment. The verdict was that I had a good chance of success. I wasn't sure whether to shout for joy or have a good cry.

With wonderful support from family, our Anne Fitch and many friends as well as two shots a week and eighteen pills a day, time passed, made pleasant by the rental of a very nice house at Savary Island for three weeks that summer. Anne played on the lovely white sandy beach with Susan and we enjoyed our many friends up there. I hadn't been to Savary since I was about eleven and was surprised to find it so unchanged. It is such a pretty island and many of the families now have great-grandchildren enjoying their summers there.

At long last, while we were having dinner, I felt the first labour pains. I put in a call to Jack Harrison and was told by his answering service that he was attending a medical dinner and they would have him call me, which he did, with instructions to go to the hospital and he would meet me there.

A Caesarean section was performed with a spinal anaesthetic so as to give our baby every possible chance. I heard, 'Nurse, please show Mrs Duffus her daughter' – there she was, a perfect seven-pound, three-ounce prize specimen. After three boys, I didn't think I could produce a daughter. No words can ever express how I felt as I was completely overwhelmed. The OR was about five floors above my room and I remember so well saying over and over, 'Thank you, thank you, God,' as we went down in the elevator.

Mort and my mother had been told I was coming down so they greeted me as I was wheeled out of the elevator. To say we were all ecstatic with excitement wouldn't begin to describe how we felt. We were going to call our 'son' Andrew so Mort said, 'We'll call her Drue.' Some days later we took her home to Susan and Anne who gave us a royal welcome.

I must mention that on the day that Drue was born, which was 18 October 1947, just after 1:00 a.m., Mort played an early game of golf so he could visit with me in the afternoon. When he arrived from Capilano Golf Club he told me he had some good news and some bad news. The good news was that he had made a hole in one – the bad news being he had forgotten to take out insurance against having one, which would have covered his 'drinks are on me' celebration – which in those days was a lot of money.

Our wonderful Anne Fitch stayed with us until she married and moved up to Kelowna. Jessie Archibald came over from the UK, followed by Miss Paton. The latter answered my advertisement for a Mother's Help. When I opened the door for her interview she reminded me of an English robin, which still remains pictured in my mind when I think of that day. She had excellent references as a secretary! The only cooking experience she had was in cakes, cookies and desserts as her sister always cooked everything else. When I queried leaving a secretarial job for a nanny/housekeeper position she said she wanted a complete change from the business world. When I showed her around the house she said she had to make one stipulation: she would never touch our bar as she had taken an oath some years before to never, ever, have anything to do with alcohol.

I cannot begin to say how deeply we grew to care for Marion Paton. The girls were devoted to her and she soon learned to add to her cooking skills, so much so that I found I had extra time on my hands and decided to put my designing and dressmaking skills into use. With encouragement from Mort and Miss Paton's secretarial ability, I started a dolls clothes business.

There was a sixteen inch doll on the market that appealed to me so I designed seventeen outfits, the most complex being the exact replicas of the uniforms and blazers of all the private schools across Canada. Only one school in the east turned me down of all the schools I wrote to. As business grew I hired four needle-women to do piecework in their own homes. Armed with my samples, I called on our three main department stores and, to my delight, two of them used my dolls in their main Christmas windows. Miss Paton handled my books for me and 'Jane Rae Togs' was looking very promising until an enterprising company in Eastern Canada took a leaf out of my book and mass-produced dolls clothes that were very cheap, not well made and appealed to the masses. So, when my sales dropped, I folded my so-called enterprising wings.

When Miss Paton's sister became ill we had to accept her resignation. We remained friends for as long as she lived. I still treasure the Bible she gave me and to this day enjoy one of her decadent chocolate desserts

Looking back to 1947 when Drue was born, we went through some dreadful nights with her, as she would waken about two in the morning and cry. Naturally we assumed she wanted attention so she was changed and put down again. Not long afterwards, she would start up again. Thinking she must be hungry we would give her a bottle – and so it went, night after night. Ann Fitch was with us through all of that period, so we took turns. Thinking we were spoiling her we would try and let her cry herself to sleep. Our specialist, for sure, thought she did it for attention. Fortunately when she went on to solid foods she stopped; more about this later.

When Drue was little she hated birthday parties and her kindergarten and was much happier playing at home with her own rocking horse, her dog, dolls, or Harry – her special friend who lived next door. One day when they were playing, she came home and was obviously looking for something, so I asked what she wanted. She replied, 'Harry and I want some matches.' I played along and gave her a couple and followed to see what they had in mind. To my horror, I found that they had rolled up newspaper with kindling and fire logs up against Harry's house! If I had not been in the room to ask what she was looking for, I hate to think of the fire they would have caused on that hot summer day. If I remember correctly, I think I burnt them both with one of the matches so that they would never want to play with them again. I would probably be put in jail for that punishment today – but when I told Harry's parents and Mort, they thought I taught them a good lesson. With our cottage at Cowan's Point to think about, with only a garden hose to put out a fire and our Island Fire Hall six miles away from us, the whole island could go up in smoke, so all children had to learn the dangerous outcome of playing with fire.

When Drue was about four and a half, she inherited her sister's beautiful English geared three-wheeled tricycle, which had been the joy of Susie's life but had been replaced with a two-wheeler. She took to it like a duck to water and soon found it a challenge to push it up the hill in front of our house; climbing aboard and holding onto the handlebars, legs akimbo, down she would go.

One day my mother, who had given Susie the bike, was about to depart when our neighbour Helen Craig, whom we adored, began talking to her when Drue appeared on her tricycle. Calling to us she said, 'Watch me come down the hill, Ga Ga.' My mother replied, 'Yes dear.' However, deep in conversation with Helen, mother missed the performance. Unfortunately Drue realised her hoped-for audience had been oblivious to her great feat. As she cycled past us she said, 'Well, that was a damned waste of time.' Obviously her father's child!

Another time, Drue was riding in Southland's when her horse shied at a sudden noise from a piece of farm machinery and took off at a mad gallop with Drue's boot caught in the stirrup as she was thrown. I followed with every ounce of strength I could possibly muster, running through a wet field, crying and screaming. I will never know why she wasn't killed. Fortunately, they came to an abrupt halt at a gate leading to a road and Drue wrenched herself free. Nothing was broken but her muscles were torn in her leg and her ankle sprained.

Having ridden for years myself, I shared her love for horses and about a year later, Mort's mother 'Grandie' bought 'Glory' for her, whom she nicknamed 'Liverlips' because she said if she kissed liver it would no doubt feel the same as Glory. We were able to take her up to the island for a few summers and much to the amusement of the ferry passengers, Glory would whinny lustily during the crossing. Drue graduated to a motorboat and Glory was given to a friend, where she lived out the last of her life with very caring people. I have written elsewhere about a crossing I experienced with our daughter.

When Drue reached grade eleven at Crofton House it was customary for the girls to invite the boys to their annual dance at the end of the year. When Drue came home one Saturday from a fun time at the badminton club, she regaled me with a detailed

Drue comes out at the Trafalgar
Ball with her father.

Drue, 18 years.

account of the evening with emphasis on the super person she had met, namely Bruce Akhurst.

'Do you know his family?' she asked.

'It's not a common name. It could be that I went out with his father, and when my father was young he worked as sales manager for his grandfather,' was my reply.

'I'd really like to ask Bruce to go to the grade eleven formal with me but I am scared he will turn me down!' Drue said.

She finally got bullied into calling him, which she did upstairs. Finally, she came bouncing down shouting, 'He said he'd love to!' So that was the beginning. Yes, it was the same family. Soon her friends and Bruce's became one and they had lots of good times together.

With the exception of one other young lad that Drue had a temporary interest in, Bruce remained number one. In 1969 they were married, with Susan as her matron of honour, and Cal

Carol Martin, Susan, Drue,
Diane Campbell and Jocelyn Davidson.

Martin, Diane Campbell and Jocelyn Davidson as her brides-maids. Bruce's brother Brian was the best man and Rick Campbell, Christopher Madden, Paul Johnson and Dave Large were ushers. There was an absolute downpour the night before the big day, with rain the next morning.

Mort had ordered an awning for the church which they were putting up as I arrived to arrange the altar flowers. I recall calling up to them and saying, 'The sun will be out for the wedding.' 'Don't count on it, ma'am,' was the reply. By three o'clock not only had the rain stopped but the clouds cleared, the sun broke out and it was a fabulous sparkling clear afternoon. Drue looked beautiful, as did Susan and all the bridesmaids. Both families were happy about their marriage, which made it nice for everyone. Drue chose Ernest Krieger, a great friend of ours, to propose the toast to the bride. It was very funny and he made much of the

Bruce and Drue,
13 September 1969.

The wedding party,
Capilano Golf Club.

nickname he had given her at Cowan's Point several years before, which was 'Fearless'. This came about because of the way she handled the speedboat. The reception was held at Capilano Golf Club, which they did extremely well. We had a chap playing the zither, who was awfully good. I love background music.

When it came time for them to leave for their honeymoon, they expected to find Bruce's car at the door but instead a golf cart, nicely decorated with streamers and flowers, was waiting for them. The car was parked at a lower parking lot, so this certainly cut out any emotional moments, as we were all laughing so hard. On their return to Vancouver, they moved into the dearest little guesthouse at the back of Dr Bill and Barney Robertson's house. There they stayed until Drue was expecting a baby when they moved to a very nice family house. We were later presented with a grandson, to be baptized Graham Duffus Akhurst. His other grandparents always called him 'Duffy'. Drue was devoted to my father so chose his name, about which he was very pleased. Mort was delighted to have Duffus as he was the last of his family.

Next came Ryan James Akhurst, a dark-haired boy, as a contrast

Susan, Drue's Matron of Honour.   *Drue and Bruce share a joke.*

Matthew's Avenue. Painted by Drue.

Drue and Ryan, Susan and Guy.

to his fair-haired brother. He was born about eight weeks after Guy, Susan and Crozier's son, so the three boys had some great times together as the mothers saw each other constantly – in fact they were fast forming a best friend relationship. They took on the leasing of a cottage at Cowan's Point and shared every other two weeks every summer. They all loved life up there and the young families thrived on the simple life, minus television and electricity, with swimming only a stone's throw away.

With two children and a third on the way, Bruce and Drue moved for the third time to a charming house and Christie Elizabeth made her way into the family.

It wasn't until Drue was eighteen that it was found that she could not tolerate milk, which, regrettably, she craved, to say nothing of ice cream, which she adored. From time to time she was to suffer a great deal of pain because of the lack of tolerance.

Drue, Graham and Bruce.

Unfortunately there wasn't a substitute for milk as there is today. Later it was finally deemed necessary for her to have an exploratory operation, the tragic outcome of which was for her to be told she had cancer, with six months to a year to live. She was thirty-six years old, had a happy marriage, and three young children. After this devastating news, all that I can remember her saying was, 'Mum, I will be living with a time bomb.' She bore that news with such courage and sheer 'guts' that it was hard at times to believe it was true, as nothing seemed to stop her from carrying on with a normal life, all of which time she was on chemotherapy. If her appointment happened to interfere with her tennis games, she would wear a long-sleeved shirt with her chemo intravenous in her arm and its little motor attached to the belt on her shorts. I remember, while waiting for Drue to have her intravenous inserted, the receptionist was talking to a young man who obviously was apprehensive about the whole procedure. As Drue appeared with her tennis shorts she said, 'Drue Akhurst is going to play tennis with her chemo intravenous.' After her next appointment, Drue was told that he had said, 'If she can do it, I can.'

I am finding it very hard to write about this particular time but

Drue, Ryan and Graham.

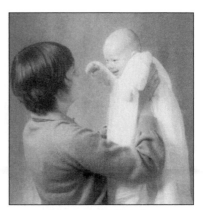

Drue and Christie.

she was such a remarkable, humorous person, she deserves to be recorded for her children and grandchildren, for all the years to come – but I repeat, it is very hard for me to write about that time in our lives.

Susan and Drue became closer and closer and were good for each other. Rick and Diane Campbell, Janet and Ernie Hammond, Cal Martin Bartolic, Nancy Edwards, Pam Harris, the Barclays, and many of her friends whose names escape me, were very supportive and kind. Bruce never failed to do all he could possibly do for her, without appearing to baby her or make her feel conscious of her illness. To my knowledge, Christie was really too young to understand. Graham and Ryan were very helpful and had their soccer and their school to occupy their days.

When it became known Yul Brynner had cancer, Drue saw pictures of him arriving at his hotel prior to a performance with a sack full of carrots. The theory at the time was that carrot juice was a great combatant to cancer, so with the aid of an electric juicer, Drue would drink quantities of carrot juice every day and, laughingly, would show off her orange fingers. This lasted until it was announced that Yul had lost his battle with the dreaded

Drue and Ryan, Susan and Graham, Guy, 'G'.

Graham, Guy, Ryan, Christie.

Drue in Maui. Her last Christmas.

Our memorial honouring Drue at Children's Hospital.

disease. I felt at the time as if part of her gave up her fight. It was already past the year she had been given.

Christmas had always been a very special time in our family and it passed onto the girls, but Drue told me she could not face up to the usual festivities, so would I please understand if Bruce took them off to Maui. It was better for everyone, as it would have been very hard to be merry. Pictures that returned with them from their Maui holiday showed them with their makeshift Christmas tree decorated with weird and wonderful innovative decorations, Christie and the boys buried in sand up to their necks, Drue reading in the shade on a Lilo, and others with their heads thrown back with laughter. Yes, they did the right thing.

On Friday 7 March 1986, Drue died, leaving an insurmountable gap in all our lives. Bruce had a huge load to carry, finally relieved somewhat by Terry, the children's much-loved nanny from New Zealand.

Bruce Akhurst

Life was hard on Bruce when Drue was ill, followed by her death in March 1986, having to have a nanny; literally nothing was the same for him. Fortunately he loved his work and the boys kept him busy attending their sports activities and time passed. At the end of a year I telephoned him and said he must get out and make a new life and that I knew a nurse at Children's Hospital who had a nursing friend who also needed a fresh outlook on life; that she was very pretty – would he permit his mother-in-law to arrange a blind date for him? He laughed and admitted that he wasn't ready, but promised he would phone me if, and when, he was ready. Three months went by and it was all set up and he would ask her out for dinner the following Saturday. Apparently he got cold feet and invited Crozier and Susan to join them. From all accounts, when Bruce called me the next day, it had been a very good

Bruce and Alexia,
24 October 1987.

Grandmother and Christie. Day of
the wedding of Bruce and Alexia.

evening and he mentioned he thought he would ask her out again. The next call I had from him was to say he had never, in all his dating days, felt as completely exhausted, because without Susan and Crozier who had helped carry the ball, he had been the sole conversationalist all evening. That was that.

Fortunately there were others out there biding their time to move Bruce out of his solitary existence. From all I heard, Alexia Woodworth had been on her own for some time and her friends decided they should meet. A pool party was arranged and Bruce and Alexia met, and clicked. She had a son Angus, the same age as Ryan, and a daughter Erin, a few years older than Christie, so when Bruce asked Alexia to go out he suggested she leave her two with his three for the evening. When they opened the front door on their return there was a ghastly silence. If I remember correctly, Bruce's comment was that perhaps they had killed each other. No,

Alexia and Bruce.

the girls were playing in Christie's bedroom and the three boys were in the playroom downstairs with a Nintendo game – so that was a hurdle well cleared. Time passed and they would meet and walk together at six in the morning. Finally, Bruce had a talk with Graham, Ryan and Christie, asking them what they thought about joining the two families and their reply was, 'Go for it Dad.' They were married on 24 October 1987. They sold both their houses and built a beautiful new one that gave them each a room to themselves with their family's dogs and cat.

I have great admiration for Alexia. She took on five children, each very different in temperament, having time for each one – and it can't always have been easy. I feel sure Alex, Alexia's mother, and her great friend Jill Currie, helped her cope many times.

Bruce has always done a fabulous job; to my knowledge he has been fair and supportive to all five, which eliminated any feelings of favouritism or jealousy.

Fourteen years later when Ryan and April were married, both Graham and his stepbrother Angus were his choice for best men –

which, I think, speaks volumes. Just under a month later Angus and D.J. were married, and Ryan was best man.

All I can think is that it says an awful lot for good parenting. To my way of thinking, one parent needs to be home for children when humanly possible, and in this case Alexia was always home. With seven to cook for, at times three meals a day, she was fortunate to like cooking and the family were always blessed that she is such a superb cook. On many occasions the entire family have sit-down dinners with as many as twenty to thirty people, and everything is delectable.

There has to be a lot said for matchmaking!

Graham

Our eldest grandson, Graham Duffus Akhurst, was born 5 June 1971 and is a combination of Mort and my Grandfather Irwin. Although Mort was 6'5", Graham is taller by a good inch. I was so excited the day he was born and held him so close to make up for the void in my life. As far as I recall he was a good baby and he grew into a most lovable little boy.

When Graham was two we were able to rent the Cherniavskys' beautiful house on Bowen Island for a month. It is a remarkable place for adults and children and can sleep sixteen comfortably. Graham spent many hours in their swimming pool, which he took to like a duck to water. Before bedtime each night he would play one, two, three, go – and run from Drue to me across the end of their huge living room, being caught and whirled around in a circle until even he was tired.

We have always had a very good relationship and I am very proud of him as I feel sure his mother would have been.

Graham graduated from high school and went to the B.C. Institute of Technology and upon his graduation from there he

Graham and Colleen.

Ryan, Graham and Christie.

was asked to join the firm Almetco Building Products Ltd., where he got his feet wet in the business world, following which Bruce claimed him for the company firm, where he has been ever since. From all accounts he has done very well, both for the company and himself.

He has had his share of attractive girlfriends but is now settled and happy in their beautiful house with Coleen, whom we all love – plus a dog and two cats.

I was thrilled on Mother's Day to be asked by the two of them to be their guest for lunch and that they would call for me. I was to discover that they had a picnic planned and it was to be up to me whether we had it on my patio or went somewhere else. I chose to remain at home. While Graham was doing a few jobs for me, Coleen produced everything – a large tablecloth, cutlery, cups, plates, coffee pot, rolls, bread and butter, smoked salmon, salads, pâté, cheese and biscuits, orange or cranberry juice, cookies and coffee!! And a sunny lovely day. I was deeply touched.

Graham.

They both play hockey – Graham on an all-male team and Coleen and a friend are the only two girls that play on a men's team. I can't quite picture it because Coleen is quite slight in build, but she must be good or the men wouldn't have her.

Think I will leave them there.

Ryan James Akhurst

Ryan was born on 19 March 1974. He is the dark-haired one of the family and is the second son of Bruce and Drue. In appearance, he is very like his father when he swept our daughter off her feet. His personality is a combination of both parents –

Ryan with an eye to the future.

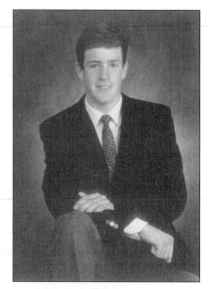

Ryan.

Ryan and April, 2001.

*Mr and Mrs Ryan Akhurst
entering Brock House for their
reception.*

Graham, Christie and Ryan.

thoughtful and kind. He is doing well in the family business, so says his father.

I have several amusing stories to tell about Ryan. When he was about four years old he was sitting on their front steps when a tall black boy was endeavouring to pick a fight with his brother Graham. Little Ryan ran out and stood between them and said, 'You leave my big brudder alone, black boy!'

A few years later, I gave Drue my sapphire and diamond ring. One day she telephoned to say that she was, at last, able to tell me that she had searched high and low for the ring, which failed to unearth itself and couldn't bring herself to tell me it had vanished. To her knowledge it had been on her dressing table. She said she had had a call from the mother of a little girl in Ryan's class to ask her if by any chance she owned a diamond and sapphire ring.

Ryan thought it had come out of a Christmas cracker and had given it to his best girl!

All this leads up to his marriage, almost a year ago, to his very special girl April. May they top Mort's and my sixty-one years. My love and good wishes to them both.

Christie Elizabeth Akhurst: born 15 December 1979

Christie was only seven when her mother died and of the three children I think her loss affected her the most. Being the baby of the family she was with her mother so much of the time, whereas the boys had their sports and school activities to throw themselves into. When Bruce employed their New Zealand nanny, Terry, Christie had the much-needed female love that she so desperately had missed.

With Bruce and Alexia's marriage some nineteen months later, Christie received a very attractive new mother, a much-needed sister, Erin, and another big brother, Angus, and a delightful new grandmother, uncles and aunts. After graduating she went to Langara college to take Child Care courses and went to New Zealand to see Terry and her family. The Olympics beckoned and she went to Australia, which she was able to see a great deal of, thanks to all the wonderful friends she made. There wasn't much she didn't do, even to parachuting at 11,000 feet and the chute not opening at first pull of the ripcord.

All good things come to an end and Christie returned to Vancouver to attend her brothers' weddings – Ryan and April on 6 July 1991 and Angus and D.J. on 4 August.

We have always had a very soft spot for our youngest. As a little girl she loved to put on skits with her cousin Caroline Akhurst (Brian and Jenny's daughter) at family Christmas dinners as they both liked to perform and were very good. They became very

At Crofton House.

close during those early years which I feel sure was a help to Christie when she needed someone her own age to pour her heart out to.

School days began at a little elementary school within walking distance. Sixteen years later she still sees her friends from those days. She entered Crofton House for her high school years where they discovered she had a slight reading disability. I am so grateful, as the teachers worked patiently to help her in so many ways. She would have floundered in the large classes that are the norm in our Government schools.

After Christie graduated she joined a wonderful European tour with her friends. Regrettably when she was packing to leave Spain she left her poems behind and they were gone forever.

The other gift she is blessed with is her love for and understanding of children. Child care is her chosen field. She is

Christie in her graduation gown.

teaching now and at a fashion show that she organized to raise funds for much needed equipment she was loudly applauded by attending parents and presented with a beautiful bouquet of flowers.

Australia she loved! Totally! When she can afford to return there won't be much grass growing under her feet, I fear.

Christie has been fortunate to have a gift of pouring her heart out into her poetry, which helped her after losing her beloved mum. I will include many of them as I feel they are an addition to my memoirs.

Whatever? My love and good wishes, Chris, dear. 'G' (short for Grandmother)

Christie's Poems

Dear G and Dad Mort,

Merry Christmas!

I want to thank you for everything you have done for me. So one of my presents for you is a copy of all my poems I have made this year, 1994. I thought it would be nice for you because they are so private and personal to me. This is a way to show my love for you both. They aren't great but I love them because I tried really hard with them. Well, I better go. I love you.

Love always,

Christie

Chris

xxx ooo

Eternal Life

She lies there
So helplessly and weak –
With no tears left.
The pain endlessly stabs her
Until there is nothing left.
She is drowning right
Right in front of me,
And I cannot even reach to give her my hand.
All I can do,
Is to give her my heart;
To love and protect,
To guide and fulfil,
And to share with everyone
Who watches over me.
Her pale face looks up at me;
With her almond-shaped eyes

Closing to a new light;
With people welcoming her –
To an eternal life.

7 November 1994

A Tear is like the Sea

Lying on my bed
With no tears left,
I whimper like a helpless puppy.
I close my eyes and
See you there –
Reaching out to hold my hand.
We walk along the endless shore
And shine like the glimmering sun.
The sea attempts to whisk us off –
Like a sailboat with no real destiny.
The day is getting darker
As the clouds start to hover above;
It is time to break apart
Like a shattered vase.
Our hands unclasp
As we walk along our separate paths;
To a different world,
In a different light.
I open my eyes
And it has all disappeared;
But I can feel you in my heart –
You will always be there.

Dedicated to my mom, Jane Drue Duffus Akhurst, who passed
away on 7 March 1986.   2 March 1995

In Memorie

It is coming to that time
That I dislike the most,
When we all have to say goodbye.
This time that I have been here,
I have learnt a lot.
Such as:
Care, support and friendship.
This special place
Has made me a better person
In more ways than I can say.
And what I love most about this place
Are the people.
They are so warm and caring.
There is always a shoulder to lean on,
To laugh with and to talk to.
I can hear the bus come for me,
But do I really want to get on that bus?
Will anyone be there to lean on, to laugh with
Or even to talk to?
Maybe, but I do not know.
Everything is so uncertain when I leave;
It is like living on shaky ground
And you do not know when it's going to collapse on you.
There is nothing I can do
But to shake it off,
And try not to think of it.
But I know that I will
And will always have to face it.
And so what I am trying to say
Is not goodbye,
But see you soon.

11 August 1995

Shadows of the Past

Sitting on the hard wood floor
I see memories in my teary eyes
People laughing, people crying
Children playing, children fighting
Shadows, busy and joyful;
The seasons pass
The events pass
Life has passed
There are no more shadows
Just a small old room
Even though there are no more shadows,
They will always be here in my eyes

The Summer Cabin

The sun shining through,
Into my sleepy eyes.
Each foot hits the cold floor;
The birds' whiz
Around and around;
The warm breeze
Brushes through the grass.
Waves crashing along
The thin white sand.
Shells shimmer on the
Beach of sand.
Cliffs hang over the
Bay of sea;
Pebbles scattered
Surround me.
The eagle circles the

Towering trees,
Just like the seasons
Circling me.
I know later in life
This special place will
Be taken over by
Pollution
And it will not be as beautiful
As before;
But in my eyes
It will always be beautiful

Friendship

A friend is someone who cares
When in need of support.
A friend shows respect
When in need of room.
A friend gives love
When in need of completeness.
A friend gives a hand
When in need of happiness.
A friend is loyal
When in need of a shield.
A friend is sympathetic
When in need of a shoulder.
A friend is humorous
When in need of laughter.
A friend smiles
When in need of good cheer.
A friend is someone who gives their time
When in need of a friend.

A Perfect World

A perfect world would not have children lying dead in the street,
A perfect world would not have children beat.
A perfect world would not have crime,
A perfect world would not have no sense of time.
A perfect world would not have flowers die,
A perfect world would not let people cry.
A perfect world would not let families part,
A perfect world would have all people with big hearts.
A perfect world would have no wars,
A perfect world would have no sores.
A perfect world would have peace worldwide.
A perfect world would have friends side by side.
A perfect world would have no pollution,
A perfect world would always have a solution.
A perfect world would always have blue sky,
A perfect world would have everyone get by.
A perfect world would have undying love,
A perfect world would symbolise a dove.
A perfect world.

Dearest Friends

Dearest friends,
When the road seemed dark
And the stars in the sky
Were all there was to lead the way –
To your eyes.
Eyes – of new paths,
New mysteries.
Seared in my heart,

I let go –
Dancing in the moonlight.
And with each turn
Things seem brighter
As the dawn rises
Before us.
Blissful dreams whelm inside
And touch each person
Who gives their hand.
Raindrops soak our
Bodies –
But we dance on
Thru the fields.
When the music
Of our dreams fade
And time comes
To recline into the
Blossoming flowers –
We lie and remember
The music that will
Always live in our
Hearts and souls.
My dearest friends –
May we live through
The music.

Dedicated to my mates from Stars N Stripes Bar, February 2000 –
June 2000   September 2000

Dearest Love

Captured by a smile –
Swept up with a
Friendship, unbeknownst
Where our footprints may lead.
Clasped hands –
Unbreakable to the storms
Ahead –
We come out stronger.
Separated by the crashing
Waves of the sea –
I still feel that smile,
Those magical touches;
Touches that embrace me
In security and warmth
Of the bitter cold nites.
It's now time our footprints
Will cross again,
I fear what lies ahead –
Until I come across your
Shadow in the lite –
Holding your hand out –
To face the world together.

18 December 2000

Memories

Memories,
So warm and wonderful;
Full of love, laughter and sorrow.
Memories,

Of endless birthday bashes,
Playing games of all sorts,
Eating cake and ice cream.
Memories,
Running through the sand
Into the cold, salty water,
Jumping continuously
Over the crashing waves.
Memories,
Eating roasted marshmallows
Around the burning fire,
Being carried to my cozy bed.
Memories,
Lingering lullabies,
Soothing me to bed
To dream wonderful dreams.
Memories,
Not in my mind,
But in my heart;
Locked dearly –
Forever.
Memories.

17 October 1994
Age 16

Parting Tears

Looking at you –
Through the whispering
Rings of smoke unravelling
From the candle –
I memorise that smile,

That smile that filled
My heart with new beginnings.
Fear struggles with
My soul –
Fear of losing your
Presence when I face
Moving onwards.
So I close my eyes
Whelming with tears –
And remember.
The struggle is gone –
And a smile covers those
Saddened tears –
For you will never be
Gone –
You will always be
Close to my heart.

Christie
September 2000

Dedicated to my friends in NZ.

Thank you, Christie dear. 'G'

22 April 1995

Dear Johnny,

This seems the best way of returning the enclosed to you as on the days when we meet at church I do not have the envelope with me – and when I do have it in my bag, we attend different services!

I know how special they must be to you and I am indeed

honoured that you shared them with me. I do hope the Italian ones were found, to add to this remarkable collection.

Affectionately,

Rosalind

(Miss Rosalind Addison was Headmistress at Crofton House when Christie attended. She was a third generation student, following her mother, Susan and me.)

Angus Woodworth

Angus was born 8 March 1974, big brother to Erin and very different from her in appearance. He is fair and she is dark and he is as handsome as she is pretty.

Angus and Ryan formed a strong friendship from the start and shared their love for sports, soccer in particular. They attended the same school, and their birthdays are eleven days apart – so Alexia

Mr and Mrs Angus Woodworth.

usually, if not always, kills two birds with one stone and has a joint celebration dinner party.

Angus has a personality that I'm sure would win anyone's heart as it did his beloved D.J. They were married a few months after Ryan and April, so will soon celebrate their first year together. They impress me as being very well suited to each other – both so natural and sharing the same sense of humour.

May you have a wonderful life together with good health and happiness.

Erin Woodworth

On 27 May 1977, Erin was born and is now twenty-five, a wonderful age. She is very pretty with a good brain and has, ever since I first met her, struck me as having her feet well planted on the ground and having a good idea what she hopes to achieve in her lifetime.

Erin.

Erin has already done some very interesting travelling – Hawaii with her father, a walking tour in Scotland with her mother Alexia, which from all accounts was a very strenuous achievement, and her latest venture to Thailand with her delightful companion Vippin. This was to be an experience never to be forgotten.

Looking back to the early days of Bruce and Alexia's marriage, it must have been very hard on Erin to share her mother with Graham, Ryan and Christie. Once more I think good parenting performed admirably as both families seem to be very well melded and happy with each other, if all the laughter and fun they share when I am there for dinner is any criterion.

Whatever life holds for you Erin, I wish you great happiness.

Cowan's Point, Bowen Island, BC

EVERY SUMMER we rented a cottage at Cowan's Point, Bowen Island, which is, as the crow flies, about twelve miles up the coast from Vancouver. We had no electricity; coal oil-lamps served us very well. Our coal and wood stove in the kitchen never let me down. The fireplace in the living room heated the cottage when we needed it. Between the two of them, they devoured Mort's woodpile. Thankfully we had indoor plumbing, a tin bath for the children and the Pacific Ocean for us. There was no ferry in those days, so we used water taxis from Horseshoe Bay to Seymour Bay where we were met by the caretaker. Mort would come up every weekend with our week's supply of food and a hundred pounds of ice. Fortunately, after a few years, a ferry service which took cars came into being and the girls would walk up the old road to meet their father each Friday. His favourite saying as he drew up to our back door – 'Many hands make light work.' The car would finally be emptied. There would be a roast, a two inch top sirloin steak for the barbecue, fresh fruit and vegetables, bottled supplies, etc. A swim was definitely in order and down our path we would go to our beloved Kinishy Bay (named by the Japanese I imagine), topped off with a drink that always tasted so good after our swim.

A creek, with a small bridge, divided the Cowan houses from the Malkin houses, and on their side they had a beautiful bay called Trinity which had a wharf, so all the children enjoyed each other's bays and beaches. On our side we had Union Bay, Alder, and, as mentioned, Kinishy, never sure if it was spelled with an i or an e. There was a field for their Sunday baseball game. There were never fewer than twenty-two children, pretty well divided between boys and girls.

Two of Mort's greatest friends, Alan Russell and Mike McLennen, were rap rummy addicts and could be seen most afternoons playing out on the so-called lawn. All the mothers would be on the beach with their families or in swimming. It was a wonderful way to bring up our children; they all got along so well together. There was no television so they used their imaginations and created endless ways to fill their days. Friendships were formed that have held fast and all the married ones are great friends.

Dear old Mrs Cowan had her log house up above our cottage. We were allowed to use her telephone, which was wonderful for emergencies or our grocery orders to our husbands. Mrs Cowan was a member of the Toc H, to which my mother belonged, and my first visit to the point was when I was nine years old and I accompanied her to attend a meeting.

When Susan and Drue were about seven and a half and five, my Wren Officer friend, Margot Redford, came over to stay with us and she spent some time with us at the Point. She loved every minute of it and if I remember correctly, she was with us when the children discovered a huge wasps' nest in one of the trees not far from our house. Mort borrowed a gun from Lila Malkin Molson and, much to the delight of the children, blew it to pieces. Such a horrible thing to do, but a far worse thing it could have been if those same children had disturbed that nest. It was the size of one of their heads.

About this time my father had a major operation in Vancouver and after he was allowed to return from hospital, I suggested he come over to the Island and stay with me until he got his strength back. He seemed to be doing so well and the girls loved him. After about a week, he complained that he had a severe pain in his back. His doctor said he must be taken to the hospital at once. Nothing was ever simple up there owing to the ferry crossing schedules and a six-mile drive across the island mostly over shockingly bad roads to catch a ferry, as well as a twenty-five minute drive into the city. As it happened that day, when we drove into Snug Cove to hopefully board, we found the ferry was not in service and was temporarily replaced by a large passengers-only boat.

As we moved out of the weather-protected bay, to my horror we found we were into a strong Squamish wind that bounced us about as if we were a pea on a hot griddle. My father's face became ashen and all I could do was pray, and pray I did. 'Please God, still the waters, as only You can do.' Believe me when I tell you, whoever reads this – we crossed in calm waters. Passengers remarked on the sudden drop in the wind, as it was so obvious, and my father lost the anguished look on his face.

As arranged, Mort was on the dock to meet us and our patient was transferred to his car. I went back to the island to the children who had been left in the care of a friend. It was some hours before I heard that the pain was caused by a blood clot in his lung. I honestly do not think he would have survived that crossing had my prayers not been answered and, thankfully, he lived for fourteen years more.

When young, Susan and Drue were very different. Susan was born to dance and Drue, like her mother, loved horses and boats and dogs and cats. For several years, Drue kept her horse up at Cowan's Point, finally parting with Glory for a speedboat. She kept us in crab from the crab pots she dropped in the bays from her boat. I, unfortunately, was elected to boil them and hated doing it.

When it would come time to take the boat over for the summer holidays, we would attach the trailer carrying the boat to my car.

To launch her I had to back the trailer into the water and remember to turn the wheel in the opposite direction, to direct the trailer straight into the water; this I found amusing. On one occasion Mort and Susan crossed in his car with all our supplies and Drue and I followed by our boat. We didn't know until we rounded Horseshoe Bay that there was a storm out there. In order for us to communicate at all we had to really shout above the wind and sea. 'If we try to turn back, Mum, we'll capsize, so we have to go on.' She handled that boat masterfully. One minute we were up in the air and the next we crashed down, sending water in every direction. I yelled my loudest, 'I'm getting so much water in my mouth!!' Her reply was, 'Then shut your mouth!' To add to the joy of the treacherous crossings, there was an aircraft circling overhead barking out orders to us, saying, 'All small craft will return to shore immediately!' My three war-time Atlantic crossings were a piece of cake compared to that experience. I don't know how long we took, it seemed like a lifetime until we rounded our point into our calm bay. Waving frantically from our verandah were Mort and Susan. Knowing what the sea was like when they crossed in the ferry, they knew what we were faced with and were sick with worry. Some experiences live in your memory forever.

Baking bread in our coal and wood stove was a favourite pastime of mine and when it came out of the oven it was as if I had sounded a bugle to the tune of 'come to the cookhouse door boys', as suddenly there was a very large hungry adopted family sitting on our canvas mat out on our bank. I have to smile whenever I smell freshly-baked bread.

One day there was a huge commotion on our back road that passed behind us, so we all went to see what was going on. To our amazement our good friends Forrie and Gwynn Rogers had in tow one of their children's tents, wooden floor and fly, to wish me

At the Point with Susan.

a happy birthday. This turned out to be a fabulous gift as it gave the girls two extra beds for the guests they so enjoyed having. I'll never know how they ever got that monstrous amount of wood and canvas up their hill from Downhill, their aptly-named house. It was a masterful achievement in anybody's language. We were all deeply touched that they would do such a magnanimous thing for our girls.

Drue loved to sleep out in the tent with her dogs, with the exception of one night which started out to be a perfectly normal one. The girls went off to bed, as usual, followed by us a few hours later. We had been having very warm weather which finally erupted late that night into a rip-roaring thunder and lightning storm. We couldn't believe Drue could sleep through the noise and flashing of lightning, but hoped she would. After about ten more minutes there was a horrendous blast that literally shook our cottage and Mort said, 'That ought to flush her out of there' – and so it did. Drue burst through the door with the dogs in hot pursuit.

I had a Hillman station wagon that both girls learned to drive in, and this proved to be a great place to learn. We were at such a private part of the world, we felt it was very safe. They both passed their test at sixteen with flying colours.

With a wharf over at Trinity Bay on the Malkin side, those who liked to fish would usually do so from there. When Bowen Day was to take place one summer, notices were sent out that there would be a prize offered to the child under a certain age who caught the largest fish that day and by such and such an hour. Drue loved to fish, so had dropped her line off the wharf. This she did the night before, not intending to look at her line until the next day. Just before dark she thought she should check to make sure her hook hadn't snagged a piece of seaweed. To her utter amazement she had a really good-sized ling cod. When she arrived back to our place it was with a very sad face, admitting that she couldn't enter it in the competition as it was three hours before the designated day. Mort handled the situation perfectly by insisting she take the fish and explain that she had caught it in the manner that she had done, so as to at least give her some fun, even if she couldn't win anything. Unknown to Drue, he explained the situation to the judge and said he was very proud of her honesty and would he award a consolation prize of ten dollars, which Mort gave. We had a very happy daughter and we had a wonderful dinner.

Colleen Walker and Susan, the former being the editor and Susan the artist, brought out their weekend edition of the *Cowan's Point Chronicle*. It was priceless and read eagerly by old and young. The two enterprising girls, then about twelve, are still very close friends, some forty-five years later. Susan told me that

Drue got into the act at some time but couldn't remember when
or how.

We spent fifteen years in that cottage. We would make our first
trip up for Easter with an Easter egg hunt for the children,
followed by every good weekend weather-wise that we weren't
obligated in town, with two whole months every summer, topped
off with Thanksgiving. We had fun and the children had fun.
They each had to use their imagination as there was no electricity
for television. We had a good battery radio which kept us up-to-
date with the news. We always thought it was the very best thing
we ever did for our children. All the parents set high standards of
discipline, encouragement, love and respect for nature.

When the Rogers bought their boat, they offered to rent their
lovely house Downhill to us, which we were delighted to be able
to do. The girls were older and took very happily to the swimming
pool and life of luxury after primitive life in our cottage. Ann and
Fred Thompson were the caretakers and were a huge help to us
and kept up the care of the property, which we could never have
done without them. We had one experience that must have shaken
Anne more than a little. Mort had been having a painful time with
arthritis in his hands and the treatment recommended was to
submerge them in hot wax. One weekend he arrived up with a
supply of wax and paper towels. He found it did help to ease the
pain. The following weekend we were invited to spend with
Gordon and Jean Southam at Qualicum Beach on Vancouver
Island. This had become an annual event of three days, water
skiing and partying with all their friends. There were hilarious
bridge sessions, one of which was secretly recorded by two of
their seven children and played back to us the next day! As we
couldn't take all the treatment supplies with us, the wax was
stashed in a pail on the floor of the laundry room and away we
went. When we arrived back, we were met by a gloomy looking

caretaker, namely Fred Thompson. Fortunately, his wife Anne was nowhere in sight, as I am sure she felt little or no sympathy for us. We were told that Anne had needed her pail and thinking the pail had not been emptied from something I had been soaking, and never dreaming it was wax, poured it down the drain! Enough said!

Ernest and Edith Krieger rented the second house which the Rogerses had built for their children, Jill, Steven and Martin. It was nice for us as we had some very spirited bridge games, when the men weren't playing their highly competitive crib.

Ernest used to marvel at the way Drue handled her boat and gave her the nickname 'Fearless'. She was a gutsy fifteen-year old at that time who, unfortunately, used to suffer from abdominal pains which eventually led to the exploratory operation some years afterwards. She used to bear these times stoically and on one occasion at Downhill, Tippy, her beloved Sheltie and I, sat beside her bed until she finally dropped off to sleep from exhaustion. I then went off to bed, taking Tippy with me and was wakened by a very loud, strange noise, followed by Tippy making a rapid exit from my room. My luminous clock said it was 2:50. I hurried to the window, not knowing what to expect, drew back the drapes and to my astonishment there was a huge cigar-shaped 'thing' up in the sky over the ocean. All I could say was 'Good God', over and over again. As much as I wanted to, I couldn't bring myself to waken Drue as she had finally been able to sleep. How many seconds or minutes I stood there in total awe of what I was seeing, I can't say. Suddenly it upended itself and, as we have all seen at launchings at Cape Canaveral, a veritable blast of fire belched out of its rear. Faster than I could follow it, it looked like a star. This took place in July 1963. I telephoned to one of the radio stations to see if they had had anybody call in to report it. They had not, but would call the airport and if they had heard anything, they would call me. I never heard from them. I phoned Mort, who thought it very funny, pooh-poohed the whole thing and said I had had quite a dream. He never did believe me, which made me furious. Within the last few years I have attended many UFO meetings with my friend Doris Manning and have related my experience. I am happy to say I have always been believed.

I don't know about other cities, but on a clear night I can watch the antics of UFOs from my bed. They make me dizzy watching them; they scamper back and forth, up and down, until I become bored watching and either turn over or become mesmerised and fall asleep. They must be incredibly intelligent individuals with a tremendous fascination with us. If they think, though, that they resemble a star up there, I have news for them – stars don't perform, except the ones we have on earth.

Forrie and Gwynn were very generous with their hospitality and every New Year was a very special time at Downhill! Cynthia and Pat Burns (he was my much-loved second cousin) and Mort and I spent many fun times with them over that holiday. Forrie's sister Elspeth was married to Jan Cherniavsky and they had a very beautiful log house – Fairweather; it was about an eight-minute drive from Downhill. They could sleep about sixteen and always invited the same group of friends up for New Year. An invitation from Fairweather to Downhill was extended each year to attend their entertainment. One year stands out in my mind very clearly.

When we arrived, they had set up a stage for what was to be a hilarious performance starring Jan. He was lying on a large double bed on top of a silk eiderdown on his tummy, wearing a voluptuous satin maribou-trimmed negligee, long blond wig, bow lips, false eyelashes, bare hairy legs, and painted toenails – all of this had to be seen to be so funny. Jan was carrying on a very flirtatious conversation on the phone with 'her' paramour. I had been sitting beside Mort but had moved behind him to sit on an elevated part of the staircase so I could see better. I leaned forward to share the humour with him and with the room in darkness, with the exception of the spot-lit bed, I did not return to my chosen seat, mis-sat, and landed on a large coal scuttle that I tipped over – then I hit the floor. To make a long story short, the x-rays showed I had fractured my fifth vertebra, which was reset, followed by weeks in bed wearing a tightly laced corset with a plywood board under my mattress.

It seems bad times come in threes, which was certainly true in my case. With me incapacitated, and our Finnish maid knowing very little English, Drue got the flu. The nurse/housekeeper we employed stormed into our bedroom to announce her departure as she was under the impression she was to look after me, not a sick child as well. Susan had already been packed off by my very special angel of a friend, Barbara Kaye, so it was hard to understand. Being totally frustrated and medicated for pain, I burst into a flood of sympathy for me. I phoned my wonderful GP Dr Jack Miller and told him my sad tale of woe. As always, he was a person who could be counted on to be there for me and this was no exception. 'Don't worry,' he said, 'I will have someone there in half an hour. She is Norwegian, with very passable English and her name is Mrs James.' True to his word, our Finnish Martha showed her up to our bedroom. One look at her and I knew all would be well. Drue got better, Martha was happy, and I finally became mobile again, thanks to that delightful tower of strength.

While Jack Miller is fresh in my mind, I must take this opportunity to expound about that very special doctor because that is what he was. He was never too busy to listen, no matter what your problems were; his office would be full of patients who had received the same wonderful care and compassionate understanding. A lot of my friends went to him and we all felt the same way about him. Eventually, our daughters went to him. They thought the world of him also. To our great sadness, he told us he was retiring, so as many as we could muster agreed to have my art teacher paint a large picture of the view from Isabelle and Jack's summer home on Galiano Island. A friend who lived on Galiano and knew the Millers took a snapshot the day after a heavy snowfall and our Constance Pomeroy painted a remarkably good picture from the photo. We then had a party for him at our house with all those who had contributed to his gift. I saw it sometime later in their dining room. After his wife died, life lost its lustre, I always felt, as they were a devoted couple.

When Mort and I were spending the weekend with Forrie and Gwynn, they had invited all the Fairweather entourage to join them for a 'nooner' as we called it, which usually meant a gin and tonic or a caesar. After they had all departed, their two sons, Stephen and Martin, said they had replaced the gin with water!

Jill and her brothers had their own house and I used to share a fellow feeling for her when she would barge in with her eyes flashing and her face puce with rage at something the boys had done to her.

When Marj and Doug McRae and Cynthia and Pat Burns were also guests at the same time as Mort and me, we tossed to see who would stay in the children's house and we won, so we stayed in Forrie and Gwynn's. After dinner, Marj used our bedroom to put on her lipstick. Shortly after she returned to the living room, I could not believe what was happening to her face. She was such a pretty person who was now turning grotesque in front of our eyes. Her lips looked like sausages, her nose was huge and her cheeks were swollen out of shape. I asked her if she was feeling all right and she said she was going to bed as she felt dreadful, with the parting words, 'That will teach me to indulge myself with your perfume, Johnnie.' She had returned to normal by breakfast.

One New Year, the Burns, Mort and I, with Forrie and Gwynn,

were met by Fred Thompson in the jeep at Snug Cove (the village on the island). There had been a heavy snowfall and freezing weather. To reach our end of Bowen Island, we had to get up Bishop's Hill and go down Granny's Hill – about a six-mile trip. Fred said Bishop's Hill was deeply rutted with snow from the cars and it was very icy. The men would have to walk up and Fred would take the three of us and bags. We got halfway up and started to slide back down; it was quite scary. Fortunately, we stopped sliding, the men caught up with us, and pushed the jeep up the hill. It was a memorable weekend – cold and beautiful with our champagne stashed in the snow. We cannot always count on snow every winter on the mainland, so when we do, our trees are a sight to behold.

A friend of mine, Bettie Myers, who grew up in Seattle, was the daughter of great friends of our parents. After she married, she moved to Portland and had two daughters, Lorri and Debbie. Every summer she would drive from Portland to Cowan's Point to stay with me for the mid-week (five days) with the two little girls. This would be in the fifties and sixties, when her car was a four-door, older vintage Chevrolet. The highway was not what it is today and the drive from her door to ours was at least eight hours on the road. How she did it, I do not know, but it was her idea of heaven to be at the Point every summer. When the girls were very much older, Bettie divorced, re-married a few years later and became Mrs Paul Keeney. He had business in Vancouver from time to time and the four of us had some very nice evenings together. He died in the early nineties, and Bettie in 2000.

Volunteering

WHEN I WAS YOUNG, we grew up with the knowledge, under the influence of our parents, no doubt, that we must help those less fortunate than ourselves. From the early days of sending children off to summer camp, I graduated to the Red Feather drive, and I was given a list of people I was to call on. Our city Mayor happened to be one of them and I remember climbing three flights of stairs and being greeted by him in a most congenial manner, whereupon he vanished for a few minutes and then came back to the door brandishing a dollar bill. I cannot believe that the Mayor of our city had so little feeling in his heart for the needy people around him.

Next on my list was to be asked to join the Junior League. My first job was to work in the Vancouver Preventorium, which was a hospital for infectious diseases, but not contagious ones. This I truly loved, and I developed a love for working with sick children. We were moved to the UK and my resignation went in to the Junior League. I was very sorry doing so as I loved my work and it was a very commendable organisation that did an immense amount of volunteer work and raised thousands of dollars to aid poorly funded places throughout our city. The young women such as I followed in the footsteps of older members who had set a very high standard that we were more than pleased to follow. It's very sad, I think, that so many worthwhile traditional organisations have been cast aside and disbanded.

Once the war was over and I was able to volunteer again, I

joined the Auxiliary to the Vancouver General Hospital as a driver. This involved reporting to the out-patients department to receive orders and a map that would take me to the home of the patient who had no other means of getting to the hospital to be treated, who would be driven there and home again. Most of these trips were quite a way out of the city, so I could only manage one or two patients a day. In no time we became friends and they were always most grateful for the drive and the company. I forget how long I drove patients, but when maternity nurses requested the Auxiliary for help, I worked there for quite a long time and loved every minute of it. When it was time for the mother to leave with her baby, we were allowed to dress the babe and wheel the mother and her prized possession out of the building and see them into the waiting car. We were a very happy team of volunteers and there wasn't a nurse on the floor that did not welcome us with a huge smile when we reported for duty.

The next SOS that came our way was to assist in the emergency department. Having always had a very keen interest in nursing, I left the babies and moved in. Once more we were welcomed with open arms by the nursing staff and doctors. We were trained up to a point, but mostly we used our own initiative and gradually took on more and more. We comforted parents and those in distress, made phone calls for them to alert families where they were, made beds, and pushed patients for what seemed like miles through the labyrinth of tunnels that wormed their way through the different buildings pertaining to the hospital. As time went on, the powers that be must have come to the conclusion that we did perform a service that released others to get on with more important things. My enthusiasm elevated me to chair this field of Auxiliary endeavours. It then became my job to train thirty-six candy stripers each summer who covered three-hour shifts during the day, as many of our usual members would be away with their families for the summer. From time to time I see one of my girls with her husband at Crofton House school, attending their daughter's functions.

All in all I think I tallied up about fifteen years, all of which I enjoyed, and I admired the tremendous job the Auxiliary did to take the tedious side of work from much needed staff. There were, as I recall, some seven to eight hundred volunteers at that time.

Sadly, the unions took over, and the Auxiliary was soon to be disbanded. If the great enthusiastic army of women were there today, our nurses would not be so stressed.

When Mort and I were in Maui one winter, we had invited friends for a drink, two of whom were Ippie and Geoff Tullidge. To my delight, Geoff asked me if I would like to go on the Board of the Children's Hospital, of which he was Chairman. I was truly thrilled at the prospect and agreed with alacrity. Geoff was a very dedicated Samaritan and to this day Children's Hospital owes a

Children's Hospital.

great deal to the years of service he donated. Thankfully, he was rewarded the highest medal we bestow, the Canada Medal.

In 1985, during my first few weeks at what is now called the old hospital, I was asked to walk around the wards and general areas with a Dr Sidney Israels, another remarkable person for whom anyone who ever knew him had tremendous affection and admiration. To each place I was shown, he would remark, 'Johnnie, do you think you could do something to improve this?' And so a very interesting field of endeavour opened up for me. It was a tremendous challenge and I loved every minute of it. There was no budget for improvements, but friends donated money to help and paint was applied throughout. We got curtains, bed-spreads, pictures, and a fabulous donation given by Margareta Brown for the Partridge Murals which portrayed the favourite fun places in Vancouver that the children love and are familiar with. These colourful scenes were there to look up to as the children lay waiting to go into the OR. Brenda Thorpe, as she was then, was the very special nurse in the OR who was filled with enthusiasm for the hours that Bob Partridge worked. Brenda and I now meet at least twice a year to have lunch together. She is now Mrs Barrie Johnston and is retired.

While on the subject of this outstanding nurse, I must share a memory I have of being shown the tiny operating table that wee babies were strapped to when she assisted our surgeons, such as Dr Phil Ashmore. He was, and is, another super person. More about him later.

There is so much to say about Children's, that my mind literally floods with memories, so much so that it's hard to place them in some semblance of order. One thing I had fun with was tracking down a mobile building that could satisfactorily be turned into a cafeteria, as the present one was unbearably overcrowded. It wasn't exactly something you could make a phone call for, so, armed with addresses, I headed out to the country where these edifices were displayed in fields. It was quite a day and I must have covered an acre, all the while climbing into those amazing structures. The salesman was tireless and very patient with me as I could clearly picture what I had in my mind. We finally found exactly what I wanted and all I had to do was find my way home and present the proposition to the Board, as those things don't come cheaply. It was passed, and it turned out to be a great asset that saw us through until we had raised sufficient money to build a new hospital. We were very fortunate to be sitting on prime land with eager buyers waiting for it to come on the market. The new hospital, which was also generously aided by both the Provincial Government and the Variety Club, was to be re-named BC's Children's Hospital. At long last, the new hospital was completed, thanks to a great many people and a Herculean effort on the part of Geoff Tullidge, and we proudly moved over to Oak Street from 59th Avenue. All I hated to leave behind were the truly beautiful murals by Bob Partridge, which I am still saddened to think were destroyed by the demolition of our buildings. Also among many irreplaceable aspects of the old hospital was the feeling I had that I knew everyone. This included the kitchen help, cleaning and maintenance staff, nurses, John Short – who kept his eye on everything – and our fabulous medical staff. We were all friends – and never let it be said that I forgot those fabulous hardworking volunteers, or the public relations personnel.

There was a huge amount to do; our walls were bare, and the parent rooms in which they could go to relax had no furniture. We seemed to need so much and I was very fortunate to be asked by many areas in the hospital to try and find donors for what they needed. My great friend Nora Gourlay donated two magnificent murals in the cafeteria as well as a huge number of her colourful paintings. My friend Madge Hogarth Turnbull gave us a beautiful fountain that still graces the entrance to the hospital and enhances the outdoor sitting area for the staff. Jean Southam gave us an exquisite doll house which the children adored. Then there was Daphne Burke's delightful and charming mother who had reached her nineties and was still making the most colourful, beautiful Christmas tree balls that you could ever imagine – and she donated dozens of them. And so it grew into a beautiful place for our province's sick children. Many people donated instruments; one person I remember in this regard was Janet Allan.

It was not all work and no play. The first get-together I remember arranging was to charter the *Beaver*, which is a large paddle steamer that departs from our harbour and cruises over the cocktail hour and dinner, then back to port. It was a huge success and gave the members of the Board and their wives a chance to get to know each other.

Over the years there were great evenings. One at the Aquarium was very enjoyable, as was another at Bill and Marjory Anne Sauder's beautiful house and garden. Two of our doctors always added to these occasions – Phil Ashmore and Rob Hill played the piano and sang their humorous duets. We all loved those two doctors, both of whom were brilliant in their chosen field.

When we invited Princess Diana to visit our Children's Hospital during her visit to Expo '86 three of us made over fifty daisy chain hoops with our hospital colours.

As many children as could be moved were brought to the large lounge area so that their special Princess could visit as many as possible. The children were each given a daisy chain, which they were able to place over her hand to her wrist. As they accumulated she would hand them over to her lady-in-waiting. She looked ravishingly beautiful in her red suit and saucy pillbox hat. The children were mesmerized. There isn't anything I can say that hasn't already been said a thousand times about her rapport with

Princess Diana with my daisy chains, Children's Hospital.

children – she really was a special person. I feel sure those children who met her that day will some day tell their children and grandchildren about talking with her. I for one, most certainly, felt very impressed with her. I always thought she must have told Fergie about the daisy chains as at her wedding to Prince Andrew, her flower girls carried a chain of flowers.

Looking back on my years, 1975 to 1986, on the Board with so many outstanding people, I really treasure that time and the friendships formed.

John Tegenfeldt, our administrator, had his finger on every aspect of the hospital and had the admiration of anyone that had anything to do with him. He was not only very competent but he had a gift of always making you feel you were not wasting his time and he had a ready boyish grin that warmed the hearts of young and old. Dr David Hardwick was another remarkable, admired and respected member who merged our medical staff – more about him later. Dr Donald Newman was another friend; he headed our radiology department and was always so grateful for anything I was ever able to do for his bare walls. Another special person was Rosalind Smith, our Director of Nursing, whom I valued as a friend until she died. All of this must prove to be boring to those who read it in the future but these were my life experiences all those years.

When I stepped down from the Board, Stephanie Southam-Carlson took my place and has more than filled my shoes.

Dave Hardwick and I shared the most beautiful retirement dinner party which was given in our honour at the Vancouver Club. Bill McQuaid proposed the toast and it was so typically Bill that I am going to enclose it in my memoirs. He was a very special man, not only capable, but also charming and fun to know. We all loved Bill and his delightful wife, Marie (pronounced Mah-rie). His death, while on their holidays, came as a frightful shock to all of us who knew and admired him so very much. Our Children's Hospital lost a great supporter and true friend and I dread to think how much his family must miss him every day of their lives.

I have hunted everywhere to try and find the copy of the speech he made at my farewell dinner and up to now it eludes me. Hopefully, before I finally wind up my memoirs I will find it as I have always treasured his now elusive speech.

Dr Phil Ashmore presented me with a corsage with an enclosed card reading, 'In the old days, we used to give our best girl a corsage and nothing has changed.' We all loved him too. As I have said before, there were so many dedicated and marvellous people in that institution that it is hard not to go on naming them. I owed Geoff Tullidge a huge debt of gratitude for inviting me to join the Board.

Children's Auxiliary asked me to join their Board, which I

accepted. I think I really couldn't bring myself to say no as I knew so many of those super women and hated to make a clean break after I had been so involved for eleven years.

The Health Centre for Children was moved from the Vancouver General Hospital over to the new Children's Hospital. They had had a very active Auxiliary and I am sure dreaded the thought of moving. Daphne Cole worked a miracle with that transition and I never heard one person complain or criticise; it could have been an ongoing unhappy union – she waved her magic wand and it worked. In all my years I have never known any volunteer who devoted more time and devotion to her work. The shop is her 'baby' and from its incubation period to the present, I could never name the amount of money she has been responsible for raising, and there cannot be a single area in the hospital that has not benefited, be it by machines, furniture, toys, or by medical instruments that can cost the earth today. If she does not receive a medal some day, I will make her one!

There are not many days that pass when I do not have to drive past the hospital and I still cast a look at it with the same pride and affection that I felt all those years ago. May it always maintain the high standards, and the dedicated doctors and outstanding nurses who give parents and patients confidence that they will do everything in their power to make their time in Children's Hospital as pleasant as possible.

I finally found Bill McQuaid's illusive speech. Also treasured is the large silver tray with all the Board signatures, as a reminder of my rewarding years with 'Children's' – and of the outstanding people I worked with who are not with us any more, such as Geoff Tullidge, Bert Hoffmeister and Bill McQuaid.

An Excerpt from 'Speaking of Children'

Planned Giving: Mary 'Johnnie' Duffus

When children and their families arrive at Children's Hospital, they are welcomed by a sculpture that lets them know they are at a place that is all about kids. The well-known, much-loved sculpture of a bear pulling a little red wagon has been clambered over by countless young children over the years; it was put there by a very special friend of the hospital.

For nearly a quarter of a century, Mary 'Johnnie' Duffus has served BC's Children's Hospital. Besides the Hospital's 'door bear' given in memory of their daughter Drue, Johnnie Duffus has provided countless hours of volunteer effort to our work. In 1975, she joined the Board of Children's Hospital, serving until 1986. That year, she joined the Board of Women's Auxiliary, which she served on for two more years.

Most recently, she has joined BC's Children's Hospital Foundation's Caring For The Future Society, which brings together philanthropists who have made planned gifts to the hospital. On 20 July, she attended this year's Society Tea held at the Vancouver Museum. This year's event was of particular interest to Mrs Duffus because the Vancouver Museum was the venue for this summer's exhibit of Dresses for Humanity: An Exhibition of the dresses of Diana, Princess of Wales.

In 1986, Mrs Duffus was serving on the Board when Princess Diana came to Vancouver as part of the Expo 86 Celebration. During the Royal Visit, Princess Diana came to the hospital and it was Mrs Duffus' idea to have our young patients present a daisy chain to her, which, with help, was made with the hospital colours. The Royal Visit and the presentation of the daisy chain is commemorated in a large photograph that hangs at the entrance of the Dresses for Humanity Exhibit.

We are grateful to Mrs Duffus for being such a long-time, committed supporter of Children's Hospital. Through her past service and also through her future generosity, she honours the memory of their daughter, Drue, and touches the lives of thousands of our young patients.

Copy of Bill McQuaid's Speech

Johnnie

This is one of the most pleasant opportunities I have had since joining the board of Children's Hospital some nine or ten years ago.

I believe Johnnie came on a year before I did, and was, as I recall, the only lady member on the board.

Actually there were never more than two or three ladies on the board for some years (until I became chairman of the nominating committee, and then we blended in the very active ladies involved with the health centre for children), because I knew who the real workers were.

Fortunately, Johnnie was able to put in endless hours of devoted duty and represented the really 'caring' side of our board as we were all occupied with budgets, space problems, funds for CAT scanners, medical appointments, etc., etc., – while Johnnie quietly and capably devoted her hours to 'hands-on' relationships with children, with the parents, and with the staff.

Johnnie always seemed to be at the hospital, working with the children, working with the Auxiliary (with our other very devoted chairman of the time – Daphne Cole).

Johnnie was always after us for funds for flowers, games, recreational activities – a pleasant change from debating sale of property, president's salary, research space etc., etc.

In any case, I can tell you that Johnnie was invaluable in all of the above and also in heading up special situations – board dinners, fundraising dinners and other such activities – so that when her final term on the board came about, we persuaded her to stay on as a special assistant to the chairman for 'special events' – and the 'then' chairman certainly needed all the assistance he could get – didn't I, Johnnie?

I used to love suddenly getting a call on – say – a Monday morning, and it would be Johnnie saying, 'I think we should arrange for the Queen to visit our hospital when she comes out next spring' – or 'I know the Lieutenant Governor and his wife and I want them to tour the hospital to get us some publicity for our intensive care unit.'

In short, Johnnie was a softly spoken, tireless power for more than ten years for our present and former hospital, contributing enormously to the public awareness of our institution, to the internal 'caring' part of our institution, and enabling all of us to 'feel good' about our contributions and not just 'efficient'.

Even now, when Johnnie has retired from the board – guess who reads stories over the hospital closed TV circuit to the children on Fridays – none other than 'our Johnnie'.

It was this unheralded, behind-the-scenes, constant devotion that inspired me to almost write one of my infamous poems, but I decided the occasion was too important to me to detract from our tribute to you (besides which I could not find a word that rhymed with 'indefatigable').

However, I can tell you that the last line ended with the words 'our own Florence Nightingale'.

Johnnie, you have indeed been our angel of mercy – we will miss you on the board, but we know that you will continue to be here, and serving our children.

Thank you for all that you have meant to our hospital; and our hospital has meant to you.

Ladies and gentlemen – please rise and toast 'our Johnnie'.

Pets

FROM MY EARLIEST recollection I have loved animals and in order of preference: dogs, horses and cats. My very first memory is of, about aged three, being sick in bed with one of my brother Bill's childhood diseases, such as whooping cough, when our Uncle Jock came into my room. He was wearing an overcoat and as he turned towards me, two sparkling eyes and a wet little black nose were sticking out of his pocket. Next came four large paws onto my bed with licking kisses, as only a puppy knows how to perform. Because of the size of his paws, we called him Boots. As we only lived a stone's throw from English Bay, we grew up on the beach and Boots loved it as much as did all the children and would be in and out of the water swimming alongside us, or off to enjoy it by himself. Even if we weren't going to the beach he would take off by himself, cross Beach Avenue and run down the little bank to have his swim. When we arrived home from school one day, our little tail-wagger was not there to give us his usual joyous welcome. The Battleship HMS *Hood* had honoured Vancouver with a visit that day and was at anchor off English Bay and greeted by every car and its driver. Obviously they had their eyes out on the water, not knowing our beloved Boots was crossing the road to go for a swim. Somebody carried him to our house and he was buried in our garden before we arrived home from school. Unknown to our parents, Bill and I dug deeply enough to feel his beautiful black coat so we could stroke him as we shed our tears of farewell.

Our father was a very keen hunter and once the duck hunting season opened, he would be away most weekends with his friends to shoot, so our dog was a cross between a Labrador retriever and a cocker spaniel, which Boots had been. We called him Barney. He was not as big as a Lab and had a long plumed tail, feathery legs, wavy black coat, long, soft ears and a nose and a mouth like a Lab. He was truly a very handsome and wonderful dog and our family adored him. Our father had to spell the word 'gun' if he ever had reason to use the word because Barney would race to the door and sit there furiously wagging his tail, waiting to go shooting. He was an excellent retriever and had a very soft mouth. Much to the disgust of the few girlfriends I had, when my father would return from his shoot, he nearly always had a teal for 'Jinx', which was his pet name for me. It was then put into my doll's pram and proudly wheeled around the streets. Next day Mother would spirit my treasure away and my doll's blankets were washed.

Jock MacLean broke his leg when he was playing polo and after he was released from hospital our parents persuaded him to spend his recuperation days with us. Barney became devoted to him. After he was well enough to drive his car, Barney would hop in with him and often spend the day or night with him in his apartment. On many occasions he would be left in Jock's car while he was in the Vancouver Club. One day somebody stole our beloved dog out of his car. We were all devastated; if I knew a stronger word I would use it. I will never know how people who do such dastardly things can live with themselves.

With my brother away at boarding school and me riding four or five times a week, we didn't have another dog for quite a while. While east with my mother we stayed with her sister in Waterloo where my little cousin Anne had two Pekinese, Wang and Woo, and they were adorable. The following spring my aunt was staying with us and gave me a Pekinese puppy. When she was older we bred her and she produced three adorable puppies. They were photographed on the palm of my father's hand, rather like hairy sausages. By the time I returned for Christmas holidays, or was it Easter? – they were going concerns. Our favourite entertainment was to let them loose in the kitchen and we would all sit around watching their hilarious antics. At times I think Mummy wondered if motherhood was all that it was cracked up to be as she was teased unmercifully. It was a very sad day when the puppies went off to their eagerly awaited homes.

Mother also had a bobtailed Manx cat called Bobby. He was an unusually bright fellow who at an early age decided there was nothing humans could do that he couldn't, so he used the toilet.

After Mort and I married, we inherited a golden cocker from friends that were transferred and couldn't take him. Peter, by name; he had a very healthy bark when anyone came to our door but the minute someone was invited into the house he would high-tail it and hide behind the chesterfield. Mort always referred to him as the cowardly lion. As we were transferred after fifteen months to the UK, we had to give him to friends.

Next came Nickie, in England, and I have written elsewhere about that wonderful animal. After the war, Mort and the girls chose our collie whom they named Buster. We all adored him and he was beautiful. He had one dreadful fault, a mind of his own. If he got out, off a lead, away he went, always to return, except once when he was killed by an automobile. More tears...

Just about this time we moved from our post-war house to a larger one close to my good friend Nora, my godson Hugo and Melinda and Mort's god-daughter Cal, who was Drue's best friend. Nora was Susan's godmother so we were all very happy with the move. We had all been too busy to realise there was one thing missing – and that was a dog.

One day after I had been visiting my parents I was about to start the engine of my car when I noticed a dog being walked by a young female. I got out of the car and approached her so I could better see her four-legged treasure. I told her I would give anything to have one like him. She said she had found him at the SPCA; he was about four years old and they thought he was a mix between cocker and poodle, but weren't sure. I thanked her for her time and my visit with her very special 'Mickey'. I said, 'My parents live over there and if you ever need a good home for him, please call my parents!' When I went home I related my story and then dismissed it from my mind. Several weeks later my mother called to say that the person I had spoken to had asked her to have me telephone her regarding her dog Mickey. Unbelievable as it seems, her husband had received a transfer to Calgary and they couldn't take their dog with them, would I like to have him? Would I!! It so happened Drue was sick and had been in bed a few days, so I didn't say where I was going or what for, but left Susan and Mort and went to pick up our dog Mickey! When I returned, after Susie and Mort had greeted and strongly approved of him, I

Drue, Mickey and Susan.

took him to Drue's bedroom. It was love at first sight and we could never believe our good fortune. There are so many things to say about Mickey, it is hard to know where to begin or end. Apart from looking like the perfect storybook dog, he was remarkably intelligent and enjoyed showing off his tricks and entertaining the neighbouring children in the playroom. He could climb a ladder, sit up with a sugar lump on his nose, and with a flick of a finger, toss it in the air and catch it. He would also crawl on command.

There was to be a 'Mutt Show' put on by the SPCA, so Drue entered Mickey. Quite a large group of us went to watch as well as support them, as did hundreds of others to watch their dog and child. The contest was to judge the dog with the kindest face; naturally every child thought their pet was to be the winner. There were three judges who lined over two hundred dogs into four rows and as they walked down each row they would ask ten to step forward, finally eliminating all but two; one being a basset hound and the other our Mickey. You could have heard a pin drop in that arena as the air was electric with emotion – with our group clutching each other's hands, we were so excited. Of course the judges played their parts well and finally, after much soul-searching, our two won and Mickey paraded his 'kindest face' – after receiving a cup and an invitation to appear on TV the following Saturday. I drove the two of them that day and was told I could follow the interview on a set in a different room. They had a very friendly young chap who asked Drue a lot of questions, with Mickey standing beside her on a bench. When the camera did a close-up of Mickey's head he said, 'How about licking your lips for us, Mickey?' which he did, much to the amusement of the interviewer.

I cannot remember why we got a Sheltie puppy but Tippy, short for Tipperary, joined the family, and the two dogs and Put, our cat, were great friends until, while waiting to cross to Bowen Island by

Susan and Tippy.

water taxi, the car door was open for a few minutes, Put jumped
out and we never saw her again. We were shattered as she was a
lovely, friendly cat and we hope she found a very good home as
nobody answered our advertisements. When Tippy was a puppy
up at our cottage, we could never leave him unattended as the
eagles would circle overhead and we were afraid he would be
snatched away.

Age caught up with our dear Mickey and he went downhill very
rapidly, becoming a mere shadow of his former self. Mort drove
me, with Mickey lying in my arms, to have him put to sleep.
When I got back into the car crying my heart out, it was too much
for Mort and he couldn't start the car until his eyes stopped filling
up.

Tippy went on to dog training classes, winning first place and a
cup over thirty or so dogs of all breeds. I was amazed he did

because he would look up at Drue and let out a sharp little bark every so often. When I was talking to the judge later I told him I was not expecting Tippy to win, in spite of his superb showing in the training aspect, and he said, 'No, that was not a fault. Tippy was happy doing his training and enjoying every minute of it.'

I almost forgot 'Thumper', the largest rabbit in captivity. He lived under our back veranda, which was enclosed with latticed wood. He lapped up half a pint of milk a day and bags of veggies and lettuce that were given to us by our supermarket. One Christmas, with the tree up and lights on, Mort and I were reading in the living room and Drue came in with Thumper. She put him down and he hopped under the tree, wiggled his nose at the parcels and evidently discovered the light flex; out went all the lights by biting it in half. Drue promptly picked him up to avoid further displeasure and sat him on a down-filled cushion. To her horror, to say nothing of mine, he was lying down but entirely encompassed by a large wet ring! She calmly got up, picked Thumper up, leaned over and flipped the cushion upside down. It wasn't until many years later that she told Mort what he missed, to say nothing of the ire she missed. After it was discovered Thumper was tunnelling himself in and out of his enclosure, we persuaded Drue to advertise for a country home. Of one thing she was to make sure though and that was to not let him go to someone wanting a rabbit pie. Fortunately he went to a farm and the man said he would be his prize stud.

And then there was Hudson, or 'Hud the Bud', as he was called. Cal and Drue each bought a hamster at the Hudsons Bay Company and I wasn't ever overly enthusiastic about that little fellow but he certainly amused Tippy as he would sit and watch the never-ending circles he ran. He was eventually given his freedom.

Mort's mother used to stay with us for two months every

Emily (Jane, Ginny) Duffus Dillon Hurd.

summer when she lived in Detroit with Jane and Norman (Mort's sister and brother-in-law). She couldn't take the heat and we all adored having her. I always thought I had the best mother-in-law in the world, but more about the three of them elsewhere.

One small pet I have a picture of is seen with Grandie, Susan and Drue, who are perched on the side of Grandie's bed, the three of them laughing at 'Furbey', Drue's caterpillar, which was walking painstakingly up Grandie's blanketed body. He had a magnificent fur coat in a smoked salmon colour and thrived on begonias, ours or others. After Grandie went home to Detroit, Lila Molson, who loved our girls, suggested the four of us drive down to Seattle for a few days. So, when we were packing, Drue asked if she could take Furbey, to which I said I thought not. We opted to stay in a motel that was within easy walking distance of our favourite shops. Lila and I were enjoying a drink before going for

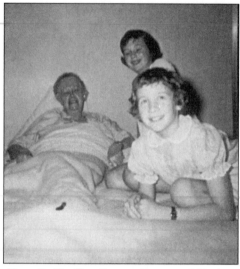

Grandie Duffus, Susan, Drue and Furbey.

dinner and Drue said she had found Furbey in her shoe that she had unpacked. 'No' often meant 'Yes', so then we were five. They put him out on a large shrub which was under our window before we went out for dinner. Next morning while waiting for Lila and me to take the girls out for breakfast, they were leaning out the window watching the people on the street. They overheard a little girl say, 'Mummy, look at this beautiful caterpillar. May I take it home, please?' to which the answer was, 'Yes dear, if you would like to.' Our two were very upset but realised they could hardly rush after her and claim him. We always wondered if one little Canadian became an 'American Butterfly'.

It was a long time after we lost Put that we got our second cat, Charlie, and he was a delight. We chose him from a litter simply because he looked at us with eyes that seemed to make us feel he thought we were just what he could live with. Once in the car he snuggled down on my lap and purred loudly all the way home. I never remember him ever causing a problem in any way so when we were going on a holiday, Susan and Crozier said they would be very happy to look after him for us (they still talk about that). It seemed Charlie liked to go out an upstairs window and wander about on the roof. One evening Susan and Crozier were enjoying their evening drink and there was a horrible crashing noise in their chimney. Crozier opened the draft and Charlie, not grey but pitch black, bounced out and fled across their beautiful rug. Strangely enough, he was never asked back.

Charlie loved to lie on his back between my legs and I would play pat-a-cake with his hind legs or front paws. He didn't seem to care what I did with him – he never bit or scratched me once. He always slept on my bed and never left me if I was sick. How he developed a matted section of fur I never knew but when I discovered it, I got some scissors and pretty well loosened it. He then took off and my feeling was that I would attend to it in the morning as I was about to go to bed. I was awakened during the night by Charlie, who was on my bed choking. To my horror I discovered he had chewed the matted hair from his body and swallowed it! We had him x-rayed but though they could see the matted hair in his lungs there was nothing that could be done to save our beloved cat. It took me a long time to get over his loss as I blamed myself for ever allowing the hair to get matted in the first place.

It was some time before we were persuaded to think of another cat. Our grandson Ryan phoned one day to say that Serena Southam's cat had had kittens and she needed good homes for them. Would we like one? Mort and I drove out to see them and there were two left. One was a pretty marmalade with short hair and one was part Persian, so we chose the latter. We called her Kate and she was a treasure. Her name was chosen because she would jump on my lap and put her mouth up and I would pretend to kiss her, so 'Kiss Me Kate' was her song. She also enjoyed teasing our dog. She would come half way down the staircase and sit there until the dog spotted her, then they could be heard rushing from room to room until they finally got tired.

When Mort died on 4 November 1997, he had been in hospital for five weeks. I was numb when I arrived home that evening, totally drained of emotion in fact, and it was quite late when I went to bed. A little while afterwards, I turned off the lights. Kate jumped up and instead of her usual place at the foot of my bed, she came up beside my pillow and settled herself. That did it, the floodgates opened. Bless her, she never stirred all night. How, I wonder, did Kate know?

Just before Christmas, to liven my spirits, I decided a kitten would be good medicine for Katie and me, so Berenice (Susan's mother-in-law) and I drove out to Maple Ridge to see some Himalayan kittens. The tiny house was swarming with Himalayan

90th birthday of Berenice, and son Crozier, 2001.

cats of all ages. We were told to sit down at the kitchen table and the breeder produced a blanket which she spread out over it. She then disappeared for a while and we were entertained by the menagerie of cats that thought we deserved their full attention. Around the corner came a basket of kittens, two white and two sable, and they were adorable. They were placed on the blanket where they played and we sized them up. The white ones were adorable but the thought of white hairs all over the furniture made me choose one of the sable females. We put her in a box on a blanket and off we went. We found a pet store where I stocked up on food, which she tucked into. We locked her in the car and headed for a nearby restaurant as we were famished. The 'babe' slept all the way home and then was introduced to Kate and also to her name – Sophie.

It was hardly love at first sight, although I think they tolerated each other in a more friendly fashion when I was not around, as there was a spark of jealousy. Once in a while they would play in

The last of my animal kingdom, 'Sophie'.

their 'duplex', or chase each other, but never slept together. Sophie did, however, miss dear old Kate when she left this world. I have toyed with getting a Himalayan kitten but at my age it would be silly. Placing Sophie some day will be enough of a problem, as who will want to have her combed out and her nails cut twice a month? I call it her 'comb-out and manicure'. She won't let me do it – I carry wounds to prove it.

They are strange cats in many ways. Sophie likes to go out on the patio, even in heavy rain, jump up on the glass-top table and lap up the rain or dew. She then shakes herself to dry off. She will come when I whistle for her and sulks if I leave her alone for too long – very feminine!

Jamaica

OH TO HAVE THE memory for dates my husband had! Without a moment's hesitation he would come up with the year we went – wherever – which made me very lazy about remembering such things. Now that he is no longer with me I am at a loss if I haven't kept a diary. It seems that in hot climates, I didn't, with the exception of our '*Bluenose*' sailing holiday in the Caribbean – but we did have 70° air-conditioning, or I wouldn't have a record of that holiday either.

A travel agent persuaded us to go to Jamaica for three weeks and arranged to have us stay at Round Hill, near Montego Bay. We flew to Toronto and spent the night, which enabled us to see my very special cousin, Anne Vincent, later Binnie. She was busy raising three little girls in Waterloo at that time, so it was a special effort on her part to meet with us in Toronto.

Our flight to Jamaica was uneventful, except to find ourselves fascinated or mind-boggled by the consumption of Martinis by a man sitting opposite us. When we first noticed him, his hands were shaking like a leaf but as time elapsed his hands were as steady as a rock.

We arrived in Montego Bay when it was dark and taxied to Round Hill. The first introduction to this heavenly place was to see the chandelier in the main entrance which was hanging from a very high ceiling; it was ablaze with dozens of candles which were encased in glass but still managed to flicker slightly from the ocean breeze and cast fascinating shadows on the walls. Before we knew it, we were settled in our suite, overlooking the water from our spacious balcony.

The bedposts were carved into wooden pineapples and there were colourful paintings and charm throughout. We were more than a little delighted with all that we had seen. As it had been a very long day, we opted for a reasonably early night – the last we were to have as there was never a dull moment at Round Hill.

Breakfasts were served on our veranda by a beaming Jamaican bearing a huge tray with a beautiful bowl of fresh pineapple, papaya and mango. All were enticingly fresh, as was the full breakfast. We were serenaded by birds that seemed to enjoy company and donations of applause.

The beach was a delight – a small raft was only far enough out to be a nice distance to swim to and the water was warm and crystal clear. It was not long before we discovered Round Hill was a favourite spot for movie actors, who were very friendly. I used to walk the beach every morning and often joined forces with Victor Borge who was there with his lovely wife and adorable little girls.

Every evening when we were dressing for dinner, a group of singers would lustily sing and play their instruments to the tune of 'When The Saints Go Marching In', which seemed to set the mood for the night. We would usually have a few drinks in the bar with John, who was quite a showman. We became very fond of him.

John and Elizabeth Pringle were the young couple that managed the hotel. She had been a Powers model, we were told, and well she could have been as she was a beauty. He was a handsome man with lots of charm and personality. They often sat near us on the beach with Moss Hart writing his plays and Rogers and Hammerstein working on a musical.

Lunch was a gourmet buffet feast that needed to be seen to be believed. Looking back now I am sure we must have crashed our heads down before we could swim again, as we found everything to be delectable and the unbelievable desserts to be quite irresistible. I don't remember whether it was our first or second holiday there that I was standing at the dessert table, filled with wonder at the selection and presentation that was before me. I heard a voice beside me saying, 'Decisions, decisions,' and when I looked up to agree, I found Deborah Kerr looking her beautiful self.

There was never a dull moment with the large number of famous people. The William Paleys had their house at the end of the walk which went to our rooms. Shortly after the Saints had marched past, they would walk by on their way to the bar or dining room. She always looked absolutely smashing. Paul Newman and Joanne Woodward, at their table close by ours, were so young and obviously adored each other. I remember seeing Joan Crawford and Clark Gable at a huge table with other stars, but regrettably I cannot remember the others.

Apparently many of the cottages were owned by famous people and when they were not using them they were available to rent. Noel Coward owned one cottage but I do not know if he rented his.

At least once a week they had an informal barbeque dinner with excellent entertainment by Jamaican groups. Bamboo poles were held by two men so the other men could bend backwards to walk under without touching the poles; it was amazing how they would hold poles low to the ground and still be able to clear them by bending so far backwards, without either losing their balance or touching the pole. They didn't seem to have normal backbones.

We made very good friends our first year, and we were asked to join a party that was going on a picnic to Negril Beach which was about twenty-five miles away. We were supplied with picnic baskets filled with a superb assortment of delectable food. The men looked after our drinks and we all took our bathing suits. It was an interesting drive over a dreadful road, so when we finally arrived we were more than ready for a good swim. An amusing little man met us and for a small sum we were able to use his 'grass shacks' to change in. The tide was in and the water was heavenly. When we had had enough, our bar was set up and drinks and a fabulous lunch were thoroughly enjoyed. All of this took place our first year and leads up to a similar picnic the second year.

Once more we made friends that we told about our picnic at Negril, so they were all very keen to go. The same little man that had met us the previous year once more rented his little 'grass shacks' for us to change in. To our surprise the tide was out and swimming was out of the question as we all walked quite a long way out and Mort, being the tallest, hardly even got water above his knees. The only thing to do was to flop around and have crazy fun. It wasn't long before we went ashore. The man who had previously set up the bar table poured our drinks and as we raised our glasses to say 'cheers', a shark swam in ten feet from shore. I picked up an orange from the fruit bowl and threw it at the monstrous thing. No doubt all our splashing and laughter had attracted the beast. Had it arrived five minutes earlier, it would have had sixteen legs to choose from. We were miles from help of any sort so we would have been one bloody mess. I can still picture it in my mind as if it were yesterday. Mort asked the Jamaican man if he ever swam there, and he shook his head firmly and negatively – we weren't exactly impressed by him. I read recently that there are hotels at Negril Beach now, so I assume they only swim in pools or they have safety measures installed.

Another experience we had that second year was to see the same man in the aircraft going down whom we had seen the first year. His hands shook a little harder and his Martinis went down a little faster.

Mort and I were otherwise addicted and that was to Scrabble. We never travelled without it as we had a magnetic set that could stand up to any kind of bouncing or jostling.

When we put down in Nassau the stewardess told us we would be able to remain on board while we refuelled. I asked her if it was quite normal for the wing to be so wet. She looked at it briefly and headed to the cockpit, soon to return with the captain in tow. He asked me how long I had been noticing the wet wing and I said, 'Since leaving Toronto.' He said, 'Next time you notice something like that will you please let us know about it? – that happens to be gasoline!' We were all herded off to a waiting area where we cooled our heels for several hours while repairs were made. So much for the old saying, 'Ignorance is bliss.' I didn't tell the captain that I was determined not to show any concern as I felt I didn't want to let on I was really a worry-wart about flying and surely the instruments would show if there was anything wrong.

Before I say 'goodbye' to memories of Jamaica: I have written about walking along the beach with Victor Borge. He mentioned he had a concert to perform in Vancouver so I told him we most certainly would be going to it and we would be very happy to see him after the performance. He said he would enjoy that, so, some months later we contacted him and spent a most enjoyable few hours with him. I remember one thing he told us and that was that he had done one thing in his life that he was ashamed of and that was owning a Cornish game farm, as the thought of killing those dear little hens made him ashamed. He was a very natural person and incredibly easy to talk to. As we were nearing his hotel one of us remarked how early he must have to have dinner when he has to be at the theatre and to our horror, found he always dined after his performance. This had never dawned on us and we had only had drinks and a cheese board. He must have wondered about Canadian hospitality!

The first time we heard Victor Borge was in Washington, DC, when Mort attended a conference. We both laughed until the tears rolled. He will long be remembered as a great performer with a ridiculous sense of humour.

While on the subject of that trip to Washington, we also were taken to hear Danny Kaye. He was an enchanting and clever entertainer. We had front row seats and at one point in his performance, he sat on the edge of the stage with his legs dangling down and asked the audience if they had any requests. I put my hand up and owing to our proximity to him, he acknowledged me and I said, 'Thumbelina, please.' Not only did he sing it but he sang it to me. Two very special entertainers are now no longer with us, I am sorry to say.

Another wonderful time we had while in Jamaica came about by an introduction to Willie Lyon-Hall, who lived high up on a hill within an hour or so drive from Round Hill. Knowing we were to be at the hotel, she left a message to call her when we arrived, which we did, and I invited her to join us for a swim and lunch. She, in turn, invited us to a dinner party. We thoroughly enjoyed our first meeting with her and received a detailed map to drive to her house. We were to be there by six o'clock. I always did the driving on holidays and Mort was the map-reader, at which I am a lost cause. The drive up was quite an experience as we met with lorries filled with field workers returning from the fields they worked in. And then their wives and children were on the road waiting for them. The last few miles were a one-way winding road scaling around the side of the huge hill upon which her house was eventually found. A tall, handsome, lean East Indian servant walked us through the house to where Willie was with her other guests. After introductions, we were able to take in the beauty of the panoramic view she had of fields of sugar cane and rice paddy fields. It was truly spectacular. We were then to be introduced to a very lengthy cocktail hour. It got dark and a fair wind appeared so we finally went in the house to find she had no electric lights, only masses of candles in hurricane glass that flickered busily owing to the wind. We were told we would not wait any longer for two missing guests, so we sat down at long last in her beautiful dining room at her exquisite table. No sooner had we done so when the front door hand bell clanged and the tardy guests arrived. Mort let out an audible gasp when he recognised Rosemary Baker (married to Wilder Ripley from Calgary, I believe). A small world, as the last meeting with Rosemary had been during the war in St John's, Newfoundland, when he commanded the HMCS *Bowmanville* and Rosemary was in the Wrens. I don't recall why they were so very late, making it the longest cocktail hour, and as I was the designated driver for the hazardous drive home I was loathe to indulge! One other remarkable event that I recall was our coffee on the patio when we were serenaded by night noises and fascinated by literally hundreds, if not thousands, of fireflies.

Dear Willie, such a delightful person, seen for the last time unfortunately. We did, however, keep in touch with Christmas cards that always enclosed her amusing newsletter.

Unlike many countries we have visited, Jamaicans produce what tourists want to buy and I have found that very rare. Items range from straw hats to table linen and both children's and adult's clothing. All the clothes were made in such beautiful colours, which were colourfast. We were never approached by beggars, as we were in Bali, for instance. There, we couldn't go to the beach without being surrounded by young boys who pestered the life out of us to buy their cheap beads. Women clawed my arms to attract my attention to buy what I didn't want and I found it alarming. You feel you want to help them but they prevent you from doing so. I seem to have wandered away from Jamaica but I wanted to draw a comparison.

Our second holiday at Round Hill was enhanced by the added company of Jane and Norman Hurd and Molly and Graham Towers. They had such glowing reports from us and they loved every aspect of their recommended holiday. We were all young in those days so we all lived it up and enjoyed everything. It is so very sad – I am the only one of the six of us that is here to remember those fabulous weeks.

Hawaii

FOR ELEVEN consecutive years, Mort and I went to Hawaii for six weeks each winter, leaving about 25 January. Our first year stands out in my memory as it was so different a holiday from Round Hill and Nassau. On the latter we only enjoyed our relatives and friends, but to each his own.

The Royal Lahaina, with our cottage on the waterfront, was all and more than we could have wished for. Swimming was at our doorstep; golf for Mort a ten-minute drive; and as so many of our friends were there the men had regular games set up. I, in turn, could go where I wished and he would get a ride back in time for the heavenly water. Dining and entertainment were always special at the hotel.

The Hawaiians appealed to both of us; they always had smiling eyes and faces, and their voices were soft and appealing. There was no begging owing to a constant development which must have filled every employment need. I doubt somehow that there would ever be begging in Hawaii.

Sadly, the Royal Lahaina was torn down so we moved the next year to an apartment on the water and we loved it also. That year it was a little different in that we had high roller waves that could be quite frightening. You couldn't turn your back on them or you would be flattened, with sand in your eyes, ears and mouth – and everywhere else that sand could go.

The next year we went to the big island of Hawaii to Mauna Kea. There are a lot of cattle ranches on this island and it is very different in every way from Maui. There was wonderful golf for Mort on a championship course and he was happy, as any good golfer would be. Although I enjoyed the beautiful hotel that was filled with artefacts, I found there was not enough to do. One memory I have is of being caught by a monster wave and being tossed every which way with my breath gone. Fortunately, Brice Evans pulled me out of it, or I think I would not have been able to save myself.

So back to Maui and Kihei, which we really liked very much. That end of the island has far less rainfall, which is a big plus in itself. We spent three wonderful holidays in a place called Kamaole One, pronounced *Ohnay*. Mort's sister stayed with us twice and Drue once. My great friend Nora was there at the same time with her sister Didge, husband Harry Boyce, and their father Gordon Farrell, and farther down the beach at the Royal Mauian was Joan Ketcheson and her husband Kip. Happy hour, as it is called in Maui, was often like 'little Vancouver'; there were always huge numbers of Canadians on Maui every year. It made a refreshing change from our cool winters. Edgar and Ann Krieger had a charming place in Hale Keana Cove and we had many wonderful times with them and stayed as their guests once.

At boarding school, I had taken special art lessons from a Mrs Utoff, who had been a pupil of Emily Carr, and, as I found I had time on my hands on those holidays, I started drawing and painting again. The flowers there are so colourful and profuse that I found great pleasure sketching, with endless encouragement from Ann.

I forgot to mention that Geoff and Ippie Tullidge came for a drink when we were staying in Kehei, and Geoff asked me if I would join the board of BC's Children's Hospital to serve under him as Chairman. I was very honoured and agreed happily to attend the first meeting on my return home.

The *Bluenose II* Diaries

Sunday 12 February 1967

Sam drove us over to English Harbour and told us the history of the island. Saw the US tracking station and the natives going to church. The children looked adorable, particularly the little girls in their crisp spanking clean dresses and flowered hats. When we arrived at Nelson's Dockyard, we had our first glimpse of the *Bluenose* lying at anchor in English Harbour and we were absolutely speechless at her magnificence! We were finally seen by those aboard and the captain's son picked us up in the whaler. The captain greeted us as we stepped aboard and Joe, the steward, greeted us with a large tray of planter's punches. After a drink together, we were taken on a tour of the *Bluenose*. Our cabins are air-conditioned and the *Bluenose* is spacious beyond our wildest dreams. Alan Miller appeared in a dinghy and he and Kirsteen were invited to come aboard at 9 o'clock. Had a fun evening with them, sat out on deck for an hour or so and then went below. They departed at about 11:30 and Ralph, Mort and I sat on deck until about 12:45, far too excited to go to sleep.

If possible, the *Bluenose* looks even larger at night. Looking up at the masts they seem to reach the very heavens.

Hope we will have some time on our return so we may more thoroughly see the sights and absorb some of the history that lies in the buildings and on the surrounding hills. It is incredible to think that Nelson harboured his fleet here.

The Bluenose.

Monday 13 February

Sailed from English Harbour at 9:02. Jean and I felt a little green but were revived by fresh air and Gravol pills from Gwynn and a pink gin from Mort. Saw lots of flying fish. Everyone very happy with blue skies, white caps and the lush and beautiful island of Guadaloupe off-shore. It reminds us of Bowen Island only it is a little more mountainous. The captain said we might find porpoise but so far none have shown their noses. Have never seen water coloured such a deep blue which makes the white caps so white by contrast.

Just heard it is 14 degrees below zero in Nova Scotia.

Tuesday 14 February

Anchors up at nine, no wind so used our engine with the exception of the jib and foresail. The French houses all look much alike with their flat roofs in pink and white. There are some beautiful houses set high on the palm tree'd hills which appear to be very lush.

Lay in the sun on a mattress most of the afternoon.

All the girls were greeted by large mushy Valentines at the breakfast table. Sailed past the Iles des Saintes – the sky was clear and beautiful and the sea so blue. Arrived in Iles des Saintes – anchor dropped at 14:20. Captain went ashore to clear customs.

Decided it was too warm to go ashore before 4:00, so everyone had a quiet hour. The captain, Mrs Coggins and all of us went ashore and walked up and down every available road. Said '*bonjour*' to all the children who looked a little aghast but replied politely. Babies looked adorable with their little naked bottoms. Came across an old cemetery. It was depressing to see how many graves were those of little children. All the graves were so well loved and cared for, dating back to the 1700s. We tried to find our way across the island to see the surf but walked a mile or so and never did find the way. Saw goats, sheep, a pig, cows and a peacock all in his glory and then returned aboard and had a dip off the ladder – not a very comfortable dip as the shark situation was unknown. The sunset and a half moon appeared for the cocktail hour, which was followed by an excellent duck dinner. Mort and Forrie played Scrabble and Pat and I watched the others play bridge.

Wednesday 15 February – Iles des Saintes

Dull and no wind to speak of. The French navy joined us during the night. A large warship of no definite class, named the *Jeanne d'Arc*. It had three helicopters on deck and representatives from all their forces. They were as interested in us as we were in them. Obviously they were in port to celebrate the opening of the airport. Bunting was flying everywhere for the occasion.

Picked up wind and set sail for Dominica. It was a nice day and we were all very taken with what we saw. The captain and Mrs Coggins went ashore at Portsmouth for supplies and we bargained with the natives to take us up the Layou River. Jean, Mort and I went in one boat with our native called 'Mike on his bike', who said he was an actor and would like to entertain us this evening. All the others piled into the other boat with Pat making alligator noises, much to everyone's amusement. Got stuck several times and Jean and Mort hopped out and pushed. Took quite a few pictures; it was very tropical looking and one expected to find monkeys swinging from the branches or alligators sunning themselves. But only heard bird noises and Burns!

Returned to *Bluenose* for a quick dip and a zizz before dinner. Fun cocktail hour, followed by lobster dinner. All sat out on deck after dinner. Huge bat-like birds flew over the water all evening and fish seemed to be very plentiful, so threw bread overboard to try and encourage them to bite at it but they simply flipped their fins and sailed by.

Everyone got a burn today through the clouds and sunny patches.

16 February

Weighed anchor at 0700 and proceeded south until the southern point of Dominica was abeam. There we ran into a beautiful sailing breeze. The mainsail, foresail and jib were set. An hour later the winds increased to almost gale force and the *Bluenose* was doing 15 knots with the rail under at times.

Jean asked me to set her hair with her Swedish machine and it turned out very well. Too bad the weather was so hard on it. Felt a bit green but thanks to Gwynn's Gravol pills it quickly passed off. Going below when it is rough is not for me.

Got soaked with spray and saw a school of lazy whales lying aimlessly on the surface of the water.

A large sailboat appeared well to the lee and ahead of us. She raised every sail she could but we caught up to her and passed her as if she were a flatty instead of a 65 footer.

Mort. Bluenose *holiday.*

Mort, Pat and Ralph went ashore to look around Martinique but it was late and overcast so we gals will go ashore tomorrow.

The *Independence* and *Homeric* were both in port and a good showing of other sailboats and a catamaran.

Played Gwynn's game of Booby Trap after turkey dinner.

The captain said we would be lucky if we saw better sailing than we had today. Would like to have been able to watch her from another ship. What a sight she must be!

17 February

Clearer skies greeted us this morning and we all donned dresses to go ashore. Two boatloads away by 10:30. Martinique has lots of charm with its narrow streets, quaint architecture, balconies with potted plants and flowers. There were taxis by the dozens. Some very nice shops filled with tourists; large, small, fat, thin, short and tall – they were all there. We from the *Bluenose* kept bumping into each other in the oddest places. Forrie and Gwynn taxied off to see the sights and told us later they had seen the Lido Hotel and

The Bluenose *Duffuses.*

that it was nice, so Pat, Jean, Mort and I went by cab and had a planter's and an excellent lunch of avocado pear, crab, scrumptious French bread and cheese and wine, topped off with delicious coffee. A thoroughly enjoyable lunch and lots of fun.

Roamed around the attractive hotel grounds and pool and took pictures. Met our taxi at three and went back into town. Bought a very pretty charm for Drue.

Sat out on deck and enjoyed the starlit night. The crew had some young friends aboard.

18 February

Good sail to St Lucia. Gwynn and Betty got drenched with spray twice. Fairly rough sea. Tied up alongside the dock and all went for a walk in the sweltering streets. Nice to hear our own language again. Everything looked so much cleaner in every way. Mort bought a bottle of Mumms champagne for $3.00; also teabags, so his troubles are over.

Had cocktails aboard and then two taxis took us all over to the hotel. It seemed a long way with endless turns in the road. The air was filled with a symphony of noises made by crickets, frogs and God knows what. It was quite windy and the palm trees swish-swashed in their inimitable way.

The hotel was quite pretty, although it would never appeal to me to stay there. Had our cocktails outside, fairly good dinner and danced afterwards. One of the taxis had a flat tyre which they changed with great alacrity.

19 February

Susan and Chris celebrate their 1st anniversary today.

Cynthia and Allison left for Europe (Pat's wife and daughter).

The *Bluenose* went off to Marigot Bay, St Lucia – only about a three-hour run from Port Castries. Wash day for the crew and most of us, with lines strung from the rigging.

This is a beautiful harbour and it seems to be a veritable boat haven. The bay is so small and the *Bluenose* so large she had to drop anchor in the middle of the bay and secure her stern to a palm tree ashore. Although the bay is very small there is a 100 foot yacht anchored in it, along with about twelve sailboats, as well as ours. As we entered the harbour a Canadian flag waved from one of the houses.

We all changed and swam ashore and the water was perfect, warm and clear. After lunch, a brief siesta, then Forrie went snorkelling and I went skiing. He also tried to get up on skis but couldn't quite make it.

All went ashore for a look around and had a drink at the hotel.

Early to bed for most of us. Full of fresh air and exercise. Even Gwynn's batteries needed re-charging – she was first to bed tonight.

Monday 20 February

Peaceful, pleasant day in Marigot Bay. Went for a long walk and saw all the lots that some unfortunate people are going to be horrified to discover they own, as they are on the side of a precipice. Can't figure out why anyone would buy a property site unseen.

Feeling warm and ready to sit down, we dropped into the hotel and had a long, cool drink. The whaler picked us up and we changed for dinner. The Cogginses went ashore for dinner so we had a rowdy, fun, dinner. We are off at 0700 in the morning, for St Vincents.

Tuesday 21 February

Sailed at 0700. Didn't get up in time to wave goodbye to all the nice people that apparently came out of houses and hotels to wave goodbye to the *Bluenose*. It must be quite a sight to watch her edge her way out of the little bay and away from 'the palm tree'. Captain Coggins is an amazing little man.

We had a good sail today, not rough and yet a good wind, as well as a cloudless, beautiful day. Flying fish zoomed along beside us all day. I love to sit up on top of the cabins on a mattress and watch them out-fly each other. St Vincents is a very lush and beautiful island and is quite mountainous. The ground is very well cultivated with no evidence of poverty. The natives are industrious in a way we haven't seen before.

Ralph took the helm for half an hour. We were anchored at Kingston and the customs came aboard and after we were cleared, we all went ashore to stretch our legs. It was as hot as Hades.

Pat, Betty, Jean, Mort and I took a cab and went to see the Botanical Gardens. We were very fortunate in having a cab driver who spoke very good English and the children made a business of giving us pods of nutmeg and showed us how all the spices grow. The flowers were truly a sight to behold. We saw a bread-fruit tree, said to have been planted by Captain Bligh. Could have spent the whole day there instead of about forty minutes.

Drove over the Queen Elizabeth drive, uphill, down, up and around we went until we had covered the four-mile distance the *Bluenose* had sailed without us. Wouldn't have missed the drive for anything. St Vincents is indeed a beautiful island. If irrigation can produce so much it is a very sad situation that the other islands can't have help to develop a water surplus.

Saw the *Bluenose* getting a soaking from a rain cloud while we were up on a sunny hillside.

The whaler picked us up at the Youngs Island dock.

Played Scrabble after dinner.

Wednesday 22 February

Went into town with the Rogers and the captain. Returned the dress I bought as it was too tight and got some very attractive ashtrays instead.

Came back to the *Bluenose* by taxi on my own and then we were all dropped off at Youngs Island, where we soon lost ourselves in admiration for the lovely hotel and cleverly designed plan of the bar, dining room, cottages, etc. Had a quick dip after a rum punch and having seen the puffins being fed by Julie Houser. Was well licked by their tame lamb that roams around the bar. Thoroughly enchanting place.

Back to the *Bluenose* and off to cross the channel to Bequia. There are some magnificent beaches, from which we lost no time in going ashore to swim. Unfortunately ate a bite out of what I thought was a Caribbean type of apple. How wrong can a gal be? It was no apple. My mouth feels as though I have been given a double lebangi treatment – to say nothing of the golf ball in my throat and the hot potato in my tummy.

Early to bed!

Thursday 23 February

How the time flies! All went ashore this morning. Mort was anxious to cash a travellers cheque. There was an information office at the wharf, so he asked the native girl where the bank was and she said quite casually, 'It won't be here until tomorrow.' She is probably still wondering why all those rude people laughed so hard.

Walked through the village and along the beach and found a very attractive shop. The first good one we have come across. Got the girls a dress and a hat.

All went next door for a drink at a hotel owned by two Canadians. They served the most lethal over-proof rum drinks we have had to date. Priceless people drifting around. It was hard to keep our faces straight, particularly as the drinks packed such a wallop. Forrie said they had LSD in them.

Admiralty Bay is a perfect yacht anchorage. Have never seen such a fleet of beautiful sailboats. Each one that came in I felt must surely be as large as the *Bluenose* but when they finally dropped anchor, they looked small by comparison.

Took a picnic over to Princess Margaret's Beach. It was a fun day. Hope all our pictures turn out well; it was such a perfect spot for cameras. We walked, swam and drank excellent punches made by Ralph from his beach bar. Sandwiches made by Ken were served on a silver tray – either in or out of the water. Jimmy Aitken was supposed to look after us but we didn't need or want him around so he moved in on two attractive girls and set them up to come aboard this p.m. The crew are most amusing the way they find their girls in every port of call.

We leave here early tomorrow for Tobago Cays – about thirty miles away – supposed to have even better beaches if that could be possible.

Friday 24 February

Thirty knot blow and a big sea. Perfect sailing for about three and a half hours. Captain Coggins said he had never seen it as rough as it was today.

The *Ramona*, a 120 foot white ketch, is already here. We are close enough to almost make out their faces, so we amused ourselves, as they did, by giving them the binocular treatment, a favourite sport down here.

Tobago Cays, except for the beautiful colouring of the sea due to all the coral reefs, is rather disappointing to say the least. Went ashore for a swim and the beach wasn't 1, 2, 3 to Bequia so we cut our stay short by a day.

Ralph's birthday and Captain and Mrs Coggins' wedding anniversary so this was 'Gala night'.

Everyone in a very gay mood to celebrate. Clean, or never seen before, white shirts, shorts or slacks appeared for the cocktail hour, with Jean stealing the show by batting artificial eyelashes and the Captain even donned his epaulets. The Cogginses went to another boat for cocktails so we had most of the cocktail hour by ourselves. Ralph wore his French beret with the label from Abercrombie & Fitch, sewn on by Gwynn.

Turtle soup, roast duckling or turtle steak, topped off with two decorated cakes with candles for economy class and the Captain's table. Champagne corks popped in all directions. A speech by Ralph to the Captain and Mrs Coggins, and a speech by Jean to Ralph.

Sat out on deck and watched the full moon come up over the hill on the island. The stars and moon seem so close and so much larger, maybe the rum punches improve the vision.

Gwynn appeared on deck with a full beard, straw hat and flour sack shirt, introducing 'Dolly', Dolly being Pat in a padded stretch bra that no doubt has had it, and a long skirt of Jean's with slits up the sides which he used to great advantage to show his hairy legs. On top of his head he wore one of the gingham turban hats the maids wear and lipstick-painted cupid bow lips. He really made a ravishing 'Dolly'. He made advances to all the men, insisting upon sitting on Mort's knee. He then took off and danced to the fo'c'sle to see the crew. He made a big play for Mr Snow, who I'm sure must have thought he was having a nightmare. The boys flashed their cameras and thought it was great.

Definitely made up our minds to move on at 0800 for Grenada which is a fifty-mile sail.

Saturday 25 February

Grenada is indeed all we were told it was. The town of St George is fascinating, with beautiful white sandy beaches. It is a very lush island with a spicy odour to it. Grenada is famous for its spices and exports – nutmeg, cinnamon, cocoa, arrowroot and a little cotton. It is very picturesque, with pretty winding streets and old churches.

We had one of our best sailing days. The wind was about thirty knots. Sat up on the cabin deck and shelled peas and enjoyed every wave and gust of wind. Saw a school of porpoise that tried to keep up with us but gave up. Forrie spotted what he was sure was a shark.

After we had lunch and a half-hour zizz, Mort and I went ashore and taxied over to a beach and swam for an hour. We all went ashore for dinner to one of the oldest hotels in Grenada. It had a little wharf out over the water so we watched the fish swimming in schools and circling around and around.

The moon is losing its fullness. It is strange to see its face at a different angle from the way we always see it at home.

Sunday 26 February

Grenada has won all our hearts. It is a truly beautiful island with its pink tile roofs and lush foliage. The people are very pleasant. The temperature 84° or over, and the water and beaches are superb.

Forrie, Gwynn, Mort and I took a taxi and the other four also took one and we drove to the new development on the other side of the island. There were some very pretty houses and it is no doubt cooler, but I wouldn't care to live there. Drove past the sugar factory, then to the Grenada Beach Hotel where we all met and had punches to cool off. Changed and swam for about an hour, topped off by quite a good lunch. Hated to leave that lovely beach.

Monday 27 February – Grenada

Had an early breakfast and went ashore with Mort to do some shopping. Found a ring for Susan in a surprisingly nice jewellery shop. Mort left me to return to the ship.

After finishing my shopping I tried to raise an eye in my direction from the *Bluenose* but finally gave up and accepted the offer of a native to row me out in his old boat. Having settled for 25 BWIs as his fare, away we went with Constantine in the bow with oars that extended fully across both sides of the boat and a little brown hat pulled down over his chocolate-brown face. Betty, Jean and Gwynn were sitting in the stern and happened to glance up and see the arrival of the shopper in the grubby little boat, so took some pictures which I hope will come out as they should be funny!

Ralph and Mort arrived aboard just before noon grinning from ear to ear, having sampled rum punches in every bar all the way around the harbour.

All felt sorry to say goodbye to Grenada as we slipped away from the dock at 1330. The sailing was very good but quite rough.

When Gary reported for duty on the wheel he was still licking his lips so we said, 'You must have had a very good dinner.' 'I did,' said Gary. 'We had roast beef and it was delicious.' We asked him if he had had Yorkshire pudding too and he replied, 'No, we had ice cream.'

Dinner was in two sittings this evening as we were not able to use the small dining table as it was quite rough. After dinner I had a long talk with Mr Snow. He told me about the hurricane that he was in on the maiden voyage of the *Bluenose*. Apparently there was one woman on board. It must have been a horrifying experience.

Ralph, John and Mr Snow all played their harmonicas and it was one of the most beautiful nights for an all-night sail. Really hated to go to bed, although Mort and I did get up and see the sun rise at 0600. It really wasn't very spectacular.

Tuesday 28 February – Independence Day

Sailed 135 miles to Castries Harbour. The town is gaily decorated with bunting to celebrate their big day. After taking on 250 gallons of water, we moved out and went back to Marigot Bay and tied up to our palm tree again.

Swimming was the fun of the day and Forrie took me along with him when he took out the sailfish and I lay out on the bow and hung on for dear life, in spite of which we dumped twice but managed to climb aboard again. It certainly is a thrill when it suddenly catches the wind and takes off.

Had lunch on deck under the awning. We thoroughly enjoyed our first avocados.

The crew went ashore to join the Independence Day celebrations. They apparently rented a couple of Hondas and drove into Castries.

The bay is filled with large boats – the captain said the bay was harbouring the best of all the West Indies charters – and *Bluenose* is the greatest of them all.

Wednesday 1 March

Sailed at 0600 from Marigot Bay to Prince Rupert Bay, Dominica, and it was quite a sail. TheCaptain said, and I quote: 'This wind is a real bugger.' We covered 115 miles – 38 knot wind across the Dominican Channel and we were doing 15 knots. Pat, Ralph, Forrie, Mort and I remained on deck, wedging our feet for support in order to stay in our deckchairs. It was a thrilling experience. Cameras were busy trying to catch the crashing waves against the bow and the water rushing through the scuppers with the rail under at times.

Had our buffet lunch on deck during the brief period that we were protected by the lee of the island. As we had little or no breakfast, our lunch was a very welcome sight. Ken deserves a medal the way he always produces a delectable meal, no matter how rough the conditions are.

As we seem to be surrounded by fish I tried a little fishing with George's rod and reel. Mort had gone to bed so didn't snag him in the pants again – didn't snag a fish either.

Thursday 2 March

Left Prince Rupert Bay at 0900 and crossed Guadaloupe Channel at an average of 13 knots – 30 miles across. Good breeze with gusts up to 30 knots and a slight sea. Very comfortable sailing. Great goings on ashore with some Frenchman yelling his lungs out over a loudspeaker. Read and dodged showers. The temperature has dropped from 92 to 80 degrees and everyone is cozied up in sweaters.

Played bridge in the saloon. The girls drew a partner from a hat. Forrie and Gwynn, Pat and Jean, Betty and Mort, Ralph and me.

Mort and Betty were the big winners, with Ralph and me in second place. Bee Wee's changed hands in all directions.

It will probably be a rough crossing tomorrow from Guadaloupe to Antigua. Can't believe our trip has almost come to an end.

Friday 3

Left Dominica about 08:30 and barely rounded the point before the wind and sea hit us. It really was a long day of slugging against the weather. About six and a half hours of winds gusting to 40. High seas and unable to use our sails. The flying fish put on a tremendous performance and never cease to amaze us. Only two other sailboats on the sea with us and a lobster fish boat was bobbing on the high seas.

A US Navy plane flew over us several times at low altitudes so we decided they must be taking photographs of the *Bluenose*. It was too bad our sails weren't up.

None of us were sorry to see English Harbour or to hear the anchors dropping. It really was a long day. Hurried into our bathing suits and went ashore for a swim. Had only been in the water for about fifteen minutes when a terrific shower came down on us.

Mort and Ralph went ashore to try their luck at the casino. The lighting display at Nelson's Dockyard was very well done. Was sorry not to see it from shore as it's supposed to be excellent.

Saturday 4 March

All good things must come to an end – so it was a different day from any other.

Breakfast at 08:00, packed a box of laundry and bathing suits and all went ashore to Nelson's Dockyard to do a variety of things. Some of us to see the Dockyard and Mort and I to taxi to the Height. Corky and Stanley Hecker were to meet Gwynn and Forrie at 11:00 with all our northern clothing.

We took a taxi and went up to see the old British forts and a cemetery. Felt a lump in my throat when we read an inscription. It was inscribed 'Elizabeth, wife of – and her two infant children, 1851 – aged 22 years.' They must have suffered dreadful hardships from the heat and lack of water, to say nothing of the constant battle for survival against the French.

We were told that all the bricks were brought from England as ballast in the ships that returned to England, laden with rum and sugar.

Had a planter's at the Admirals Inn and signalled the whaler to take us back to the *Bluenose* for a swim and lunch with Corky and Stanley.

Had fun water-skiing but the engine kept conking out – but with 80 degree water one does not mind.

Excellent dinner with a speech by Pat to the Captain and the latter's response.

Packed and so to bed. What a perfect holiday!

Sunday 5 March

Said our goodbyes to the *Bluenose*, Mrs Coggins and the captain, then George and Don took us ashore in the two whalers; two taxis to the airport for a lengthy wait for our flight north.

In the years to come, we can re-read Forrie's log and this diary and recall what a wonderful holiday we had. Also some of the laughs we had over Ralph and his Abercrombie & Fitch wardrobe, Betty and her slave, Gwynn, who kept her cigarettes going for three windy weeks. Those Thomas girls! Forrie's rear-end popping up out of the water when he was skin diving without enough weight. Jean jumping into the Layou River to push the boat. Pat dressed as Myrtle, among many other things. Mort, for his ability to make the best 'red snappers', and myself for taking pictures of the late, late sunsets. The Captain and Mrs

Coggins for being themselves, Ken for his good-natured grin and eagerness to help make our meals as good as they always were. Joe for his Jackie Coogan cap, if nothing else. Jimmy, George, big Jim, dear Mr Snow, John, Gary and Ricky and Don, for being a terrific crew.

We all wished Cynthia had been with us and I'm sure Pat will welcome his own 'wife noises' again instead of all of us.

Bluenose 1967

Foreword

In 1920, Senator Dennis, publisher of the Halifax *Herald and Mail*, offered the 'International Fishermen's Trophy' for a competition between commercial sailing vessels of the Grand Banks fishing fleet. The first series of races were won by an American vessel, and efforts were immediately instituted to build a ship which would 'bring the cup back to Canada'.

The result was the *Bluenose*, designed by W. J. Roue, built in the yards of Smith and Rhueland and launched in 1921. *Bluenose* under command of Angus Walters not only brought the cup back, but successfully defended every challenge thereafter. She became something of a legend for Canada, a postage stamp bearing her picture was issued in 1929, and since 1937 her likeness has appeared on one face of the Canadian ten-cent coin.

With the coming of war in 1939, *Bluenose* was laid up along with the rest of the sailing fishermen, and in 1942 she was sold to be used as an inter-island trader in the West Indies. She was wrecked on a reef near Haiti in January of 1946.

Many efforts were made to have a new *Bluenose* built to perpetuate this famous vessel, but the task of raising the necessary funds seemed insurmountable. Eventually the firm of Oland & Sons, brewers of Halifax, agreed to underwrite the project and

Bluenose II was built from the same plans and in the same yard as her predecessor. She was launched in July 1963.

Great care was taken to exactly duplicate the hull and rigging of the original *Bluenose*; however, below decks there can be little resemblance as the present vessel has comfortable well-appointed staterooms and a sumptuous saloon, all of which are air-conditioned for tropical cruising in winter. The overall length of *Bluenose* is 143 feet, her draught 15 feet 10 inches, and her total sail area is 10,901 square feet.

Cruise of the *Bluenose* II

(Forrie Rogers 'Saga' with permission from Gwynn to include with my diary as the two accounts are different).

12 February to 5 March 1967

Guests for the cruise arrived as follows:

Ralph and Betty Farris and Jean Rogers flew down by way of New York arriving on Saturday 11 February. Then by previous arrangement they went directly aboard *Bluenose* II, which was lying at anchor in English Harbour, Antigua. The rest of the party came aboard the following day. Pat and Forrie had flown down a day or two before from Montreal and had stayed ashore for two nights at the Barrymore Hotel. Gwynn had come by way of Jamaica, where she visited with the Evans, and she too spent one night at the Barrymore. Johnnie and Mort Duffus had arrived in Antigua a week earlier, which they spent at the Anchorage Hotel. Sometime before noon the whole party was on board and it was decided not to set sail until the following day, as some time was taken up in unpacking and the captain suggested it would be advisable for us to become familiar with the ship. Apart from this there was plenty of time for a swim ashore at a nearby beach.

The Bluenose, *left, in Nelson's Harbour, Antigua.*

Ralph Farris was put in charge of the liquor locker and presented with a key for this purpose. A few notes regarding the operation of the bar might be appropriate at this point.

Since the locker was located on the port side in the dining saloon and since in our travels south we were always on the port tack it became difficult, if not impossible, to open the locker when the ship was heeled over because on doing so the bottles would cascade out onto the floor. Apart from this, it was difficult to pour drinks and carry them above when the ship was under way. For this reason the bar was seldom open before 11:00 to 11:30 in the morning, by which time we had usually found some shelter behind the lee of an island. On the journey home the problems didn't exist in the same fashion, as the bottles would stay in the locker when we were on the starboard tack. However, the same rules applied and the bar was not open until we gained the shelter of an island. To begin with it was expected that the steward would pour our drinks for us, but as he was so terribly slow the male guests soon found out where the ice and mixers were kept and the operation of the bar continued quite successfully until the last day, when someone lost the key. This was not an insurmountable problem as the steward had a duplicate, which we are fairly sure he used for his own purpose from time to time.

The crew on board consisted of the following:

Captain Ellsworth Coggins, a short, cheerful man with wide experience in sail, as he had captained the *Bounty* which he took out to Tahiti for the shooting of the film *Mutiny on the Bounty* some years ago. He, of course, had many interesting tales of his experiences to tell us.

The Mate was Mr Skojde, a very quiet-spoken but efficient Norwegian, who obviously was highly thought of by the crew under him.

The Chief Engineer was Mr J. Weeks, who was in command of everything in the engine room but seemed to spend most of his time fiddling with his ham radio equipment.

The Cook was Kenny Beckford, a very cheerful black Jamaican, who supplied us with very excellent food, and since he was also required to feed the crew, he almost single-handedly produced sixty-six meals a day, which is a quite a feat in itself, as it was frequently done while the ship was under way.

The Steward was Edgar Joseph, also a black Jamaican, but who was not too cheerful in disposition. About all he was good for was waiting on tables and cleaning up the cabins once a day. When you gave your order for breakfast – say orange juice, poached eggs and tea, Joe would serve you tomato juice, fried eggs and coffee.

The Mess Boy was Jim Aikens, who also played a full part as deckhand. He was an expert on swimming, scuba diving, water skiing and practically anything in the way of aquatic sports. He was a very cheerful boy and was liked by all aboard.

The Bosun was Mr Snow, who at seventy-four was by far the

oldest man aboard. Mr Snow had served previously on the original *Bluenose*. He was an extremely quiet man, but obviously very experienced, and the captain told us that he dreaded the day when Mr Snow would leave the ship.

There were two individuals classed as seamen. These were Big Jim Porter and George Deering. Jim was a rather cheerful, fat boy and was usually the one to climb the rigging when the mainsail was set. More about this later.

George, we think, was the more efficient of the two and seemed to be dedicated to a career at sea.

There were four ordinary seamen. Garry Berkman was probably the youngest and a very cheerful, good looking lad. Mike Wigger always performed his tasks properly, but sometimes with a bit of a hangover. If anyone was to get into trouble ashore it would inevitably be Mike. Donald Coggins, son of the Captain, we gathered was not too popular with the rest of the crew and had a slightly arrogant, know-it-all attitude – and finally, John Butters, who was probably the best seaman of the youngsters aboard and a well-behaved, quiet lad and the best skier.

All in all the crew seemed extremely happy and one of the first things we noticed was that all work operating the ship was carried out efficiently and with an absolute minimum number of commands from the Captain or the Mate.

On Monday 13 February we set sail and left English Harbour. We had a good breeze and ran along between eight and ten knots. All the passengers were immediately intrigued with the many flying fish that we saw about the ship. These we were to see every day from then on and we never ceased to be fascinated by their antics and the distances which they could fly.

We reached Guadeloupe about two in the afternoon where we anchored in De Sayes Bay. The village there was most grubby looking and certainly not inviting. However, Pat and Jean went ashore and managed to procure a taxi which took them over to the Fort Royal Hotel. On returning, they advised us that this establishment was full of French fruits, and some of the sexy sights that they saw were rather difficult to describe. The rest of the passengers stayed aboard for bridge and Scrabble.

On Tuesday 14th, we made our way down to the Ile des Saintes, but as there was little wind only the foresails were hoisted, and we proceeded under engines. On arrival we all went ashore to inspect the village, which was rather grubby. We also walked over to the cemetery which had some rather interesting tombstones, and up past the only hotel which consisted of a two-storey wooden building with raucous music blaring forth and the owner's daughter leaning seductively out of the window. During a tour of inspection a very attractive French maiden raised a laugh by calling out to Mort in a loud voice, 'De Gaulle, De Gaulle!'

On Wednesday 15th, we awoke to find a French Naval vessel, the *Jeanne d'Arc*, anchored nearby. At nine o'clock we hoisted anchor and sailed with light winds and occasionally rain squalls to Prince Rupert Bay on the Isle of Dominica. Most of the gang went ashore and took a boat trip up Indian River. We did not get very far as the river was rather low and the local rowboats that we were in ran aground fairly frequently.

Back on the *Bluenose* that evening Johnnie Duffus told us that she had once seen a green flash just after the sun had gone down and she came in for a fair amount of good-natured kidding as to whether indeed such a flash could be seen, or whether possibly she had been looking through the bottom of a glass of crème de menthe. At any rate the subject of the green flash came up every day from then on at sundown and although many of us watched this phenomenon was never observed.

On Thursday 16th, we weighed anchor at 7:00 a.m. and went under power down the lee of Dominica. Once into the Dominican passage we found an excellent wind which during the crossing gusted up to forty-five knots. The sea was slightly rough but *Bluenose* ran beautifully along at speeds of up to fifteen knots and on several occasions we had the lee rail under. We were advised by the Captain and Mate that they had never experienced such good strong winds before at this season of the year. *Bluenose*, of course, behaved marvellously with these breezes. However, we learned that two smaller charter vessels had been completely dismasted during the time that we were crossing.

During the crossing we noticed that the crew was carefully watching the main mast. This is because on a previous voyage the mast had cracked and it had been repaired by fitting a section of steel tubing, about thirty feet long, around the mast just below the spreaders; this repair being a temporary one until such time as a new laminated mast could be secured from British Columbia. It was this steel bracing that made it sometimes necessary for one of the crew to climb the rigging as the hoops of the mainsail would not always pass over the lip at the bottom of the tube. Also, on account of this temporary repair the topsails and staysail were never set during our cruise. However, with the winds that we experienced, *Bluenose* sailed at times up to her maximum speed without the benefit of topsails.

Crossing the Dominican passage with us was a small red ketch and a staysail schooner, both of which we passed and left far behind, as we did any other sailboat that we encountered on our cruise. There can be no doubt that when it comes to speed, *Bluenose* is queen.

In the lee of Martinique we passed a school of dolphins that were apparently basking in the sun and at about the time the bar was open, drinks were served and by mistake two rum punches were mixed using the Captain's special liqueur rum. This error was not committed again.

On arrival in Fort-de-France we found the cruise ships *Independence* and *Homeric* at anchor and were told that there were several others in the inner harbour. From this we knew that prices in the shops ashore had all gone up. It was raining hard and we stayed aboard ship.

On Friday 17th, the sun was shining and we all went ashore to buy wine, brandy and champagne and do some window-shopping. The party then broke up and went their various ways.

Gwynn and Forrie hired a taxi and took an hour's drive around the city and suburbs, while others explored the bars, shops, etc. In the course of their drive the Rogers found the Lido Hotel which seemed to be quite attractive, so Jean, Pat, Johnnie and Mort made their way there for lunch. Mrs Duffus went all out in the wine department and they reported that it was the best food so far.

On Saturday 18th, we set sail at eight o'clock and had good winds for the crossing to St Lucia. We averaged ten knots for the trip and many times were up to fifteen or better. For a while Captain Coggins thought we might have to lower the mainsail, but this proved to be unnecessary as the wind did not become as strong as expected. However, we took a good deal of spray aboard and at one point the top of a wave was washed aboard soaking several of the passengers, especially Gwynn and Betty. Betty decided to go below and change into dry clothing but then fifteen minutes later another wave came aboard and she and Gwynn were completely swamped once more.

On arrival at Port Castries we made fast to the wharf and all passengers, together with Captain and Mrs Coggins, drove off to the St Lucia Beach Hotel for dinner where we were told that a casino was in operation. However, no casino existed. We had a good dinner which Ralph insisted on paying for as he said that he was 'up to his ass in beewees'.

Our taxi ride back to the hotel was not without excitement as we had a flat tyre to start off with, and then found that the local sport appeared to be playing chicken on the highway and as this was narrow and winding we had a few hair-raising moments. The only other item of note is that it was in Port Castries that Pat managed to lose his glasses. This he reported to the police, in the hope that they would be recovered – but without success.

On Sunday 19th, we left Port Castries and went under power for four miles to Marigot Bay. This is the most beautiful, almost landlocked, little cove and as there was not room for *Bluenose* to swing, the anchor was dropped in the centre of the cove and a stern line tanker ashore and made fast to a palm tree. Not far from us was a large plastic imitation of a snail shell which had been built for shooting the film *Dr Doolittle*. We spent the day swimming, scuba diving, sailing the little sunfish. Forrie made an abortive attempt to get up on water skis, but only managed to swallow a fair quantity of sea water, lost his trunks, and was put to shame by Johnnie, who proved to be an expert. We went ashore for cocktails at a small hotel operated by a couple of Canadians, who also operate a rather fine charter schooner, *Ramona*. We were not surprised to find that with such a delightful cove, somebody has tried to start a real estate development but some of their purchases will get a rude awakening when they come to see the lots they have purchased, as many of them are on extremely steep slopes and it would be difficult, if not impossible, to build houses on them.

On Monday 20th, we stayed in Marigot Bay and continued with somewhat the same activities as the day before.

On Tuesday 21st, we left Marigot Bay and had a very pleasant sail down to Kingston on St Vincent Island. Here the captain went ashore as usual to clear with immigration and customs and some of the passengers went with him. However, as Kingston is not a comfortable anchorage we went a bit further and dropped the hook behind Young Island, which is a small island within swimming distance of St Vincent.

At one time or another everyone went ashore to drive around the island and visit the botanical gardens where Captain Bligh is reported to have planted the first breadfruit trees brought from Tahiti. Everyone agreed that this was the prettiest island that we had visited so far and, as a matter for future reference, we thought that the small hotel on Young Island was very attractive. This island is unspoiled and prosperous, and in contrast to Antigua all the native cottages are well kept and well painted. The island has diversified crops of berries, sweet potatoes, yams, cottons, citrus fruits, bananas, spices and sugar.

On Wednesday 22nd, we went under foresail and jumbo jib to Bequia. This was a slightly rough crossing but we were told not nearly as bad as it could be. There was an excellent beach at Bequia and people should be warned not to try eating the fruit from the trees that grow near the shore. Johnnie tried this with rather unfortunate results.

We went to Barclays Bank, who are agents for the Bank of Montreal, and were informed that 'The bank isn't here until Friday.' Forrie posed for a photo in order to prove it at the next Directors' Meeting. Incidentally, the bank looked much more like a garage than a bank.

For Thursday 23rd, we remained at Bequia where we spent most of the day ashore, visiting the very small village and drinking very potent rum punches at the small hotel. Later, we had a picnic on the beach and did some biological research on a sea urchin. It was on this day that Pat tried to frighten some of the others by calling out that a barracuda was nearby, but he spoiled the whole effect by saying barbecue instead. It might be mentioned that our picnic was held at Princess Margaret Beach.

On Friday 24th, we had a good fast sail from Bequia to Tobago Cays and we anchored with the *Ramona* nearby. The water here was absolutely crystal clear and all went ashore for a swim and to do some snorkelling. While the small islands here are supposed to be uninhabited, we found that there were three men from Bequia camped ashore where they were earning a living by catching turtles and lobster which they sold to the various yachts visiting this spot. That night we were treated to real turtle soup and turtle steaks for dinner and while on the subject of food I should mention that at lunch that day we had a very excellent salad made from conch meat. This day was Ralph's birthday and the Coggins' wedding anniversary so we had a gala dinner with champagne and all the trimmings, after which Pat and Gwynn dressed up – Gwynn as a gentleman with whiskers and Pat as a rather disgusting looking lady. Pat later visited the forecastle in his regalia and sat on Mr Snow's knee, much to the delight of the young members of the crew, most of whom instantly brought forth flash cameras to record the occasion.

A little boat propelled by an outboard motor circled the *Bluenose* and suddenly a voice called out, 'Are you Canadians?' On giving the affirmative, we were asked whether we knew Bryce and Daphne Evans. This turned out to be a friend from Winnipeg, Barbara Baldwin.

While it had originally been planned to spend two days at the Tobago Cays, because it was somewhat windy we decided that the extra day wasn't worthwhile and so, on 25 February, we sailed to Grenada. We had good winds all the way south with occasional rain squalls that chased most of the passengers below. In due course we anchored at St George's Harbour with two stern lines taken ashore to the wharf. That night all passengers went ashore to the Silver Sands Hotel for dinner. Gwynn, Forrie, John and Mort went for a drive to see the rural parts of the island. They saw a large new subdivision where a number of modern looking houses had already been built.

On 26 February we all went ashore to investigate St George and its surroundings and then drove to Grenada Beach Hotel for swimming and lunch. In the evening, before the sunset, we strolled in town and found it most picturesque as well as very clean. There seemed to be numerous churches and very attractive and well kept up gardens behind stone walls. This was the farthest south that we got and, therefore, the warmest place that we visited and, of course, this was the one place where the air-conditioning decided to pack up during the night. Fortunately the repairs did not take long to be put into effect.

On 27 February we moved from anchor to a wharf where fuel, water and other supplies, including booze, were taken aboard. There was some delay in getting this latter important item on board and so it was not until two in the afternoon that we set sail. We had a fair breeze and sailed all night – a distance of one hundred and forty miles – back to Port Castries, where we arrived at nine o'clock the following morning. On the previous evening we had a mouth-organ symphony concert at the stern of the ship with Mr Snow, the Bosun, being one of the principal players.

We arrived in Port Castries on 28 February and, having cleared customs and immigration, decided to move immediately to Marigot Bay and since this was to be Independence Day for the island, it was expected that there might be some troubles ashore. We learned later the festivities were carried out without any disturbances and units of the British and Canadian Navies had been on hand to help celebrate the occasion and to remove the Governor to Barbados, as it had been agreed beforehand that he and his family were to leave immediately after midnight on the Day of Independence.

In Marigot Bay we had more of the same – sunfish sailing,

swimming, etc., and there were many other boats at anchor in the bay, including the *Ramona* and *Lord Jim*. That night, Johnnie Duffus tried her hand at spinner casting for fish and succeeded in hooking a large prize – namely Mort – whom she got in the ass.

On 1 March we left Marigot at six in the morning and had sloppy weather for a short while. However, at Martinique we picked up an excellent breeze and for quite a while were travelling along at a good fifteen knots. Then for a short while we were in the doldrums, with winds coming from almost any quarter. However, once we got into the Dominican Channel we had heavy winds with gusts up to forty miles and, once again, *Bluenose* was rail under and we had some real sailing. During the passage, we sighted a full rigged ship nearly hull down on the horizon, travelling in the opposite direction to us. Some of the crew aboard claimed that she was the *Libertad*. However, no-one was too sure.

We arrived at Prince Rupert Bay at sundown and Pat, shortly afterwards, bargained for a steel band to come aboard and entertain us in the evening. This ended in failure, as despite all promises no band appeared, which was probably just as well.

On 2 March we left Prince Rupert Bay and sailed directly back to Des Hayes Bay on Guadeloupe. We had excellent sailing all the way and averaged a speed of twelve knots across the channel, which meant that at times the ship was travelling at sixteen knots and more for a considerable distance.

In Des Hayes Bay it was quite windy and there were quite a number of rain squalls and as the village ashore held no attractions, we stayed aboard.

On 3 March we started under foresail and jumbo jib and engines to make the crossing to English Harbour. This was rather an uncomfortable crossing as there is a three-knot current running through the channel to eastward against the prevailing north-easterly wind. On arrival at English Harbour all went ashore for another swim at the beach on the easterly shore and had a pleasant time, until a rain squall came up and Garry came to our rescue with the larger of the whalers.

That evening, Ralph and Mort went ashore and visited the casino with no great financial success. They returned about two in the morning and reported next day that there was not much action to be seen. An amusing Damon Runyonesque touch – Ralph met a well-known Vancouver bookmaker who, believe it or not, introduced them to the newly-appointed Governor of the island.

On 4 March we stayed at anchor in English Harbour. Everyone went ashore to visit the museum and to examine the old dockyard which is being renovated. We had drinks at the Admiral's Inn with Stanley and Corky Hecker, who had very kindly stored our northern clothes in their house while we were away cruising.

Stanley and Corky came aboard *Bluenose* and, after a swim over the side, we all had lunch under the awning at the stern. During the course of this, Captain Coggins decided to shift his position, much to the delight of Stanley who said that he could now say that he had sailed in *Bluenose*.

Quite frequently on the trip, Pat had been asked when he was going to ascend the rigging and take a picture of the ship from above, and he claimed that this would be done, but kept putting it off. On this day, Pat secretively went below with Jim Aitkens where they traded clothes and Jim then went scampering up the ratlines in Pat's clothes carrying his camera and proceeded to photograph us from above. Unfortunately on this day too we were required to get out our suitcases and pack up for the journey home.

On 5 March, we arose fairly early and by 9:30 were all in taxis which took us to the other side of the island to the airport. We arrived there in ample time for our flight north and so used up the last of our beewees at the bar. All of us boarded an Air Canada flight to Toronto, but Pat, Betty and Ralph took off for Montreal, while Johnnie and Mort, Jean, Gwynn and Forrie flew directly back to Vancouver.

Thus ends the saga of the Cruise on the *Bluenose* II.

Europe 1967

Mort and I had a lovely trip planned where we would spend the first part in England and with friends in Northern Ireland, prior to which I was to have an operation in my foot. Plans went ahead very nicely with Jane (or Emily) and her husband Norman Hurd to meet us in Lisbon after we had been to Barcelona from the UK. As luck would have it, my foot didn't heal properly and my doctor said I must not think of travelling. I called Mort at his office to break the bad news. I insisted he carry on without me but to take Drue in my place. Susan had had her trip abroad, so he agreed, if Drue could obtain a passport in the three days ahead of us. At that time Drue was working at Simon Fraser University so was completely stunned when told she was to give her notice, stop on the way home and have a passport photograph taken, pick up the necessary forms and fill them out, then drive the application to the airport and it would be couriered to Ottawa. In the three days she had her precious passport and some new clothes, and off they went without a dry eye between us.

They spent about a week in and out of London and then went on to Northern Ireland. While at the latter they were taken to the races and Drue was drenched in a downpour and subsequently was chilled to the bone. Meanwhile, my foot was healing miraculously, thanks to a remedy which was given to me by a friend who instructed me to rapidly flick my fingers in the hand opposite to the ailing foot; this would bring a flood of circulation to the blood – which it did! When I phoned them in London and woke them both up, I was forgiven, when I sheepishly admitted to my miraculous recovery. Mort said they would proceed to Barcelona and I was to meet them in Lisbon where we would join forces with Jane and Norman, who would be flying from Ottawa.

I was the first to arrive and was catching a little 'shut-eye' after the flight over, which was made quite comfortable thanks to seats being made available to me so I could keep my foot elevated. Mort and Drue walked in on me and it was a very special time for us as we never thought when they left Vancouver that I would be able to join them.

Jane and Norman followed soon after. We had a fabulous dinner that night to celebrate. Drue adored her Aunt Jane and Uncle Norman as they did her in return. Unfortunately Drue had never properly shaken the chill caught in Ireland so had a visit from the house physician who had her on the mend within twenty-four hours. We had an excellent driver and a good-sized car to accommodate all of us.

It has been said before that Mort and his sister Jane were tarred by the same brush, as they had to test their skill at the casino, so Norman took Drue and me to the Fado and we were as delighted with our evening as they were with theirs.

We had a very interesting tour through a winery which was famous for its port and madeira. We placed our orders for many we sampled. We also went to a cork factory which was fascinating, as it also is one of Portugal's main industries. There are great forests of cork trees to draw from. We all enjoyed Portugal and the people with their softly spoken language. We also loved their seafood and fish dishes.

To our delight, Paddy and Mike McLennen contacted us and invited us for dinner at their hotel. It was a very special evening, they being about the first couple Mort met when he moved to

Vancouver from Calgary, later to become best man at their wedding. They also had a cottage at Cowan's Point and had known Drue since the day she was born. They loved our girls as we loved their Pat and Glen. I have a very good picture of Mort proposing the toast to Glen at her wedding.

We drove to Estoril and stood on a high cliff overlooking a beautiful beach with a fair number of their colourful fishing boats pulled ashore. A little boy of about six had adopted us and was wearing a straw hat, of which he was extremely proud. Suddenly a gust of wind caught his hat and sailed it out over the cliff. If Jane hadn't caught him, he would have thrown himself after his precious hat. I can't bear to think of how dreadful it might have been.

After Jane and Norman flew home we went to London and took in a few shows and on our last night, Finlay Mungall invited us to be his guests for dinner and a little gambling at the Twenty One Club. There was only one catch: Drue would have to be his young married friend for the evening and he would lend her a ring belonging to his wife who was on holiday in the States. Drue thought the whole idea was too good to be true and rose to the occasion, looking as pretty as a picture. After a scrumptious dinner we moved in to the tables and Drue joined Finlay at '21'. Being a chip off her father's block, she knew what she was doing. Mort had settled himself at another table and I cruised around, not being a gambler. It wasn't long before it was obvious Drue was causing quite a stir, as there were never fewer than three or four men standing behind her and her chips were mounting. By this time, Mort was anxious to call it an evening and finally said I should tell Drue it was getting late and we were flying home the next day. I made a few 'wife noises', as we used to say, that this was an unforgettable evening for her and to find a comfortable chair and stop growling. The time did come when even she was tired so she cashed in her chips, gave Finlay his ring and a huge hug and we taxied back to Jermyn Street. It was a never-to-be-forgotten experience, having garnered the equivalent of three hundred and fifty dollars!

Early the next morning we struck out for the Burlington Arcade where she had seen a gold charm that she coveted for her bracelet, so that was soon tucked away in her purse with several cashmere sweaters and a very nice gift for Susan and Bruce.

Home sweet home, after a truly wonderful holiday – the memory of which would be greatly treasured.

It wasn't long after our return that we needed some repairs done to a built-in bookcase in Drue's bedroom. In her haste to leave the house one day, she had neglected to put her treasured possession, the very valuable gold charm bracelet, out of sight. Tragically, it was stolen from her dressing table by one of the carpenters. Fortunately the memories that inspired her collection that each charm represented remained.

It is such a pity not to have kept a diary when we made that trip but I think it can be blamed on post-op foot. I had to elevate it as often as possible and keeping up with a busy schedule was quite demanding. By the time it was bedtime, I was zapped and writing a diary was far from my mind. One thing I am sure of is that I wouldn't have missed it for the world.

Looking back now, it was wonderful for Mort to have had that time to himself with Drue. So often, with daughters, there is more time spent with their mothers. He adored his girls and I am sure having them to himself without me were special times.

Drue had missed Bruce (Akhurst) terribly and had kept letters flowing back to Canada, so it was a happy day when she returned home after her totally unplanned trip.

Although Susan was married then, they had a remarkably close relationship that grew stronger with each year.

Europe 1969

Villa d'Este – Lake Como

12 May 1969

Drue and Bruce drove us out to the airport at 11:00 a.m. and we dutifully checked in and got our insurance. Had a cup of coffee with them and sent them on their way. Had a brief chat with John and Jean Mann before taking off on the first leg of our journey.

Refuelled in Amsterdam which was most pleasant as they allowed us to roam around the duty-free shops, which helped to stretch our legs. Good flight with a very pleasant little German girl who was returning to Berlin for a visit with her mother.

Thought we were being so clever in Frankfurt, hopping a flight that would see us in Milan a bit earlier, but found when we arrived that our luggage wasn't with us, so we had to wait and wait. Our taxi arrived and two very, very weary people climbed in. Try as I would, I couldn't keep my eyes open driving to Villa D'Este on Lake Como. Today I have little, if any, recollection of our drive, except to say that we went like a bat out of hell. However, we weren't too tired to quell the excitement we felt when we saw this beautiful old palace sprawled along the shore of the lake in the most serene manner.

We were shown to our room which was truly gorgeous. Too bad Drue isn't along as there is a dear little room which I imagine is for a maid. We have a garden all of our own leading off our bedroom, with French doors. Across the front view we have our own fifteenth century balcony with table and chairs. It commands the most breathtaking view of the lake and hotel.

We put on our dressing gowns and literally died for three hours. Wakened refreshed, bathed and dressed and wandered over to the hotel and sniffed out the bar, which is most colourfully decorated in delphinium blue, white and gold. A young French girl was singing to the accompaniment of a talented pianist. Our dinner which followed was most disappointing as we neglected to inquire if the lamb would have garlic – indeed it did, so we had our soup, strawberries and ice cream. Drank a toast to our Susie's 24th with a bottle of Rhein Riesling. We then strolled around the magnificent grounds of the palace. It would take a far greater pen than mine to do justice to the beauty of it all. The flowers, the trees, the mosaic walls, fountain and garden steps that lead up and up, and which are bordered by water dripping down from a statue, played upon with lights. We were much too weary to climb up to see of whom it was.

13 May – 9:00 a.m.

My darling Mum and Dad,

Am sitting on our verandah made of fourteenth century stone overlooking beautiful Lake Como. There is a castle above us and estates of such magnitude and luxury on the surrounding jutting pieces of land, that there is no way I can describe their beauty. The hotel has many picturesque fourteenth century buildings, all landscaped to perfection.

It's warm and there is a haze that is filtering across the buildings, giving them a look akin to an ancient painting.

We were terribly tired after our sixteen hours of travel, some of them spent sitting in airports waiting for a plane, or our luggage in Milan. When we finally walked into our beautiful room we simply peeled off our clothes and went to bed as fast as we could.

Strangely enough, we only slept for a couple of hours, bathed and dressed for dinner. Had a drink at the bar and went in for dinner. To bed at 11:00 and slept like the dead until 7:00 this morning.

Hope all is well with you both. I feel a long way away from you but in actual flying hours it really isn't so very far away today.

Have no idea what we will do today, but will write my next letter to Susan and Drue and keep you all up-to-date on our enjoyable experiences.

Hope Bill will be able to visit you often as he is so close. Do give Doreen and Bill my love when you see them. Lots and lots of love to all of you. Please keep my letters so I can make a diary when I return. Tell Drue to pick this up and she can read it to Susie.

Love again,

John

There is an arbour of wisteria that leads to our residence and also to the moat where boats come and go, to and from the hotel. The swimming pool is quite something. It is on the lake itself and has been encompassed by a wooden deck that is kept shining with cleanliness that reminds us of the *Bluenose*, only it was highly polished.

Had an early breakfast out on our garden balcony. Unfortunately Mort had forgotten his bathing trunks so we walked up to the shop to hopefully acquire a pair. He was shown quite a selection, which he gathered up and proceeded to a dressing room. After what seemed like an interminable length of time, he called me. I honestly thought I was going to expire, I laughed so hard at him modelling the Italian stovepipe little numbers!! We both had the tears streaming down our faces. It must have sounded dreadful to the girls in the shop. They were skin tight, striped and obviously they were never meant for any man of his height. He ended up with the least of three evils. Even the girl had to laugh when he paid the bill, although thankfully she didn't see him wearing the wretched things. While I was cooling my heels, I found a very nice luncheon set of twelve place mats and napkins. Will pick up some for Drue's trousseau. Also found a very attractive evening jacket.

There has been a haze shrouding the lake all day, which has given a mysterious beauty to everything we can see looking across and down the lake. The trees appear much darker silhouetted against the mountains that strangely enough resemble cotton wool. The weather is superb, 75-80°, so we are as happy as happy can be. We sunbathed and had a swim this afternoon, with Mort cutting quite a dash in his costume. I'm sure he only felt content with his lot when he was submerged. I never could, in my wildest dreams, call that thing he has to wear, trunks!

Had our cocktail hour outside in the garden rather than in the bar, watching the lights on the lake and the boats moving about so quietly. We felt sure they were enjoying the glorious voice of the French girl. Fairly nice – they do have a very good band in their new night club.

14 May

Made the mistake of thinking we could find the address of a silk shop in Com. First of all, no ferry at 10:40 weekdays, so took a cab and the driver not only didn't understand English, but hadn't a notion where the shop was – so we walked up and down lane after lane, until finally, after what seemed an eternity, we bore down on the blessed place only to find it was locked tighter than a drum for siesta. Had a sidewalk café beer to recoup our energy as it was HOT, HOT. Luckily the ferry was just about to take off so we dashed aboard and headed for Villa D'Este and a swim. Lunched outside with a delicious omelette and excellent salad, then crashed our heads down for a few hours. Am always delighted when Mort says he is wiped out, so it isn't just me. Later, we climbed to the top of the old fort which is above this palace and had a thoroughly strenuous climb. Watched some tennis on the way home, followed by some writing and sewing, then dressed for dinner – the latter not too successful in the clubhouse owing to our usual problem, the language barrier, but greatly helped by some excellent entertainment, which we enjoyed outside after dinner. Danced and generally lapped up the beautiful evening. A gaily lit boat drew alongside the hotel playing great music, so quite a few of the guests here went to the railing, waved and made happy noises, topped off by one fellow calling out 'Aloha!' It doesn't seem funny to write about it but he certainly got a lot of laughs. To bed about midnight, to the sounds of lovely music.

15 May

Our first day with our driver, René, by name. Young fellow and a superb driver. Didn't at any time, all day, feel the least bit nervous with him at the wheel. Left here about 10:00 and as our plans had been to go into Switzerland, we changed them due to it being Ascension Day, and all the shops would have been closed. Every man and his well-dressed child were on the road and at one point we were bumper to bumper for half an hour. First of all we went to Isola Bella, a picturesque little island almost entirely covered with a very ornate old palace, the actual place where Mussolini and Neville Chamberlain had their meeting to cement relations prior to World War II. We hired a little boat to take us out, only to find that we couldn't see through the palace owing to it being siesta time. Will we ever learn? We then drove to the Grand Hotel in Stresa and had an extremely good lunch, quite the best we have ever had. Saw some very pretty houses, vineyards on the hills and the most outstanding display of azaleas in every colour imaginable, some of which were at least twenty feet high.

René then drove us to the Giardini Botanici in the Villa Taranto, where we joined up with a guide, because we had to, and toured the gardens. The tulip season was over and we were in between flowers. The azaleas once more were incredible so we took many pictures which we hope will do the gardens justice. It became unbearably hot, so we escaped from our guide and caught up with another one heading to the exit. We hated to miss the rest of the tour but we were weary and very happy to collapse into the car, whereupon I dozed most of the way home. Had hoped to arrive before the pool got into the shade, but ended up by flaking out for a read and zizz.

Dinner at 9:30. Sat out listening to the night club swingers and to bed around 11:30. One good laugh today was when I sat without being observed, in the car, and Mort had wandered away from it to stretch his long legs while we were waiting for the ferry at Pallanz to cross to Laverno. When two young men saw him they waited until they were just past him, grinned, and gave Mort a smart salute – followed a few minutes later by a girl pointing his way. She drew herself to her full height and said 'Commander.' He towers above the Italians.

16 May

Lovely day today. René picked us up at 10:00 and drove us to Lugano in Switzerland to shop. We were across the border in ten minutes, much to our surprise. Got quite a few gifts and could have spent a fortune, then had an excellent lunch at a restaurant called Bian. We heartily agreed with the Millburns; it was a five-star rating with us also. Went for a delightful drive along the lake and were very impressed with the view. Quite the most spectacular we have seen on our drives, so took pictures to preserve the memory.

Another very pleasant happening was stopping to see the Swiss miniatures. We were staggered to find castles, cathedrals, churches, railway yards, villages, farms and rivers. You name it, all in miniature and built to perfection in scale. We felt like a couple of kids, we went around them as excited as all the little children. I got a book so I can show all of you at home. It was some person's brainchild, believe me. Ferries and trains were all docking, shunting or whatever else they had to do to perfect the scene they were depicting. If only we could produce a portion of it at Children's Hospital. Arrived home in time for a swim, rest and quiet dinner, for which we were not in the least hungry.

17 May

Dearest Drue,

Early this morning I was awakened and was wished a happy birthday by your mother. Then I proceeded to open my parcels and when I came to yours – imagine my delight when I discovered a beautiful bushy shaving brush. I just don't know how you knew I needed it and it is just the kind I like. Thank you ever so much, darling daughter. It was sweet of you, but much too extravagant on your part.

Your mum and I are starting off in about half an hour for a speedboat trip up Lake Como. You have probably been told how lovely it is. Yesterday we took a drive to Lugano, which is in Switzerland. Had a good lunch there and returned in time for a swim and a late dinner.

You and Bruce would love this place for a honeymoon – too bad it is so far away.

We drive over to Venice tomorrow, stopping at Verona (*Romeo and Juliet*) for lunch. As your mother is writing a diary you will be getting all the details – especially as you will no doubt be given the job of typing it.

Must run now. Thanks again, sweetheart, for your lovely gift. My best to Bruce and all my love to you.

Dad

Villa d'Este – Florence

18 May

What a very special day this has been. We left the villa at 8:30, having been awake since 6:00, so we were all set to be picked up by René. The morning passed very quickly and the first thing we knew, we were in Verona and we were more than ready for lunch. We were driven up to the top of a hill to the Reteodorico Restaurant, which was every bit as good as our 'Fieldings' said it would be. We were surrounded by the most beautiful old buildings with the Adige River winding all around the city, which was walled and very well preserved. Prior to lunch we saw the famous Roman Arena in Verona and Juliet's famous balcony of the house of Capulet – certainly a very romantic setting. After lunch, René took us to the tomb of Juliet. It was a most impressive place that we were glad to see on a sunny day as it would have been dank and dark otherwise.

On to Venice where we arrived at about 4:15 and simply parked in a large square, changed our luggage to a Canal boat, said goodbye to René, of whom we had become fond, and went directly to our hotel, which is the Gritti Palace.

To say we were excited would be an understatement. We couldn't take it all in quickly enough. The gondolas, the traffic of boats, the singing, the buildings and the ancient beauty of it all left me feeling full in the throat and moist in the eyes.

Stepped out of our boat right at the Gritti Palace and were duly ushered in. Our room is charming. It is filled with antique furniture on exquisite Persian rugs and with a double bathroom. Unpacked, changed, and went for a walk to St Mark's Square. Being Sunday, nothing was open. I imagine there must be many more people during the week. We were enchanted with the people, the canal life, and everything we could see. Wended our way back for a nap with an excellent late supper at Harry's Bar, a world famous and fun place that serves superb food. Walked home and listened to the sidewalk café orchestra. A truly perfect day with one exception, no mail. Surely tomorrow.

We thought it was going to rain so changed our plans for the day and decided against going to the glass blowers and took off on an exploratory walk, our first stop being at St Mark's cathedral. We were enthralled with the beauty and detail of the gold and jewelled mosaic work. There must have been a thousand people there. After some time, we went to the square and saw the Three Wise Men circle and bow to the Virgin Mary on the large clock. They only do so on this special day, so we were very fortunate to have Ascension Day while we were there.

When we arrived back at the Gritti Palace, it was sunny and bright so we had a salad lunch on the river. It was simply thrilling sitting there watching the gondolas being poled around our corner right beside us. Fortunately I had my camera with me so took a picture of one just to prove it. The gondoliers have such an ingenious way of poling their boats without appearing to put out very much physical effort. Mort enjoyed his excellent omelette and my crab salad was perfect. Quite the best gateau we have had since Round Hill.

As it was still a nice day we took a gondola and went via the Grande Canal, finally to cross over to the Cinco Cenedest, Isle of Murano, where they manufacture artistic blown glass. We now have a listed order number – 1684. We spent several hours there and hated to tear ourselves away as it was fascinating watching the most delicate crystal wine glasses being made.

Coming home, we struck bad weather and had to move as fast as our chap could pole, but finally had to draw alongside a lace and linen manufacturer and take shelter. Before we were able to take off on the last lap, there were quite a few of us, and much kidding took place between the gondoliers. By the way, he was a very special kind of man. Although we had been pretty well covered with tarpaulin sheets, we were quite wet and cold so had a hot bath, a game of Scrabble, read and dressed for dinner, which we had at the Grand Caffè Restorante Quaddre. It used to be frequented by the Windsors, Princess Margaret, Byron and Ruskin, etc. The food was excellent but we both nearly passed out with the heat. Also, there were two men who sat nearby who spoke so loudly to each other that we found ourselves listening to them rather than talking to each other. The rain had stopped so we went for a long walk before turning in.

A good clear day for sightseeing, so we were out and at it very early. First to the Doge's Palace, which took several hours. It is simply enormous, filled with paintings, murals and the greatest array of armour that was worn by the Dukes. How they lifted some of the swords we saw is beyond me. The marble floors amazed me. It seemed that we covered miles on them, ending up by going to the prison cells, which we reached by crossing the Bridge of Sighs. How they must have suffered, those poor devils, kept in those dark, dank, cement hovels.

Next we went to the tower, called the Campanile, and up by elevator to see a most spectacular view of Venice. It really is a fascinating and exciting different city with walking and boating their way of life. Haven't seen a car since we arrived. Everything is delivered or taken away by boat.

Returned to the hotel to change for lunch, hoping beyond hope to finally receive some letters from someone, but no mail again today. We know there is mail out there somewhere but it must be coming by slow boat. Soon we will have been away for two weeks. We console ourselves that no news is good news.

Had lunch at a very interesting, outside but under glass, restaurant, called Fecine Tavern, recommended by Ted Wilkinson. Both enjoyed it and our lunch was very good. On our way back, Mort took a picture of me covered, literally, with pigeons, from the top of my head down. Strange as it may seem, I came away from that experience unscathed.

Went across the Grand Canal to the Hotel Cipriani for dinner. It was a five-minute boat trip. They have the largest and most attractive swimming pool I have ever seen. Good food and very well attended. Later we went for a walk and met some amusing New Yorkers in Harry's Bar. Six of them were celebrating their 20th anniversary. They were a fun group and they, as did we, enjoyed meeting our friendly neighbours.

21 May

This morning we took off by foot to the art gallery where we spent hours trying to absorb the magnitude of the art works. All very beautiful individually but we found it too much to absorb. We then walked to the Rialto Bridge and back to the hotel. Sad to relate, yet good to learn, that the reason we haven't had any post is that outgoing mail goes but incoming mail is not moving, owing to a strike that they are having over here. We could weep! All this time and no news from home and as far as we can see, none until Vienna, which being Austria is not affected.

We had enjoyed Harry's Bar so much we decided to return for lunch today. They make hamburgers that are to die for. We are determined to know their secret before we leave Venice. We hired a gondolier and he poled us for two hours as we just wanted to savour this wonderful place. We made only one stop, which was to see the Fraisi Church which is said to have the most famous painting of the Virgin Mary. We were not disappointed as it truly convinced us it had earned a well-deserved reputation. Sad thought, we had our last dinner in Venice and packed.

Florence from Venice

20 May 1969

Dear Susan and Drue:

If you have anything really important to say you should send a cable by night letter following our itinerary. Telephone CPR, telegraph and say, 'I want to send a night cable to Duffus Hotel Eden Rome.' If we don't hear anything, we will know everything is OK. Hope my 'diary-letters' are getting through to you – it takes time to write it and as we are on the go all day I am a bit weary when I get down to it. We are off again tomorrow on an all-day trip to Florence. Miss you all terribly but really enjoying every minute.

Lots of love,
Mum

22 May

We were called for by speedboat at 8:00 and taken to the bus terminal where we met the others that we will travel with on our trip to Florence. A mixed bag of about ten couples. We were very fortunate to have a female guide and an excellent driver. They took us to many beautiful churches they felt we should see. We went to the National Monument in Padua – the mosaics were spectacular and depicted the life of Christ.

Next came our first glimpse of the Adriatic Ocean and the River Po. We were held up on the road for some little time, owing to a head-on collision where four people were killed. Having seen the two cars, it would have been a miracle if anyone had survived.

On to the Basilica and through several beautiful cathedrals. We cannot get over the beauty of the mosaic work, it is unbelievably beautiful. Stopped for lunch which we had with a very nice doctor and his most attractive wife, and on the road again over fairly mountainous roads and very pretty scenery. Went through the famous village of Ruffino where Chianti comes from.

Arrived at the Grand Hotel in Florence around 7:00. Our room is huge, with twenty-foot ceilings and windows that overlook the famous flooding river of Arno. You could have a ball in our bathroom; it is vast. Both bathed and tucked into a late dinner downstairs.

Getting around Florence is really quite something. The streets, if they can be called streets, are so narrow, on top of which they have single line sidewalks, so if I wanted to stop and look at something, Mort would be under full sail ahead of me. I never dared cross a street without him as the cars and motorcycles go like the very devil, so you have to keep your wits about you or you would be whacked to the ground in no time flat – the old horse and buggy days had to be the answer.

Went up to La Loggia overlooking Florence, with a copper 'David' and a fabulous view. Really a most rewarding morning topped off with a fairly good lunch. Of course I took pictures, so trust they come out well. Taxied back to the hotel to rest a while before starting out once more. Bought a pair of shoes at Ferragamo's and I can't get over how comfortable they are. The shops are simply fabulous and hard to resist. Had our dinner in the Grill and it was only so-so.

RED LETTER DAY. OUR FIRST LETTER and it was from Dianne Campbell, giving me her glove size and drawing of her hand. Thank goodness the strike is over at last, but there will be such a backlog of mail we will be lucky to get any more until we reach Rome.

With only our one full-day in Florence, we did most of the really important things we wanted to do, such as the famous Pieta by Michelangelo and the Academy of Arts. Went to the Prezzo where we, thankfully, took a translator guide in English – that was a great help explaining the art works we saw. We were sorry to have so little time here but we have deadlines to meet.

24 May

From Florence to the Isle of Elba by car and driver, making one stop in Sienna, where we went through the cathedral and were more impressed with it than any we have seen so far. The floors were all done in mosaic but more closely resembled a painting as it was such fine delicate work. The city is walled, as most are that we have seen, and situated on two hills. The residents must have very strong hearts and legs. The countryside was beautiful, most of it hilly, with great fields of scarlet poppies. They never fail to thrill me and I must try and get a good picture of them as nobody will believe me if I don't produce a photograph.

Lunch proved to be a disaster at the ferry wharf. Mort wasn't feeling awfully well so it really was no great loss. Nobody spoke English so they had no idea what we wanted. Our driver, by the name of Caesar, came to our rescue and we finally ended up with a sandwich that we couldn't eat. Mort had a cup of tea and ice cream and I had a beer.

The trip over was quite amusing; all sorts of people and masses of children on a small ferry. The weather had clouded over so the colour of the sea etc. wasn't as exciting as it could have been.

We have a smallish room, tiled floor, nice verandah overlooking a large terrace with pretty tables, a flowering hedge and the blue

Mediterranean Sea. There is a very pretty bay with white sand. Only a handful of people enjoying it.

We unpacked and Mort had a rest and I sewed. Dressed for dinner which we found to be excellent, both food-wise and service. Interesting families with small children, German and Italian, with only one other English couple who looked awfully happy to see us. Early to bed, with Mort feeling almost himself again. With good weather here we should have a lovely time.

Druesie, a letter from Dianne the day we left Florence. Can't understand how her letter got through and not some of yours. A lot of letters held up somewhere. Two weeks tho' is a long time to go without hearing. However, it will right itself eventually. Love and buckets of it to you, Susie, Ga Ga and Granddad, Bill, Doreen and a hug for Tippy and Mick.

25 May

Dearest Susie and Chris,

Red letter day today!! Your letter, written on the 29th, arrived today. Our first from family – the other from Dianne Campbell with the outline of her hand, which, by the way, I never got from you. I will need it, dear, when we are in Rome. We were so relieved to hear news of all of you at home and that the home fires are OK. Your furniture sounds lovely and will give you so much pleasure for a house or your apartment. We are hoping you won't choose to live on the other shore as we would see much less of you both, but what will be will be.

Only one more day here. We catch a ferry at 9:45 to start our drive to Rome. It's been a delightful rest. Florence really wore us to the ground. We go to sleep listening to the waves on the beach instead of the roar of traffic.

Long to see Drue's dressmaking efforts. Good for her! Please call Ga Ga and tell her we finally got a letter and happy to hear they are keeping well. Lots of love to all of you and thank you, dear, for your very welcome letter. Dad joins me in sending lots of love.

Mum.

Had a very good sleep and I'm happy to say Mort is feeling himself once more after his slight tummy upset. Not warm enough to have our breakfast on our own verandah, so had it in the breakfast room which is used as a TV room at night. It rained lightly when we were starting off with Caesar, our driver, but it soon stopped and the sun came out. Drove the west side of the island, going across the island to Marina di Camp and around the coast, which was very lovely. On to Marciana where we stopped long enough to look around and take in the quaintness of this typical village, which is set 1,000 feet up and was built in 35 BC. We went through one of the old gates on to Proggio and for lunch of cold lobster mayonnaise at Marciana Marina. We were gone about four and a half hours and enjoyed it very much. With the sun out, the Mediterranean lived up to its reputation, with a very special blue which is a beautiful colour.

Excellent dinner, beautifully served. Had an interesting talk with a Swiss couple and also with an English couple who Mort described later as being a couple of thoroughly nice hockey sticks. Their name was Seaton.

To bed and our books that we found when in Marciana Marina.

26 May – Del Golfo Hotel

Out on the road to see the sights by 10:00 o'clock. Invited the Seatons to join us as they don't have a car. Went to one particularly attractive fishing village called Porto Azzurro. Very colourful and quaint. If I lived here I would never have a paintbrush out of my hand. Bought an ashtray for the den, then drove up to a prison where they had a shop open to the public – some very frightening art work done by the prisoners. It's no wonder they are locked up.

Had lunch at our own hotel, a snooze, a good long walk and then read. Had the cocktail hour with the Swiss couple, then chatted with the Seatons and a very nice English lad, played Scrabble, read, and off to bed around 11:00. The weather was mostly cloudy with sunny intervals – so no swimming.

Dearest Mum and Dad,

Thought you might like a letter for a change from all the postcards that must be harder for you to read, I'm sure. Have been keeping a diary and sending it to the girls, as someday we will enjoy reading it. I have asked them to pass them onto you to read. I know you have been to many of the same places many years ago, Mum, but I doubt that there has been a great change, even in that length of time. If the girls have neglected to pass my diary on to you, ask them for it. This way I send all the news without having to write the same thing over and over again to each of you.

The mail strike being over makes us very happy. Yesterday was our red letter day with our first letter from Susie, telling us she had seen you both and that you were both well. Dad, I hope you are drinking lots of water and fruit juices. Please be sure to do so or you will be in trouble.

What a superb holiday we are having; to see the places we have read about over the years – and each place we go to is so different. I give full marks to Mort for choosing the places we have seen and will see. We wish the girls were here, as it would be an education for them they would never forget. Wish it was easier to describe.

Mort joins me in sending lots of love. Take care of each other. Love to Bill and Doreen when you see them.

John

27 May – Elba

The sun looked promising to take the chair-lift to the top of Monte Cappane, so Caesar drove us, with the Seatons, to where it is and we climbed into a basket, the two of us in one and the Seatons in theirs. We had to stand up in it. It came to about my waist – mine, not Mort's! We proceeded to go up and up and up. The wild flowers below were so beautiful. Clumps of yellow and purple violets everywhere. We climbed 5,000 feet to find we were in cloud wisps with the odd break, so you could see the villages and sea below, but no way could we see Corsica, as we had hoped.

Arrived back for a late lunch at the Hermitage, a very attractive hotel about two miles from here. Had my hair done in the village while Mort had a swim. Beat him at Scrabble before dinner, which was preceded by drinks with the Seatons. Said goodbye to the delightful waiters and gave Walter, the English lad of whom we have become so fond, our address, on the off chance he ever visits Vancouver. He has reminded us of Hugo Martin; they could be twins. Walked up to the village and were fascinated by all the fireflies. Off tomorrow, so we packed.

28 May

Sue. Strike tie-up still with us, so only your letter to Elba so far. Three weeks on Sunday since we left home. It's maddening! Hellish!

Seen off by the Seatons and the staff of the Del Golfo. A lovely day for our trip. Left at 9:30 for the ferry and finally tracked down a hotel for our lunch *en route* and it turned out to be a winner. It was situated high up on a hill overlooking the most glorious view. Excellent lunch of sole and to our amusement, Orson Welles was at the table next to ours, with, we assumed, his wife. Mort thought I was seeing resemblances again as he has never let me forget dragging him off a bus in London because I said I had seen Johnny Rose. After having chased this person down the street, I realised it wasn't Johnny. However, he had to admit it certainly sounded like his voice. When the waiter came to bring us our bill and the couple had already left the room, I asked if I was correct, which, thankfully, I was. With the odd glance in his direction, I noticed he hardly ate anything, which surprised me as he is as broad as he is long. What a pity it couldn't have been Gregory Peck!

Arriving into Rome wasn't very spectacular and it was hard to see anything except St Peter's cathedral and Vatican Square. Said our farewell to Caesar, who has driven us for many, many miles and always been so helpful and interesting and certainly an excellent driver.

Settled and unpacked. Took our lives in our hands and set forth to walk. How the lame and the halt get around here I simply cannot imagine, you have to run for your lives to cross the streets. The traffic defies description. We thought Florence was bad, but Rome makes Florence look like a country village. It's hard to conceive living here from choice. I like the sidewalk cafés, although they appear to be very expensive.

Not being very hungry, we went to a well-recommended restaurant that understands the meaning of a small snack. The restaurant is called the Nuova Coloni and is directly behind the Excelsior Hotel. To bed and dead tired at only 10:00 p.m., quite the earliest since leaving home.

29 May

Still no mail. One letter in three weeks, it is unbelievable. Saw a picture of the mail tie-up so no doubt we have a pile of it in some of those bags.

Mort and I walked our legs off nearly all day and managed to find all the places we looked for. The traffic is dreadful and we found crossing the streets a death defying experience. I collected masses of pamphlets of all the places we went to, so we will be able to better describe everything to all of you. Better this than me trying to write it all down when at the end of the day, I am deadbeat.

Did manage to find the gloves I was after. Looked at materials and couldn't find anything except the most beautiful bridal white, which of course I did not buy or even price. Too bad Drue isn't along with us as there are some exquisite materials. Went to Mort's tailor then to George's for lunch, a very attractive place and close to the Eden Hotel.

Made plans to take two tours tomorrow. Went to Mort's tailor for a fitting, then back to the hotel for a rest, bath, and change for dinner which we had at the Cesarina. A swinging place, unlike anything we've been to and we both thought it was great. Funnily enough, who should be there, in all his vast bulk, but Orson Welles, once more – forty miles from Rome where we first saw him way up at the Hermitage.

Topped off our dinner at a sidewalk café on our way home, to soak in some of the atmosphere. Vancouver was never like this.

30 May

No mail – now we are having a garbage strike so that doesn't appeal too much either.

We were called for at 9:15 by a coach and driven to a terminus where we boarded another one with only English speaking people. Quite a good guide who had a sense of humour.

We went directly to the Vatican Museum and neither of us had imagined it to be as it was. We walked for miles it seemed and were very impressed. Amazed at the size of the place and totally overwhelmed by the treasures it houses. We couldn't begin to see everything, it would take days. As it was, we walked until our legs ached, looking through the galleries of statues, maps and tapestries. Saw frescoes by Rafael that were wonderful. Ended up at the Sistine Chapel, with frescoes by Michelangelo. There were masses of people who were as breathless with admiration and awe as Mort and myself. It is beyond comprehension how any man could have achieved all that he accomplished in one lifetime.

Had a light lunch and a sleep. Picked up at 2:30 for our afternoon tour. Saw the Church of St Peter in Chains and Michelangelo's statue of Moses, which we all thought impressive. Then to the Trevi Fountains, but we were not allowed out of the coach owing to so little available parking. We were then taken to the Roman Forum, which was a fantastic sight, where fifty thousand Romans sat. On to the Basilica of Saint Paul, then to Gianicola Hill for a panoramic view of Rome. Home by 6:00. What a fabulous experience.

Took a cab to a well hidden restaurant called Hostaria Dell Orso. It was a winner! The place itself was quite lovely and used to be the private home of Dante. It seemed to be on three levels. There was a bar on the ground floor with an excellent piano player who made it hard for us to be ushered upstairs. It was fairly dimly lit and we were led into a beautiful dining room which also had a pianist and violinist, as well as a couple of wandering minstrels who could play anything. When they came to our table, we requested Drue and Bruce's special song, which they played to perfection.

Dinner itself was a masterpiece, quite the best we have ever had anywhere, and we think we are fairly good at judging them. It was, in fact, a memorable evening which Mort topped off by ordering a bottle of champagne.

Be sure and keep all my diary in good order, kids, or I sho' am going to wish I had never thought of writing it, or at least posting it.

P.S. Susie dear, we leave here early Monday by train for Sorrento and still only your letter under our belts, received in Elba. The concierge says that practically no mail is being delivered. Gosh, it has been a tough break for us. We are longing to hear all your news. For a couple of doting parents, this has been very hard to take. For your information, dears, Mum and Dad are having their wedding anniversary on 5 June. It would please them if you were to give them a card. I long to hear how you are.

Loads of love,

Mum and Dad

P.S. WRITE TO VIENNA – no strike there.

31 May – Rome

We took off bright and early for St Peter's Cathedral. The day was brilliant with sunshine and we were both deeply moved by all we saw. We were fortunate in that we walked into a special service with a Cardinal in attendance. The choir and organ were outstanding. The acoustics so incredible that as we walked, wherever we went, we could hear every word, even if we couldn't understand the language. The Pieta was all that I hoped it would be and more. We even heard a mass being said in English. We finished our tour by descending to the tomb of St Peter and found many others as well, including that of the late Pope John.

Had our lunch at the sidewalk café on the Via Veneta. In the afternoon we simply did nothing but have a thoroughly lazy time. I call it recharging our batteries. Wrote some letters, read and sewed. Walked to the tailor to pick up Mort's suit. Unfortunately, I couldn't get the material I am after for the bridesmaids.

Our only mistake of the trip so far was to take the night tour of Rome. It was a real pain – too slow – too many languages – so we escaped as fast as we could. The fountains were beautiful.

Still no mail. Damn the postal service.

1 June – Sunday and our last day in Rome

Took off for All Saints Anglican Church and was so very glad that I did. The service was very good and the church most beautiful and unusual. Instead of pews, they had oak chairs with rush-bottom seats and velvet kneeling cushions. Met the minister who struck me as being a very fine man.

Mort walked to meet me and fortunately anticipated that I would return by going up the Spanish Steps, so we met half way. We went to the zoo which was full of interesting animals, but I was disgusted with the dirty conditions and filled with sympathy for those poor beasts.

Hungry, at last, and enjoyed our lunch at La Flavia, a quaint place that served excellent food and had excellent service.

Had a snooze and dressed for the opera, *Aida*, which was an experience neither of us will ever forget. The Opera House alone was magnificent! I swear the main chandelier was as large as our living room, with balcony after balcony with red velvet cushioned easy chairs to sit in. They were so comfortable that my skinny bottom was happy for once. The performance itself was absolutely fabulous. Voices, staging of sets and costumes. The orchestra was outstanding, in fact, everything was perfection and we were both thrilled to the core. I couldn't believe it was possible to stage anything as perfect.

When we came out it was raining quite hard, which surprised us as it had been quite nice earlier. Neither of us was dressed for rain and I had on my pink linen dress. We looked at each other and said, 'What are we going to do, as we will never pick up a taxi.' A young fellow just ahead of us turned around and in broken English, he said, 'Stay right where you are. I will get my car and drive you home,' which he did!!! In we came, dry as beans and so grateful not to have gotten soaked and have spoiled a memorable evening.

Dinner in the hotel and packed for Sorrento, in the morning.

2 June – Grand Hotel
Excelsior Vittoria
Sorrento

Trip from Rome very frustrating due to it being a holiday in Italy. Our normal fast train service went into low gear and it took about three hours longer. Finally arrived in Naples and were met by C.I.T. and driven to a place for lunch. It was quite a spot and every man and entire family were there, with so much noise you couldn't hear the musicians, who, nothing daunted, passed their hats. The whole scene was very colourful. There were swimmers, boats of every description and sunshine unlimited.

Joseph, our driver, finally got us out of Naples, which is a filthy city set in a truly magnificent bay with the bluest of blue water. The drive to Sorrento was very pretty and mostly along the coast. It took about one and three quarter hours.

This hotel is set high on a cliff overlooking the water and is very quiet, being almost a block off the main road where the heavy traffic is. Our room has to be the largest we have had. The floors are yellow and blue tiles with scattered Persian rugs. We have a huge balcony where we sat and watched a wedding reception and had our drink before dinner, watching the beautiful sunset. It's all very relaxing and lovely after the mad hustle and bustle of Rome. The highlight of the day being a letter from Susan, written on 27 May, her second to reach us. None from Druesie. No doubt hers are jammed up in the larger cities. Fortunately Susie gave us lots of news about everyone and everything, except Tip and Mick, so we are feeling much better.

Dinner downstairs. Lots of Americans but we were the only Canadians as far as we could tell. Wandered up to the hopping little town of Sorrento. Fortunately for us we are off the beaten track or we'd never get any sleep. Have never seen so many shops, mostly full of things you don't want, but their lace and linens are very pretty, along with their woodwork. Went to a factory and watched the man doing inlay work. It was fascinating and quite wonderful how they turn it out.

It rained off and on in the afternoon so we played Scrabble and I had my hair done in the hotel. A very good man here so I'm presentable once more.

Had a letter from Mum and Dad which was the highlight of the day. Had lunch in a quaint *ristorante* full of Italians, one English couple and ourselves. The Italians can certainly tuck away the spaghetti; it amazes us how much they eat.

Dinner in the hotel and a long walk after, topped off with an early night.

Tried to take the hydrofoil to Capri but it didn't go from Sorrento that day, so took a small boat that was very slow and cold after the big thunder and lightning storm. Capri proved to be very lovely. We took an open car so as not to miss anything and toured the island. Stopped for lunch at Gracie Field's Lido restaurant. Saw her when we arrived and departed and both times she greeted us. Had a very good sole in wine sauce for lunch, then sat outside around the pool for a rest. Drove up to San Michaeli's Villa, which was most intriguing, with a fabulous view of the Bay of Naples, Vesuvius and Sorrento.

Managed to pick up a much faster boat home. Played a game, had dinner, walked and packed for Vienna. We depart at 7:15!

Vienna

5 June – Up with the birds and called for right on the dot. Blessed again by a beautiful sunny morning for our drive into Naples. Hopped aboard an Air Italia bound for Milan, where we sat around for one and a half hours at the airport, waiting to take our Austrian Airlines flight to Vienna. We were met by the C.I.T. and driven directly to the hotel where, to our delight, were letters from Drue, Bill, Nora, Peg and James Evans, and Ted Reynolds from Berlin. Let's hope we receive lots more before we leave here.

Our room in this exquisite hotel is quite lovely. Three huge windows on the corner with a little balcony, an L-shaped living room that has a chaise-longue, an antique desk and easy, comfortable chairs. In the L, there was a king size bed, fortunately with two mattresses, and the most enormous pillows that I have ever seen. There were two of the biggest and fattest eiderdowns that will be removed, like all the others we have met in our travels. There are enough crystal chandeliers around the room and in the hall to light a theatre. Oh yes, the bed has some very heavy brocade hangings that can be drawn to conceal the bedroom area Too bad we don't have anyone to ask in for a drink with us as I would like to draw them.

We unpacked and went for a walk and managed to obtain two tickets to *Salome* at the Opera House. It started at 8:00, so we had a light supper first. It was another great experience and once more Mort and I were bowled over by the performance. The orchestra alone had at least one hundred and twenty musicians and they played superbly. The girl who took the part of Salome put on a perfect performance. There were no intermissions and it was one hour and forty minutes of straight singing, with excellent, strenuous acting.

The Opera House was not as impressive as the one in Rome, except for the great staircase and it was beautiful.

Coffee and dessert at the Sacher after the performance. A young American and a young German boy sat at the table next to us and we enjoyed their conversation as much as they seemed to enjoy ours.

6 June

Started off to go for a walk, picked up tickets for a tour of the Historical Buildings, then found we wouldn't be back in time for a 12:00 o'clock appointment with the concierge at the Bristol, so will take it another day. Went through an art museum where we saw Michelangelos, Rubenses, Turners, etc. Could have spent many hours there but both find you can only take in so much. Stopped for a coffee and a biscuit at a tea shop, then wrote a few letters and had lunch at the Sacher sidewalk café.

Mort went for a long walk and just made it in as the rain started. Lightning, thunder and pouring rain so we played Scrabble and dressed for the opera, *Don Carlos*. We were both well and truly thrilled to the core. It was marvellous. The voices were quite the best we have heard and that is saying something. There must be one hundred chandeliers in the Vienna State Opera House, that were at least the size of our den. We walked all around as much as we could during the twenty-five minute intermission. They certainly pack in people. Standing room only in the Gods and they stood for three and three quarter hours.

Had a light supper after the opera and went for a walk. It started to rain just as we arrived home. Blast the change in weather, and oh, for a good raincoat and umbrella.

7 June

Drue dear,

This will be a combination diary/letter as we just received yours of 24 May, also one from Ga, having just posted one to them saying no mail from them, so please thank them for me. We are shocked to hear about Bruce being hit. That was dreadful, he ought to throw the book at that boy. Your father says he would sue him. You can't go around hitting people. For the wedding, too; let's hope it heals quickly – shaving will be difficult for a while.

Longing to hear about the hen dinner. Hope it was fun, dear. We are so pleased you have the house; did you get July and August gratis for putting money into it? All for now.

Diary – Sunday morning

Although cool, at least there are patches of blue. Took a cab to the famous Hofmusikkapelle and the Hofburg Chapel to hear the High Mass sung by the Vienna Boys' Choir, men's choir and orchestra. Fortunately we had tickets that we had obtained months ago as there were hundreds of people and not a large chapel so there were dozens who had to stand throughout the whole service. The singing was absolutely beautiful and I, for one, was deeply moved. We couldn't see where the boys were but did see them later in the courtyard where they boarded their bunny bus. They wear very well tailored navy blue sailor suits, white collars and sailor caps with blue streamers down their backs. Very fine looking boys who were obviously taken aback by the stir they created.

We then wandered into the Opera Museum and spent a good hour or more looking at all the pictures of operatic sets and singers, conductors, composers, letters and death masks, etc. All very interesting.

Had lunch at the Hotel Imperial and enjoyed it very much, particularly the waitress who was so good that Mort gave her a happy smile and said, 'donkey field mice', as suggested in Fieldings Guide, when you are truly grateful. Much to his delight he was bowled over by a beautiful smile and we laughed all the way home.

Had a light salad and took off to see *Electra* at the Opera House. I'm afraid it was way beyond my operatic comprehension and I'm still wondering what it was all about, but the Viennese went completely mad so I have a great deal to learn. Sandwich and tea after a very good walk.

8 June

Sad, sad day – it poured all day, so much so that it was too wet to go out to buy an umbrella until well after lunch, when we finally ventured forth to look at some of the shops, and my golly, they close on Saturday afternoons. We walked until it really started to pour again so dashed to the hotel to dry off. Read *Time* and the newspaper and then had a zizz.

Had a delightful evening at the Three Hussars Restaurant. It was a fascinating place and absolutely hopping with Viennese, all very elegantly dressed. Pictures of horses on every wall. Best dinner we have had since Verdi's. Speaking of horses, to our utter dismay we find we can't see the famous Spanish Riding School. The horses have been sick for three weeks with colds. We are dreadfully disappointed. They won't even allow visitors to view the stables.

Walked for nearly an hour after dinner and saw some beautiful shops. The antiques here are so lovely.

The pace of Vienna suits us perfectly, although we begrudge the endless time it takes to be served. We hate to waste the time when there is so much to see and do. The sunshine burst out all over today. Clear blue sky, warm and perfect for our chosen day to have a car and driver. At 9:30 promptly, Gunther called for us and in very understandable English, we were guided all around the city and shown all the points of interest. It is such a beautiful city and I love it. Our car, although we stopped in the oddest places, was never honked at nor did anyone even look the least bit annoyed if we held them up. Saw the River Danube. The old part is blue and the new is very dull river water. Went over the only bridge that wasn't blown up during the war. Out to the Vienna Woods, which was a delightful drive. The sunshine was dancing through the trees just as I always thought it would be. We had no idea the Vienna Woods covered such a vast territory. Cahlnburg was our viewing spot and it was so clear not only could we see all Vienna below us, but Czechoslovakia and Hungary as well.

By this time we were all ready for lunch, so went to Coblenz, as the other spot we hoped to go to was closed on Mondays. Gunther regaled us with tales of his four months working for a group of actors and actresses, including the Richard Burtons. From all accounts, they are a shocking pair.

Next we visited a very large cathedral and monastery owned by the Vatican, and on to the dearest little village which has a wee garden at the back of the winery where people sit around at night and drink wine, sing, dance and generally make merry. We are going to try and go there one evening.

Walked over to Demel's and had some tea and cakes – they have to be the best! In the evening we went to the Volksoper *Der Zigeuner*, or Gypsy Baron, one of Johann Strauss's and it was very well done and the music terrific.

10 June

Off on a tour this morning to see Belvedere Palace, the home of Prince Eugene, who kicked the Turks out of Austria. It's a lovely place and for a palace, not too large. Then on to the Schönbrunn Palace where they were busy filming a movie. Dressed to the nines in white wigs, etc. There are about twelve hundred rooms and we went through forty-six of them. It was in perfect condition, renovations and restorations having just been completed. The colours, furniture, paintings and possessions in general were truly lovely. It felt homey in spite of the grandeur. They had sixteen children, although six died very young. Probably it felt homey because of their large family. The girls all did the most exquisite needlework and even embroidered family scenes which were framed as pictures. All in all the tour was well worthwhile, although hard on the ears.

Walked over to the tea garden to hear some Strauss music, then had my hair done and cut, which it really needed. In the evening we went to the ballet and then to the Balkan restaurant, which was different.

11 June

Druesie dear,

A letter from you written 2 June and posted the 4th – all about your cold. What a beastly thing for you to go through and how kind of Bruce to look after you. You never mention Brenda, Luna or Monica – ! Sorry about Tippy too, what a strange thing for him to get. Must close dear and get out, it is our last day here.

We both send lots of love to all of you. Looking forward to big hugs on Monday. Here is our flight, Air Canada 10:30 p.m. Sorry it is so late.

Love

M and Dad

11 June – diary

Walked all morning. Visited St Stephen's Cathedral, which all the Viennese call 'Old Steve'. Despite the bomb damage during the war, we really had no feeling that anything had ever happened to damage the beauty of it.

Tossed off a nummy cake and a cup of coffee to gather our strength to go to the National Art Gallery. We couldn't begin to believe the collections we saw, nor could we believe one man could have painted so many art works in one lifetime – Rubens, Rembrandt, Velasquez, Raphael, Titian, and so on and on. Truly awe-inspiring. We walked and we walked until we couldn't walk another step, so crawled back to the Sacher for lunch on the sidewalk and basked in the sunshine. We have reached the awful time when we know we have done it for the last time.

It was such a beautiful day that after a brief rest we took off once more by foot to the Belvedere Palace. Took pictures and devoured the beauty of it all.

At seven, we crossed the street to the Opera House to see *Cosi fan Tutti* by Mozart. We couldn't believe our good fortune as to see such a finished and exquisite opera for our last night. We loved every minute of it, in spite of the squirming little boy who sat in front of us.

Had dinner very late at a place called Stadcrug and a very pleasant place it was. The after opera crowd burst in all at once, which seems to be the way of things here. The pianist strummed away for about an hour and a half of our time there and was super to listen to, as well as to watch as he so obviously enjoyed playing. Left there about 11:45 and walked the long way home, talking nineteen to the dozen about everything we have done, seen, listened to and enjoyed so immensely. It will seem strange to have our dinner at an earlier hour when we are home again.

Such was the ending to our perfect time in Vienna. We hope we will return some day.

12 June

Oh sad, sad day! Really hate to think of leaving Vienna as we both feel we have only scratched the surface of this fascinating city, but the time has come and I packed during the a.m. while Mort saw to all the essentials and then went for a walk. After he had packed, we both went for a walk. Had a good lunch in the Sacher and our driver called for us at 2:30 to take us to the airport.

Germany

Caught our flight to Munich and waited there several hours to board for Berlin. Both our flights were about an hour. I can't get over how short the distances are in Europe.

Ily and Ted Reynolds were at the runway to greet us and she is everything that I was told. They drove us straight to the Schloss Hotel Gehrus, which is situated about a twenty-minute drive from the city centre, surrounded by acres of grass and trees. There is an abundance of bird life of all descriptions, that are obviously very happy with their chosen habitat. The hotel is difficult to describe. It is a castle structure with a huge staircase that leads up to a balcony that almost entirely surrounds the drawing room, some forty feet below. Our rooms are so large you could fit a small house in them. Mirrors, gold framed wall panels, tapestry upholstered furniture, and beautiful rugs. Quite the most unusual hotel I have ever been in. We were greeted at the door by Herr Gehrhus who bent down deeply over my hand, which I thought for a moment he was going to kiss but no, not quite.

Freshened up and went to the Reynolds' charming house, a five-minute drive away, where we had a delicious supper and enjoyed talking to Ily, Ted and their son. Had fun with their Japanese dog. They drove us back and we unpacked and crawled into bed under masses of feathers, which were pulled on and thrown off all night long. How the Germans sleep under such warmth is beyond us!!

13 June

Breakfast in the sitting room and ready by 10:00 to meet Ted for our tour, and indeed it was a very comprehensive one as we covered quite a bit of territory and some very interesting things.

First of all we went to the US consulate offices and met Ted's staff, and as the American Ambassador, he had a considerable one. We left there for the US Mission where Goering had had his headquarters. This building was very impressive and has a bronze life-sized statue of a US soldier standing at the foot of a beautiful staircase that went up to Goering's office. Unfortunately Ted was unable to show us the office because there was a meeting in session.

Picked up Ily and drove to Brandenburg Gate to see the Reichtag (parliament buildings) and 'The Wall', or zonal border, dividing the Federal Republic of Germany from the Soviet Zone. This is a tragic sight that has to be seen to be believed. We went up on a platform to see over the Wall, where we were eyed by the Soviet binoculars from their machine-gun lookout posts. Barbed wire, mined areas and concrete posts, as well as the fourteen-foot wall that is covered by a revolving pipe that moves the minute your hands could clasp it, so that nobody could get a grip on it to jump over.

We then drove past the Victory Column (Sieges-Saule 1870) to catch sight of 'The Onion' in East Berlin, as it is called, or a needle, as I might call it, with an onion on top. To what must be the everlasting chagrin of the Soviets that had it erected, a most astounding phenomenon occurs. When the sun shines on the onion it develops a huge clear cross. This we saw with our own eyes and I had shivers run up and down my body.

We then drove along the famous Tiergarten, the former centre for the Embassies. Past Bellevue Palace, which is the residence of the President and on down to the museum at the Wall. This is a rattle-trap of a very old building that is filled with wall after wall of pictures of the people that were killed or were actually trying to cross into West Berlin. There was so much to see and Ted was able to translate for us, which was a great help. It is aptly called The Agony of the Wall. It is a wicked tragedy.

On to brighter things and to see the 3,000 year old head of the Egyptian Princess Nefertiti, who was queen of ancient Egypt. She is a breathtaking beauty and remarkably well-preserved, even to colour.

Across the street to the Charlottenburg Palace. During the war it was almost demolished, but it was finally decided it should be restored, which they have done remarkably well. It was built for Frederick III's second wife, Sophie Charlotte, in 1695. We didn't like it as well as Vienna's Schönbrunn Palace. The German furniture is heavier in every way and their tapestries and silk wall coverings lacked the gayness of Vienna.

We were finally taken on a slippered tour with Ted interpreting and it was very worthwhile. We kept saying how grateful we were for his knowledge and patience with our questions and intense interest in everything he showed and explained to us.

Back to have a rest at the hotel, then after a restful bath and change to dinner clothes, we taxied to Ted and Ily's to attend a very lovely buffet supper party with fourteen guests. It was a very international party. One from Australia, two from the USA, four from Canada and the others from Germany. Fortunately the last spoke quite good English. The dinner was delicious and beautifully served. Afterwards we played amusing games – one in particular, played with a glass covered with Kleenex, edged with beer to make it stick tightly, a coin and lit cigarettes. Each person takes a turn burning the edge of the paper until finally the coin drops into the glass. Whoever has this happen to him or her has to kiss one of the ladies or men present. I was kissed once. We were driven home around midnight, tired but very happy.

14 June – The Queen's Birthday

Ted and Ily had been invited to two functions in honour of the Queen, to which they had obtained invitations for us. It was a great experience for us and the day was warm, clear and lovely. Ted, Ily and Nicky arrived at 9:30 and we drove to the Mayfield Olympic Stadium where the General, the officer commanding Berlin (British sector) Major General James Bowes-Lyon,

inspected the Ceremonial Parade. It was perfection. The colour of
the uniforms, the kilts, the precision of the marching and
ceremonial rifle drills, were so absolutely flawless, people gasped
in admiration. All this ended after an hour with a twenty-one gun
salute that must have made the East Berliners hope the Wall had
been blown to bits. Met the French General and several other very
interesting people, then proceeded to Checkpoint Charlie, which
is the crossing into East Berlin.

Ted, Ily and Nicky dropped us off before we reached the gate as
we couldn't cross in a consulate car, so we walked, with our
passports in Mort's care. It's hard to express the feeling one has
being faced by guards with machine guns and Russian soldiers
glaring at you as you walk toward their immigration office with
your passports. The little shed-like place was filled with young
people mostly. It was very hot and we waited and we waited and
finally had to fill out a form declaring who and what we were,
how much money we had with us and, finally, were given a chit of
paper for our passports. Ted had told us that he would be about a
block away waiting for us. Our impression of East Berlin was of
still, bleak, desolate streets facing us, fortunately with Ted's
smiling face on the corner of one. He looked so relieved as he was
becoming very worried and concerned that something had
happened to us. We were all ravenous, so headed for the only good
place they have on Unter den Linden and, to our surprise, had an
extremely good lunch and excellent beer. The people stared at us
as though we were from outer space. After lunch we walked up
Unter den Linden and looked at the few very good shops that
have been built where the tourists would see them. Then Ted
took us back to the car which by this time was entirely surrounded
by children, or I should say, boys. Obviously they were spellbound
as they were looking at their reflections and stroking the fenders.
When we walked up to them they looked a little apprehensive at

first and when they saw us smiling, they relaxed and laughed. Ted gave them some change and they ran off waving happily. We were then driven all around so we could see the desolation of war-torn buildings and the new ones that have been erected. Very good ones they are, but oh so few of them.

Thunder and lightning plus heavy rain brought our tour to an abrupt end and in a lull of rain, Mort and I ran as fast as we could for the border crossing and with no trouble, picked up our passports and were across to West Berlin. The Reynolds were already across as they simply place a card given to the Consuls in the car window and over they go, without being checked at all. We obviously looked very happy as Ted remarked on our joyous faces as soon as he saw us coming. Indeed we were!!! It was as if a dead weight had been lifted from us. It was an experience neither of us would have wanted to miss and certainly will never forget.

Back to the hotel to rest and change for the reception in the London Block, Olympic Stadium, given in honour of the birthday of the Queen by Major General and Mrs James Bowes-Lyon. Red and white flowers were everywhere, along with British flags. There were masses of people from all over the world, Consuls, Ambassadors and all the services. Ted introduced us to everyone that came within reach. The British General and US General were delightful, as was Bowes-Lyon himself. Champagne flowed and we had a fascinating time and hated to leave. We both found it difficult to look at the person who was talking to us with an interpreter, as we found ourselves conversing with the latter.

Off to dinner to a typical German restaurant called the Hofbräuhaus, with music and dancing. To see the barmaids, buxom gals they were, walking down to the tables carrying 6-8 steins at one time, to say nothing of watching the people drink them, was most entertaining. I could have lifted one of those steins and then I might have dropped it. We had so much fun there. Mort was in great form trying every German word he could muster on the waitresses and a lot he didn't, much to their amusement, and ours. The huge weiners called *bockwurst* were delicious and Mort made a meal of them. Finally tore ourselves away as the *haus* was really getting warmed up. People were standing on the tables, all holding hands and rocking and singing and generally having a wonderful, noisy, time with everyone joining in with all their hearts. They certainly know how to enjoy life.

Walked on farther and across the street to a Konditori. It was so full of goodies that we had a hard time knowing what to have. Full of food and laughter, we went home, tired after an absolutely perfect day, thanks to Ted and Ily, who are an outstanding pair to represent their country.

15 June

Our last day, it doesn't seem possible! I had a good lazy morning. Mort walked around the golf course while Ted and his three friends played. Had lunch out in the garden with Ily as my guest and she stayed with me until the men returned.

We hated to say goodbye after our days with Ted and Ily and can never begin to thank them for all they did to entertain us. We will hope to see them when they are able to visit Vancouver again, and in some way return their hospitality, if that could ever be possible. They saw us off at the airport, so it is home sweet home.

A Cruise,
February-March 1983

3rd February – D Day – SAN FRANCISCO

Won't go into goodbyes. I hate them! Good flight down, then to the pier to leave our luggage. Would love to have gone aboard. Went by taxi to Union Square. Neiman Marcus was our first stop for my stockings – even they had a limited selection. It's unfortunate when you can't wear hose. Put in the day but found it tiring. Shopping isn't for Mort! Caught the pier shuttle double-decker, too tired to go up. Waited forty-odd minutes before boarding. Spotted a few soul mates, but only a few. Pictures boarding. Happy moments and our steward, Assassi, greeted us. Our cabin is much larger than I anticipated; as long as our living room but not as wide. A wire, opened by Mort who couldn't read it out loud for the lump in his throat, so I read it and got one too. God bless our four – they are the greatest. Super letters, a bottle of Champagne from Marta etc.

Unpacked and, to my amazement, we both have adequate hangers and cupboards. Totally lost but very impressed, seem to have everything to make our voyage a happy one. May see the purser re our table. Five women and Mort, not good from any point of view.

4th February

9:00 a.m. The purser says it's still only twelve degrees, although we are two hundred and forty miles south-west of San Francisco.

Sunny and clear, so by this afternoon it should be a lot warmer. That didn't really happen. A mist came up and then a little rain.

Had a delightful day. After breakfast, attended a flower arranging class. Forget his name but will get it tomorrow. He travels all over the world exhibiting his prowess and spends two months of every year with the Queen Mother. Relates fascinating name-dropping stories – true ones – all the time he is demonstrating. Can learn a lot from him so will attend all his classes, also an artist who teaches in the afternoons. All the classes are very well attended and are well worthwhile.

Saw the purser and asked for a table for two. They didn't have one so we are at the Deputy Captain's table. I sit next to a very nice man from Vancouver, Matt Fischer. English Jew (I think); we get on famously. The others are women, English, extremely nice, obviously loaded. The Captain's reception at 7:45. Everyone in their number ones. Beautiful gowns and jewels flashing every-where – mine are in the safety deposit at home; this amused me.

Had no sooner walked into the Pacific Room and been given a drink when a very pretty and attractively groomed person with an equally nice looking husband, came up to me and said, 'You must have boarded yesterday. Welcome! We are from England and boarded in Southampton.' They are Susie and Charles Banks. We got along so well I can only think we will see a lot of them. Captain's dinner was fun and I hope I remember all the details. 10:40 when we finished and last out of the dining room! Entertainment was in every direction until heaven knows what time. We powdered out at 12:40 and it was still going strong. Cabaret evening entertainment, very cleverly done by a mind reader. Temperature going up but too breezy to be outside for long.

5th Feb.

Slept like a baby and very comfortably. Able to turn down our thermostat so our cabin is cool. The flower arranging was potting of plants. He used a round copper pot about fourteen inches across and five inches high. It was very well done and learned a few tips for including fresh flowers and the use of charcoal to keep the earth sweet. Wish the Garden Club had him around to give us some of his knowledge.

Light lunch with only six of us. We certainly have a very congenial table. Susie and Charles introduced me to friends of theirs, she is a delight. Had a nap. Arrived late for the art class, wrote down the wrong time, damn it. Will be better tomorrow!

Several games of Scrabble with Mort and before we knew it the afternoon was over. Marta had sent us a bottle of Champs, so we invited our table to join us with the aid of another bottle. They were not reluctant to accept. An excellent concert pianist played to a full look-out bar. I went and Mort was persuaded to join Susie and Charles with the quiz game.

Bed around midnight. Almost forgot our tour of the bridge, which was fascinating. We generate enough power to light the whole of Shaughnessy.

6th Feb.

Slept like a babe. It's the most glorious day, smooth blue sea, some white fluffy clouds and glorious sun. Had breakfast on deck which we won't do again and then had our first really good walk. Saw our friend Ed Paulson on deck. Such a nice man. Mort went off to a backgammon tournament and I went to the captain's church service. Lots of hymns, packed attendance in the theatre. Joined Susie and friends to watch the most entertaining Hawaiian fashion show. Six of the males were from the ship's officer's entertainers. Complete hams and most amusing. One of them did a strip tease with five pieces of shining trunks, each pair a little smaller than the first. Clothes were very reasonable and some of them were attractive. Went up on deck afterwards with Charles and Susie, then met Mort in our cabin. He got into the finals and then got sadly trounced.

Lots of laughs at the dinner table. Captain asked us all to have a drink with him afterwards. Pity really, because we missed the concert we had planned on.

7 February

The flower lecture today was a showing of slides of church flower arrangements. I now know I know nothing about such things. I wouldn't have believed it if I hadn't seen it. They have church flower festivals to raise money. It's really quite an idea. Bears thinking about.

Had a sun-bathe on the upper deck, but not for many minutes as it's very hot. Lunch on deck, changed and went to the art class. Excellent teacher.

Played Scrabble with Mort, then bingo. Dressed for dinner and went to bed as we are up early tomorrow. Must call Steph Douglas as I promised to do.

8 February

06:45 – saw a ship! First sight of anything since our first morning – for me anyway. Early breakfast; to be on the dock by 9:00 to go to Pearl Harbour. We did a complete tour by boat with a commentator who was extremely good. Was very moved at the same time, horrified that the security was so shockingly bad to have allowed such a thing as the tragedy of Pearl Harbour! It took three hours by boat and it was also a beautiful way to see the city.

Had lunch aboard – seemed very quiet where we were. Oh yes, indulged ourselves with a drink before lunch. Mort had a

Singapore Sling and I had a Pimms No.1. Slept it off for about half an hour, then went ashore to walk and look for a pair of sandals, Valentines, etc. Gorgeous day. There are some very nicely laid out malls, flowers and shrubs hanging and growing. All happy. After about an hour and a half, we ambled back to bathe and dress in order to go ashore before the gangplank was removed as they are going to change our berth at 6:00 p.m.

As we weren't due to be at Steph and Fenner's until 7:00, we taxied to a flower shop where I got three branches of orchids for a little prezzie, then we drove to the Colony surf to wait. Also placed a call to Susie and Drue and, to everyone's delight, they both answered the phone immediately and couldn't believe their ears. Hated to hang up as it will be a long time before we talk again. Nice to know all is well at home and they now know we are both well and enjoying ourselves.

Steph and Fenner were waiting for us in their very attractive condo. We all talked ninety to the dozen over our drinks and then ambled next door to the Outrigger. It is all that I had heard it is. Truly a very attractive place to dine. The setting is unbelievable and has to be seen to be believed. Three of us had tempura. Fen had the duckling. All of us delighted with our choice. By the time we had finished it was time to catch a taxi and head for Pier 31. It was a lovely evening and I hope enjoyed by the two of them, as it was by the two of us. Stayed up on deck to see us sail away from Honolulu at midnight.

9 February

Such a gorgeous day. Warm and calm. We couldn't ask for better weather. After my flower class, we all made small silk flower gift arrangements, so I gave mine to the girl who runs the shop where I made a few purchases this morning. Happened to hear it was her birthday and she was delighted with it. I got a great kick out of the old darlings that attend the class. They have no idea what they are doing and are so funny. He certainly packs them in.

Mort and I met after I finished and had a sunbathe on the top deck and then a swim. More sun and changed and had lunch, followed almost at once with the art class – perspective – at which I am poor, outside on deck. Susie and I went together and hope to get back to our new spot tomorrow, where we paint with water colours.

Hawaiian dress tonight and a revue. Lots of weird and wonderful clothes worn for cocktails and dinner. Hope pictures are good. Very clever show in the Carousel Room, followed by a sleepy game of Scrabble. Everyone finds it hard to keep awake.

10 February

Howard Franklin introduced Julia Clements, or Julia, Lady Seton, the world-famous judge of floral design, author of nineteen books on floral design and with the distinction of having three roses named after her. Well – that was a little less than I anticipated, as well as everyone else. Several walked out although an awful lot didn't. There was very little flower talk, mostly people, such as her great friendship with Princess Grace. (See notes I made at the back of this diary. Said Caroline was overshadowed by her famous mother but feel she will come into her own now.)

Susie and I painted outside – water colours are hard after acrylics, particularly when it dries so quickly.

Had a beer out on deck with Vi Hillman and Elsie Robins. They are such a nice couple. Mort played bridge with Elsie this afternoon. Missed our swim but got in a walk. Matt gave me a tin of macadamia nuts, he's a nice little man. Looked like a midget beside Mort but is always pleasant and helpful. Loathes his daughter-in-law, which is unfortunate. Piano concert after dinner.

Mrs Thomson had on the most gorgeous gown once more! The Captain is besotted.

11 February

Saw our first birds while having a beer on deck after our swim. We aren't far away from the equator now and found ten minutes in the sun about all we could take, so cooled (?) off in the pool, which is thirty degrees celsius. The birds, we think, are albatross, but will find out from our art class teacher, Margaret Lawman. She is a bird fancier and is the vet for any birds that come a cropper on the ship. She says from my description it was a booby. The Captain says we are hundreds of miles from the nearest island so one would wonder where they ever came from.

Swam and bingo. Bridge for M.S., cocktails with Susie and Charles. Good dinner. Hope they get a salt-free diet worked out for Matt soon, it's rather tiresome. The crew put on *The Jolson Story* and it was awfully good. How they work all day and have rehearsals and two performances is quite beyond us.

Scrabble with Mort and beat him quite soundly, for a change.

12 February – Derby Day

It's now 1:20 a.m. and writing a diary is not exactly what I feel like doing, particularly when it's been a full and fun day and evening.

Made my Ascot hat last night with the finishing touches this morning, after seeing some of the ones they did at Howard's class this morning. I didn't go because Mort wanted to see the slides on Suva. Was sorry in a way that I hadn't gone because they made the most beautiful flowers out of crepe paper. They were so real it would be useful for the Hospital Auxiliary to know how. Suva looks beautiful. We will have a three-hour tour while we are there. Wish we were staying in Fiji on the way home.

Had lunch on deck today as it was too hot to be bothered to go to our cabin and change. The buffet is good but it's too much of a hassle so we don't care to do it too often. A drink in the look-out bar and later went to Tiffany's. There are quite a few kindred spirits and a nice couple from New Zealand. Mort thinks she is a bit loud. I don't, she's a peach. She knocked the top of her cigarette off and at first we couldn't find it. Unfortunately it was busy burning a hole in her beautiful chiffon gown.

After dinner (Captain absent and sick with a flu bug), we, being about thirty-nine women, all appeared wearing our Ascot hats. There were some fabulous ones. The hours some of them must have put in. We were paraded and judged. Mort, bless him, loved mine but the judges thought otherwise. They gave nine first prizes which made sense. No hurt feelings and everyone agreed they were fantastic.

Next came the horse races. Mort went to the concert so I played the horses with Vi and Matt. Won our races so I just about broke even. Lots of fun and very cleverly arranged. We then went up to the Carousel Room where we were entertained by a comedian and an orchestra. We all had a drink and went to our respective cabins. A fun day with lots of laughter.

13 February

Very nice church service – theatre full and hearty voices. Nice to hear everyone really singing. The Captain took the service and what an inspiration he must have been to his men when he commanded the *Cumberland* at the Falklands. He has the most wonderful face and kind eyes.

The flower class became a Valentine making session. Always learn something useful.

Mort and I then took off with our bathing suits for our favourite spot on deck. At noon, I took Mort's picture with no shadow – it is the most amazing thing to see. The pool was fun as there was enough sea to make it full of motion and being so salty, you could lie full out and ride the roll.

After lunch, a short cat-nap and off to the art class. She is a marvellous teacher!

The bingo big prize is up to the two hundreds, so we took a try at that but didn't win anything. After dinner, Susie came up to us with two people in tow and said they lived in Reigate. It's a very small world! Fred Russell was his name and he turned out to be Owen Evans' business partner. Owen was Mort's best friend. Incredible!

14 February – Valentine's Day

Another lovely day. Had my bath and dressed and up on the lawn deck to see the sun come up at 5:50. Watched the pilot take us into Pago Pago, the US Samoan island. It looked very beautiful with the sun playing on the emerald green mountains. When we landed alongside our mooring, a band struck up and a large group of royal blue uniformed girls appeared to dance and sing for us. All along the wharf were lined row upon row of the artistic endeavours of dozens of natives. Our tour, by bus, was tee'd up for 9:30 so five of us went together. No air-conditioning in the country style bus of course, so it was HOT. Drove all along the lush coast backed by mountains and hit a rainstorm but were in the coach, so it mattered not. The family plots were in the front of all the houses and each expensive-looking grave was covered with flowers. Vi found a very good art object for me to turn in to the competition exhibit and I got a weird piece of coral.

Finally got back to the ship, had a brief rest, changed and had lunch. Later I took off alone to see the display of baskets etc., on the wharf. Couldn't find much. Wanted so badly to buy some flowers for our cabin, finally asked a little girl to find some for me.

She said if I would wait she would be back from the hills before the ship sailed. She arrived back, a little breathless, but clutching the most beautiful bouquet of mixed tropical flowers you could ever imagine. I sent her off happy and I was exactly that. The perfume is so pungent I will keep them in the bathtub all night.

Pleasant evening with a concert put on by the Pat Boone of Scotland, at least that is what I call him. He has the most beautiful voice.

15 February

Everyone a bit bushed after our big day yesterday. A few clouds for a while today but glorious sunshine all afternoon. Art class today; Howard Franklin's slides of his converted stable. His flowers were all Constance Spry at her best, all through his house. Terrible name-dropper.

Elsie Robins was telling me about her life. She seems like such a happy-go-lucky type, it's hard to believe she has had a miserable childhood and two rotten husbands. She is always so bubbly. Mort played bridge with her while I had my art.

Am going to cut this short as I'm dead beat and we are up early tomorrow to go ashore to Suva. Strange to think we never lived Tuesday! (Crossing the date line).

17 February – Suva

Up fairly early to get up to the promenade to see our arrival. The sun is just up on the greenest of green mountains, covered with the greenest trees I have ever seen, which of course could only get that way with heavy rainfall. Dashed off a few cards and a letter to Susie and Drue etc., then went ashore to go on a tour we had booked. Tried to get out of it as our table wanted us to go with them. Thank heaven we didn't, as we were so delighted with our two and a half hours in a government sponsored culture centre. The gardens were beautiful and each little thatched house held something of interest, either by pictures or a talk – mostly by native Fijians, who were fully dressed in their native costumes of flowers and ferns and tampa and reed skirts. They were so gracious and pleasant. They are a deeply religious people and mostly Methodists. Not one of them even mildly looked as if they expected a tip, which these days is *most* unusual. The hibiscus in every colour imaginable were all through the gardens, making ours look like miniatures. Orchids, tropical shrubs of ginger, etc. I can't name them all but they were everywhere.

Another very interesting thing we saw was a charming, pretty and extremely well-educated English woman who devoted her life to raising iguanas and breeding almost extinct varieties. She also had a tame flying squirrel and, cuddled in her arms, was a mongoose!!! She was a fascinating person and everything she touched loved her.

We were all loath to leave this happy place. The men had the bodies of warriors but the smiles of friendliness. I for one, won't forget today. It all ended with all the women singing with the men, a farewell song to us. It was very beautiful and moving.

After we returned to the ship, we decided to catch a cab and go out to the Trade Winds Hotel and have lunch. Expected to find Elsie, Vi, Norah and Matt, but they never did show. Lunch was very indifferent and we were sorry we had left the ship.

We were returned to town where Mort left me and I roamed all over looking for a white purse. Meantime, the heavens opened and down came a cloudburst that went on and on bursting. How to get back to the ship was the question! Finally deduced I would be better buying a cheapish umbrella rather than going by taxi as they couldn't drive right alongside, so I would get soaked getting from A to B. Bought a lightweight collapsible one that got me back with only wet feet, and damp, not drowned.

Shampooed my hair with Doris' super 'Mink', and let it dry under the lamp. Black tie – my smoked salmon and gold – and off we went to the Captain's cabin for drinks. Met a charming couple from Florida, Iris and Lewis, I believe. A lot of fun but deafeningly noisy! Dinner very good, followed with the cabaret. The mind reader hypnotised a passenger. Quite something.

18 February

Working our way down to 'D' day. I will feel very sad saying goodbye to all the nice people we have met. Assassi, who has looked after us so conscientiously and happily – I'd like to wrap him up and take him home. Vi Hillman is a peach of a person, I hope to meet her again. And Elsie Robins, who asked us to stay with her in New Zealand, is such a nice person.

Went to the Sydney slides and talk, which was very interesting – it looks like a beautiful city. Art class was charcoal figures. Wish we had more classes but tomorrow is the Pacific Princess' First Art Show and exhibits of artistic findings ashore. Should be fun.

Matt has invited us to his cabin as a farewell party for us, which is nice of the little fellow. Susie and Charles had drinks with us this evening and we listened to the Scottish singer. I love his voice and personality.

Clocks go back another half hour. Not as hot today and the pool cooler. No more warm water out of the cold tap and all because we are now about five hundred miles south of the equator.

19 February

Dried flower arranging class and our last of the course. It was very interesting and I learned a lot. He certainly produced some beautiful Constance Spry arrangements. Made a few notes in my other diary.

Lay up on the lawn deck, met Mort and had a gin and lime before having the buffet on deck. Couldn't go to the dining room because we had to take our art piece and walk up to the Carousel Lounge where we were to have our exhibit (for a prize) and an art show. The pieces were placed on card tables and our paintings, etc., were placed against the backs of all the seats. It was astounding how many there were as the majority had been at it since Southampton. To my amazement, I got the second prize for the piece of coral I found on the beach in Pago Pago. It is an interesting piece.

Had a game with Mort. Got Graham a birthday gift. Met Charles and Susie for drinks. Good dinner. Went to the concert and saw most of the Cole Porter show. First one I haven't enjoyed.

A little bit of a roll tonight. Packed all my evening gowns.

20 February

Mixed up day. We had to have all our bags packed by dinner time, so shot Mort out of the cabin and finally got it all finished by 7:00. It's so easy to pack when everything is in one area instead of all over the house.

Managed to be on deck to see Lord Howe Island. An amazing sight, tucked all by itself, miles from anywhere. People actually live there and are wanting to make it into a resort. I would be stir crazy in no time.

Went to the church service taken by our Captain. Met Mort and lay up on the verandah deck – sunny spot we like so much. After we felt we had had enough, we had a Singapore sling and the buffet lunch. Played in the bridge tournament with Mort from 2:30-4:30, then to the final bingo game. The jackpot's two hundred was won by a lady. Very tense and exciting.

Matt had a farewell party in his cabin for us, which was nice of him but we would have gone to our usual bar with everyone.

However, it was very nice of him. Dear little Elsie gave both of us
a pen with a dear note saying:

> *Happy to have met you*
> *Happy knowing you,*
> *And very happy happy to have*
> *shared so many happy days with you.*
> *Goodbye, God bless and keep you.*
> *Elsie*
> *Hope to see you again. E.*

It's a P&O, SS *Sea Princess* pen. It was so nice of her. Haven't seen
Mort's note as yet. He was so tired he went off to bed fairly early. I
too must get some sleep. The last one in my comfortable moving
bed. I will miss the ship's noises. I have had such a happy time.

21 February

We got up at 6:30 so we could go up on the bridge and see our
entrance into Sydney Harbour. Unfortunately, it was dull and rather
like a cloudy Vancouver morning, so didn't get any pictures. It is all
I had ever heard and more. I always have thought Vancouver
Harbour was so very special; now I have seen Singapore, Hong
King and Sydney, I'm not so impressed with ours. Said all our
goodbyes and left the ship around 11:00 a.m. The Captain was
ashore to say goodbye. I liked him but really did think he made a
bad choice with his beloved Jean – she gives me a pain – Mort also.

Finally got a taxi and took off for Randwick. Our flat is lovely –
air from the ocean that we have a glorious view of is fresh and
breezy, which comes as a surprise. The sun soon came out and the
clouds all vanished. Our flat is delightful. Very large living room
and dining area, good sized sun deck with a table and four chairs,
kitchen, breakfast room, laundry, and two bedrooms. Large bath
and shower and a separate john. We are up one floor so can leave

everything open. The houses are fascinating. They have so much character.

Our mail was produced – one from Drue telling about Christie not wanting to go to the Planetarium party because she really thought she was going to the moon! Nice to hear, although the latter was written before my phone conversation when in Honolulu. Letter from Jane from Barbados, also Margot and Catherine, my nice nice nurse from years ago!

We unpacked, more or less, and decided to take a bus into town as we are four miles out. Everyone we talked to for information was so kind and helpful. One lady even suggested she could drive us into town at 5 o'clock, if we wanted to go then. We could have got a cab but we were much happier going by bus, it was a means of getting to know where we were and the cab's so fast you can't see a thing.

The shopping consisted of going in one store and out the other, with me in hot pursuit of Mortimer. We did sit long enough in one place to buy some black shoes to walk in as the elastic on mine has stretched too much from my swollen feet in the ship. Looked at opal rings and saw one I loved. The shops, large ones, have the most beautiful merchandise and have marble floors and crystal lighting. Everyone so helpful. Finally exhausted ourselves and did some grocery shopping for breakfasts and taxied home.

Slept soundly until someone's horn got stuck so we switched on the TV and what should be on but Alan Alda in M*A*S*H. Had two drinks and walked to the French restaurant we had been told was close by. Turned out to be Monday closing. We were a little disgruntled, and as we walked back a man was draining his shutters on his drugstore so I asked him if he could tell us the name of a good place for dinner. To our amazement, he said he could recommend a French one but we would need to take a cab. When we told him that was okay, he looked up the phone number and address and made a reservation under the name 'Smith'. Little did he know Mort's second name is 'Smith'. We could hardly believe anyone would go to so much trouble! Dinner was very good and we both enjoyed it very much. A long but pleasant day.

23 for 22 February

Here it is the 23rd and so much happens each day it's quite impossible to write it all down. Left my glasses at the restaurant last night so couldn't write my 'day'! Still no glasses but will try and recall.

We left for town early and took a special bus for eighteen stops, each stop being a place of interest. Indeed they were, from the Opera House to old houses packed with antiques. A walk of some miles through the Botanical Gardens to Mrs McQuarrie's chair on the point. Kept bumping into Betty from the cabin across from us, also Jim the Canadian, ex-Commanding Officer of a Canadian corvette. It seemed that everywhere we went we saw *Sea P.* passengers. Had a very good dinner at the Palmer Room, but left my glasses!

Excellent lunch on the wharf by *QE2*.

23 February

I was determined to see the zoo, so we left here around 10:30, having talked to Susie. Woke her up, I'm sure, as their air-conditioning wasn't working very well, so hadn't slept. Crossed the water by ferry boat with twenty other *Sea Princess* passengers that sat near us in the dining room. After docking, we bussed up to the top of a steep hill and we wandered all through endless pathways to see the animals and birds! It was a very well planned and cared for zoo, with every imaginable bird or beast in as natural an environment as possible. Walked our legs off. Were so weary we decided against going into town to get my glasses and had dinner instead.

We went to the French restaurant around the corner. The food was superb, unbelievable! We simply could not believe it. Just after our dessert, the young couple next to us asked if we were Canadian. One thing led to another and, to our amazement, they are calling for us at 7:00 a.m. to drive us to the Blue Mountains! What a pair they are. More of this tomorrow, I must get some sleep.

24 February

Here it is, 12:55, and I have a wonderful day to write about. Mark, our friend of last night, arrived sharp at 7:00 without Janeen as she couldn't get out of her duty at the hospital. Off we went carrying sweaters and wearing my golf skirt, which was just as well as I was in the back with the two bucket seats pressed well back against my knees. It didn't take long to realise he was a very experienced and competent driver. It took one and a half hours to get into the country and then before we knew it, we were at the Blue Mountains.

It was misty, with the sun struggling to get through. Smoky blue everywhere. It's a great valley, surrounded by blue mountains. Took pictures, bought cards and a gift for Janeen as it was her birthday. We then said we had time to go to the caves. We travelled fast, good and fast, but neither of us was the least nervous. The caves required one and a half hours to tour properly, so we only did a very small portion and were so glad we went as it was very different from anything we had ever seen or done before. The height and complexity of them was exciting and the colours quite beautiful.

By this time it was getting onto noon so we went to the bar in a very nice hotel. The men had a beer and I a gin and tonic. A very good buffet lunch after, then the long trip back. The latter route was much prettier than going. Lots of hills and valleys, sheep, cows, flowers and trees. Mark is a very nice young man and he is a corporate investigator. Very relaxed and pleasant. It is surprising to me how fast they travel in cars, no police ever to be seen anywhere, excellent road manners, no honking, pedestrians popping up like corks every so often, crossing against signals, but all the drivers are so disciplined and pleasant. Drivers trust each other to do the right thing.

Got back on the dot of 4:30 and said goodbye to our delightful host. Although we had been walking our legs off, we had to pop up to the little market for our breakfast supplies. Dear little village area close by. Left for town at 6:35 so we could stop by for my glasses then on to the Sydney Opera House. We joined many others around one of the circular bars and had a drink. They also have very high circular stand-up tables for those that might like to have a sandwich with their drink.

We wandered around for a while as we were a little early. No words of mine could adequately describe the Sydney Opera House. It is ultra modern and yet has a gracious dignity about it. Our box was beautifully situated so we could see everything. At 7:30 the curtain went up on Bonning conducting *Romeo and Juliet*. The cast was young and the singing superb, along with their acting. Both Mort and I were enchanted with the whole performance. The applause proved everyone felt as we did. Quite a day!

25 February

My one-time nurse, Catherine, arrived to see me at 10:45. Mort went off to see the Entombed Warriors at the art gallery, which I would so love to have seen also – maybe tomorrow. Peter and Helen were with her, darling children. They swam and were taken to Helen's godmother's to have lunch and a rest. Catherine came back for me and then we drove out to the prettiest bay and had a seafood platter for two. It was delicious and we ate most of it. We talked our heads off and filled a twelve-year gap in a few hours.

Got back at 3:15 and Mort got in about 4:00, having had a strenuous but rewarding day. Went up on the revolving restaurant – both the Art Gallery and the latter are a must. Went to our favourite French restaurant and had noisettes of lamb. Unbelievably good food! Walked there and back. Lovely evening.

26 February

They can't all be good and this one wasn't our greatest! Started off all right, in a way, by me trotting off at 7:45 with two pairs of Mort's trousers to be cleaned. The place we had seen, 8:00 in, out at 12:00 on Saturdays, was a fiasco. He's open but no cleaning. So – I walked and walked to the next shopping district. Arrived back at 8:25, hungry, to say the least. As I wanted to do some shopping in town, Mort arranged to meet me at 1:00. I suggested the waterfall and French café we had seen several days previously and I said it was the Hilton. I was wrong! It wasn't the Hilton at all, so he paced the hall and lobby and looked everywhere, then taxied back to the café then to the Hilton. Finally at 1:50, I gave up and took the bus home. He arrived around 3:30, not amused, naturally. To top it all, our flight is delayed and we don't take off until 2:30 instead of 1:00, which makes it very late arriving in Auckland.

Felt a little brighter after a read and a sleep, then a drink before leaving for our Le Dauphin, where we had dined three nights in a row. A family business, he cooks and she serves. Never have I tasted such food. If I could achieve cooking like they serve I would do little else. We have now almost worked our way through their menu and it was lobster for me this evening. I'd dreamt about that, to say nothing of their lamb and the crepe soufflé with the most superb sauce. Tonight we had their fruits with strawberry soufflé.

And so to bed! They may move to Vancouver one day, so gave her our address.

27 February – Auckland, NZ (Population: 800,000)

The usual kind of day when moving from A to B, up early and pack and wait around in the airport. Our flight to New Zealand was delayed by two hours, so they said, but we didn't actually take off until close to three hours late. A super crew of New Zealanders – as far as I'm concerned, they are the nicest of all people. Warm and friendly and nicely spoken. Made chatting friends with the crew, wish we were flying to Tahiti with them.

Our hotel greeted us warmly and said we had the honeymoon suite – king size bed and all. So tired we died, so I am writing this from our next un-honeymoon room in Wellington!

28 February – Wellington, NZ

Our flight was interesting due to a delightful lady next to me. Had sailed thirty-six thousand miles in a forty-five foot sailboat which moored alongside the Bayshore for a month. She's going to help me locate Graham Read's parents (Fleet Air Arm, NZ). Was also going to help me locate Elsie Robins, thinking I had thrown out her address. While looking through my wallet to show Mort something, I came across a picture of her with her son on an island she wants us to visit. Fortunately, we may now be able to. I am so pleased to have found it.

Wellington cold and so windy. Would probably love it if it was warm and sunny. Perfectly joyous dinner. *Red letter day. Found Elsie Robins' address, in the island off Auckland! Ad reads: How to keep your fashion balance in wonderful windy Wellington!!

1 March – Wellington

Up bright and early, good breakfast. Dull weather. All sorts and types of us gathered in the lobby to board our coach tour to go back to Auckland. An excellent driver and guide and a lot of the group have been together for ten days, so seem to be a happy gathering.

We spent the morning touring Wellington. Went to a perfectly beautiful old church, St Paul's. I was very impressed with it. The windows were exquisitely beautiful. White dried flowers and a money plant were on the altar and a large bouquet on a stand at the chancel steps. The stand was gracefully draped by a white linen square, hung in folds. Simple and very effective.

Went up to the Botanical Gardens. It was quite breathtaking. Beds upon beds of red begonias massed in huge areas. Then we went into the greenhouse where they had the finest display of begonias one could ever imagine. Every colour. I swear some were as large as my face. Pale pink with yellow centres. We have nothing to equal their display.

Up to a look-out, quite high, and it gave a panoramic view of the city and harbour. Although it wasn't a good day, it cleared a bit. Had a very nice lunch, the two of us, in a good Chinese restaurant.

Left Wellington to wend our way to North Palmerston where we are spending the night. Four people from our ship and we didn't recognise them or they us. Tried to play bingo. Mort and I felt like fools, the caller went so fast we couldn't keep up. Alarm set for 6:00 a.m. Jolly day.

2 March – Rotorua

Up at 6:00 and into our coach by 8:00. Everyone full of good humour but heads falling to our shoulder for at least the first hour. Today was very interesting to everyone as we headed toward Rotorua. We must have seen thousands upon thousands of sheep, very few people and billions of trees, mostly planted to prevent erosion. This centre of the North Island is a wide plateau of lakes, rivers, mountains, scrub, barren wilderness, and strange, other side of the moon landscape that masks a horrendous upheaval about AD 120, when this countryside belched itself inside out. Smoke rings puffed from what is left of Mount Tongariro, the volcano that literally blew its top. Our driver wants us to take a half an hour flight over it tomorrow, but I think I will pass.

In the Wairakee Valley we saw where geothermal engineers have bored down through the earth's thin crust to tap hellfire beneath! The whole valley sprouts cauldrons of steam. Saw where the Maoris live and work and cook and steam their food in the natural waters. There was a cold water lake on one side of us and a boiling, bubbling lake on the other. They can catch fish on one side and cook it on the other. Took quite a few pictures which I hope will come out. Some forty years ago a scientist discovered that spreading cobalt and super-phosphate on the soil evolved healthy farm pasture land. Pine forests that had wilted in the volcanic soil suddenly took on healthy and huge growth.

We checked into our hotel around 5:00. Rested, dinner, walked, and now to bed. A very interesting and educational day. Staying here two nights.

3 March – Rotorua

We travelled many a mile today, seeing all the places we could see in one day. First of all, we went to a wood carving building and really wasn't very impressed after Bali, then walked down a hill past spewing hot, steamy pools to the old Anglican church that has a sand-blasted figure of Christ as a Maori. It is alone on a large window that is silhouetted against the sea, so He looks as if He is walking on water when you sit looking at Him from the pews. All graveyards are above ground because below ground, three feet or so, is *hot*.

Then to Rainbow Springs. This was a very unusual place with clearly swept pathways leading past pools and pools of varying sizes filled with trout that were kept together in age groups, from newly-hatched eggs to eight-twelve pound fish. The young Maori that took us around spoke beautifully and treated all the fish and birds like humans. He even had the large fish jumping to take food off a spoon he held out for them.

Tore ourselves away from there and moved on to an agrodome. It was a nineteen ram parade to show the variety of breeds that are popular in this country. It would fill a page to describe it all thoroughly. I didn't know sheep don't have upper teeth, they eat all their waking moments very well without them. The sheep were individually chained in a cubicle and upon release of their chain, they literally pranced down a railed walkway and up on a platform to a specified place on a stage. Each promptly tucked into a tin of nummies that was meant for only that sheep. All in all, the nineteen did just that. They were attached to their little food stands as they scrambled up there and then stood like angels looking positively angelic.

Next, the sheep rancher whistled his whistle noises for his sheep-dog and put him through his paces, even to walking up the backs of all the sheep and then crunching down on the designated one. I ended up in the wool shop making some purchases and unfortunately missed the dog trials, which Mort said were marvellous. The evening was a Maori dinner and the entertainment was of traditional stunts, actions and war-cries. Really a very good programme.

4 March – Leave Rotorua for the Waitomo Caves

Oh dear! So weary last night I never got around to saying a word about our full but very interesting day. The highlight of the day had to be our guided tour of the Waitomo caves – can't pronounce it. This turned out to be a very special experience. We were carefully guided through the caves which were weird and wonderful, capped by a hushed subterranean boat ride under a canopy of glow-worm stars. There were about eighteen of us to a boat that moved in total darkness and silence through the weird shapes of the caves. As one looked forward it was as if you were looking at the Milky Way, the glow-worms were so brilliant. The acoustics are perfect. Our group sang 'Waltzing Matilda' before we went into the boats. The Vienna Boys choir have sung there also. It was a delightful experience.

The countryside we went through on the way to Auckland was very restful – sheep, sheep and more sheep. Also, bull farms, deer farms, cattle farms, and agricultural farms. The volcanic soil apparently is very fertile as everything grows very rapidly; they have two potato crops a year. The corn and tomatoes and fruit were outstanding. Did a small tour and up to the look-out site in Auckland. Finally saying goodbye to all the nice people we met coming from Wellington to Auckland.

Vale Harvie from Canberra is going to call Johnnie Bull for me. I tried so often to reach her. Called Elsie Robins and we are going to the island that her son is on to spend Sunday with her.

5 March

We were both weary, put a sign on our door 'Please do not disturb' and slept until close to ten, with the exception of two disturbances. At 6:00 a.m., the *Viking Fairstar* blew her way into harbour, which is directly outside our windows. We thought she was the *Canberra*, having heard she was due in, but with Mort's binoculars I soon found otherwise. No sooner had we settled off to sleep than a large blast from the whistle woke us up once more. This time it was the *Canberra* and she nestled in outside our windows alongside the *Viking Fairstar*. It was all too exciting to really catch on paper.

We were so late we missed breakfast, so walked out for a Continental bite and Mort picked up an Auckland tour for us that made for a very happy and interesting afternoon. It's a city that resembles San Francisco. Hilly, clean, bridges, water, interesting old architecture. I love it!! Mort aided an air stewardess with her heavy case and asked her to recommend a restaurant. We took her advice and dined at Number Five Restaurant, 5 City Road, and it was excellent – particularly my caviar and vegs and dessert. The lamb was spoiled by them piercing a hole in the centre of the dear little chops and stuffing it with a savoury sauce. Beautiful service and a most attractive setting. Really a very nice evening.

The *Viking Fairstar* sailed off into the lights of the night around 10:00 p.m. The *Oriana* departs at midnight, no doubt just as we get to sleep. She looks heavenly out there. We both wish we were aboard instead of flying!

6 March

Didn't know the clocks went back last night so lost an hour's sleep and went across to our ferry to find it was only 8:15 instead of 9:15. Back to the hotel to put in time, so packed our Tahiti bag as much as possible. Caught our ferry and were met an hour later by Elsie, looking very spry and pleased to see us. Her son John was at his house which is soon to be totally renovated. It's over one hundred years old and will be made into a Holiday Campers Inn. It will be a very exciting challenge to create the place he has in his mind.

The beaches are safe for swimming and they are still covered with shells. Sailboats everywhere. I would swear every man and his dog has a sailboat. Elsie will come over tomorrow and have lunch with us and perhaps one day will visit us in Vancouver. Vi Hillman too, we hope. Elsie didn't seem to think Vi was very well. Apparently she told Elsie she had had a cancer operation before she left England. Why does it strike the nicest people?

When we returned with all the trippers, we had a drink then went to the seafood restaurant in the hotel. We had John Dory with asparagus and hollandaise sauce. Wish we had that fish at home. I can imagine all the things one could do with a firm white fish like it.

The *Canberra* blew her whistle at 11:00 p.m. sharp and two tugs eased her out with all her lights blazing. She is a beauty. Mort and I had our after-dinner stroll out on the wharf walkway alongside her. I'm sure she must be close to a block long. Hard to imagine her at war in the Falklands. Mort too tired to care if she sailed or flew out of the harbour. Mort came home with the most beautiful roses for me. Am going to *hate* to leave them behind.

7 March

After a light breakfast, Mort took off to check on a restaurant we had seen on Sunday that was closed. If he likes it, he is going to make a reservation for us for lunch with Elsie. I festooned our room – beds, tables, etc. – with suitcases and clothing. Hard to believe order could ever come from chaos, but with careful packing it was amazing how well it all got divided into two parts. One case is to be left unopened in Tahiti and the other to see us through island-hopping and our eventual flight home next Sunday. While our room was being tidied we sat outside by the pool enjoying the warm, sunny day.

Elsie arrived on the dot of 12:30, with Joe, whom we met yesterday at Whaihcke. She didn't join us for lunch but came to say goodbye to us. We went to the buffet in the hotel as the food here is excellent. It turned out to be a wise choice and we all enjoyed it. After saying goodbye and a small shut-eye, we walked up hill after hill until Mort left me to it and walked back by himself. I caught a cab and went up to the top of the shopping centre. Had been developed from the old houses. It was very cleverly thought out and a bit like Carmel. Bought a few things and waited a good half hour for a bus. Mort said he was beginning to worry about me.

Found Antoine's in the Parnell village, so told Mort it looked as if it might be good so we got a reservation for 8:00. If it hadn't been for the party of NZ women at the next table, it would have been very good because the food was excellent, but the women were like forty cackling hens and we could hardly hear each other.

7 March _again_ (Date-line)

Flew all day, hour after hour after hour. Our first stop was Nadi Airport, the scene of the big hurricane a week earlier. Western Samoa, Rarotonga, was a lively place. Having crossed the date-line, we gained another day, as well as two hours that we put our clocks on. Finally, half-dead, we arrived at Papeete, Tahiti, and drove out to the Tahiti Beachcomber. Most attractive hotel. So tired we barely looked around. Took a pill each (my first) and died.

Light breakfast, packed and separated our bags that were to be left and out to the airport to a little puddle jumper of an amphibious aircraft. After much pushing and pulling and squeezing, Mort finally got his legs in! Ten minutes in the air and we were there in Mooria and met and driven quickly to our Bali Hai Hotel. I will describe it tomorrow. I'm too weary!

8 March

Good sleep, with four huge screened windows open and our ceiling fan whirling silently overhead and, of course, only a sheet. The hotel is fascinating. All guests have their own thatched roofed, very high ceilinged, house, that is almost totally windows. They are all privately situated in acres of gardens, each one surrounded with all colours of shrubs. We are beside a fourteen-foot waterfall that runs down off a huge rock-formed covering for the pool equipment and waterfall shed. Very clever and beautiful huge pool with a thatched roof house at one end that must be used as a bar.

The lounge and dining room all face out to sea. It is full of windows and tiled floors. The beach is pure white, soft sand, only tiny shells. Palms lean out to sea. There is a well concealed good tennis court. Too hot for most, I would think. The barmaids and waitresses are friendly, smiling and lovely; be they fat or slim, they are lovely. Flowers in their hair or halos of flowers that they make themselves each day.

A good tropical downpour just before we thought of dressing for dinner, so sat it out with everybody else at the bar as guests of the manager, who served a Mai Tai punch and canapés. As soon as it eased off, we nipped back to our grass 'shack' to change.

Very nice dinner, the white tablecloths all have a wide red floral centre straight down the middle, with matching bright red table napkins. Lots of flowers. Couldn't keep my eyes open so we went to bed around 10:30, which for us is very early.

9 March

Today started out to be a normal day, with a very nice breakfast. Lazy morning on the beach talking to the odd couple, when the wind came up and the people occupying the thatched roof cottages on low stilts in the water were told they were being moved back around us as there is a bad storm expected. This was confirmed by the manager and everything is being battened down. The sea is growing and so is the wind. However, the big strike at the island is due in during the early morning. The last cyclone was in 1905, Mort's birth year. We are all naturally apprehensive. Can't believe any of the roofs will stay on. We figure the safest place is in our cupboard. The scary thing to me is all the lights will go out. Hope the girls don't hear about it until it's all over. Real trouble certainly breaks down all barriers. There are only thirty-five guests, so we all had drinks, more or less together. About seven of us joined forces and John, the manager, would come and sit with us every so often and tell us the latest satellite reports. We are in a direct line of the cyclone that is moving slowly towards us. We asked what we should do to try and protect ourselves and he reassured us that we should go to bed, with only coconuts to worry about getting from A to B. There would be a radio-watch kept all night and we would be called to all closet ourselves together in behind the stone walls of the office that he considers the only safe place to be.

Made a dash over to change for dinner and everyone was presented with a halo of flowers to wear. Red, white and green, so cleverly made. Mort was sorry we didn't have a flash to take a picture as he said it was most becoming. After dinner (which wasn't all that special), the dancers, male and female, with their music, put on a performance for us. They all wore beautiful flowers on their heads, around their necks and even around their shaking hips. At the end of their entertainment, the prettiest one went to Mort and got him to his feet and one of the older ones pulled me up. Away we went, much to everyone's amusement. I caught a glimpse of Mort whirling himself around and having a great time.

Sat around afterwards, hoping to hear some good news but

none was forthcoming. Off to our thatched houses, each wondering what future lay ahead of us. Having Mort with me, my mind went to the girls. I couldn't shake the thought of holding Susie as a tiny baby for the first time, and carrying Drue out of the hospital. Those two pictures kept coming to my mind over and over again. I didn't need any persuading to sleep in Mort's double bed as my single one was under the window. With a sheet over us, we talked above the battering wind. Finally dropped off, to awaken and find it was only 12:15! So it went all night. Both hoping daylight would come so we wouldn't have to beat our way to the main office in the dark. Finally it was daylight, so Mort went over to the office to find that the cyclone had veered and headed for Bora Bora instead of us. Thank God. Now we wait to hear further news of Bora Bora. So ended our experience we will never forget, or be more thankful to have avoided.

10 March

Everyone feeling relieved to have last night behind us. The weather BLOWING and GUSTING. In between showers, I tried to walk on the beach, but at times was nearly knocked off my feet and the sand on my legs was piercing, so gave that up. Very quiet around the hotel all day, except for work parties of natives looking brown and lean and bedecked with halos of flowers on their heads and brooms in perpetual motion, working on the water coming in on the tiles and the blowing sand. No news of any sort, except that flights are all cancelled. Many people wondering where or how they will make connections. Can't get out to see the island as we hoped to do, taxiing around in this wind and rain hardly makes much sense. Said goodbye to the Dick Welches from Portland.

11 March – Homeward Bound

After breakfast at the Bali Hai, quite a few of us departed for the little airport. Fortunately, Mort decided to go earlier than as first planned as the little nine-seater goes back and forth with its running mate about every twelve minutes and no sooner had we received our boarding cards for number 3 flight, when into the airport came about fifty people. They had a couple of hours wait. We expected it to be terribly rough and bumpy with the wind the way it was blowing, but it wasn't too bad. Heaved a sigh of relief when we landed all the same!

Back to our old haunt of several days ago, the Tahiti Beachcomber. At noon we had a drink at a makeshift bar and lunch in a sealed-in dining room. They seem to be much better prepared for the cyclone than we were at the Bali Hai. All their windows were taped and heavily plasticised over the large dining room windows. They were in the line of the storm also and obviously weren't going to be caught napping. Managed a tiny walk before it poured.

Ernle Morgan Carroll.

Dinner and entertainment break and female Tahitian dancers. Saw various friends. Bed early, with a 4:50 a.m. call!

12 March

Could be called our longest day. Up at 6:00, half dead, only to wait hours in the airport. News that the cyclone had now swung around and is heading towards Papeete. Got away at 3:30, thank God. Wind and rain working overtime. Endless hours until we finally settled down in L.A. with great cheers from all the passengers!

13 March

Home sweet home! How good it is! We slept like the dead and were up early to catch our flight by Western. Had a light breakfast at the airport. Talked to Bruce to tell him about our arrival time. Very good flight and an easy time with customs and then greeted by all the family, except Bruce and Graham who had work to do and came down later. Susie's hair looking awfully pretty, all short and curly. Ernle and Charlie at home to greet us and all the gardens looking unbelievable, colourful and beautiful. They all had tea and we talked our heads off. Ernle had prepared a scrumptious dinner for us and Eliz had the house glistening. Charlie soon on my lap. Mort not feeling awfully well, so on his pills. Such a pity.

Our trip:
Vancouver to San Francisco (air). San Francisco to Australia (Sydney ship), to Auckland and Wellington, N. Zealand. Rotorura, Papeete, Tahiti, Los Angeles, home.

Round the World Cruise,
March-April 1984

8 March

Always such a sad day – how I do hate leaving all the family behind – particularly this trip with our distances so great and no letters or news until we reach London! Kate didn't add to the whole situation, poor little darling. Evidently a raccoon clawed her back, unknown to us and it wasn't until I patted her on my bed this morning that she cried out with the pain. So off to the vet, which meant she returned to our house to Ernle, not Mort or me. I felt worse than awful about the whole thing.

Drue drove us out and Susie met us at the airport. Before we knew it we were saying those awful goodbyes and being boarded. As it wasn't a full complement, we had three seats between the two of us and for thirteen hours we read, Scrabbled and snoozed. Was disappointed in Cathay Pacific. It always appears to be so special on TV. First class, perhaps, but ours was only average. No afternoon tea or a cookie, just juice. Having had lunch at 2:00, we were starved by 7:30, particularly as I didn't care for my lunch. The flight itself was as calm and pleasant as could be, finally landing in Hong Kong with a perfect touchdown. The city wasn't clear – low cloud and misty, which made all the lights eerie and soft.

After checking in to the Regent we went for a short walk and to bed. Too tired to sleep.

9, 10, 11, 12, 13 March (really all rolled into one)

Laziness due to jet lag and cold, drizzly, dreary weather. Even coats worn by the locals, no doubt longing for the opportunity to do so for months. Nevertheless we have worn our sweaters and anything cosy we could pull on out of our English, or should I say UK, suitcases. The weather certainly slowed up our sightseeing. Low cloud has been with us all week, along with a cold wind. Mort went his way and I went mine. He, for shirts, ties and trousers. Fittings for me. Nice to see old friends and find my measurements hadn't altered.

Had dinner at Hugo's, which was quite as superb as our last, two years ago. It is such a treat to be served food cooked in every respect to almost perfection and service to match.

The next night we dined at 'Plums'. I call it 'La Plume'. There are screeds written about it and I must admit it would be hard to fault. We were lucky our last night to get a cancellation at the Peninsula. We were turned down this morning and they called at 5:00 p.m. to say they could take us at 8:00. We were delighted as it is rated No. 1 in Hong Kong. One would think we only have thoughts of food – NOT SO!

We took a tour to the New Territories yesterday and *en route* drove miles through poverty-stricken areas where families up to 8-10 are delighted to have a good housing flat of about 8-10 square feet per family – no plumbing, no kitchen facilities. How much we take for granted. The four-hour tour was very depressing, miles of misery. They never throw anything away but they don't have any place to store anything, so the untidiness is unbelievable, not like Japan.

We packed in the morning and I had a last fitting, then we drove over to the ship and deposited our luggage. Boarding time is 5:00 p.m., so went for a walk and got a few gifts. Got settled into our cabin as much as I could Our cabin steward is called Iggie. Big handsome fellow that comes from the same town as Assassi who looked after us last year.

Several familiar faces that were aboard last time. The bridge 'master' is the same, also one of the entertainment groups, 'Tommy', who everyone loves.

Off to bed around 11:00. She was still in dock but we were too tired to keep our eyes open. Mort slept through the announcement that we were going to be sailing at 2:45 a.m. I pulled up the blind on our window and put on a warm coat and watched all the lights in Hong Kong gradually fade away. It was a pity we had such poor weather. The sun only peeped out on our last day, and then it was very humid.

Thursday 15 March

We both had a good sleep. I got up at 7:00 and went below to the indoor pool, hoping to have a before-breakfast session, only to find the pool hadn't been filled. I should have known better as they are always emptied when in port.

It was the most superb sunny day. The ocean was glistening with diamonds, with a warm breeze and as calm as a mill pond. Absolutely no feeling of motion to the ship at all.

Started my slow-tanning process by spending only about half an hour out in my suit by the pool. Talked to a delightful Swiss lady.

Mort and I entered the bridge tournament and won our first four rubbers that counted for the total score. We have to play tomorrow. Unfortunate it is, that the bridge and art conflict. Perhaps Mort will find a better partner, although I must say I enjoyed myself and didn't make too many booboos. Who knows, one day I will stop saying I don't play afternoon bridge!

Saw an awfully good film with Michael Caine, with several Irish jigs.

18 March

Singapore and a big wish come true for me, to arrive by ship. It's such a magnificent harbour, third finest in the world. Up very early to see the beauty of it all. Ships, ships, so many tankers, I couldn't count them. When we were finally drawing alongside, the entertainers arrived. A large drum-like affair, but like a steel one you'd see in the Caribbean. Four people got into two outfits that became a couple of lions that danced and played with each other to the music and I could only wish our grandchildren could have seen them.

No telephone was available for ship-to-shore calls and as we were to call friends of Tim and Mardi's, we finally took the shuttle bus into the city and called from there. They were out, so we taxied to Raffles and had a Singapore sling. They were filming the third part of a BBC series called *Tenko!* It was fascinating watching it all, but oh, was it hot. Finally spoke to Mr Boon and brought him up to date with Mardi's great progress and we had a very good conversation. He was sorry not to see us but was flying that afternoon out to one of the islands on an oil deal. Perhaps we'll meet in Vancouver.

Took a cab to the Shangri-La Hotel for lunch, by a waterfall and under paddle fans. It is a magnificent hotel and makes most hotels I've seen seem very second-rate. Mort says it is one of the top in the world. I wouldn't doubt it.

Queued for a taxi for twenty minutes and finally arrived back in time for a swim and dinner. Agatha Christie movie and bed. Very good. Expected to sail around 11:30 and gave up waiting at 1:00 a.m. Got up to look out the window around 5:00 and all the Singapore lights were still visible.

19 March

Two good things today. Mort and I came fourth in the bridge

and if we get any kind of break in cards, we should do a lot better. I'm attending a tough school! The scenery all through the Singapore straits is very interesting, we aren't close enough to really see anything, other than islands, but it's the Malay Straits, I believe. We attended a super recital given by a concert pianist who has been on board for the whole cruise and will be leaving the ship in Sri Lanka on Tuesday. She is quite outstanding as well as beautiful, young and charming. Meeting more and more people all the time. Had drinks with a very nice English couple. He is retired from the Prudential Life. Tom and Norma Greenhalgh are their names and we seem to have lots to say to each other. Still too pink a back to expose myself to the sun, unfortunately.

Happy birthday, Ryan.

20 March

Working like mad on my knees from 8:00-8:45 every morning in the indoor pool. Wish I knew whether I should or shouldn't, but will continue and hope for the best. I end up in the sauna and feel as if I could take on the world.

We are between Sumatra and Malaysia. The Bengal Passage next and close enough to see houses, beaches, palm trees and hills that are tree'd and cultivated. They must get quite a rainfall as it's very green, although very hot. We are only two degrees north of the equator. On board, the breeze is cooling and delightful. Ashore I would not be very happy.

The bridge was fun and we won all our games. Mort had unintentionally put us down for duplicate so we bowed out of that and played rubber bridge in another room.

The Captain entertained all the guests at a noon party. That is to say, all new arrivals that joined the ship either in Hong Kong or Singapore. There were about one hundred and thirty people there. The Captain is quite young, tall, dark and very good looking and charming. Gave us all a royal welcome and a very nice party. Had no sooner arrived than once more we were fortunate to be spoken to by the most delightful couple. Strangely enough I had taken an instant liking to her as we all queued at the Shangri-La for taxis. They are English – Hong Kong for thirty-one years. He is RNR and was in command of the Port of Hong Kong. She is exceptionally attractive and charming. They are seriously considering retiring in Vancouver. Hope they do!

The Fancy Dress Parade in the Pacific Lounge was most amusing. Some of the costumes were terribly clever, unique, or amusing – some all three.

21 March

They are always dreaming up some idea to entertain us. This time it was spoil your husband evening. They wore carnations in their buttonholes, we had to buy all their drinks etc. All very silly but it's amazing how everyone enters into the spirit of things. Our bridge turned out to be a change of five partners playing one rubber with each partner. I was terribly nervous at first but finally relaxed and quite enjoyed it. They all play different systems and a weak no trump, but were kind enough to play what I play.

A beautiful sunset on the Indian ocean. A hot day. Met two Canadians who have lived for years in England and even look and sound English. Had drinks with them and then met Norma and Tom to watch the show. With our clocks going back half an hour every night we seem to stay up quite late but sleep like babies.

22 March

Arrived a few hours late due to one engine being replaced. It affected some of the tours but not us. Thought we would have heard from Tim's friend Anton Wickremasingh, but by 11:00 we still hadn't heard anything so walked around the town, which is filthy with beggars everywhere. We got a government guide so he came with us, taxi and all. He hoped we would hire the taxi all afternoon, but we decided our air-conditioned town buses were preferable. Luckily, we were able to join the 2:30 tour, so had a cooling drink and salad for lunch and sallied forth.

The poor and the weather seem to live cheek to jowl, the poverty is appalling. I can't pass them, but the crowds do come if you show any sign of aid. Had tea at the Mount Lairnia Beach Hotel and enjoyed the air, sea and beach with good surf, for half an hour, then on to the zoo. We were terribly impressed with it. Every animal had a clean, well-planned area. We could have spent hours seeing it, along with at least one thousand school children – all in their heavy blue and white, crisply clean uniforms and shiny beautiful teeth and laughing, sparkling eyes. They hooted with laughter at Mort. Children always seem to find his size amazing. It happens all over the world – even France. The show put on by the elephants was superb. There were four babies and big dad and mum – as I figured they were, only naturally by different mums! They performed in a sunken circle, entirely surrounded by children and people, sitting and standing. They did everything, from dancing to playing a mouth organ and obviously loved doing it all, and the hearty applause. The dad picked up the trainer in his trunk and held him in mid-air encircling his waist; also the trainer appeared to put his head in his mouth. The babies were adorable and did almost every trick done by their seniors.

Sailed at 10:00, which we watched and to bed. Dead tired at 11:00.

23 March

Lots of fresh air today. Attended a lecture and slide presentation in the theatre on Djibouti and Safaga Luxor and the Valley of the Kings. They are the most interesting lectures. Informative, beautifully presented; simply pours out to us while the slides are being shown. Wish our grandchildren could be exposed to such a person.

We put our clocks back every night for half an hour, which is a very painless way of arriving finally at Greenwich time. Didn't play bridge today as they were having a duplicate tournament and that is not for us.

Attended a concert in the theatre after dinner and found it very hard to stay awake. Listened to the dance band before going to bed. Had Dover sole for dinner that was delicious.

24 March

Saw some flying fish and three ships. We've been alone on this huge, to us, Indian Ocean, for quite a few days. Mort says we are almost exactly half way around the world right now. It's a strange feeling to be so far away from the family – no news has to be good news, one hopes.

Enjoy all the regulars that go into the pool and sauna at 8:00. A lawyer from Hong Kong and I have a great chat while stewing each morning. One never lacks for someone to talk to at any time.

Played rubber bridge, changing tables at the whim of the director. Made one major booboo. Find the noise somewhat disturbing but know it's good for me.

Mort's throat and glands started up again so we are all tucked away early tonight. Every time he gets rid of it, it comes back again. Maybe a good sleep will do the trick. Not our day! I went to cross my leg and struck my bad knee on the corner of the bridge table. I hope it never happens again. I thought I was going to be ill with the pain and no way could I hold back the tears.

Had our pre-dinner drinks in the Look-out bar tonight and the trio they have up there is terrific. We could have danced up a storm if I wasn't such a crock! Early to bed.

25 March

8:00 a.m. pool and sauna. Good breakfast and to the church service given by the captain in the theatre. Very well attended with a rousing God Save The Queen to round off the service. Sunbathed for over an hour before Mort joined me for a swim. He can't take the sun for more than a few minutes at a time. The pool is 82° and it's 84° in the shade, 130° in the sun. How some people sit out all day is beyond me.

Bridge all afternoon. Lousy cards most of the time. Sat out on deck until 5:45, then up to the Look-out for an hour's Scrabble. *The Jolson Story* was the cabaret. Will be saying goodbye to the Arabian Sea tomorrow, I believe.

26 March

The days are flying by. The mornings particularly seem to vanish so quickly. I was writing letters and cards in my cabin when Mort came in to tell me I could see my first sight of Africa if I hurried. I went up on the bridge area that is permissible at certain times. I was glad I did as I have never seen land anywhere in the world that looked like it. I couldn't even describe it, except that nothing could grow or survive on the land we saw. There was a heat haze settled down for a good hot day. Thank God for a breeze and air-conditioning. Some people stay out covered with oil all day long. Their skin must feel dreadful.

Roweena Lack found us at the pool and invited us to meet them for drinks in the Tiffany Bar at 7:15. It was known as the Black and White Charity Ball in aid of a sunshine bus for Britain's handicapped children. Made a very handsome black and white carnation for Mort's white dinner jacket. Really amazed at how gorgeous they look. The men pretend to be dreadfully hurt and neglected if they don't get one. Really good fun all evening.

Started off to bed and bumped into Tom and Norma, so ended

up in the Carousel Room listening to a very amusing Scot who had the greatest collection of funny stories we have heard in a long time. They raised close to £1,000 by auction, raffle etc. Everyone threw themselves into the spirit of the fundraising evening.

27 March

We entered the Gulf of Tadjura off the western edge of the Gulf of Aden this morning. We then sailed around Musha Island and approached Djibouti from the north. I stayed in the stern the whole time wearing my bathing suit as it was very hot and I could pop into the pool to cool off. The pilot came aboard around 11:00 and we were alongside about noon.

Had lunch and twenty buses, each holding about twenty people, took us on our tour.

Djibouti is situated on the eastern coast of Africa and is sandwiched between Ethiopia to its north and west and the Democratic Republic of Somalia. We drove twenty-five miles to Arta, which is high enough up to command a good panoramic view of the Gulf of Tadjoura and the Day Mountains.

Terrible, unbelievable poverty – indescribable – with goats and cattle all over the streets. It really was an eye-opener. Would love to have bought from the stalls but the begging is such that you can't cope with it so you give up and return to your bus.

It was quite a day, but just a sample of what is to come on Friday.

Bed early! But first a thought: Why can't the wealthier countries teach the poor people to make things that will *sell*. Nobody wants 98 per cent of what they have to sell, so they think we are selfish when we all go ashore hoping to be able to pick up gifts and don't buy anything.

28 March

Awakened this morning in the Red Sea, having left the Gulf of Aden. It's so strange to look out to sea and realise you are doing something that you never thought you'd ever do. It's a wonderful way to learn geography. Yemen on our starboard with Saudi Arabia on the other side of it. Lots of shipping to watch all day. Japanese cars, I was told. Spent most of the day outside, it was such a beautiful day.

Mort has finally started to read a book. He couldn't settle down to one – it's now two weeks tomorrow since we sailed.

Asked Norma and Tom to meet us for drinks. She thinks she is coming down with a cold. Heaven help her Friday if she does as it's going to be a gruelling trip.

Went to a movie, *Without a Trace*. Very good.

Have my nose in a very good book, so this diary will suffer, or letter writing. The book is *The Judgment*, by Ian Messiter. True story.

29 March

Port talk on Athens by Frank Jackson. That should be a lovely day and one to make us want to return. Lots of sun. We don't put our clocks back tonight, for the first time since Singapore.

Invited Wendy and Nick, Roweena and Alan to have drinks with us. The latter were putting a phone call through to their son in England just prior to his departure to Hong Kong for his school holiday break from Charterhouse. Saw a bit of the Cole Porter show. Good, what we saw.

Throughout the day we steamed up the Red Sea, passing Sudan and around 6:00 p.m. we passed the border between Sudan and Egypt. Saudi Arabia is out there too but out of sight.

Bed early, by our standards.

30 March

Big, long day. Breakfast at 6:30 and ashore by tender at 8:30. All our so-called favourite friends, Laks, Calverts, Greenhalgh, Wendy and Nick, all on our bus, and away we went on our hundred-mile drive through a mountain range before crossing the flat Eastern Desert. Picked up a guide at Kania, who never stopped talking and whose voice was very garbled at the back of the coach where we always sit, for Mort's long limbs. So, we didn't glean anything from him. Finally reached the fertile area which is irrigated by the River Nile. The crops being worked by oxen, donkeys and camels. Lots of mosques, temples of Luxor to be seen. Clean countryside.

Finally arrive at Luxor, on the east bank of the Nile, for a brief stop for pictures of the Temple of Luxor. This was built in the most trouble-free time in the history of Egypt. On to the Etap Hotel for lunch and a comfort stop, as it's called, then on to the Karnak Temples. There is no way that I can begin to describe their magnitude. Mort and I simply wandered on our own. It is impossible to retain the information that pours out of the guide and apart from anything else, it's too hot to stand for any length of time. We took quite a few pictures that couldn't possibly do much to portray what we saw. To think such architectural splendour was produced five thousand years ago is mind-boggling. The colours they used still looking as fresh as if it had been done yesterday.

We then boarded a ferry, of which there are umpteen, and crossed the Nile, which wasn't very wide and was clean and colourful. Stepped ashore at the Western Bank to visit the vast City of the Dead. The Pharaohs of the 18th, 19th and 20th dynasties were buried in the Valley of the Kings. Royal consorts and children from the 19th dynasty were buried in the Valley of the Queens, noblemen had their tombs dug at various cemeteries in the foothills.

The three most interesting in the valley were on our agenda. The Tomb of Tutenkhamon was the most famous and was discovered intact, quite by accident, by Howard Carter in 1922. Most of its treasure has been removed to the Cairo Museum. Only the inner mummy case which contains the Pharaoh's mummy remains. It is the smallest tomb in the Valley of the Kings, as the first two chambers are bare. Only the burial chamber is decorated with paintings of religious scenes and inscriptions retaining the vivid colours of the day they were painted! Then to the Tomb of Ramses VI. It had three entrance halls, a further two chambers and corridors, an ante-chamber, and the tomb chamber. Even to dig these tombs out of the rock, built deep down like our undergrowth, must have taken hundreds of workers and man-hours, with no forty-hour week or money being considered. The tomb chamber is one of the most important painted ceilings in the whole valley. Every inch of that immense tomb was inscribed, painted with large and minute paintings, all so beautifully done.

Mort and I passed on the third tomb. I couldn't climb one more step. Next we drove to Queen Hatscheprut's Temple. This is built, or being built, as a series of terraces on a grand peak with colonnades blending in with the grooved mountainside. Very impressive indeed. The Egyptians are an amazing race. We found them friendly and happy.

Back by ferry as the sun was setting on the hill. An amusing shoe cleaner appeared to shine shoes for forty people. Our shoes were white from the sand dust.

Comfort stop! Coach and the three and a half hour drive back to our launch and late dinner, served to all three hundred of us at 10:30. To bed, to bed – all in all a never to be forgotten day.

1 April – UK Mother's Day
Suez Canal Transit

A very special day it was from start to finish. We were the lead ship in our convoy for the first half of our sail north in the Suez Canal. The day was sparkling. Everyone out early and cameras were clicking in every direction. There were ships from every country imaginable, except Canada! Two Egyptian air force aircraft kept roaring over us, soon joined by two more. Although they didn't break the sound barrier, they must have been close to it.

Our heads were spinning on our necks all day and we hated to go below to have our meals in case we missed something. The fertile areas were so green and beautifully groomed. Palm trees lined the canal, all nourished by the Sweetwater Canal which comes from the Nile. The Egyptians have a very efficient way of handling the world's shipping. No hold-ups anywhere. So, our lovely day passed up on the top deck surveying what I would have thought should be one of the 'wonders of the world'.

I wish I had a Xerox machine. Writing letters is hard work, after keeping up a diary.

Vincent Belington's forty-five minute concert at 10:00 was thoroughly enjoyed by Wendy, Mort and me; then to bed. We sailed from Port Said about 8:30 but were not allowed ashore unfortunately, as it looked clean and attractive. There must be fifty ships in harbour with all their lights glowing in the dark. A most spectacular sight.

2 April

On the East Mediterranean, steaming towards Greece. In the early morning we passed between the islands of Kasos and Crete, entering the Aegean Sea. The pools were cooler and there was a bit of wind that you could avoid quite easily if you wanted to. We played rubber bridge and for the first time we had a decent break in the cards, so we weren't ashamed to hand in our cards.

After dinner we went to the cabaret in the Pacific Lounge. We have a new comedian called Mike Goddard who really broke everyone up. Quite one of the most amusing I have ever heard. Hope we see lots more of him.

3 April – Athens

We docked at Piraeus, it's only about five miles from Athens. Our arrival was very interesting. There are ships in this port from all over the world. We had two Soviet cruise ships alongside us all day. There are so many ships they are like a tin of sardines, one beside the other.

We were all bundled out to our coaches at 9:00 a.m. and off for a sightseeing tour and then into Athens and up to the spot where they park the coaches. From there we walked up to the Acropolis.

Another cruise.

We took lots of pictures and the ship's photographer also took two of us up there so, hopefully, we will have some good pictures to remind us of a very exciting experience. It was clear enough for us to get a good panoramic view of Athens. It is a very unusual city, packed with history. The Persians certainly tried hard enough to take it away from the Athenians.

Wendy, Mort and I roamed the streets after lunch and did a bit of shopping in Piraeus. Wished it had been Athens, but we were all too tired to cope with taxis and a shopping spree. We had a lot of fun and we both think Wendy is a very special person. Nick was tucked away in his cabin with a rotten cold. Wendy did a *Zorba the Greek* dance in the music shop as she was unable to make them understand what record she wanted. They caught on very quickly and were highly amused.

Tom and Norma had drinks with us and watched the Greek dancers which were very indifferent and lightly applauded. Mort went off to the music quiz and Tom, Norma and I went for a walk on the dock.

Wakened about 1:45 when the warning went that we would be departing at 2:00 a.m. Put Mort's coat on, drew up the blind and watched all the ships and lights of Athens as we slowly steamed away. It was another very special experience.

The bridge scores went up and Mort and I were second. If I hadn't blown the first hand, we'd have been first!

4 April

Today is our very first cloudy day. The sun tried and tried to get through and did from time to time, so the Mediterranean wasn't Mediterranean blue but English Bay grey. The decks were pretty well cleared all day. Without the sun, it's quite cool outside.

Mort played bridge with Enid, the director's wife, and I bowed out. Looked in on the art class and read. Invited Wendy to join us for a drink and heard all about Nick's fascinating background. Cossack father, English mother. When he escaped from Russia with his friends, they went to Paris and did exhibitions riding horses, Cossack style. Met his wife in Paris, were married and went to Mexico where they had Nick (proper name is Nicola), and lived for eight years, then to England to educate him. At eight he spoke Russian, Spanish and English. She was born in the mountains in South Africa and educated by her mother, rather like the Trika story in *Masterpiece Theatre*.

Watched 'The Best of British' musical show which was very good, particularly the dancing and then went up to the bar and had a brandy with Guy and (?) Willets, forget her name, but she is a 'B' to that darling man, who has had two strokes. It is a very small world to think he grew up almost next door to my first caring person for me and a great friend for fifty years.

5 April

Our first dull day and too cool to walk in the very early a.m., and in fact the whole day was different. Listened to the bridge lecture with Mort at 11:00. I'm sorry I didn't start them long ago, but it's the old story aboard, you can't do everything. The walking, sauna and pool exercises start my days and a brandy and soda finishes it – and I sleep like a babe.

Mort got a partner for bridge and I read and had a perm at 4:15. Finished by 5:30 so played Scrabble with Mort. Wendy and Nick asked us to join them for a drink, which we did, and thoroughly enjoyed their company.

We passed the southern coast of Sicily and Tunisia and are set on a westerly course along the north coast of Africa.

Went to the music recital with the Knotts then had a brandy with them, and to bed. Mort won a bridge prize of one pound!!

6 April

We continued on a westerly course along the North African coastline of Algeria and later in the day, Morseau. A perfectly lovely day which we spent together doing a little of anything, except sun, reading and bingo. Scrabble and deck chatter. Met John and Diane Peacock and were invited by Alan and Roweena to have cocktails with the four of them, to celebrate Roweena's 52nd birthday. They are all so interesting. Feel sure it won't be too long before Roweena and Alan will visit Vancouver.

Clocks back half an hour for the last time.

7 April

Got up at 5:00 a.m. hoping that Mort could see Gibraltar, but binoc's and much squinting couldn't penetrate the darkness, although we were only five miles south of it. We then started our passage through the straits. We approached Tangier from the north and were alongside at 8:00. Had breakfast out on the Lido. I made a big booboo. My purse slid off my shoulder and struck a silver jug of milk. It went flying! The young lad that is the assistant head dining steward gave me a bad time all day and was quite amusing. I've never seen so much milk.

Our tour left at 9:00. We were in a van with a good driver and nine passengers altogether. Wendy and Nick were with us, which was fun. The dock-side was rapidly turning into a row of shops – dresses, bags, brass, jewellery – everything one could think of and a beautiful display of flowers – sweet-peas, Calla lilies, stalks of freesias, marigolds, etc. Huge bunches for one pound. It wasn't long before we realised how very much we were going to enjoy our three and a half hours.

The city itself is so well laid out and they have metal flower shapes, crowns and different designs that are attached to the light standards and are quite large. Each one is outlined in little lights.

I would so love to see it at night, they must be beautiful. Tangier really appealed to me. It's so clean and the people are not pushy or persistent in their selling, like so many places we have been to.

The residential area is beautiful, with palaces and residences of the King's relatives. They all have guards at their gates and immense magnificent homes, mostly white. I'm not sure what they are constructed of. The rolling North African countryside was spotlessly kept. We stopped briefly at Cape Spartel to admire the view. Seven miles of perfect beach and surf, but we were forewarned there is a bad undertow. I didn't go down into the caves of Hercules with Mort – and apparently it was very dull compared to New Zealand.

We then left our coaches and walked through the Kasbah and the old Harem Gardens, finally coming out of the maze of narrow streets and lanes to find our coaches waiting to take us back to the ship.

After lunch and a drink, Mort had a cat-nap and Wendy, Nick and I went ashore to look over the wharf market. These jaunts have to be experienced and the more times you do it the better you get at bargaining, which must be done. I did very well this time. Got Mort a brass elephant to remind him of our trip and Sri Lanka elephants. Dromedaries for the three boys.

8 April

Weather beautiful. Finally got an appointment for a perm which hit the bridge time, so Mort played with someone else. We are cruising within sight of the Portuguese coastline and saw the most westerly point of Europe where Norman, Jane, Mort and I stood and the little boy's hat blew off and we were all terrified he was going to leap after his prized possession. Fortunately he didn't or that would have been the end of one hatless little Portuguese boy.

Terribly impressed with the salon below. I was in and out (wet) with the best perm I've ever had in years, in one hour!

Dolphins played around us for a while. Seagulls, of course, and even a flight of homing pigeons that were banded and beautifully coloured, and one of them surprisingly tame.

We were asked to have a drink with Wendy and Nick. They are such good company. Dinner and a show that wasn't really very good. First roughness we've felt, so packed one case.

9 April

Bay of Biscay, and calm seas once more. Mort and I got some order into our packing and were amazed that there was no problem. I'm sure he never dreamed I would get it all in. Bags had to be outside our doors by 6:00, with only carry bags left and our travelling clothes on us.

Had noon drinks as guests of Monica and Brian Beckett from South Africa. He is the end, but she is delightful, and liked their friends.

Sunny day that we all made the most of. Sauna closed when I went down at 8:00.

Joined Wendy and Nick for farewell drinks before dinner and a visit with Roweena, Alan, Diane and John, all so nice. Addresses being exchanged with our newly-acquired friends.

Neither of us particularly hungry and ended up going to a movie which we shouldn't have done as we missed the best entertainment since Singapore. Tom and Norma had been looking everywhere for us and we had totally forgotten that they had asked us to join them for a drink after dinner. Probably because we don't, as a rule, drink after dinner, we never gave it another thought. When they spotted us coming out of the film they called us to have a nightcap. We felt very badly, naturally.

Can't believe we will be sailing up the Solent at 6:30 tomorrow morning.

Highlights in England were many. The Boat Train was waiting on the wharf for us to board and everything fell into place. No trouble getting a redcap or porter and cab. A royal welcome waiting in our No. 16, 22 Jermyn Street. Flowers and masses of mail. Wonderful to hear at long last that all was well.

Margo phoned, talked to Sonia and will go out for the weekend to Sussex.

I didn't keep my diary, so nothing will be in order, highlights only.

The Embassy (Iran) rally ended in the shooting from within the Embassy of a British policewoman. As the rear of the Embassy faced the front of our hotel, we were totally involved in the whole affair. Police with guns held at the ready were everywhere. Bullet-proof vests were worn at all times. Two police officers came into our rooms, probably to look us over as I had been standing on the window seat looking out at all the activity. They said to keep away from the windows and throw ourselves on the floor if there was any further shooting. We certainly were fortunate to be spared that.

We weren't allowed to return to our hotel after we went out the first time, but finally got through the barricades around 6:00 p.m., in time to get dressed for the theatre.

Speaking of theatres, we saw *Cats*, which was superb. Also, *The Aspen Papers*, *Run For Your Life*, a *Pack of Lies*, and *Evita*.

Home sweet home.

Our trip: Vancouver to Hong Kong (air)
From Hong Kong we sailed on the South China Sea through the Malacca Straits to Singapore. Across the Bay of Bengal to Ceylon,

the Indian Ocean and Arabian Sea to Djbouti. The Red Sea to the Mediterranean. The Atlantic Ocean to the Bay of Biscay to the English Channel to Vancouver by air.

Sea Princess Cruise: September 1987

12 September 1987

Can't think why I stopped writing my diary as it was a fabulous holiday filled with interest. Having neglected to keep a diary of our *Royal Princess* Cruise from San Francisco to San Juan, I don't dare miss again or my picnic friends will be most annoyed.

Marta Friesen picked us up at the house and a sad, sad Kate and Selma were there to see us off. Drove right to the dock and boarded immediately so we could get some unpacking done before going on deck to see the family. Crozier, Susie, Graham,

Mort and Johnnie, Sea Princess *cruise.*

Guy, Ryan and Christie were all there and Graham had made one of his banners with his computer, reading as follows (with a beautiful ship at each end): HAVE A GOOD TRIP. He had only just finished a massive affair for my birthday and it must take quite a time to produce such masterpieces.

The sun came out briefly as it has done off and on since we sailed from Vancouver, therefore didn't look as beautiful as she can in brilliant sunshine.

We were all settled in by 7:00, so had a stroll to see all the changes since the seventeen million dollar renovation. Was to find next morning, a vast change in the indoor pool, gym and sauna rooms. They have separated us from the men, which is sad. That is where I met the most delightful people. Everything looking very comfortable and nicely decorated – low-key, soft colours, and comfortable deck and indoor furniture.

Dining steward is from Rome and the busboy from Mexico and

Cruise.

the one that makes a great fuss over me is a section head, we gather. He makes the best Crêpes Suzettes I have ever tasted.

Barbara Burns Sturgess and husband are aboard, along with Don Lauder and his wife, all of whom are going to Honolulu.

As of this morning we are seven hundred and forty miles from Hawaii, so we are well on our way.

I go to bridge lessons every morning and Mort and I have played in two tournaments and won first prize both times – Mort's brilliance, without a doubt.

We have the same Captain as we had when we sailed in the *Royal Princess* through the Panama Canal, Captain John Young, by name. Most amusing and attractive, and makes the best speeches.

Arrived Honolulu and rented a car. I drove, Mort map-read, and off we went to familiarise ourselves with the route to Diamond Head and Micheles, where we were to take the Cathcarts for dinner. One way streets predominate so we were very careful. Lovely, hot day, so we drove out to the golf course and eventually to the ship for lunch. Jack and Allison joined us in the afternoon after we made our arrangements to change our cabin. Our drive wasn't too inspiring but they are good company.

Back at 4:00 and then the move. Why do I bring so many suitcases? The only things I forgot were a spool of black thread and one of Mort's sweaters. Packing and unpacking are not my favourite indoor sport.

Off to Micheles at 6:30 and to precede dinner with a phone call to Susan. Fortunately, she answered the phone and was as excited as I. It is such a joy to be able to talk to those you love when you feel so far away. All well at home, thankfully.

Micheles was all and more than we were told it would be. Perfect day with the water lapping just below. Boats of all kinds and colours, beautifully flowered throughout with candlelight. The service was perfection. We all had Caesar salad which was delicious and paka paka steamed in a champagne sauce, served in its entirety across the lower portion of the hot, attractive platter. The fish was covered with the sauce and decorated with skinless halves of grapes. The evening was a huge success and everyone was on deck to see the lights of Honolulu fade into the distance.

The week passed at sea. Two birds, one on deck briefly resting, flying fish, much smaller than those seen in our *Bluenose* Caribbean sail. One ship was spotted by some and a few jet streams. Otherwise, the South Pacific Ocean was ours!

Made more friends. A delightful Englishman – around forty, named Phil Baldwin, who we would meet for drinks and all talk our heads off, naturally about our travels and England, or Charles, the young enthusiastic English bar steward.

Perhaps one of the highlights was Mort and I winning first place four times at bridge, ending up with two large trophies! The family are going to expire when they see them, if I can squeeze them into our luggage. I attended bridge lessons every day and hopefully I have benefited, although at times Mort isn't quite sure!

Kobe, and farewell to some very nice people. They went their way and we boarded our coach to take our three-hour tour. The highlight was a typical Japanese garden. It was very beautiful, with one white duck sitting on a rock. Also visited a sake brewery and its museum and a shopping mall. Prices are very high and Kobe on the whole did nothing for any of us.

Meant to say we had open sitting for dinner that night and two couples were put at the table we were given as ours was already occupied. They couldn't be more fun or delightful. Vilma and Bob John and Maureen O'Sullivan. John is as naughty and delightful as only an Englishman can be.

27 September we celebrated our fifty-first anniversary, as at home it is the 26th. We kept it quiet as possible but it was a special

night, being the Captain's cocktail party, which we topped off with a bottle of champagne. Didn't feel like the cabaret show so went to a Paul Newman film. Mort couldn't keep awake so we toddled off to our cabin. Had to be up early to tour Nagasaki.

Can't begin to say how much I like Nagasaki. It's a clean, friendly, attractive city and everyone felt happy with our tour. We climbed one hundred steps and had two elevator rides to reach a park, the centre of which was where a prison had been. There was a magnificent sculpture of a man holding one arm up to the sky where the bomb came from and the other arm stretched forward to peace. I hope my pictures come out. It is a huge white sculpture. At the other end were beautiful fountains of water, representing the thirst for water the victims had. I will write about the children later.

Mort being so tall attracted the schoolgirls in a most amusing way. They would gather together in a group, point at him and giggle uncontrollably. Finally, one of them worked up the courage to ask him to pose with her for a picture. Being the good sport he is, he agreed, never dreaming he was opening the gate to all the girls clamouring to also have their pictures taken! They were such an attractive group, with glistening white teeth and sparkling black hair, well cut and styled uniforms that made them an impressive group. Have often wondered how many of them kept his picture framed in their bedrooms.

Our trip:
Sea Princess from Vancouver – Hawaii, Japan, Korea, Hong Kong.

To Dad/Mum, Dad Mort/"G", Mort and Johnnie.
Married for 60 years!

A <u>very special</u> occasion for our toasts & cheers
September '36 brought you both to Church
And for 6 decades you showed us how it's better – not worse
Soon after that the war years began
Taking you over to dear old England
With Dad at sea and Mum ashore,
Those times apart couldn't lessen L'Amore!
Six years later - the war now over
It's time to return to your Vancouver.
From Aylmer to Kelly Douglas & Super Value
35th, 54th, 33rd and Matthews Avenue
St. Mary's, Children's Hospital, painting & flowers –
Mort, the years just don't have enough hours!!
Wonderful Summers & times spent at Pt. Cowan
Finds "Tall" down at Russels, alias "Boys Town"
Long week-ends of Bridge, Crib and Gin Rummy
"I'll be home soon, girls, go and tell Mummy!"
From newly weds to parents – then Grandparents of four
Quiet changed meaning when they'd burst through the door.
Many stories & memories too numerous to mention,
Now brings many friends & your family to this question!
Soooo – when are you going to start acting

like an old married couple?

Composed by Susan for our 60th dinner party celebration.

Journey to Britain,
May-June 1998

Sadly, leaving a huge void in my life when Mort died, I will make my first solo holiday which is as follows.

18 May 1998 – Day 1

Susie and Crozier arrived to pick me up, followed by Isabel Lockridge, who will stay with Kate and Sophie. Felt simply awful walking out on them and hate to miss Sophie's precious antics. Kate had it all figured out – crept into bed with me for the night with Sophie pressed tightly to me on the outside, so not too much sleep.

Started the day by being at St Vincent's Emergency to have my second antibiotic intravenous. (I walked against a lady's umbrella that she had sticking out as she examined a container of food in Safeway. It became infected.) They were wonderfully kind and generously gave me all the dressings I will need.

Sad farewell to my darling Susie and Crozier.

Wonderfully comfortable seats in Canadian business class but had to up-end my small case and put a little pillow on it so my leg would be up. Got restless but nice Caesar and lunch was very good.

Toronto is *huge*. Beautiful highway (five lanes in and out); good driver. Plaza is a lovely hotel. Message from Ernle and John Belyea. Phoned Anne Fitch Stevens and she will come in tomorrow with her niece – no, won't see Ernle unfortunately.

John will pick me up and take me to Susan and Chris's for dinner. Will meet William and Spencer.

Don't feel hungry, so skipped dinner – should have had a drink but with the three-hour difference, I never even thought about it. Now 11:55 new time. Ready to read a bit and, hopefully, sleep. Leg okay.

19 May

Awakened before the birds, so watched TV and read. Dropped off and slept until 9:15. Several chats with Ernle and Lindy and both have me delighted with my change in plans. On the Saturday I return to Toronto from Ottawa, Ernle will meet me at the train and we both will stay at Esme's and I will taxi to the airport Sunday. Next, Lindy and Ken are driving me to Stoney to meet Anne and we will have lunch *en route*. Wonderful!

Anne Stevens and Laura arrived as planned at 12:00 and we had a long lunch with much conversation. Laura then went shopping and we sat in my room and talked steadily for an hour. Anne is a precious old lady with the same lovely smile and complexion. Sad to think I will never see her again. She is eighty-nine.

John picked me up to take me to Susan and Chris's for dinner. Chris, Susan, William and Amanda greeted us very warmly, along with their enchanting son Spencer. Their house is quite unique and attractive. Drinks and dinner were delicious. Liked Chris very much. William is a going concern and a little shy with me but loved him. Look forward to their visit next year.

Back around 10:00, asleep by 11:30.

20 May

Up very early and up to the roof for breakfast. Amazing what they charge for orange juice, boiled egg, toast and coffee!

Ready and waiting for Lindy and Ken who arrived at 10:15,

having so kindly volunteered to drive me to Stoney Lake. They are a super couple who obviously enjoy each other. We had an excellent lunch and a weird and crazy drive as the roads weren't properly marked and we back-tracked in many places. Finally arrived at the proper marina and located Anne. She had changed as much as I have, but the same wonderful person.

Hated to say goodbye to Lindy and Ken. I did so appreciate all they had done for me.

Heaved my luggage into the whaler, mostly done by Anne, and off we went, wending our way through all the islands. Passed Headlands and Mother's 'Tree Tops', now owned by Libby – Anne's eldest – that Granddad built for her to persuade her to come east no doubt, with us – Bill and me.

Anne's charming house cat, Misty, greeted us, with Faerie Lake in all its glorious splendour weaving its size into little bays and coves, with a beaver enjoying his life in the water. Lilies by the hundreds. Pine trees of every size and shape abound by the lake and Anne is the Lady of the Lake, having the only house on it. I try to imagine mother, Elizabeth (the three Irwin sisters being Elizabeth, mother of Anne, Aunt Anne – who died when she was forty, no children – and my mother Evelyn, or 'Eve', mother of my brother Bill and me), swimming and playing here. It is a solitary sanctuary.

Anne opened a bottle of champagne and we drank to our past, present and future. To bed reasonably early. The leg not so good.

21 May

Off to Peterborough to check in with Dr Wilson. Expose it to air and up when possible. Purchased good bandages in case of trouble. Took Anne for lunch. Very good.

Anne performed miracles in the microwave, even to boiling her water, to say nothing of everything else – meaning porridge!

Anne shocked to find a raccoon had opened the door to Steph's house. (Behind her, but on Stoney Lake.) He had made chaos out of her kitchen. Cereal boxes devoured, even the stove was vandalised by the animal. Anne disappeared in the afternoon to clean up.

22 May

Drove from the landing to Peterborough early enough to go to her beautiful apartment to rest prior to meeting a super group of friends at the restaurant for a drink and dinner. Did some shopping a good boat ride from here. Super sandals, some Christmas gifts, to say nothing of wonderful furniture at respectable prices for Cowan's, if it ever materialises.

23 May

Another beautiful day, just the right temperature. Faerie Lake reflecting trees and stone with the occasional ripple from a jumping fish. The birds swoop and swallow a bug or a drop of water. Otherwise gentle shimmers of light and shade. If I never saw anything for the rest of my life I would always have this glorious place to think about.

Time flies.

(Our mother was half-owner of Headlands and the lake but sold her share to Anne's mother as we never had used or would use it. Three thousand miles to travel was a great deterrent, plus the electrical storms that Mother hated.)

Saturday – Theatre and Dinner Night

The day flew, with Anne's skinny-dip and a trip down the lake past all the big and very little islands – some really minute with quite good-sized trees growing from the crevices in the stone. Port and starboard lights line the way through the islands because of the stone throughout the lake. The houses are beautiful and all have their own boathouse with various types of boats pulled up or tied to the wharves.

Decided to drive to Peterborough early enough to have a rest after a brief stop for film before crossing the street to meet Anne's friends at the restaurant. They were all charming and friendly; liked them very much. Had a drink and an exceptionally good seafood salad after a gin, which was a really good drink. Were driven to the theatre by Bill Hamilton and wife who I had met in Vancouver.

The play was *Beyond the Fringe*, a British satirical review at the Lakefield School of Fine Arts. I found Brian Jackson hard to hear. The pianist, Richard Hayman, was very talented. Thankfully Anne felt as I did at intermission, so we departed, knowing we had an hour ahead of us to reach Faerie Lake, in the dark.

Didn't realise what a difference there is in our mobility, but climbing in and out of the whaler is not an easy feat for 81s! Fortunately Anne handles her boat like Drue did hers and we docked safely at her wharf. Lovely night with masses of stars and every island silhouetted against a brilliantly clear sky. The battery light we used for the walk up the hill and through the woods petered out and I was afraid to take a step in case I fell. Anne said to stay where I was and she went up to the girls' house and put on their spotlight for me, so the elderly guest got up the steep wooded path safely, thanks to my very special 'Cuzz'.

24 May

George Baird, who bought Headlands, invited us over for coffee at 10:00, so we boated over. It once more gave me a strange and marvellous feeling to go through that unbelievable house – which they called their 'cottage'. Room after room I was shown, with the old original furniture, even to a beautifully upholstered chair with the original leather. I saw the sideboards, dining room table, chairs, dishes, lamps, desks and dressers and beds. Rocking chairs on the huge verandahs which stretch across two stories of the front of the house. Took pictures of what I could including the original outdoor bathroom with a commode (quaint and pretty) and the old water tank and tap.

Sat around with coffee for about an hour and then home. Hope my pictures come out well. Am sure Anne must be bored with my enthusiasm for all of Stoney Lake and Faerie Lake history that I lap up. It is so different for her, she grew up here. Mother couldn't bring herself to leave our Vancouver summers for the heat in the east. She hated lightning and thunder storms and the heat and flies they apparently had during the summer.

Had a gorgeous dinner which Anne cooked to perfection. Atlantic char and fiddleheads that Roma Henderson brought us by freezer box. We will have the other half tomorrow. Roma and her husband Hendy drove all the way from New Brunswick, with a stopover to visit other friends, to have lunch with Anne and me. Roma was on my Canadian Wrens OTC. I am so very fond of her and Hendy is a most likeable person.

Anne went to bed early and I watched a Canadian film depicting the Japanese after the war in Canada. Wish I was going to see the Canadian series on the war that starts next Sunday when I depart. Talked to Susie which was great.

25 May

Called the doctor early to see what he could do for my latest problem. Prescribed medicine which meant poor Anne had to take me to Lakefield to pick up a prescription. Just about the last thing she needed. However, we enjoyed it once we got going and the boat ride was smooth and not windy. Saw Bill on the dock and asked us to drop in at their island. We didn't, as the timing was wrong, but his wife Elaine (?), called while we were having dinner, so we are going to have a drink with them tomorrow at 5:30.

Had a rest on our return – wrote some thank you letters and talked to Isabel. Says she doesn't think Kate likes her. If not, it won't be easy for her as Kate can take skunners to people. Sophie being over-fed, I fear, but here I am and there are they! Doubt if she will ever brush them but will suggest it.

Lovely dinner, bit of TV which neither of us could hear, so opted for bed.

26 May

Another beautiful day. Unfortunately my film has expired so can't keep up with all the changing colours. The lake never looks the same from hour to hour.

Half an hour by Anne's whaler, in and out of all the beautiful islands; we drew alongside Walter and Wendy's very nice dock and were greeted with bear hugs from Walter. Wound our way up the hill to their winterised beautiful home. Wendy greeted us and after a few minutes had a long cold drink in our hands. I couldn't begin to describe their house. I adored their new edition which was beams and cedar panelling and huge windows overlooking the islands. Walter is a great sailing man and was very interested in our *Bluenose* charter, so I will send him the video and two diaries. They are such a nice couple who obviously are very happy. It would be nice if they moved from Maple Bay to Cowan's Point but it will doubtfully ever happen.

Wendy had prepared a gorgeous lunch – shrimp, rice, peppers and mushrooms in a heavenly flavoured sauce, strawberries and blueberries with a delicious yoghurt sauce and brownies made in the microwave. We had a lovely time and I really loved their house but prefer the Irwin end of the lake.

Got home in time to get our heads down for a nap. Anne did

but I didn't as I really had to get my nose into my packing and washing, then to get ready to go to Bill and Elaine's for a drink. Into the whaler and off we went. It's quite an experience to have to go by boat everywhere.

Very nice visit on their nice enclosed verandah. Two from Vancouver were there that I had met before when they invited Mort and me to a party in Richmond.

Got most of my packing done and then to bed as we leave for Peterborough tomorrow.

27 May – Peterborough

Awakened at 5:00 and that was it, so got up and finished my packing and off we went to Marni's 10:00-12:00 party for her friend from Quebec. Met the man who designed the Pearson College and knew Gordon and Jean very well. Charming couple, both of them. Quite a gathering of all ages and I enjoyed it.

Picked up my films of Kate and Sophie – really adorable of both.

A friend of Anne's joined us for lunch then off to have hair done. Quite happy with it.

Back to the flat to rest with Misty, dear little cat. Dressed and out to have drinks with Don (major-padre). Delightful man who served us his home-cooked macaroni and cheese; and a 'delish' salad. He knew the Ferguson house at Stoney, and Agnes Jeffries and Norman, so phoned him to say hello. Sounded very nice. Knew Granddaddy when he was very young and taken to Headlands.

Tired – VERY!

28 May

Very sad goodbye to my dear, dear Anne, who saw me off at the bus in Peterborough. I had such a wonderful time with her.

The bus drive was so-so. No spectacular scenery and a cranky driver, but it brought me here to be greeted by Judie (Mort's sister's daughter) in Ottawa. Jane very forgetful now. Judie took me to a charming restaurant so we could talk and prepare me for my two days. Picked up an azalea for Jane and she was as happy as I was to finally have a big hug. She really is far more agile and 'with it' than I would have thought, but forgets she has been told something, so there is lots of repetition over everything. Judie stayed until 9:00-ish and made our dinner. A friend came for a drink; an extremely nice person (Flo).

Judie brought in our dinner which was fabulous. Best soup I have ever tasted and was topped off eventually with a fresh fruit cheesecake. After much chit-chat, we got ourselves to bed.

29 May

Cloudy and a bit cooler, which appeals to me. Judie came over about 10:30 and we were driven all through the loveliest areas in Ottawa. Spectacular houses. Quite a bit of tree damage from the ice storms they had from freezing rain. Streets of elm trees are gone. Saw Government House – acres of property well protected, obviously. Bus tours do walk through the grounds. Saw all the lovely Consulate houses and those of Members of Parliament.

Back for lunch. Judie looked after my train ticket and picked it up for me. She has been absolutely marvellous.

Stirling is an awfully nice, kind young man. Brought us both a bouquet of flowers! I feel honoured to be his Godmother.

Had a drink here and then went out for Jane's dinner treat. We had such a nice evening, with a fabulous dinner. Home to look at pictures.

30 May

Judie arrived early to drive me to the train station. Jane all set to go along for the ride. Judie has been absolutely kindness in itself and she leaves tomorrow for her holiday, so she had her hands full with Jane and me to cope with. Poor Jane, she has a combination of a great memory for some things and none for others. Repeats her questions over and over and thinks Norman will be coming at 6:00 o'clock and finally said, 'I wonder why I talk about Norman that way, as I know he isn't with me any more. Do you get along well with Drue?' etc. She says this as she's dancing a merry jig with a loud word-perfect song. Would love to come out to stay with me but I think I would be lucky to survive the visit. We love each other dearly but it's a difficult situation. Judie must nearly lose her wits. Sad farewell to both but awfully glad I came.

Train, four hours, to Toronto. Very well looked after with a Caesar, nuts and chips. Could have had a full lunch but opted for a salad, dessert and coffee. Was happily met by my dear old friend Ernle, and driven to the joyous home of Esme and Earl and two daughters, Caitlin and Lyndsay. Earl is away and I was sorry not to see him again as I thought he was a very special man (doctor). I was terribly impressed with their house, every detail so well thought out and in very good taste. He apparently is the perfectionist. Esme is the President of her advertising company. Attractive and charming. Ernle, of course, is both.

31 May

Became besieged with problems due to my umbrella-stabbed leg. I've certainly run the full gambit with the wretched thing. Suffered a miserable day due to the reverse of my trouble in Stoney and due to the antibiotics I was allergic to. Spent a *bad* night but was grateful I was in Esme's house, not a hotel. Hope it's all over with so I can enjoy every minute with Sonia and Rupert.

31 May

There was a tornado that demolished a town in the States – hit Peterborough and knocked down trees in Ottawa. Esme drove me to a drugstore and branches whirled across the street in front of us and it was all I could do to walk from the car to the store. That is my second encounter with a freak wind, the first being in Papeete with Mort. Fortunately we only got the tail-end of the storm.

Had a nice visit with Ernle who was most kind and considerate about my problems.

Talked to Jane, Isabel, Susan and Crozier, John Belyea and Lindy. All is well and happy to hear Kate is being a little nicer to Isabel. It must be hard on her to adjust when she is so used to me.

My driver arrived right on time and farewells once more. The cost of a limo (small), was only $36.00 – our taxis charge that for much shorter trips. Got through everything in no time, thanks to needing a wheelchair. Not too long a wait to be wheeled aboard. Here's to a smooth, pleasant flight.

1 June

So much for British Air.

We were one and a half hours late taking off and my leg-rest didn't work. I had an alcoholic lad next to me who lay out almost flat, so I was stuck and couldn't climb over him to go to the john. Had a salad which was good, champagne and cheese. Dropped off eventually and the lad came to at last to spring me and he drank scotch for breakfast. Sat on the tarmac for nearly two hours, knowing I would be late for my driver at 9:30. Golf carted a short distance then out on my own, minus a wheelchair. Fortunately I found a redcap for seven pounds who, thank God, stuck by me through the endless wait for the luggage, which he eventually found at a different roundabout. At least three-quarters of an hour

Sonia and Rupert Ross's 50th Anniversary, Poppy and Johnnie.

later, was looking for the driver and fell into each other's arms when we finally did meet.

Nearly a two-hour drive to Sonia and Rupert's, who met us down their driveway. Wonderful beyond words to see them again. They look so well and we non-stop talked. Champagne before and with a delicious dinner. Sonia produced a remedy for my problem, which was a huge relief.

2 June

To Rye for something I wanted to look for and then went to the bank to cash some travellers cheques – finally succeeded at Barclays, who didn't charge me. Took Sonia for lunch at a fish restaurant, which was very good. News came that their Claire had a better bill of health than they expected, which cheered us all enormously.

Lovely dinner. Watched an hour's review of Diana's death.

Tried unsuccessfully to call home – can't seem to do the right thing. Weather a bit rainy and little sunny spells but a complete delight after the heat.

3 June

Rupert drove us to see a National Trust estate which was very interesting. It was finally owned by a wealthy American who donated it in his will to the National Trust. They have spent a veritable fortune on it in restoration.

I took them for lunch, which was a huge success. All enjoyed our lunch. Drove to see Fiona's roses which were fabulous. (Fiona is the daughter of Sonia and Rupert.) We were all a bit weary and had a quiet evening. Will be up early tomorrow.

4 June

Up at 6:30 as we left the house at 7:45 to drive to the Tunnel. What an experience! The car, with us in it, was driven aboard a double-decker train and after a thirty-five minute ride in a well-lit train space, we arrived in France. It was quite unreal. Very silently we took off with little motion at any time, only music and a few instructions. Thought I might feel a bit claustrophobic but, to my surprise, I didn't feel anything.

Picked up a bottle of Scotch for Margo at the duty-free shop. Would like to have bought more things but our time was limited.

Had lunch first, as Rupert and Sonia's guest. He was cross about the general lack of interest shown to us by the staff. Our waitress was a dour, cross looking girl as was the owner of the Auberge. Was disappointed for the most part in the scenery we saw, Calais, etc., flat as a pancake. Pretty geraniums in the flower boxes but for the most part the houses were dull and drab.

Had a terrible time finding our way to the Tunnel but finally made it with a very short wait.

So nice to get back to the beauty of East Sussex. I love the trees and flowers along the narrow roads and the farmland is spectacular.

Talked to Isabel and Susan. Think Sophie must be in heat, she is behaving so weirdly. Hate to have her spayed but will do so on my return. Tired.

5 June – Happy Birthday, Graham (our eldest grandson)

Today is Sonia and Rupert's luncheon. Met Colin and Shirley, both extremely pleasant. It is a very small world. She attended a concert at Strathcona when I was there to see Vera Sharland in it, as she was the daughter of her mother's great friend. Awfully good cold lunch made by Sonia. They left around 4:00 and I cleaned up while Sonia had her hair done.

I took them out for dinner and we all ordered the duck. It was so awful we couldn't chew it. Much to the proprietor's disgust, we turned it back and ordered prawns which were delectable.

Such a sad day tomorrow.

6 June

Mr Headly arrived on the dot of 3:00 and we had a sad farewell. Rupert and Sonia were so kind and hospitable and are such true friends. Sonia and I had a walk to see the house they hope to buy, their present one being no place for older people. The stairs are a disaster. I took great care while there to watch every step I took or it would have been a very serious fall.

The drive to Oxted passed very quickly. Mr Headly is a wonderful driver and a most pleasant person.

Dear Margot, now ninety-one, was at the door to greet me. She looks wonderful; a bit heavier but hardly a wrinkle. We were soon talking ninety to the dozen and time passed quickly. Had a drink, was picked up at 7:00 by her taxi and driven to my B&B, the Croft. Had a quick look and dropped off my luggage and Margot took me to the Plough for dinner. She wouldn't hear of me paying for anything. We had Dover sole and masses of vegetables. I was disappointed a little in the sole as it was not cooked the way I think it should be; naturally said I thought it was delicious.

The taxi picked us up at 10:00 and I came home to my B&B. I like it very much. Such a nice family run it. I have the whole floor to myself, which is very nice. To bed at 11:00.

7 June

Didn't sleep too well due to a duvet – I was roasted, so asked for blankets. Nice breakfast, except for not fresh orange juice which, I think, is the end after what I drink at home.

Was due to be at Margot's at 11:00 so set off to walk, with directions given. Well, I ended up in fields with horses, ponds of ducks, turnstiles and then a huge hill that nearly killed me. Finally I stopped a couple who drove me and knew Margot! My leg evidently didn't take too kindly to all the exercise as it was painful all day.

Had a roast lamb lunch with all the ladies and a wonderful fresh fruit flan. Very lazy day with conversation and TV. Golf and cricket news. Margot gave me such a pretty dress she was tired of – beautiful material.

Back by cab at 9:00.

8 June

Highlight was being able to talk to Susan and catch up on all her doings. Clear as a bell. All well at home and with Isabel. Susan had been swimming so they must be enjoying hot weather. Not so here – coolish with the odd shower. WINDY.

Betty and John drove here to go out for lunch. Margot doing the lunch. I hope to catch up one day before I leave. Had a lazy time after they left. It was very good of John to drive me to Barclays bank to cash some cheques as nobody wants to accept them. Absolutely infuriating. My credit card they will take.

Also talked to Paddy and am definitely going to be with her for a night or two and she may cross over to Ireland with me, which will be wonderful for me. Ian not very well but Paddy says it will cheer her up to see me. It is nice of her to make me feel I won't be too much trouble at this time.

Goodnight to Margot at 9:00, after a very pleasant day. She is amazing for her age. Wrote to Susan Belyea but don't have her address!

9 June

Leslie Todd very kindly drove me to Margot's. They don't trust me to walk there after my fiasco my first morning. Millie Gresham picked us up at 12:30 and drove us to her place. It is such a lovely house. It's my second time visiting. She really is such a nice person and a wonderful hostess. We had a gin and tonic, cheese biscuits and shrimp in pastry shells. Lunch very special with three courses – made me feel I'm a lazy hostess now. Asparagus served with a sauce instead of butter. Had a beautiful salmon mousse, tossed salad and French bread. Dessert was a lemon mould that was topped with crunched cornflakes. Would love the recipe as it was beautiful. She served it with fresh raspberries and cream. Delicious coffee was served next in the living room.

I have invited Millie to stay with me and hope one day before I am too old, she will do so.

Millie drove us back to Margot's where we finally dropped off for forty winks.

Out again to have wine and smoked salmon from 6:00-8:00 with Pat, Margot's very charming neighbour, who I liked so very much seven years ago. She is such an easy person and thoroughly nice. Her apartment was charming. Beautiful things and very attractive in all respects. Was married three times. The first husband was killed after three months of marriage, in the war. Following two died – one a big-shot with PNO and the other equally big in the railway. Wish she would come to Vancouver.

Returned at 9:00 by my taxi.

10 June

Picked up by Margot and her friend David. He and his wife invited us to their place for coffee. They have a very unusual house. It's most attractive with a verandah off their large living room that has a fabulous view of Surrey, Kent and Sussex. Extremely nice family, with a sixteen-year-old granddaughter. Lovely garden. They are driving north Monday and I go by rail Tuesday. David was a great help to me, giving me directions for my trip north. I should go from King's Cross at 12:00 noon and to Stirling which is 5-18 and then to Perth 17-55 by the Highland Chieftain. I will check with Alan and see which is the most convenient for him.

Margot and I joined all the ladies at Abbeyfield House for lunch and some wine. Took one mouthful of the meat – I had liver! If there's one thing I can't bear, that is it. So, enjoyed all the veggies and dessert. The average age must be eight-seven and they are quite a group. Scotty was an undercover agent with the Free French. She is ninety-three and as sharp as a tack and pops around like a seventy-year old. Has asked us for tea.

We donned our sweaters and armed with our 'Macs', we set forth by taxi for the town. Margot bought Susie a gift and so did I. Some very nice shops. Hope my darling daughter likes my prezzy.

Had to walk back which Margot did remarkably well. She really is quite a person, terrible eyesight and two replaced hips, one good and one bad and although she walks fairly slowly, she gets there.

Had our evening drink and a heavenly stuffed smoked salmon cold entrée and a celery root salad.

My cab brought me back at 9:45. If I am tired I wonder how she feels!

11 June

Call from Sonia, found my avocado shirt in the dryer! Fiona has the rest. So ashamed not to have checked that drawer!

Very cold, wet day but luckily we never got wet. This was my day. Roger picked us up and we drove to Reigate. All very changed. The Tunnel was closed to traffic. Went up and down Wray Park Road but our house was either bombed or torn down, as it was all built over. St David's Boys School and playground is now all housing but a street has been named for it. Drove over to 'Little Bats' and although it was there, all the property was covered with houses and the house had been turned into two. What wonderful times we had there with the Evanses (Nimmer and Dood) and Betty Birks, as she was then. Nostalgia really brought the tears in town when I looked up the Tunnel where I walked with my basket every day to shop or have coffee at Robertson's. A police lady was talking to Roger, my driver, and he explained what I was doing, so when I walked up to them, unable to speak, she patted my shoulder and said I should purchase the new book showing how it was and now is.

My little fire station where I was a telephonist the first part of the war is now a huge station on an entirely different street. Redhill is quite unrecognisable, as I expected. Finally wended our way to a very attractive pub for our lunch. All was well until six women took the table next to us and that was the end of our peaceful meal. I have never heard more raucous laughter. The waitress was very upset but what could she do?

Lunch was delicious and I hoped my last meal of the day, but no such luck. Margot had smoked salmon and salad. With so little activity, I can't cope with it.

Went home at 8:45 and the children called on me to say goodbye. They are delightful. Spent the next one and a half hours packing. Can't believe how time flies! Margot will probably live to be one hundred at the rate she is going.

12 June

Had a bad night. Enjoyed my B&B. Such an interesting collection of nice things and furniture. Roger arrived in good time, as usual, and off to Margot's for coffee, then a vodka followed by a delicious lunch. Nice group of women that get along surprisingly well.

Two o'clock rolled around and it was goodbye to dear Margot. Can't believe I will never see her again. Off to London, actually a lovely day at long last. Roger gave me a tape of the nightingales singing as I had remarked to him that Mort and I used to hear them in the church cemetery when we walked from Redhill home to Reigate – so many years ago.

22 Jermyn Street. All settled in and not feeling like budging, so made my calls to Margot, Sonia and Alan. The latter has A.K. and his wife dining with us. It will be wonderful to see him again. We liked him so much.

Ordered my soup and roll as I wasn't hungry – very warm, with fan going full pelt. Must get to bed. Very happy here.

13 June

Here I am on the 16th in Scotland and my London days not recorded. Will try and go back.

I do know I was absolutely zapped. It would have taken a derrick to move me out of my lovely room and bathroom. I revelled in the luxury and comfort to simply relax on my own. Had a lie down and dozed off for a while. Opened the bar at 7:00 and poured myself a drink of gin from one of the many wee bottles. Perused the menu as there is no dining room, only room service. I ordered soup and rolls as I was still far from hungry after the farewell lunch with Margot at her place.

Had a very poor night – far too warm, as usual, so ended up under a sheet.

14 June

Breakfast very light as I really haven't had much of an appetite. Hair appointment with Lizzie Arden who has a salon in Simpson's, or what was. Nice Italian did my hair, only fairly well, and with all the rain, I fear it won't stand up to much. Walked for miles, had lunch and walked some more, finally getting caught in a rain shower. Back to the hotel and changed, rested for an hour and walked again. Had my drink and soup and a roll and to bed reasonably early. Talked to Paddy re next Saturday, also Sonia and Margot. Jackie Roe, Margot's young friend, called me and is driving me wherever we decide to go after church tomorrow.

15 June

Up early and over to see favourite church by 8:00, only to find I was too early – 9:15, so went back to 22 for breakfast, then to church. There were about twenty of us with a female priest who was very worthwhile. Fascinating plaques dating back to the 1700s.

Met Jackie at 11:00 and she asked where I would like to go and I suggested the Spotted Dog, where Mort and I used to go and loved so much. It is in Penshurst and although Jackie used to live there, she didn't know it and would love to go. Finally tracked it down and it hadn't altered a scrap that I could see, in almost sixty years. We had a gorgeous lamb lunch and a drink. It was wonderful to be there again. Jackie was extremely nice and we got on very well. She is coming to Vancouver in September so I will be able to drive her. She is staying in Bellingham for three days so can drive her there.

Quiet night with only an apple for dinner as we had such a huge lunch.

16 June

Much better night. After breakfast I went for a long walk in between rainy spells. Fortunately I can dry my shoes and other things in my lovely, warm, bathroom. The bath plumbing is weird and un-wonderful to me, so I fill my bath with the very hot water half an hour before I need it, then it's just right, but God alone knows how to get cold water!

Walked down to Trafalgar Square and dropped in to Canada House as I wanted to see the Karsch exhibition. He certainly turned out some wonderful pictures. Churchill's was remarkable as was Laurence Olivier's. I swear I covered miles. I could walk forever in England and, of course London. Every street is of interest one way or another. Wish I could have taken in some shows but alone is not for me. I miss Mort terribly. We always saw everything worthwhile seeing, to say nothing of all the good restaurants.

Finally returned to 22 to have my legs up and a few shut-eyes. Margot persuaded me to take only one suitcase and leave the smaller at 22 until I return. Agreed it might be less of a problem, so spent a good time re-arranging and packing. The weather has been so wretched it makes it difficult.

Last night until I return from Scotland and Ireland.

17 June

Arrived at Arden's at 9:00 to have a comb-out, but nobody there so had breakfast and then was told they could take me at 10:00. Breakfast at Fortnum's, which really wasn't all that great.

Checked out and into my cab for Kings Cross. The service at 22 certainly is ★★★★, if not, five. Service personified!

A great little redcap looked after me and my bag, even switched my seat so I wouldn't be travelling backwards. A really nice bright and sunny day, so the country was looking like a well-kept sparkling garden. The fields so immaculately kept. Lots of sheep and lambs. Wished I had had a map to follow the route – went through Peterborough and Stirling, the latter being where Grandfather Ferguson was born.

Had an excellent lunch. I had extremely good tomato soup, salad, shrimp pâté (type?) with chopped up bits and pieces within rolled up smoked salmon and topped with watercress. Lime flavoured mayo dressing surrounded it all. I will be serving that many times in the years to come.

It was a long train trip but I'm glad I did it as I really wanted to see the country. When I came to Newcastle, my thoughts turned to Mort as he had to go there on business in '38 and '39 and part of '40. I swear to God he was with me as my whole body was filled with his spirit – as it has always been with Drue. Nobody can ever tell me our spirits don't live on.

Got some help off the train with my bag and looked around to find Alan walking towards me with a big bear hug. I think I might not have recognised him on the street. Seven years has changed him and only in a natural aging way. White hair instead of black, and heavier, but still the same nice, nice chap.

Quite a drive through beautiful country to my B&B where I was left to settle in. To my joy I discovered a *huge* Himalayan cat who struck up a purring friendship with me. Nice country place and family business. Their daughter breeds King Charles spaniels and they go all over our side of the world.

Alan arrived back at 7:30 and took me to his 'pad', as he calls it. What a gorgeous place it is. The huge top floor of a lovely house set up on a hill with a spectacular view (westerly). I have never in my lifetime seen any view to compare with it. Everything about his 'pad' is beautifully done and in such good taste. Masses of rooms – four bedrooms, dining, beautiful kitchen with table and chairs. He is finishing a book on his experiences during the war in which he mentions Mort and then both of us, after my arrival into the Wrens. Read over some of it and it is a well-written manuscript that Mort would have loved to have read.

18 June

We went for a good drive and walked and walked. There were sheep grazing, with their young never far away, and a huge lake that is their supply of water to Glasgow, etc., nestled in a valley. Gorgeous day and warm in the sunshine. Hope it lasts.

Drove in to the butcher which was, as I remember, mine in '38-'39. Alan bought two beautiful fillets and some ham which, with a glass of sherry, we made into sandwiches, topped off with cheese and biscuits. All very delicious. He is very organised in everything he does, as well as being easy to talk to. We collapsed in the drawing room and dozed off for fifteen minutes.

We then drove to the castle we had tried to visit earlier and found it opens at 2:00. Drummond Castle is really in two parts. The old is only to be viewed from the outside as the steps are so steep it is dangerous. The other half is fully occupied by a family! No admittance of course. However, the gardens are quite incredibly spectacular and I took quite a few pictures. Peacocks are roaming around showing off until you want a picture and then they lower their fans, so I didn't achieve a good one. We debated descending the great stairs leading to the garden and then went, knowing what went down had then to be got back up.

The design of the gardens is taken from the Drummond Arms. I bought a book that describes the gardens. It would be impossible for me to do justice to it. We must have been there about one and a half hours and bravely set foot on the bottom step of the many, many, we had to climb up. Sat briefly on a bench (Lizards Rest we called it on Grouse Mountain, years ago).

Dropped off to recoup and dress for the big event in the evening.

Alan called for me at 5:30 and went to his place for him to have a drink and to wait for Pat to arrive. Took an instant liking to her and we had a drink then went to the meeting of their group to hear General Sir Robert Gow's talk. Before the talk, we went to the ancient library of Bibles, etc., dating back to 1600, all beautifully preserved. The cemetery was filled with tombstones that could barely be deciphered, they were so worn with age.

Proceeded to join the group that by this time had grown to about thirty. Alan introduced me to most of them, all very friendly and charming. Three of us discovered we had all been in the Wrens at the same time so instantly hit it off. As it turned out, we were all invited to the same dinner party and at the house of Jean-Ann, the person that introduced the speaker. Very interesting man who regaled us with the history of Scotland.

Drove to Jean-Ann and Jack's beautiful house and garden, where drinks were served in their upstairs room overlooking their joyous garden and thirty peacocks!

Finally went down for dinner to a huge dining room with a very large table beautifully set with three crystal wine glasses, a heavenly table centre of mixed flowers and candles, etc. Exquisite linen and chandelier.

They have no help, any of them, Alan said. Plates left from our first course of hot tomato-based soup – don't know what else, but very good – were passed to one person and stacked and carried out by the host, Jack. Jean-Ann meanwhile had everything set up on the sideboard and I, as the second guest of honour (the General on my left being number one), was asked to please help myself. There were chicken breasts in a creamy champagne sauce, a huge mousse of shrimp and smoked salmon, tossed salad, and beautiful bread. I enjoyed every morsel.

My two dinner partners, the General and a very nice man who I only got about a ten-minute talk with, got along swimmingly. The General devoted himself almost entirely to me. A great big good looking man in his tartan. We talked about our ideas on the world we are leaving, our grandchildren, travel, Canada, religion and experiences. I did so enjoy him. My other partner had been a prisoner of war by the Japanese in Singapore for three years. Intensely interesting and very easy to talk to. Dessert was lovely but couldn't finish it. Cheese board I also had to pass up. Coffee, liqueurs and conversation flowed. Got home at 12:30. Oliver, the huge Himalayan, joined me and slept on my bed until four, when I went to the bathroom. Never forget this day.

Alan arrived at 10:30 to drive to Scone (pronounced Scoon) Palace, the home of the Earls of Mansfield, in Perth. The drive there was exceptionally beautiful. Vast spaces of finely groomed farmland, well kept cottages and exquisite houses and the odd hotel. Sheep and more sheep, and cattle. Finally arrived and parked with a fairly nice walk to the palace, sprinkled all around by peacocks. We were met by a charming, beautifully spoken volunteer who directed us and described the history of her area. I bought their book which has better pictures than mine will be, I feel sure, so I won't go into details here. Suffice it to say I was overwhelmed by the collections of treasures – furniture, pictures, cabinets of china etc. There were pictures around of the Mansfield family, all handsome and outstanding.

We both felt we could have spent a day there and never have seen it all, but as Pat had invited us to have lunch with her, we cut it to an hour and a half. The drive there was once again superbly pretty. Thousands upon thousands of fir trees are planted everywhere. It is the livelihood of the landowners and they are packed together in great squares or oblongs and as healthy and systematically placed as it's possible to imagine. Being a brilliant day, everything stood out. I have run out of all adjectives.

Finally arrived at two large cattle gates which I opened and closed (nothing like our gates) and proceeded on a horse and buggy type of road and ahead of us was a cow that was obviously heavy with calf. She gave a few harried trots and realised she couldn't do more. She moved over once and as soon as we started to pass, she did a quick turn in front of us. Alan commented, 'There is only one animal more stupid and that is a sheep.' After about ten minutes she found a place a bit roomier and we sailed by. Pat awaited us and my ooh's and ah's left me speechless. Her stone house is in two parts, set up above the River Tay. It is across from fields, a castle and huge hills (or baby mountains!). She is quite the most intelligent female I have ever had the privilege to meet. The main house was changed by her design and we were ushered into her huge kitchen with an immense work table in the centre. There was a three-oven Aga cooker serviced by gas, with a tank buried at the foot of her garden, a refectory table and separate chairs in the dining area, windows, all with a nice view, sea green slate floor and partially painted white walls. A gem. Saw the formal drawing room, big hall and a staircase that went part way up and then divided into two with a turn off to the right to the guest room en-suite. On the left lay the master en-suite. Every window had a view, as I said before.

We sat outside and had a drink then went in for lunch. Delicious bowl of vegetable beef soup and wonderful bread, then a salad topped off with cheese, followed by coffee.

After lunch she took me over next door to what once had been a barn, converted into a guest and children's house. She had found most of the furnishings including old-fashioned bath tubs. The dining room table was about seven feet long and opened up on both sides to show the seed dividers. The chairs had little cubby-holes at the back of them that the children could put their crayons or little toys in. Running along both concealed sides were tunnels for the children to play in. They were opened from both sides and were lighted so they wouldn't be frightened! I totally fell in love with it.

Finally tore ourselves away and had a light supper and home by 10:00. All in all a marvellous day, topped off with a long talk with Susan and a few words with Crozier. Clear as a bell. Have my seat changed, I'm happy to say.

19 June

Last day, which is sad as I really have had a marvellous time. Alan has driven me in every direction, two castles and a palace. Today, to Stirling Castle. Grannie Irwin's ancestral home. Never thought I would ever see it. Really a lovely city and so old. Not raining but very misty. Stopped to buy veal for dinner with A.K., peapods, asparagus, French bread, new potatoes and fresh strawberries, which all turned out beautifully. Also went to a glass blower's that was fascinating. Both collapsed when we returned from Stirling Castle, having had a shandy and a sandwich outside a pub – the former being in an incredible Marks and Spencer's!

A.K. arrived quite late for dinner, so enjoyed seeing him again. He is the head of the Argyll Regiment now and lives and breathes his enthusiasm. Have yet to meet Carol, but hope they will both come to Vancouver when they are moved to Virginia in November.

Cooked Veal Scalopini, asparagus, peapods and new potatoes for them and we sat down to dinner in grand style. Alan is now so capable and organised to the hilt. I didn't realise Kirsteen died four years ago, so he says he has mastered cooking and has a lady who cleans and irons for him, at which he draws the line.

Although I like the family that run and own my B&B, I shall not be sorry to move out. King Charles spaniels yap their heads off when they are in their day kennel and all the doors are slammed and would literally rock my bed.

Such a nice lady next to me for breakfast, waiting for her newly bought house to be available to her. Knowing I was very much on the go, told her daughter about me and the message came back if I had any laundry, she would be more than happy to run it through for me!!! I declined with profuse thanks.

Am waiting to be picked up by Alan to drive to Inverary, where we meet Paddy Stewart for lunch, then Alan will drive back on his own. It seems dreadful but he says it is a beautiful drive. It is a cloudless, heavenly summer day so once more I am blessed with a super one.

21 June

Must get Pat's name and address. Had a call from Jean-Ann saying how delighted she was with my planted hanging basket.

Our drive to Inverary was, as told, very beautiful. I really am amazed at the spacious farmland there is and how few houses and people.

Alan is a real tour director, knowing where and what to look for and seemed so enthusiastic to see it all again. We made very good time, no nervous moments as he is an excellent fast driver.

As we were early, we went for a walk around the shore and by the time we got back to the George, Paddy was there looking almost the same after seven years. Had lunch and a drink and as I thought, they knew nearly all the same people! After lunch we ambled back to the cars, moved my bags from his to hers and had a hug and two cheek kisses with a thank you from Alan for giving him such a happy interlude. I certainly loved my time there and am so grateful to him and all his friends.

Made amazing time driving to Campbeltown due to Paddy's very good driving and not too much traffic. Very nice scenery. Arrived about 4:00 and both had a rest. She must have been very tired after a four-hour stint of driving on curvy roads. Had a very brief few words at that point, with Ian, but a nice chat later. He is such a kind, gentle person.

We dressed and drove miles out along the coast, hoping to be able to see a beautiful sunset from the restaurant, but it was not to be; it rained quite hard. As it turned out Ian and Paddy were terribly disappointed as there were two huge dinner parties and their raucous laughter made it totally impossible to hear. Finally took off to a bar table where they agreed to serve us. Rear Admiral Robin and Betty Mayo joined us. They are such a nice couple, he particularly. I had had dinner at their lovely home seven years ago.

After our late dinner, to my utter amazement, they were invited back to the Stewarts for coffee and a brandy. Unheard of in Vancouver. Paddy must have been bushed by bedtime, around 12:00.

Breakfast at 8:40. Very good night in my lovely guest room overlooking the bay, the same room I had slept in before.

We looked at some of my pictures and then goodbye to dear Ian. Off we went to the dock to board the Seacat to take us to Ballycastle, where Winkie is to meet us. She didn't know Paddy would be with me for a one-hour visit before her return journey. They hadn't seen each other for fifty years, with one exception, my luncheon, years ago in London. Wonderful to see Winkie again. She looks very much as she did when in Vancouver. Such a lovely, easy person. We proceeded on to our hotel for the night. Nice hotel overlooking the ocean and many children on the beach. Had a good rest and got together for a drink and dinner, after which we went for a walk and watched the boys trying to surf. Luckily, got nearly back before it started to rain quite hard, and we weren't dressed for it.

Winkie off to bed early so have been able to catch up on my diary. Tried to phone Paddy but didn't call properly. Can't believe I am back in this beautiful country. It is so kind of Winkie to have me. I do hope I won't wear out my welcome. I really shouldn't be here so long but it just seemed to happen that way in trying to tee up dates.

The Duffus Celebration in Duffus, Scotland – June 2000

A LITTLE TARDY in starting writing this on 28 June instead of the take-off day, the 26th. Lucky to get away owing to bronchitis, but so far so good.

I'm settled in Elgin, six miles from Duffus, in a beautiful old house on Duff Avenue which is a B&B. I am very comfortable except for the lack of my own telephone. There is a pay phone in a cupboard on which I waste money through my ignorance.

Really sad saying goodbye, but very content to leave home and the cats are with Mary Foster. They will soon adjust and be happy. Graham drove me out and Alexia arrived for a quick hug. I heard that Cal had upped me to First from Club. The most caring stewardess adopted me and we got along famously. Managed to lie out and had about three good hours sleep. Ended up at the Royal Auto Club, which was very nice in most ways. Will not be there when I spend two nights in Glasgow prior to training south.

Snapped into action so I could catch the 10:10 train to Inverness. Not a redcap anywhere these days. Driver got me a cart and loaded it for me, so pushed it to Information to ask for help – this I got, finally. Ushered into a small first class which only had room for about ten people, all of whom were wonderfully nice, one couple in particular, who were also going to Elgin, so ended up by carrying all my bags with theirs. New Zealanders. Have their card; hope to see them in Vancouver one day. Arrived about 5:00 at my B&B on Duff Avenue! Really very happy, mother and two great-granddaughters and dog. Only have breakfast here.

Sleep doesn't seem to come easily, probably because we dine so very late and I am either too hot or cold, as the latter is what it has been. Ten degrees and a wind that cuts right through you. Thank goodness I do have three good sweaters with me. Today, Thursday 29th, I was taken to the tragic battlegrounds staged by Bonny Prince Charlie and his ill fed, under supplied army with no up to date war equipment. The drive in a coach was beautiful – field after field of plump, well-fed cattle and sheep. Except in the small towns or villages, you never seem to see anybody, much less a cat or dog. Quite incredible to me. Finally got back, had a rest and then joined Lorna and Grace for dinner. Had a talk with Susan.

Am now well settled in Douneside and I never seem to have time to write it all down while it's fresh in my mind.

Saturday – Canada Day – was very special. In the morning I walked to the cathedral as I had arranged to meet Lorna and Grace there at 12:00. Meantime, they had been offered a lift to Duffus for the three of us, so missed seeing the Holy Garden which I had been so strongly recommended to see. Only caught a glimpse of some dedicated ladies working in the bit of the garden I could see; met up with the nice couple that drove us. Arrived a bit early at the Community Centre, but finally the Duffuses arrived about 1:00, I think, and we then went in a coach to drive to the Duffus Castle. No rain, fortunately, as we were out for hours. There were flags of every country attending, except nobody had brought a Canadian one which we were sad about. The best we could do was wear our Canadian flag badges. One lady had about one hundred of them which she passed around. One extremely nice couple from St. Louis asked if they could wear one so people would be nice to them. We were duly walked through a cattle gate and trailed ourselves up and up and up to the Duffus Castle. I did so wish Mort and family east and west could have been with me as it was very exciting. There were Duffus pennants flown as well as the flags brought by David, the wonderful David. Guests of honour were now the owners of all the land for miles around. Speeches by David to welcome all attending, also from the guests of honour.

After all the fanfare came the contest. The tallest Duffus, 6'7", won. Look-alikes – I had spotted a young 16-17 year-old who reminded me in so many ways of Graham when he was young, only our 16 year-old was much better looking! But there was the back of his head, chin, expressions and ears that were Graham's. David had him come and stand beside me and our pictures were taken. David was very impressed by our family crest brooch as in all his research he had never seen an old one – so he had me display it and all interested came to look at it. I have worn it for sixty-four years and Mrs Duffus before me and goodness knows how many others, so it is very old. Was glad I had a safety clasp put on it. They then had a few more games and then we all trooped down the ancient roadway made of every size and shaped stone. I really had to watch every step of the way.

There was one exciting event I have overlooked and that was a single fighter aircraft display put on for the occasion. The noise was deafening, but what a display of pomp and flying ability it was! It went on for about twenty minutes around the castle area.

Back to our walk down – ended up being able to buy our lunch from an erected tent affair. Wonderful chicken sandwich, chocolate bar, chips and a 7-Up, half the size of ours which they also sell over here. (Why not in Canada?) The latter, plus cookies, were produced by Lorna and Grace. We had all taken cushions, as directed, and Lorna brought along a lovely Shetland rug for my legs as it was not warm, but at least no rain or the beastly wind we had been having. Everyone was doing the same thing. A shuttle bus went to Duffus for necessary visits, so after lunch we went to and fro! Many people had their own cars there so we finally went back to Elgin with our friends. I was able to buy one of the pennants, sorry there weren't more of them. A brief rest and change of clothes and back again to attend the farewell party. We enjoyed a piper, a small orchestra and Highland dancers who did the 'Highland Fling'. We all chipped in to present a silver tray to David Duffus in small appreciation for a magnificent job, so well done. Over one year of e-mail pursuit of Duffuses, plus all the incredible organizing over here. He, by the way, has more personality and warm charm than anyone I have ever known and a smile that beams from his face. His knowledge and research for 'The Thousand Years of Duffus' celebration took him one year and he gathered 150 of us together. Scottish reels were done by about twenty of the guests and thoroughly enjoyed by all.

The haggis was piped in as the custom demands. Our first course for dinner was a dessert-size plate with mashed turnip, mashed potatoes and haggis. I had always refused to have it in the Navy years, but was told it really was mild and delicious, which to my amazement, it was. It was after 11:00, so we said our goodbyes. A big hug from David and his lovely wife and daughter. The warmth and friendliness of everyone was as if we were all related. I felt very sad saying goodbye. I adored all the children. They were so good. I never heard a cross word or a cry from a child and there were toddlers around at all times and all hours.

One little four-year-old was a study – a boy, obviously a future brainstorm or genius. I told his mother I was fascinated by his knowledge, inquiring energy and brain. His kindergarten teacher said he was way above average for his year; I could have stolen him.

Were driven back to Duff Avenue and got to bed at 12:30. Lorna and Grace were to meet me at the Rail Station at noon. Packed all morning. Hated to miss the church service at Duffus Church and the tour of Gordonstoun School which they were to do today – but I didn't know this and all my reservations were made. My taxi driver said he would be able to drive me to Douneside rather than train to Aberdeen and hire a taxi from there. After giving it further thought, I said my very fond farewells to Lorna and Grace, of whom I have become very fond. They were so good to me and I was indeed blessed when they found me on the Internet.

Changed from the back seat up with my nice driver and away we went lickety split down the highway. Beautiful highway, light traffic and a super driver – informative, not too strong a brogue, and we got along famously. The scenery was unbelievably beautiful every inch of the way. What a country it is. The forests of trees alone defy description. Some of them are planted close together so they are high, straight columns like thin telephone poles with the foliage only on the top, which enables you to look through the forest and I swear someone must clear every vestige of waste material on the ground.

Finally arrived up a beautiful long driveway to Douneside. It is all and more than I could ever have hoped for. Being Sunday afternoon, I stood in a huge hallway in this remarkable place. Finally tracked down a nice dining room attendant (I think), who called for someone to take me to my room. I am very comfortable – green fitted rug throughout, built-in double wardrobe divided by four large drawers with ancient, heavy handles. Also an antique, three mirrored dressing table and stool, twin beds, white duvets with clusters of pink flowered vines and white wallpaper with pink honeysuckle that perfectly matches the bedspread colours. Old gold-framed picture of two young lovers leaning against each other and a shocked adult male approaching. Bronze sequins on either side. A framed mirror I would adore to own. Antique rose-buttoned upholstered chairs. Also, on a mahogany table is a tricky kettle, two glasses, two cups, etc., container of coffee, teapot and cookie jar. A super bathroom, enormous bath, towel rack and folding steel rack for any hand laundry required. This you open up and place in the bath to dry. Figured out the flush system easily for once!

I was asked if I was hungry and said a bowl of soup would be super and this I got – it was 2:30 – and tea would be served with it. Had a cup and re-met a charming couple of women who had helped me with my lack of actual cash and paid my unexpected taxi bill as he didn't want Amex cheques. Old friends, one lives in the States now. Both charming and friendly.

Had an hour's rest, made a few phone calls and changed for dinner. Nice barman. No sign of the Fields, who manage Douneside. Must have slept well in spite of my earlier snooze.

Had a message to call Rupert and Sonia, which I did. Can't wait to see them again, they are treasures in my life.

Nice dinner, enough for two – the dessert was to die for. Homemade rhubarb ice cream, molasses-rolled treacle, lace cookie with cream filling – plate splashed well with pureed raspberry sauce. Perfect. Watched the end of the Rugby World Cup. Sorry the French won. I should be watching the tennis but must get back to my writing.

Here it is, Monday 3rd, sunny and warmer – window open. Met the Fields – both charming and interesting, quite the youngest grandparents I've ever known. Cashed some Amex cheques for me. Kipper for breakfast – had my first one in Glasgow in 1938! Love them.

Nice man at the next table whose wife has been very sick with bronchitis – familiar name. Thankful mine is so much better. The air is so fresh and clean – perfect for me.

Went for a walk around the estate. The gardens are spectacular; not many steps before a tiny bunny scooted by and was soon followed by another. Dear little things. No veggie garden in sight; I imagine they can survive.

Lunch was buffet, every conceivable type of salad, cold meats (I passed), oh yes, spiced parsnip soup, creamed and it was a taste treat. Never would have thought of parsnip soup. There was also cheese, fruit and coffee.

Phoned Susie and Crozier around 4:45. Great chat, hated to hang up. Had to walk through the dining room to get some help with my endeavours to call Alan. Tea was set up for 5:00 o'clock, dinner is 7:30. If I had had that tea I would have had to skip dinner. Gorgeous pancakes, whipped cream, strawberry jam – huge plate of them. A two layered sponge cake with jam in the centre and whipped cream on top! The best looking shortbread I have ever seen. Long, thick slices, cake-like squares and rolypoly whatevers – cookies. I left the room quickly or I would have had no desire for dinner.

Talked to Paddy Stewart, my guest, and she arrives tomorrow, driving from Campbeltown, where I have stayed twice with her. It will be nice to be able to drive around and see something of the outside world, as unless I hail a taxi I could never walk to the village. Well, I think I have caught up – so until tomorrow...

Paddy drove all the way, having said she would stop over and then changed her mind. Five and a half hours, it took her, and on these twisting roads, I shudder to think of it. She is in great form – lots to tell me – which gave my voice a rest as she arrived at 5:00, which is tea time at Douneside. It revived her but she was able to rest before dinner and our drink at the bar. Watched Wimbledon most of the afternoon while waiting for her.

We are invited out for dinner tomorrow. John and Jane live a fifteen minute drive from here and he will call for us at 7:00. John used to stay with Paddy and Ian as he was a great friend of their son.

After breakfast, we picked up our picnic and took off for Balmoral Castle. My darned camera isn't working so only have postcards. Fortunately, Paddy took some. We were allowed in the ballroom to see some of the treasures of China – silver pictures, etc. Very interesting, but we were disappointed in the over-kill admittance. It's too early for the garden as it has been so cold. Drove to a pretty view spot by the River Dee and ate our very filling lunch of a thermos of cream of mushroom soup, cuc's and tomato in a bun, cheese biscuits, banana, potato chips and fruit cake and coffee – stuffed!

I had pulled muscles in my hand and wrist at Douneside and it acted up with shooting pains. Finally got a pain killer and ointment which took effect, fortunately.

Drove to Braemar. Paddy bought a sweater but I am forced to pass as my cases won't hold any more. Phoned Margot who was a bit upset that I hadn't called her, as she was worried that something had happened to me. People mean well but wish they wouldn't worry about my independence.

Arrived back in time for a hot cup of tea and more Wimbledon, changed and was picked up by John. A perfectly delightful chap. They have a nineteen year-old daughter – John must be about fifty-two. Lovely drive to their most attractive house and loving dog who rushed out ahead of Jane. Perfectly charming person. I was quite enchanted with both of them and their house. Very different. It had been two houses but they joined them together. Jane poured me a good drink which I enjoyed through dinner, while they drank wine. Wonderful dinner – three courses, in their kitchen family room with the largest Aga cooker I have ever seen. A very special evening it was.

Forgot to mention a small world experience. I was reading the register after seeing a car arrive earlier (Douneside), and to my surprise saw that the car was owned by a person called Deanna, address Redhill, Surrey. We lived in Reigate which was the neighbour to Redhill. We had some American friends that lived in Redhill and we used to walk to their house from ours, going through a cemetery where the nightingales sang their heads off, to our delight. When I saw Deanna later, I introduced myself and we got on beautifully – in spite of our age difference. Paddy liked her also. The latter left around 10:00 next morning after taking several pictures. She might do a Canadian trip next year, all going well with both of us. She will be eighty-six in December but seems to be in very good health. It was a bit sad saying goodbye as one never knows.

I was most anxious to get my hair shampooed as it is such a long time since I had it done, on 25 June. Thanks to our delightful dining room maid who overheard me say I was going to order a taxi, she volunteered to take me and Deanna. Picked me up after her drive to Aberdeen. She is such a nice person.

Watched the tennis, then walked around the beautiful property and gardens. Packed for my drive to Aberdeen, taxi coming at 11:00. Takes about fifty minutes; my train to Perth goes at 12:35. Felt quite sad leaving. Everyone so nice and the place itself absolutely superb.

The train trip quite pleasant. Nice American couple and the conductor helped me with my luggage and Alan was at the station to give me a huge welcome. He had gained more weight, but just as nice as ever. Drove to my place and I settled in while he waited downstairs in the pretty drawing room. (Very pretty room.) Took off to Dalruach (Alan's) where he settled me to watch the tennis. Serena was beaten – the sisters are quite something. Alan brought me a prettily set tea tray and then later a really well cooked dinner. Huge tender double loin lamb chop, carrots, broccoli, potatoes, salad, raspberries and cream. We talked a blue streak and then he drove me back to my very nice B&B. He is a very relaxed, natural sort of person and we knew so many of the same naval types from Plymouth and mutual friends in Scotland.

The weather, although warmer than Elgin, is teasing us with Scottish mist so keep hoping the sun will pop through.

Saturday, Alan picked me up and we drove to the beautiful school closing of A.K.'s daughter. (A's Grand). It was a never to be forgotten experience. The boys and girls were up to our elementary age and all boarders; ancient historical school. All students in kilts, green knee socks, white blouses and matching green v-neck sweaters. If the family had their own tartan, they wore it, otherwise tartan of the school. As the students moved, their kilts tossed in unison and all the colours of them contrasted so nicely. The Head spoke beautifully of every aspect of the years – prizewinners, etc. A.K., who sat next to me, has his third daughter there and is now to serve on the Board of Governors. More about him later.

What I will never forget was the students' orchestra; there must have been over forty of them who gave a fabulous recital with their music teacher playing the piano. They were so mature and confident and the eldest couldn't have been more than twelve. The choir was also awfully good. Academically, the number of awards indicated they had a very studious and inspired lot of students. All sports were also covered, even to one girl for shooting. A.K. said she will compete in sixteen and under for all of Scotland and she is twelve. It was interesting seeing all the trunks being loaded into family cars by the fathers, some of whom were also in kilts as were many of the baby siblings. How I *do* love kilts.

A.K. and his daughter (Iona), were at Alan's briefly before going home to Edinburgh, where we go tomorrow. After they left, we had a gin and tonic and a light lunch. The tennis was on so watched Davenport go down to defeat to Venus Williams. I was hoping so as I love to see the black people rise to fame – plus the fact that her tennis was exciting to watch. What a future she has. Hope we get a chance to see the men's final.

Alan drove me home for an hour and a half rest and change. Picked me up at 6:30, back to his place for a drink and then as my guest out for dinner. We went to the Grill which was full of interesting people. The hotel itself is world renowned and is filled at all times. Would love to have really toured it as it was a fascinating hotel. Very good dinner but after late lunch, one course was all we could manage.

Had a much better sleep with a light quilt. Can't understand how anybody can sleep under a duvet.

Sunday, last full day. Today is very special. Alan picked me up at 10:45 and we drove through every type of weather to the luncheon party given by the Hon. Lord Kincraig, known as Bobby. There were fourteen of us, most of whom go as a group of good friends to golf in South Africa every year. Our drive to his heavenly 'cottage!!' out of Edinburgh was in a deluge of rain and low clouds. What I could see at times, was beautiful – awful for Alan who is an excellent driver, signs for directions being lost to sight until we had almost passed them. Overshot a few times but finally arrived. Bobby emerged with a huge grin and welcomed me with 'Welcome, Johnnie', and was soon to be given a gin and tonic and introductions. When I came to the tallest and best looking one and his wife, namely Ian and Cora, he said, 'I didn't expect to meet you *here* – Rupert Ross said to look out for you at Douneside.' Small world it is! He is so like Rupert it is ridiculous – even his voice and they were best friends, or I should say, are. They were charming as were all the others.

Another strange thing was that one judge, of which there were three, knew my wonderful Scottish friend Lyndsay Mavor (later Lyndsay Sandeman). I stayed with them in '98, but Lyndsay died later. We got on so well in Glasgow in '38 and her parents were so kind to me and us.

First of all, the 'cottage' was perfection. Although smallish, it coped with all of us very comfortably. A sun-room off the living room that opened up on the rose garden with every flower in bloom, all colours, with the shiniest, healthiest leaves I have ever seen – doors opened out onto it. The bar was in a beautiful old cabinet with every known bottle. Bobby served all of us constantly. The dining room table had white plates with smoked salmon, three good sized pieces with a lemon wedge and rolls or whole-wheat bread. When Bobby rang an old fashioned bell, we went in and picked up our plates and sat wherever. I have *never* tasted the equal; it was wonderful and quite a course in itself, but then his maid proceeded to laden the table with a huge platter of cold meat and every known salad. All delectable. Then came two enormous Pavlovas topped with raspberries. Only one was eaten – I never expect to enjoy a more delectable one, or one as attractively presented. All of this with a vast cheese board and coffee.

We all moved around so felt I knew a bit about all of them. Having arrived at 12:00, we departed just after 3:00. Not raining, but a bit overcast. Tried to persuade Alan to just drop me off but he said we must have a drink and some kind of a snack, which we did.

Drove home at 9:30. I'm sure he was exhausted and he faces two hours of it tomorrow. The highways are wonderful, three lanes each most of the way, but the others are one turn after another, clearly marked and everyone obeys the rules of the road – no honking, courtesy for everyone. I've never seen a piece of paper or anything untidy or dirty. The impressions I formed of all of Scotland that I have seen, and that is plenty, is that it is immaculate as are all the people – young and old, male and female. No obesity, slovenly clothes or coloured hair; they maintain a great sense of pride in Scotland and themselves. I can't say enough about them.

Last day in Crieff has come and gone. My B&B people were charming and we enjoyed each other fully. He had a coronary when he was forty-five so had to stop working. They bought their large house and totally renovated it beautifully and in very good taste. Do hope his health will get totally better, but she says he has to be very careful.

Alan picked me up at 10:30 and off we drove to Glasgow and to the Western Club. The porter gave Alan a jacket and tie as he didn't understand that I wanted him to have a drink and lunch before driving back to Crieff. He has been so kind, driving me all over the place, wouldn't hear of me taking the train. Felt badly saying farewell and hope he will come to Vancouver before we are all too old to do things and drive our cars.

Had a lazy time after he left and a very light dinner. Talked to Susie which was just what I needed. Slept well and walked my legs off. Got a pair of Black Watch troos.

Glasgow has changed so much. Some streets don't allow cars so people walk on them – seemed strange. I am *so* impressed by the trim figures on everyone – only saw one bulky female all day and she looked American or Canadian. The men, young and old, are so well turned out. Dark suits, white shirts and tie always. The young men and boys are spotlessly clean, hair cut nicely, no cut-offs or layered clothing. Can't get over them.

Really didn't achieve much except to write my thank you letters to Bobby, A.K. and Carol and Alan. Phoned him to thank him for driving me and to see that he got home all right.

Good sleep till 6:00 and was ready to leave by 9:20. Had help ordered, which is what you do with luggage such as I have.

It was a long six and a half hour journey but had a drink and a grilled ham and cheese sandwich. Snoozed off a few times and finally whizzed into London's King's Cross. Taxi to the Sloane Club, past Buckingham Palace. Reminded me of 1938 when I did it for the first time on my way to stay at a club near Ernle and all her wonderful friends. I guess I will get used to the casualness or lack of smiling welcome that I hope our clubs produce for strangers.

I was given a huge key – 118 – and was pointed in the direction of the lift that happened not to be visible. Left my three precious suitcases, assuming they would be sent up to where I finally found my room. Not so. After about fifteen minutes, phoned down and they said they would attend to them. Some time later, they phoned to say 'Are your three bags flowered?' 'Yes, they are,' I replied, and up they came. Nice little brown-faced young fellow brought them and has been a great help to me ever since.

At first, my room looked miniscule, but only because of a double bed and quite a lot of furniture. Good sized bathroom so sorted myself out. Packing and unpacking is not my most favourite sport but am getting good at it..

Finally found the bar and waited and waited – the service there is ridiculously indifferent and slow. Ordered a gin and tonic, or at least I popped down some liquid with my 1 ounce (if that). Next one I ordered was a double, also if that, and said I would like some potato chips that one other table had in view. They finally arrived after I caught her eye when she was busy shining bar glasses! Ordered Scotch salmon and small salad which I greatly enjoyed. Dessert was supposed to be hot, but the man was busy doing account chits and the girl was shining the glasses to perfection. He came to his senses and brought me my tepid dessert and tepid coffee. £28 was the cost of it and I swear I could produce the whole thing for a pittance. If I sound a bit browned off, I was. Not so much as good night or thank you. Our Vancouver Club is so different! If I could have cancelled my further reservation, then I would have.

Phoned down three times regarding a replacement for my feather pillow. Finally discovered they didn't have any so I suggested a plastic bag over one. After all this, I'm happy to say I slept well and was up bright-eyed and bushy-tailed, as Mort used to say.

Breakfast was better because of a nicer, caring staff. Did a bit of packing, chopping and changing so I could handle my travels to the Rosses. Realized I could solve all my problems with a canvas type of case to balance my other weekender. Walked up to Peter Jones on Sloane Square and got exactly what wanted. Glad I did as it worked out very well as there is never a helper at small stations and my train time ended up being different from Sonia's directions – new timetable.

Waited in Staplehurst for them to pick me up. I was an hour early and have been able to sit quietly and warm in this wee country station and write my diary. It is so much milder than Scotland so am very happy. So looking forward to – was going to say meeting Rupert and Sonia again – and up they drove! I was early and they were smack on time for the train I was supposed to be on. Huge hugs; how I love them.

Nonstop talk – drove home to their heavenly house and garden. Spurts of sunshine, bit windy. Sonia made me tea which was greatly appreciated. Strolled around the garden. All sorts of goodies! Lots of plants I have never seen before. The house is very old, hundreds of years, and very attractive with beautiful old pieces of furniture.

I had asked them to make a reservation somewhere they equally liked so I could take them out for dinner. Sonia has a luncheon arranged for me Sunday, so thought we should stay home Saturday night and go out tonight. We had drinks here and then drove quite a way it seemed, as the roads are winding; one darned curve after another.

Excellent dinner. Sonia and I had Dover sole and Rupert opted for a lovely piece of salmon – Scotch – nestled on a mound of spinach. We all chose a different dessert. Our waitress was a peach of a young girl and very pretty. When she found out I was from Vancouver, she said she was going there with a grass-hockey team. I gave her my address and phone number and said I would love to put her up with or without a friend and I really would love to have her. Martha Nuthall, by name.

Off to bed around 11:30 after a lovely day. Must have lost my nice pen.

Saturday, meant to say I talked to Susan and Crozier. They seemed so close. Great to have these calls.

Drove over to Fiona and Simon's. They are in Devon but I had to see their Shitsu puppies. They were a pair of knockouts, cute as anything I have ever seen. Took some pictures of them playing, then went shopping.

Home for a short gin and tonic, then they took me for lunch at a delightful pub. Gorgeous lunch. Shrimp tempura and salad. Scrumptious. We then went to a supermarket. I am having to use great control not to buy all the delectable things I see. Such variety and quality. If I had room in my suitcases, I wouldn't know where to stop.

Shocking news about the storm in Alberta, seen eighty miles away from Calgary.

Sales are everywhere for summer wear. I really haven't missed hot weather a bit but have felt cold many times, partly because of being sick, I'm sure.

Sonia very kindly set up an appointment for me with her hairdresser, so am feeling a bit more acceptable. Delicious smoked chicken and avocado salad for our dinner. Lovely dessert and large argument about slang expressions for the world population. Sonia and I against Rupert.

Can't believe we are already at 16 July. Just over nine days and I will be boarding the *QE2* for home. So far I have handled everything without a problem – may my good fortune continue. Hoping when I return to London tomorrow that there will be some communication.

My last day and always so sad to part with such great friends. In 1939, we introduced Rupert to Sonia. It is amazing, I think.

Up a bit early to have breakfast with Rupert as he was off to play golf. Pictures and hugs, hope the former turn out.

Sonia and I then proceeded to ready ourselves to drive to Tentenden, first to visit (Lady) Sheila Bates, who was here at the luncheon given for me that I fear I didn't mention! I had met her before as she spent part of her life in Vancouver at the convent, no less. She is my idea of a truly delightful person, warm, most attractive and charming. She invited us to drop in around 11:00 for coffee, which was a huge treat for me. Her house was absolutely delightful. I could have moved right in. Not large, but filled with lovely furniture, pictures, etc. and a view to die for – rolling hills with grazing sheep. Fortunately, a lovely warm day so could see for miles. Sheila does watercolours very well, and pastels. Hated to leave but we had a bit of shopping to do and wanted to peruse the masses of antique shops etc

Took Sonia for lunch to a delightful antiques and restaurant place that Sheila told us about. Finally, after a delicious Stilton broccoli quiche, we headed to the station. Arrived as my train pulled out so put in a half an hour waiting for the next one. Sad farewell once more, waved and waved until out of sight.

Shoddy first class, so different now to the way it used to be. Made good time and was in the Sloane Club by 4:30. Same room as I had before. Phoned Sonia and Rupert to thank them, also called Margot. Big happy face when I was given a fax from our darling daughter. She is up to her ears, sorry will miss the P.P.P.

this year, particularly as she is so involved in it. Had a call from Jackie Roe. Meeting her at the theatre Wednesday, so looking forward to it.

Apart from a real London walk, I simply cozied myself and stayed put, but suddenly found it was 11:30. Fortunately, like home, it cooled off at night and I slept very well.

Always seem to wake up around 6:00, but happy just to lie there. Had a Continental breakfast and walked miles. Ended up in Harrods, which was like a madhouse. It has changed but the meat and food of every description is breathtaking, to say the least. I have never seen its equal in Canada. Found a 'ladies' with several comfy chairs so availed myself of one to recharge my batteries, though not sufficiently enough to walk back so hopped into a taxi. Traffic is heavy everywhere and many busy streets are dirty, messy and un-British. Tourist season, I imagine. I keep my handbag clutched firmly at all times as I gather wallets are easy prey.

Decided to go to the dining room as it now has the assistant chef from the Connaught. I was hungry so had my dinner at 1:30 and haven't had anything since. Should sleep well.

Went out again and walked my legs off. The antique shops fascinate me. Hoped to catch Ian in the office but left my fax and phone number with his answering service. Had hung up only a few minutes and he was on the phone. Great chat, he had had a very good holiday in Malaysia and brought his mother back with him. Sorry I won't meet her. Also talked to my Machrihanish friend Nora Malloy who lives in Bath. We enjoyed each other's company in the Wrens. Big write-up about Cecil Merritt. He really had quite a war record, VC to prove it. Our heroes are leaving us rapidly.

Tomorrow is a busy day. Meeting Jackie Roe at 1:30 to see the musical *The Lion King*, then here to change to go to Fiona and Simon's for dinner. It should be a lovely day. It is now 10:30 so will make my large bed to suit me (minus blankets) and get to bed with a very heavy heart for little Sarah's parents as the poor child's body was found. Life can be so cruel. Men that commit such heinous crimes should have the lash.

Such a contrast in temperatures! Scotland is 10°. East Sussex, warmer out than in. London, hot. I certainly have a problem with my wardrobe. Two large windows and I am hot.

Left here around 10:30 and walked to Peter Jones, then on to Harrods. The latter was filled with sale seekers so did quick scan of the food floor which was mind boggling. I could have spent hours. Cuts of meat we never see. The wee squabs reminded me of a birthday dinner I gave for Mort in Reigate, pre-war.

Talked to the family, all well there. Also spoke to Sonia and Jackie. Dinner here and watched TV; good lazy day.

Wednesday, caught a bus to Hyde Park Corner and there I hit the tie-up of London traffic. Bomb scare due to the Queen Mother's 100th. Saw the Horse Guards arrive at the palace. Finally, after an hour or more, my number 9 appeared. We were bumper to bumper for another hour and time was running out. Got off at the Savoy to order Margot's little birthday cake for Sunday. Also got a ticket for my last night at the Savoy Theatre, Donald Sutherland in *Enigmatic Variations*, 8:00 to 9:30, which gives me time to finish my packing for the ship. Nice way to end my wonderful adventure.

As I still had a half hour before I was to meet Jackie at the Aldrich for *The Lion King*, I spotted a very nice place to have a sandwich. Very good it was. Down to the light and up to the theatre. She arrived at exactly 1:30 so had a hug and went in. She is such a nice person, pretty and very easy to be with. Owing to the bomb scare, they held the show back half an hour, so we sat in our very comfy seats and caught up on all our news. Packed house. It is a Walt Disney story about the animals in Africa and there must have been thirty of them, many of whom came down the aisle, including the most fabulous elephant. Can't imagine how they _ever_ were able to dream up the clever way the cast were the animals that talked for the animal they represented, but manipulated their mouth or beak as if it was doing the talking. The applause was deafening at times and the most delighted audience I have ever seen. Jackie had got two turn-in tickets months ago and we were lucky she happened to try for them when the two were turned in just ahead of her. Just wish everyone could see it so we could all talk about it as it is totally impossible to describe.

Took me ages to get back to Sloane. Endless tie-ups everywhere caused by the Royal 'do' and the bomb scare. Just in time to change and hop in a taxi for Fiona and Simon's.

Greeted with happy hugs and the puppies and mom, brought to London by Fiona yesterday. Their house is four stories. Susanah is away but Claire was there – can't believe she is now grown up and very attractive. Simon (Barrister) arrived on his motorcycle which saves him hours a week in traffic. I liked him so much as I really didn't get to know him years ago in Vancouver or at Sonia and Rupert's 50th. Fiona, Susanah and Claire all paint very well in oils; the house is full of their talent.

Lovely dinner, beautiful smoked trout to start, lamb chops, peas, carrots and raspberries and ice cream. Finally, around 10:00, I said my goodbyes. They called a taxi for me and to my horror I found they had already had it put on their account! Lovely evening.

Up reasonably early to be called for by Jackie to drive to Oxted to take Margot and Jackie for lunch. Margot was at the door with a huge happy smile. Ninety-four this Sunday, no less. Her face never seems to age but she has got smaller and does suffer back problems. It was a lovely time to be together, it's such a long friendship. She wrote me a treasure of a card and gave me a silver brooch which is very nice. She is also sending Susan her silver bear and necklace (chain) she wore all through the war. Dear Mag, as I have always called her. I will miss her, but she may outlive me!

We went to an outstandingly good pub for lunch. All had a Pimms, which was not as good as I remember them to be, then we all had Dover sole which was perfection. Topped it all off with a delectable sweet. We all enjoyed ourselves.

Back to Margot's for an hour and on to London, a good hour's drive. So full of lunch I simply skipped dinner. Talked to Susan and watched golf. Tiger Woods is tearing St Andrews apart. Phoned to see if I could get a seat at the Drury Lane to see the *Witches of Eastwick*. Got one, so walked over, not far from the Savoy. It turned out to be an anticlimax after *The Lion King*, although I enjoyed some of it. Was thankful to be in the balcony as it was noisy at times. Thunder when you least expected it. The best part of it was the three witches in full evening gowns. Gave a spectacular performance flying all through the theatre; it made Peter Pan look like Mickey Mouse.

Better night's sleep – it is my 11th bed since leaving home.

Up fairly late for me, breakfast overlooking the Thames at 8:45. On the whole, not a very inspiring gathering of people. Some very well behaved little children with nice looking parents. Men for the most part badly turned out, but London is very casual now as witnessed at the theatres and on the streets. It is swarming with tourists. Trafalgar Square is a veritable mass of humans and pigeons with no space between them

Jackie and Margot picked me up at 12:15. Drove around a bit and then to her absolutely charming house. As usual I didn't have my camera which is a pity and her garden was a mass of colours. Her lunch was delicious. Champagne for Margot's 94th and my Savoy birthday cake, which was a delight. Jackie is off to the

Cotswolds at 6:00 a.m. tomorrow, so while she tidied up the kitchen she put on the tape of the Queen Mother's 100th celebration in London for us to watch.

Drove back here by 5:30, supposedly to meet with a Cunard representative. Finally got a call from her so met in the reading room for a slight briefing. Have to wait until the morning for the fax number of the *QE2* that Susan wants. So, full of my big lunch, once more I couldn't face dinner – always wish I could just have a bowl of soup like I do at home.

My evening gowns have been squeezed into my unopened suitcase since I packed at home. They will look like accordions so will be given to the ship's presser pronto!

A day of frustration is my last day in London. Got up early to have breakfast in order to be at the Wheel by 10:30. They said at the concierge's desk that it would take about fifteen minutes to go there so left at 10:15 What a fiasco! There was one of London's famous tie-ups, some engineering problem, so with no progress and a £5 taxi fare, I said, if I get out here will I have far to walk? Oh no, about a fifteen minute walk. So away I went over the Thames and finally found where I would pick up my ticket, only to discover the hotel should have given me a voucher, without which I couldn't go on the Wheel! I walked and walked, back over the Thames, traffic still jammed so a taxi was out of the question. Decided I would opt for the underground. Lots of guidance, climbed aboard with dozens of young schoolchildren. Very impressed with a large sign that said, 'Don't wait to be asked, give your seat to someone that needs it more than you.' A young lad gave me his so thanked him profusely. Hopped off after two stops to change to the Circle Line, thought I was pretty smart. Up from the bowels of the earth to Charing X and I walked back to the Savoy and told them my sad tale. Refunded my account and said they were very sorry.

Decided to have my dinner for lunch as I would be going to the Savoy Theatre to see Donald Sutherland. Went to the Grill and had a scrumptious Dover sole. I could die for it. Told the maitre d' about Mort's and my twelve days here in '44. He loved the story and said he would relay it to the chefs. Then I walked to Somerset House to see the famous Gilbert Collection. It was absolutely marvellous, no wonder he was knighted! What a donation he made and how well it is being enjoyed. Walked and walked, can't believe I covered so many miles today.

Back here, sent some faxes, had a nap and dressed for the theatre. To my utter dismay, they had to cancel the performance!!! Obviously not my day! Too late to go to a different show – didn't want dinner having had such a good lunch and so came back to my room and watched TV. Phoned Susie which cheered me up and had a fax from Ryan which was nice. Long talk with Margot and also called Alan to say goodbye. Will call Sonia and Rupert in the morning. It is now 11:00 o'clock so will stop here and hopefully have a good sleep. Mostly packed.

Did very well and here I am tucked into my bed in the *QE2*!! 12:18 to be exact, arrived around 4:15. Promptly had fire drill so finally had a chance to unpack and size up the situation. A beautiful bouquet of flowers and a letter from Sonia and Rupert, so took the bottle of champs that was in a silver ice bucket out and arranged the flowers in it and they look gorgeous. No fax so obviously Marta's faxes were wrong which is very sad as I know I should have had some to greet me. Thanks to Sonia and Rupert for saving me from a bare cabin.

When I find the purser's office I will take Marta's in and see where and why. Boarded efficiently, bags already in my nice cabin. 3099 – steward is Andres, who does everything I ask of him. Cabin is probably the length of Sue and Crozier's kitchen and family room. Twin beds, sitting area with table, two portholes, cupboard and drawer space everywhere. Walk-in dressing room and safe. Nice bathroom. Six days will be enough. Couldn't keep my eyes open so will back up a bit. Dressed casually for dinner. Braved a bar and to my amazement I was surrounded by screaming children – later to learn that this is a *family* cruise so there are around one hundred and forty children aboard. I don't think I would have opted for it had I known. With a hearing aid I was not happy and wonder where I can go another time. The children were adorable, but not in a bar!

Proceeded to the Princess Grill and to my table. One couple were there. He rose and big smiles from both so sat down by her and introduced myself. They are Mary and Ray Clanton from Carolina and they are celebrating their 50th – couldn't be nicer. We enjoyed each other. Finally one other female joined us and she was obviously not happy with us or children nearby. Had my favourite delight – caviar, how I love it. Baby Caesar salad, sole, ice cream and chocolate and two truffles! Slept very well.

Breakfast preceded by a walk on deck with a beautiful day – cloudless, light wind. Mary and Ray were there and we talked our heads off. Before they started breakfast, he said Grace which touched a spot with me and reminded me of Ian. Our dining steward is from the Midlands and is a delight. They told me about the Concorde crash. Ghastly!

The only one at our table for lunch, so was spoiled by our two stewards. A couple I stood beside in the boarding queue came over to talk to me; they had been at the Savoy. Consommé, omelet and fruit for lunch. Watched bridge for a few minutes and will go and size up the art class. Haven't painted for so long. Had a phone call from the maitre d' asking if I would join Mary and Ray Clanton at a table for three, so I was overjoyed. They are a fun, interesting and charming couple. Painting class was fun, masses of us and a talented teacher. Very nice Brit, who makes films, and was good company throughout. We all get on with our paintings tomorrow. Last one is Sunday.

Captain's party 6:00-8:00, so wore my jazzy black and gold. It must have been the right choice as I've never had so many compliments and by complete strangers. Quite unbelievable! Little did they know I bought it on the wharf in Sri Lanka years ago for $35.00! Two photos were taken so hope they are good. Too early for drinks, so was guided to the unique little bar beside the Princess Grill and there met up with the nice couple from the Savoy that I came aboard with. Mary and Ray popped by to say they would see me in the dining room. A most enjoyable few hours with them. I would love to see both of them again if I should live so long. At 10:30 they held a seat for me in the theatre where we saw the show. Lots of laughs at the comic from Britain.

Clocks back one hour from now on. It will certainly break my jet lag down considerable. To bed at 12:30 and slept well. The weather is being very good to us.

Nice day, heard Princess Diana's butler, who she called The Rock because she got support from him. He certainly knew her, probably better than anyone, and he said she was a real person with a kind, helpful manner with sick people. Said he has memories of her with leg-less and sometimes arm-less little children that she would pick up and cuddle.

Lunch alone, then a walk and painting class. Snooze. Nice evening with Mary and Ray.

Seem to have missed a day but they are all much alike. Had a bridge lesson, rule of twenty and one other. If I go again I will take a paper and pen. Hard to digest it with my three men all joking and laughing. Went to the library to look up Sir Samuel Cunard. He was married for twelve years to Susan Duffus (!!!) who gave him nine children and died when the last child was ten months old. With the help of their grandmother he brought them up. I will copy the part out for the Family Bible. So much Mort would have enjoyed about this trip.

Played bingo – no win, but pot tomorrow, $1000.00 I believe. Hair appointment at 4:00 so will miss it, never win anyway. A perfectly gorgeous Saturday – blue skies, water a picture of baby whitecaps. Everyone that dares is lying prone and many in the shade reading. Heard Paul's farewell on 'Di' – he is a delight. Huge receptive audience. My other nice couple were there with me.

Wasn't going to watch the chefs but did for about half an hour. Make ahead ideas were good. Then went up to the boat deck and walked a mile in only my sweater and t-shirt. Simply glorious, shall go again after lunch. Can't believe I pack tomorrow. Hope I can make it all fit in! Probably drink my champs while I'm doing it because I am truly tired of packing. Overweight, I am sure to be. Hope I have enough US to pay for special tips and air expenses. Sterling Amex cheques are only useful to pay any charges I have made – they won't cash them, damn.

Weather is cloudy with a chance of rain; guess I missed my chance for snapshots this morning. Mary has taken some but not the kind I should have been taking. It's been quite a day. Don't like my hair but Mary liked it very much so . . . ? Listened to Paul again – fascinating life he led with Princess Di, all about Christmas and Easter at the Palace, etc. He says Di's youngest is the one with masses of character.

Took in a bit of the cooking demo with two chefs – already wrote that! Never had so many compliments over dresses. One little lady said she looked forward to seeing me every evening and my gowns are so regal. Age doesn't deem to matter if the materials are beautiful. I must tell Mrs Heese, who did such a superb job designing the dress and jacket. Had a couple of glasses of champagne while dressing as I wanted to have early dinner due to all the entertainment this eve. Missed most of the play which was very good and is going to New York. We then went to a piano concert given by a twenty-two year-old lad. He was outstanding. The world will see him for many years to come. It was the first time he had performed in front of an audience and it was anyone's guess as to whether the audience or he was more excited. His name is Daniel Vaiman, born in Latvia in 1978. That seems like yesterday to me and look what he has achieved.

Now have to think back to yesterday. Settled my account, walked and finally took pictures as it was a beautiful day. Used the wide lens, just missed seeing a whale by three minutes. Attended the children's choir performance which was very good. Spoke to the captain after church about Susan Duffus, wife of Sir Samuel Cunard, and he was anxious for me to go to Halifax to see the preservation of their house and memorabilia. If only Mort was alive we would do that.

Early dinner with Mary and Ray – such a nice couple next to us who feel as I feel. Food definitely low rating. Very nice table steward but not fully trained which the girl (French) who works with him, is. I really had some very indifferent meals. I think a family cruise is not for this 'girl' who does truly appreciate good food.

On to the last concert. Screamingly funny chap that I could watch and listen to every day and he's not vulgar which is a treat. Mary and Ray are devout Presbyterians, to the point where they are verging on being Quakers. No matter, they are special.

Packed furiously and achieved miracles. The largest and a smaller suitcase outside by 6:00 p.m., then a light one to carry with my sweaters, jewelry and cosmetics. Very proud of myself. Bed early as I wanted to be on deck entering New York.

Awake from 3:30 on and up at 5:15 to see the Statue of Liberty – so much for my efforts. It's damp, foggy and hot so here I am writing and waiting for 7:00 a.m. to meet the Clantons for our last time together. Have to be in the waiting area by 9:00. It's going to be one – long – day. I go by coach to JFK airport. Glad the gun man did his thing the other day. Don't take off until after 2:00. A shocking night, excited I guess, no sleep after 3:20, so very happy to have it reach 5:15. Had my bath, dressed and clutched camera to take New York and statue – whoops – I did that while waiting for 7:00 to go for breakfast. Sad farewell with Mary and Ray. Mrs Phillips came over to the table to say goodbye and steward and maitre d' wished us well.

This could be the worst of all, wait for this, wait for that. Swelling in my feet and legs is awful. Finally in the TWA airport, almost struck down twice by airport people who didn't even say 'sorry'. One official knocked my pile of suitcases over and couldn't have cared less. Thank God I'm going first; at least I don't queue for hours and I was chaired up ramps and miles of walking area. Only 1:15 and don't take off until 3:30. *Yuck*.

Am now home and will think back on this saga, as the flight is worth recording. Time finally passed. TWA ought to go back to the drawingboard. No comfort, narrow seats. One empty beside me but divided by a wide permanent container for a telephone that is no longer usable. So, unable to stretch out sideways or put my seat back to relax properly. 'Would I like a snack?' 'Would I!' I was starving! Late taking off for St. Louis. When we arrived, I was told: 'We have ordered a wheelchair as this aircraft will not be going to Vancouver after all. Your flight is from the far end of the airport.' Off we went, I swear a mile away, with a nice black 'pusher'. No chair visible, and up jumped a very nice looking young man and gave his chair to me. We became friends. Canadian, from Nanaimo. About twenty-nine I think. Been on business in New Orleans. Looked after my carry-on and helped pass the long waiting period. Talked about restaurants, right down my alley. Finally settled in same seating situation. Saved eventually by the trolley bar and a mediocre supper later. When we had reached about midway, the captain announced we had a problem with an odour. As there had been a plane down with an odour a few days ago, we passengers raised our eyebrows at each other and he continued to say we might have to land if they couldn't find where it came from. The stewardesses turned off all the lights and we waited. A little later he said, 'As can happen in our own homes, we believe it to be a blown fuse.' About an hour later they reported more of the same but no more talk of an emergency landing. Finally, coming into Vancouver, he said, 'We are now approaching one of the most spectacular cities that I know of.' It was a beautiful evening. On departing, I spoke to the captain who had congratulated and thanked us for being so calm under stress. I patted his shoulder in the cockpit and thanked him. I said I would fly with him anytime.

Ryan and April were waiting for me which was a wonderful welcome home. Even got a warm one from Sophie and Kate which was a very nice surprise. Everything looks wonderful!

As I was so late arriving home, Susan was terribly worried something had happened so phoned her as soon as I could.

So nice to be home, but it was, all in all, a fabulous holiday and only wish Mort could have been with me, in Duffus particularly.

My Faith

WHEN I WAS AT boarding school all my Anglican friends were going to be confirmed. As my parents and grandparents were Presbyterians, I wrote home saying that I, too, would like to be confirmed. Strangely enough they didn't think it was a good idea and would rather I didn't. What they didn't realize was that Miss Gildea was a very devout Anglican as well as being an inspirational preacher. Certainly she sowed seeds in me that lay dormant for many years.

Susan was baptized at St Mary's Anglican Church which was a very short distance from our house. Dudley Kemp was the inspiring minister at that time and soon, with his wife Muriel, to become our treasured friend. Drue was also baptized by Dudley followed by my wish to be confirmed in the Anglican Church. Harry Boyce was in the same class. I always remember at the very end of our classes Dudley asked if we had any questions. My turn came, with the mixed feelings I felt about the communal Cup, to which Dudley hastily replied, 'Johnnie Duffus, do you think Jesus Christ would leave this memorial to Him with an impure Cup?'

It wasn't long after, I was asked to join the Chancel Guild. It's so long ago now I forget who invited me – so – forty-five years later I'm still there. I don't feel like a very efficient member, I'm ashamed to say, as all I do and have done is flowers.

During Rev. John Bethel's time at St Mary's I was a lay assistant and reader which I truly loved. Over the years I used to read to Mort and with the public speaking I did for Children's Hospital it was very nice to be able to read the Lessons. Regrettably, my throat became very sensitive and I had to stop.

Before 2002 says goodbye I will resign as 'Flower Lady' and enjoy more leisure time. I will miss my many friends. Ifon Boone has been in charge of my group for many years, such a super person. Mary-Jean Otway Ruthven is another special member as is Chick Bachop and too many others to mention.

We have always been very fortunate to have excellent preachers. At present we are blessed with Kevin Dixon who is young, gifted and inspirational. I am also devoted to his wife, Dianne. I won't be around to see it but I have the feeling he will climb to the top.

The Venerable Alan Jackson has been a wonderful friend who is always there for me; he teases me unmercifully most of the time which ends in laughter. Thank you, Alan, for your friendship over so many years.

John Bethel, Elizabeth Northcott and Michael McGee are all such dedicated people.

Next in my thoughts are our Vergers. Jim Rattee served us for years with his beloved wife Lillian. They knew everyone and all the children loved them. Very recently when Lillian died the service held for her took place at St Mary's and the church was filled.

After Jim came John Taylor. His lovely wife Elizabeth works so we don't see as much of her as we used to see of Lillian. John was the host to a Vergers' Conference held at St. Mary's. I was able to do the flower arrangements on the banquet tables for him and placed four passion flowers at each table. Kevin Dixon had never seen them before so I explained the meaning of them to him. He, in turn, enlightened the many Vergers. For some weeks after I received the most beautiful letters extolling the beauty of the passion flower and its meaning, with gratitude for introducing them to this hitherto unknown vine.

Thank you, John, for all you have done for me.

I have often been asked why I am such a devout Anglican; it is a hard question to answer. I don't think I could have survived mentally if I hadn't had that anchor in my life. To lose three infant sons, and then our daughter, needed something beyond earthly comfort. This I found.

A Cross to Bear

Before I leave this world I want to do something to stop young girls from becoming addicted to smoking. If anybody had told me how cigarettes could have affected my whole life I hope I would have had the intelligence to heed the warning. Unfortunately we were never warned of the damage we were doing to ourselves. My mother smoked and was delighted to share our breakfast coffee and cigarettes together.

When I was sixteen I developed a congested lung and rheumatic fever and had to leave school and spend six weeks in Kelowna as the change of altitude would clear my condition, which it did.

As a paying guest of a delightful young widow who had a four-year-old daughter to raise, I was thrilled to be welcomed by her entire family. Her younger brother arrived from army camp and we fell in love. He smoked and persuaded me to join him. I was a very willing student.

If anyone had ever suggested to me that smoking was so damaging I would have wanted to cut them right out. Unfortunately it was many years later that my doctor, Jack Harrison by name, who went through so much with me, said, when I went to see him, 'If you are still smoking so much, there is my door. I will not look after you.' I never smoked again, and I am forever grateful to him, as I am very sure I would not be alive today if I had continued to do so. If all doctors were to take the same stand with their patients they would clear a great deal of the congested

535

traffic out of our hospitals ... to say nothing of cutting the taxes that foot our health care programs.

In the garden of B.C.'s Children's Hospital there is a bench Mort and I donated after Jack Harrison died, honouring his memory, and at the entrance to Emergency is our memorial to Drue, both of whom were very special people.

Some forty years without smoking has not left me un-tarnished. I cannot be in a room when someone is smoking; I go into severe convulsive coughing which can be very embarrassing at times as well as frightening. Now that smoking is being eliminated from so many places and smokers are sitting and standing outside buildings, I am finding I am forced to hurry past them or I start to choke.

Now having an extremely sensitive throat, diesel fumes that are puffed out of trucks can be very trying on my throat and voice. With population explosion comes the automobile explosion, so I can only hope and pray they will finally eliminate health-destroying fuel, and also that cigarettes die the death they deserve, having taken so many lives.

Friends

MUCH HAS BEEN written about my friends throughout the years but not about my life without Mort. Everything changes if you are on your own. Fortunately we are quite a sizeable 'club'. I used to swear I would never play afternoon bridge, but now we have a great time. It took a while to adjust to it after the strict school I was subjected to – from, namely, M. S. Duffus. Where we used to play eight rubbers in an evening, we are doing well to play four in an afternoon. There is a lot to talk about and our teas defy description, interspersed, monthly, with bridge – lunch bridge – starting at 11:30.

J.D. Doreen Ferguson (sister-in-law) with daughters Ann Lowery (seated) and Gill Schramm behind. Birthday party.

Thank you Joan Ketcheson, Joan Clark, Ruthie Brazier, Rita Thurston, who moved to Montreal, replaced by Berenice Lucas. Naomi Hopkins and Doris Manning are willing spares. We have a lot in common: we have all lost our husbands.

Other wonderful friends are Herb and Jane Randall, Tom Brown, Doreen Walker, Janet Allan and many others who are already in these memoirs.

Ian Mak

After Mort died, a young Malaysian man by the name of Ian Mak has, fortunately for me, been able to advise and cope with this elderly spoiled person, whose husband looked after all business details. Ignorance was never bliss, as it wasn't for me. It doesn't matter what needs attention, all I need to do is call Ian and my problem is solved. Nothing is ever too much trouble.

Ian is married to his attractive wife Schuling. They have a son and a daughter.

I can't expect my sons-in-law to have the time to cope with my problems; they are business men working hard to survive in the rat race that is out there today.

When my two Trust 'girls' Margaret and Johanne have lunch with me I always include Ian, who knows them well, and he is able to discuss any problems or questions that I am interested in that arise from time to time. They look after Mort's estate and Ian looks after mine.

Every Monday morning I receive a call from Ian to see if I am all right; in fact there are very few days that pass without a call. When I had bronchitis this past winter he would check twice a day to see if I needed anything and when I was feeling better after two bad weeks he wanted to take me for a drive. His kindness and thoughtfulness constantly amaze me, particularly as he puts in at least a seventy hour work week. I often say how kind he is to me and his answer is, 'You are my Canadian Mum.'

If you ever read this, Ian, you will know how much I have appreciated you and how grateful I am to have had you for my financial adviser and true friend. Thank you, Ian.

Manny

Manny, or Manfred Haizman, is another person who has, over the years, been such a help to me in so many ways. I've always felt I could call on him at any hour and he would be there for me. Manny manages parties for many of my friends, with the able assistance of his friend Harry.

Apart from catering he helps me with my fifty-odd pots of plants on the two large patios I am fortunate to have. There isn't very much he doesn't know about gardening, which he told me he learned from his father in Germany. He has the most remarkable memory. He remembers what everyone likes to drink and what they like with it.

Long may you be with us, Manny, and my thanks to you for all you have done for me and your friendship.

2003 Since writing the above I regret to say that Harry died suddenly in February.

Finale

THERE IS ONE satisfaction I will experience with this chapter and that will be to live in tidy surroundings once more. There has been so much paper around. I was encouraged to buy a computer which I found fascinating but too demanding a mental strain to learn at my ancient time in life, so I returned to my trusty typewriter. All my rough copies were re-typed by Guy firstly, then Christie when she returned from Australia and latterly by Jo Robertson. My sincere thanks to all of them, particularly Jo as she had time on her hands to compete with my needs.

It was very much easier to remember the past than conclude the present. I have so thoroughly enjoyed delving into memories and it has filled many hours with what might have been lonely times since Mort died in 1997. Many friends have asked me what will fill my time now? As I have only produced three paintings since I started writing I think I will pick up a brush. Bridge, of course.

With all the empty wall space looming in our grandchildren's houses they may be grateful for my efforts in the art field. Their parents always seemed to be politely grateful for all donations! Five hours used to vanish so quickly when Nora Gourlay, Joan Silbernagel, Faith Halse and three others met weekly with our outstanding artist Constance Pomeroy who taught us. We had such fun, and laughingly called ourselves 'The Group of Seven'!

I am writing this chapter in the UK saying hello to my special ex Wren Officers who I was fortunate to have in my quarters.

Margot Redford in Oxted, Nora Carey Malloy in Bath, Paddy

(Ailsa) Massey Stewart from Campbeltown, and Winnifred Hawkesworth Simpson in Hillsborough, County Down. We seem to pick up where we left off. Quite wonderful, as we have kept up our friendships since 1942.

Mort used to say I always found it hard to say goodbye – nothing has changed.